CLEOPATRA AND ANTONY

Power, Love, and Politics in the Ancient World

DIANA PRESTON

Walker & Company
New York

Published by Walker Publishing Company, Inc., New York

All papers used by Walker & Company are natural, recyclable products made from wood grown in well-managed forests. The manufacturing processes conform to the environmental regulations of the country of origin.

LIBRARY OF CONGRESS CATALOGING-IN-PUBLICATION DATA HAS BEEN APPLIED FOR.

ISBN-10: 0-8027-1738-1
ISBN-13: 978-0-8027-1738-2

First published in somewhat different form in the United Kingdom in 2008 by Transworld Publishers

First U.S. edition 2009

Visit Walker & Company's Web site at www.walkerbooks.com

1 3 5 7 9 10 8 6 4 2

Typeset by Westchester Book Group
Printed in the United States of America by Quebecor World Fairfield

In memory of Henry and Lily

CONTENTS

TRANSALPINE
GAUL
CISALPINE
GAUL
Danube
ILLYRICUM
Mutina
Perusia
Rome
THRACE
MACEDONIA
Dyrrhachium
Philippi
THESSALY
Brundisium
Tarentum
Corcyru
(Corfu)
Pharsalus
Actium
Athens
Ep
Samos
Corinth
Sicily
Methone
Carthage
Thapsus
MEDITERRANEAN
Crete
Cyrene
A
CYRENAICA
Siwa
0
km
400
0
miles
200

Black Sea
Caspian Sea
ARMENIA
BITHYNIA
PONTUS
Mount Ararat
hesus
Lake Van
CILICIA
Tarsus
Carrhae
Tigris
MEDIA
Antioch
Phraaspa
Rhodes
Euphrates
Cyprus
SYRIA
PARTHIA
S E A
JUDAEA
Gaza
Jerusalem
lexandria
Lake Mareotis
Pelusium
Petra
Cairo
Memphis
NABATAEA
EGYPT
Nile
Red Sea
Dendera

PROLOGUE

"THEY OPENED THE DOOR, and saw Cleopatra lying dead on a golden couch, dressed like a queen, with one of her two ladies-in-waiting, Iras, dying at her feet. The other, Charmion, was so weak that she could hardly stay upright but she was trying to adjust the diadem which adorned Cleopatra's brow. One of the men hissed angrily, 'A fine deed, this, Charmion!' and she replied: 'Yes, nothing could be finer. It is no more than befits this lady, the descendant of so many kings.' "

So the ancient historian Plutarch portrayed the death scene on a stiflingly hot day in August 30 BC* of the thirty-nine-year-old queen of Egypt, Cleopatra. Captured by Octavian, who would become Augustus, the first emperor of Rome, she had triumphantly taken her destiny back into her own hands. Rather than be paraded in chains through Rome by her conqueror, she had poisoned herself with the bite of a snake. A few days earlier, her lover of eleven years, Mark Antony, bloody and sweat-soaked following his own botched suicide attempt, had died in her arms after she and her waiting women had hauled him painfully into the fortress tomb where she had taken refuge as Octavian's victorious armies advanced into the broad, colonnaded streets of the Egyptian capital, Alexandria.

Thus ended the lives of the ancient world's best-remembered celebrity couple—charismatic figures who died at the height of their fame and whose

---

*All dates are BC unless otherwise specified.

physical appearance still provokes debate. Their depictions on coins of their time are not flattering. Cleopatra, in particular, appears hawk-nosed and imperious. However, a model of her head created for this book by an archaeologist specializing in facial reconstruction and based on a wider range of evidence offers another image—a woman who, though striking, was also more than a little plump.

Cleopatra and Antony lived unconventionally and to the full. Their deaths were sudden and the subject of conspiracy theories. But their enduring place in our popular consciousness derives from more compelling reasons than our interest in celebrity and romance. Their personal love story was an integral part of a great military, political and ideological struggle, the outcome of which still affects us. Had they triumphed over Octavian and recast Rome's territories in both east and west as they planned, the history of the Roman Empire and of what followed might have been very different.

The backdrop to Cleopatra and Antony's story was one of the rise and fall of empires. The once great power of Egypt was waning while that of Rome was aggressively on the rise. Cleopatra's Egypt had been founded by her opportunistic Macedonian ancestor Ptolemy I, who was one of the generals of Alexander the Great and also his distant cousin. Ptolemy had taken advantage of the chaos after Alexander's death in 323 BC in Babylon to seize Egypt and start a dynasty. Ptolemy had chosen well in selecting an ancient, established land united for more than three thousand years under its pharaohs. It had good natural defenses—invaders from east and west faced arid deserts, and invaders from the north could only attack by sea. Southward down the Nile, just beyond Aswan, were the tumbling waters of the First Cataract and then the gold-rich lands of Lower Nubia, which, like the pharaohs before them, the Ptolemies swiftly occupied.

At first Ptolemaic Egypt had flourished, but by the time of Cleopatra's birth in 69 BC, though it was still wealthy, its political and military fortunes had long been in decline. In need of a powerful protector, the Ptolemies had adopted a policy of appeasing and pleasing Rome but faced the possibility that the expansionist republic, by then the dominant power in the Mediterranean, might gobble up Egypt as just another Roman province. The risk was a real one. Rome's only serious rivals for the status of "superpower" were the Parthians—the rulers of Persia (Iran) and many other lands besides. Rome's ambitions seemed boundless and her military momentum unstoppable. But her internal political tensions would also affect Egypt's fate and how Cleopatra and Antony's struggle with Octavian would ultimately play out.

The Roman republic had been founded in 509 BC when the last of Rome's kings, Tarquin the Proud, was driven out by citizens under the leadership of one of the Brutus clan claiming that Rome would never again be subject to the tyranny of one man. Rome, though, had become the victim of its own success. By the time of Cleopatra and Antony, the pressures of trying to reconcile a system of government originally designed for a small city-state on the east bank of the River Tiber—not only with the requirements of law and order in a rich and fast-growing empire but also with the personal ambitions of power-hungry generals, businessmen and politicians—had become impossible to contain. Although Rome's rules of government provided for a form of democracy, albeit imperfect, which gave every male citizen (though not of course their wives, daughters or slaves) some sort of voice, a growing number believed this to be incompatible with Rome's growing status. Power, they argued, would be better exercised in the hands of a few men or even in the hands of only one. This ideological debate—which often spilled out bloodily onto the streets—had become a contest between the collective power of an autocracy personified by the Senate on the one hand and a series of strong men on the other who used their legions to back up their aspirations and bribed or sometimes coerced the people to support them, thus lending their regimes a veneer of legitimacy.

Both Antony and Octavian took part in these struggles, sometimes as allies but, as their ambitions clashed, finally as enemies. Both of them craved power and both circumvented the established structures of government. However, Octavian was the more single-minded and ultimately triumphed. The dual suicides of Cleopatra and Antony effectively marked the death of the long-ailing Roman republic and the rise of personal rule as embodied by the emperor.

Shakespeare's play *Antony and Cleopatra* is one reason we naturally think of the couple's names in that order. Yet—as the title of this book suggests—Cleopatra perhaps deserves first place. Her tenacity, vision and ambition would have been remarkable in any age but in a female ruler in the ancient world they were unique.

This successful and liberated woman seduced two of the most powerful leaders of her day. The first was Julius Caesar, thirty-one years her senior, who became her lover after pursuing his enemy Pompey to Alexandria. He restored Cleopatra to her throne and then dallied in Egypt to take a Nile cruise with his pregnant young mistress. (The historical records call it a "royal progress.") Returning to Rome, despite having a wife of thirteen years' standing, he invited Cleopatra and their son to join him in his capital, and to the outrage of the Roman political classes, even installed her statue in the Temple of Venus, the first human image ever to be placed in such a location.

After Caesar's murder by one of the same Brutus dynasty that had rid Rome of King Tarquin and who claimed that he too was liberating Rome from tyrannical oppression, Cleopatra fled back to Egypt as Rome disintegrated into fourteen years of civil war. At the end of that conflict, Caesar's onetime most trusted lieutenant, Antony, now joint ruler of the Mediterranean world with Caesar's adopted Roman son Octavian, summoned the Egyptian queen to Tarsus. A consummate mistress of stage management, Cleopatra wafted upriver to meet him at dusk on a scented, candle-lit barge, displaying an image of beauty that even Shakespeare suggested beggared description. Here began the long, passionate affair that would rightly place Cleopatra and Antony in the ranks of the world's greatest lovers, and the political partnership that would shake the ancient world.

In that partnership, Antony was more than a foil to Cleopatra and much more than, as he is so often portrayed, a graceless, hard-drinking womanizer. From impoverished beginnings Antony had become Rome's most powerful general and politician in an age when it had become increasingly difficult to separate the one from the other. Cleopatra—an outstandingly shrewd and politically astute strategist herself—became one of his closest advisers and together they planned on a grand scale. She aided him in his campaign against the Parthians. Had Antony succeeded, he would have cleared the path to India, massively extended Rome's empire and made his own position so secure that Octavian never would have dared to challenge him. Yet even when the Parthian venture failed, neither Cleopatra nor Antony gave up their ambitions. They wanted to forge a new bipolar world order centered on Rome and Alexandria. Under it, Rome's military might and administrative skills would, with the backing of Egypt's wealth, have formed a partnership with the culture of the Greek or Hellenized society to which Cleopatra's Macedonian dynasty and capital belonged.

Their ultimate defeat by Octavian, however romantic they may seem with hindsight as doomed lovers, was by no means inevitable. As the balance of advantage swayed, the couple often seemed to have the upper hand and almost to the last held realistic prospects of success. But history is written by the victors and in this case truth was warped and hidden to an even greater extent than usual through an intense propaganda campaign. This barrage of invective was deployed against Cleopatra and Antony by Octavian while they were still alive and continued well after their deaths, selectively sorting and distorting the facts of their lives and careers. Octavian's motive was pure self-interest. Cleopatra and Antony were his final opponents in his campaign to make himself master of the Roman world.

The Romans were thoroughly tired of civil war. Therefore in his struggle against Antony, Octavian needed to exploit the Romans' innate sense of superiority and their xenophobia and misogynism to turn a civil war of personal ambition into a patriotic war of self-defense pitting the civilized, ordered West against the decadent, barbarian East. It suited Octavian's purpose to make the Eastern foreigner Cleopatra the villainess of the piece—a wily oriental and a woman to boot, enticing Antony, a formerly good-intentioned if dissolute Roman, from the path of his duty—and to portray himself as reluctantly assuming power to defend his homeland.

Octavian led a team of propagandists as skilled at the art of spinning as any today. In addition, after seizing power, he simply had two thousand documents that did not support his version of events burned and had the supposedly sacrosanct Sibylline oracles edited to reflect his thesis. As a result, Cleopatra, a charismatic, cultured, intelligent ruler who spoke seven languages and lived at least half of her adult life celibate, was transformed into a pleasure-loving houri, the very epitome of fatal beauty and monstrous depravity, bent on bringing animal gods, barbarian decadence and despotism to the sacred halls of Rome's Capitol.

So successful was Octavian's propaganda that, fed by snippets of both fact and romantic fantasy, it evolved into the myth and legend of Cleopatra and Antony that has continued to develop, mutate and fascinate over two millennia. In early Christian times, Cleopatra became a kind of seducing Eve to Antony's naïve Adam. To Chaucer, on the other hand, she was a virtuous and steadfast woman consistent in her love, for which she died. Dante placed the "licentious" Cleopatra in the second circle of Hell among the "carnal sinners," who also included Dido of Carthage and Helen of Troy. Shakespeare produced a tale of obsessive, doomed love and, as was his wont, endowed his characters with complexity, humanity and universality. To the Victorians, Cleopatra was an exotic and dangerous dominatrix whose home life was so unlike that of their own dear queen.* In more modern times, she became the great love of Antony's life, the woman for whom he gave up the world, something the Romans would have considered unequivocally a serious character flaw and vice but which to contemporary eyes becomes a romantic virtue. Some have seen in Cleopatra a prototype feminist, yet others an outsider metaphorically and just possibly physically black in a hostile white male world.

Cleopatra's supposed physical allure has always been a potent part of the myth. In complete defiance of all the ancient sources, which, unanimous for once, state that she died dressed in her full state robes, artists through the ages have lovingly displayed her on her deathbed naked to the bite of the phallic asp and the lascivious gaze of the male patron.

Above all, Cleopatra and Antony have remained, like Julius Caesar—Cleopatra's other lover and Antony's mentor—among the very few classical figures who are still everyday names to the general public. Their lives still remain the stuff of popular drama. In the early years of the twentieth century, a German academic carefully enumerated 127 stage works about them (seventy-seven plays, forty-five operas and five ballets) produced between 1540 and 1905. Since then, the couple's greatest impact on the imagination has been through the cinema. Perhaps the film that made the biggest impression was the 1960s production starring Richard Burton and Elizabeth Taylor, their adulterous offscreen relationship seeming to mirror the sensational on-screen events they portrayed. Critics suggested Taylor, like Cleopatra, was seducing Burton from the classical stage, the natural Rome for his talents, to fritter them away amid the glitz and glamour of Hollywood. That the film went massively over its already extravagant budget only added to the myth of luxury and excess surrounding Cleopatra and Antony's names.

The truth behind the propaganda and myth is not easy to resolve and any answer is, of course, to an extent subjective. The four main classical sources for Cleopatra and Antony—Plutarch, Suetonius, Appian and Dio Cassius—were writing respectively some 130, 140, 160 and 230 years after the lovers' deaths.

---

*This comment was said to have been made by a middle-aged British matron watching a performance by Sarah Bernhardt as Cleopatra.

There are, however, some additional contemporaneous references to the couple in the vivid, witty letters and speeches of Cicero and the poems of Vergil and Horace and elsewhere, as well as inscriptions and portraits on coins and monuments. Being written under the Roman Empire, each of the main sources is considerably influenced by Octavian's propaganda, although Plutarch and Suetonius did employ some evidence of a more favorable and diverse nature. For example, Plutarch culled material from the eyewitness account of Cleopatra's doctor, from reminiscences handed down through his family, and even from his own travels in Egypt. (The greatest weakness of Plutarch—Shakespeare's source for his play—is perhaps embroidering the facts a little to produce a good story.) Suetonius used a variety of personal and sometimes scurrilous anecdotes lifted from the gossip of the time. Almost nothing survived in Egypt in written form about Cleopatra and those few scraps that do—on stelae (tablets) or elsewhere—are almost invariably the subject of heated academic debate about their significance. As is so often the case with ancient history in general and with so much of women's history of any but the most recent period, there are silences to be interpreted. Additionally, the sources often contradict each other and even, sometimes, themselves.

However, for all the ambiguities, contradictions and omissions, the sources do allow something of the characters, motivations and expectations of Cleopatra and Antony to be pieced together as the balance of power in their long, iconic, often tempestuous and rarely straightforward affair evolved. The real history behind the many myths and legends surrounding the classical world's greatest love affair offers many contemporary resonances—the political and cultural tensions between East and West, the nature of empire, the exploitation of the Middle East's wealth, the concealment of personal ambition beneath the watchword of liberty, documents forged, edited or disposed of, special relationships established, constitutional forms and legal niceties both invoked and ignored, private lives exposed for political ends as well as cronyism and personal ambition. Above all, however, there are the passions of powerful leaders and their lasting impact on our imagination, our history and our culture.

PART I

Dynasty of Eagles

CHAPTER 1

Keeping It in the Family

THE EGYPTIANS HAD WELCOMED the arrival of Cleopatra's distant ancestor Alexander the Great and his Macedonian and Greek army of forty thousand men in 332 BC as liberators and allies. He had successfully ejected the Persians who had overthrown Egypt's final pharaoh and had ever since been thoroughly oppressing the population. The Egyptians did not object when Alexander claimed the right to succeed the pharaohs by being crowned in the Temple of Ptah in the ancient Egyptian capital of Memphis, near modern-day Cairo. Alexander, in turn, took care to respect and even to sacrifice to the native gods. Before he left Egypt, he founded a new city in the sandy marshlands of the western Nile delta that, with characteristic immodesty, he named Alexandria.

Within a decade, Alexander was dead and a mighty struggle was under way amongst his followers for parts of his empire. The Macedonian general who grabbed Egypt, Ptolemy, was Alexander's food taster as well as his relation. Ptolemy's personal emblem was an eagle, which would become the symbol of the dynasty he founded. He ruled at first as governor but soon awarded himself the kingship of Egypt under the title Ptolemy I Soter—meaning "savior." With him came more than a hundred thousand serving or veteran soldiers and large quantities of civilians and their families, to whom he gave lands to farm along the Nile valley and delta. Of all her direct ancestors, he was the ruler whom the last Cleopatra—the seventh Ptolemaic queen to bear that name—probably most admired.

Ptolemy was above all an opportunist. To the annoyance of rivals who would also have liked to possess the prestigious cadaver, Ptolemy I intercepted Alexander's funeral cortege as it was traveling toward Macedonia from Babylon, where he had died, and hijacked his embalmed body, which he interred in Alexandria in a splendid tomb. Here Alexander was worshipped as a god. In his lifetime he had claimed divinity, insisting that his mother, Olympias, had conceived him through sexual intercourse with Zeus in the form of a serpent. As Ptolemy recognized, fostering the cult of the divine Alexander could only add legitimacy to successors and relations. Indeed, succeeding generations of Ptolemies would be buried around the great tomb of Alexander and, just as purple-mantled priests sacrificed to him, the Ptolemies' own priests made offerings to their dead kings and queens.

Ptolemy's greatest rivals were the two other successor dynasties to Alexander's empire, the Antigonids in Macedonia and the Seleucids in Syria and Asia Minor. Though sharing the same Macedonian Greek heritage, their territorial ambitions would clash for centuries with those of Cleopatra's family until Rome finally subdued them all.

Demonstrating prudence and a grasp of detail, Ptolemy thoroughly reorganized the management of Egypt in a way that would last basically unchanged until Cleopatra's time. He moved the capital from Memphis to Alexandria, made Greek the official language of government and fused Macedonian and Egyptian methods of administration. He also introduced what was, in effect, a planned economy to exploit Egypt's abundant natural wealth. Although 90 percent of Egypt was desert, the rich alluvial mud created by the annual flooding in late summer of the Nile valley produced bumper crops of wheat and barley—sown in the autumn and harvested in early summer—making the country the biggest grain producer in the Mediterranean. The land was at its most fertile in the delta, where, as Vergil wrote, "the river that flows all the way from the dark Indies empties through its seven mouths making Egypt green with its black silt." There was a relatively docile workforce to harvest the grain—from the time of the pharaohs the native population living along the Nile in simple mud-brick houses had learned to work hard and live frugally.*

---

*The flooding of the Nile was not regulated until the building of dams at Aswan—the first, by the British, completed in 1902 and the second and major dam, built by Egypt with Russian help, finished in 1971.

Ptolemy soon expanded his territories. To the west he annexed Cyrenaica (eastern Libya), a region long inhabited by Greeks and famous for its ostrich feathers, honey and wool. To the northeast, he invaded southern Syria four times—the region would remain one persistently disputed by the Ptolemies and the rival Seleucids. One of the lures was the port of Gaza, terminus of the great camel caravans from Arabia swaying under their burdens of frankincense, spices and jewels. These lands also gave access to the trade routes from Asia to Tyre and Sidon, to the skilled Phoenician sailors who inhabited those cities and were useful for crewing Egypt's ships, and to timber from Syria's mountains to build them. Egypt, though rich in much else, lacked trees. Ptolemy also seized Cyprus, another valuable source of timber as well as of copper.

His new subjects' manners and customs may have surprised Ptolemy. The Greek Herodotus, the world's first historian and travel writer, writing earlier in the first half of the fifth century BC, had been startled that their way of life ran counter to "the ordinary practices of mankind." In particular, Egyptian women enjoyed far more control over their lives than their Greek counterparts and could even initiate divorce proceedings. Often women were the traders and went to market and some even owned barges from which they made large profits from transporting grain. Conversely, many Egyptian men remained at home undertaking such domestic tasks as weaving. While the men carried burdens on their heads, Egyptian women bore them on their shoulders. Most striking of all to Herodotus, women urinated standing up while men squatted, although both genders performed such acts decorously. People relieved themselves indoors but ate outside since "what is unseemly but necessary should be done in private and what is not unseemly should be done openly."

Herodotus, however, noted one area where women took second place. No female was allowed to hold priestly office. He also concluded that the Egyptians were "the most religious men." Ptolemy too grasped both the deep significance of religion to his new subjects and that it provided a means of winning their allegiance, especially that of the influential shaven-headed, shaven-bodied, white-robed priesthood.*

Egyptian religion had no single cohesive theology but was an accumulation of cults derived from legend and myth and governed by ritual with a strong

*Believing body hair to be impure, they even plucked out their eyelashes.

emphasis on the afterlife. The new Ptolemaic rulers were confronted by a bewildering array of animal-headed gods, enigmatic sphinxes and vast quantities of mummified animals, from baboons and bulls to birds, cats and crocodiles, all deliberately killed to allow pilgrims to gain divine grace by participating in the funeral rites of a sacred animal.

Ptolemy participated in the rituals of his new land and, as would his descendants including Cleopatra, restored and embellished the temples of ancient Egypt while building new ones—the massive structures at Philae, Edfu and Dendera owe as much to the Ptolemies as to the pharaohs. However, he went a step further—devising a new god to appeal to all his subjects, Egyptian and Greek, and help create a common bond. With the aid of priests he fashioned Serapis—a fusion of the Egyptian cult of Apis, the sacred bull associated with Osiris, lord of the Kingdom of the Dead, with the Greek god Zeus. The new god was one of healing and of prophecy and was worshipped in a great temple, a "Serapeum" near Memphis. Another Serapeum was built on a hill overlooking Alexandria. Even in Cleopatra's day, a quarter of a millenium later, admiring visitors thought it grander than anything they had seen outside Rome. Its long flight of steps rose to a columned Greek façade faced with marble. The interior was decorated with gold leaf, silver and bronze. Within the dark incense-scented sanctuary, which only the high priest and the king were allowed to enter, the god—whose image was that of a mature bearded human male—sat on his throne with Cerberus, the three-headed dog of the underworld, at his feet. Beneath his elaborate headdress Serapis' piercing, life-like eyes of quartz and rock crystal shone mesmerizingly through the gloom.*

Around 283 or 282, the highly successful Ptolemy I died peacefully in his bed—the only one of Alexander's Macedonian generals to do so—at the age of eighty-four. His fair-haired and stocky son, Ptolemy II, found a yet more potent way of implanting the Ptolemies into the psyche of their people. He decided that, like the pharaohs before them, the Ptolemies must become gods. Claiming the title Theoi Soteres, "savior gods," for his deceased parents, he set

*The oldest surviving papyrus in Greek is a plea to Serapis from a woman of Greek descent called Artemisia to take vengeance on her behalf against "the brute who got her pregnant."

about turning himself into a deity, establishing the tradition that more than two centuries later would allow Cleopatra the status of a living goddess.

To underline this divinity, Ptolemy II embraced another pharaonic custom—incest. The ancient Egyptians had believed their kings to be the earthly manifestation of the god Osiris, whose consort was his sister Isis, and many pharaohs had married their half sisters. Ptolemy II decided to marry his full sister, Arsinoe—an act for which he later understandably acquired the title Philadelphus, "lover of his sister." He presented himself and his sister-wife to his subjects as the Theoi Adelphoi—divine siblings—and ordered their images to be placed in the inner sanctums of temples, where specially chosen priests tended them. The Greek and Roman world considered sexual relations between brothers and sisters unlawful and immoral but henceforth incest would be an integral custom of the Macedonian Greek house of Ptolemy, underlining their divinity and exclusivity.*

This exclusivity was to an extent mirrored within the ruling Macedonian elite, although without the refinement of incest—intermarriage with Egyptians was forbidden in Alexandria and the other "Macedonian" cities of Egypt. However, in the countryside Macedonian settlers quite soon began to intermarry with Egyptians, so as time passed, a family's ethnic origins became hard to disentangle—a situation some Macedonians exploited to claim and enjoy the greater legal rights enjoyed by Egyptian women.

In 273 Ptolemy II initiated Egypt's long and pragmatic association with Rome when he dispatched ambassadors there, charged with delivering gifts and flattering words. Dio Cassius caught the blend of shrewd self-interest on the side of one party and conceit on the other, describing how the Egyptian king, impressed by "the growing power of the Romans, sent them gifts and made an agreement with them. The Romans, flattered that one so far away should have thought so highly of them, sent ambassadors to them in return." It was a good moment to secure Roman friendship. The following year, the Romans took control of the entire Italian peninsula.

The next Ptolemaic king, Ptolemy III Euergetes I, "the Benefactor," invaded and plundered Syria, the core of the rival Seleucid kingdom, and crossed

---

*Another dynasty of god-kings, the Incas, also practiced incest. Their last ruler, Atahualpa, was the result of fourteen generations of it.

the Euphrates. One account even claims that, following in Alexander's footsteps, his armies reached India. This was the Ptolemies' high point. Their empire was the predominant power in the eastern Mediterranean and their capital sophisticated and rich. However, under Ptolemy III's successors, Egyptian power waned as the royal family became increasingly and introspectively entangled in its own complex and bloody feuds while invaders took most of Egypt's overseas possessions.

In 193, Egypt got her first Queen Cleopatra—the name means "Glory of Her Father"—when the daughter of the Seleucid king of Syria, Antiochus III, married the young Ptolemy V, who had no sister to wed. On her husband's early death, leaving her with two young sons, Cleopatra I ruled as regent. The first Ptolemaic queen to exercise sole power, she proved a strong, effective leader and a role model for her female successors. Most subsequent Ptolemaic queens took her name in tribute to her.* After Cleopatra died her two sons ruled in uneasy alliance. Both were, as tradition dictated, named Ptolemy, but the younger was nicknamed Physkon, "Potbelly," because of his wobbling obesity. Taking advantage of Egypt's political fragility, in 168 an emboldened Antiochus IV of Syria marched into Egypt, crowned himself king in Memphis and advanced on Alexandria. For the first but not the last time Egypt invoked the help of Rome, now emerging as the Mediterranean's dominant power.

Rome's relations with Egypt had drawn closer over the years since Ptolemy II had dispatched his silver-tongued ambassadors. Egypt had prudently backed Rome in her wars with Carthage and perhaps even sent a small force of troops to support her. The Romans had certainly felt grateful enough to send thanks to the Ptolemies because, as their chroniclers recorded, "in difficult times when even their closest allies had deserted the Romans, [the Ptolemies] had kept faith." The Romans had also recently formally consulted the Egyptian kings, with their Macedonian roots, before Rome's expansion into Macedo-

---

*The first Cleopatra known to history was the wife of the king of Macedonia, Perdiccas, in the fifth century BC. A little later, Alexander the Great had a sister of that name. In 1821, *Cleopatra* became the first Egyptian word to be transcribed from hieroglyphics, a year before the Rosetta Stone, with its identical text in Greek, Egyptian demotic and hieroglyphs, yielded many more secrets of hieroglyphs.

nia and Greece—even though the Ptolemies had been entirely powerless to do anything other than acquiesce gracefully. Still conscious of their debt of gratitude to the Ptolemies, the Roman Senate duly agreed to intervene in Egypt's favor and sent a consul to insist on Antiochus' withdrawal. Antiochus obeyed.

The Ptolemaic dynasty had been saved but at the cost of increasing thralldom to Rome, becoming only a little better than Roman "clients." Continued infighting between members of the royal family only raised their dependence on Rome and they frequently called upon the Romans to arbitrate in their disputes, like a parent sorting out the squabbles of fractious children—which, to an extent, was how the Romans viewed the Ptolemies. The Romans were also alert to any strategic advantages that might fall to them, for if the Ptolemies were children, they were wealthy ones.

When, after five uneasy years of shared rule, Ptolemy "Potbelly" forced his older brother, Ptolemy VI, off the throne, the latter hurried to Rome, where, dressed for effect in mourning, he appealed for help. This gave the Senate an opportunity not only to demonstrate Rome's position as guardians of the dynasty but also to further weaken the Ptolemaic kingdom by splitting it in two. In 163 they decreed that Ptolemy VI was to rule in Egypt and Cyprus with his sister Cleopatra II, while Potbelly was to have Cyrenaica.

Reluctantly, the rival brothers accepted Rome's verdict, but Potbelly continued to scheme and hit on a device that future Ptolemaic rulers, including the last Cleopatra's father, would employ to ingratiate themselves with Rome—he composed a will. After inveighing against those plotting "to deprive me not only of my kingdom but also of my life," he wrote, "If anything happens to me before I leave successors for my kingdom, I bequeath to the Romans the kingdom belonging to me, for whom from the beginning friendship and alliance have been preserved by me with all sincerity."

Potbelly dispatched the will to Rome and hastened after it to display the livid scars in his plump rippling flesh inflicted, he claimed, by would-be assassins. A doubtless amused Senate awarded him Cyprus for his trouble but took no further action after his brother failed to relinquish the island. Neither was Rome particularly perturbed by the ensuing chaos when, in 145, Ptolemy VI died. Potbelly rushed to Alexandria, took the title Ptolemy VIII and forced his brother's wife, their sister Cleopatra II, to marry him. As soon as he was sure he had impregnated her, he had her young son—his nephew—murdered before her eyes. The unfortunate Cleopatra II in due course bore Potbelly a son.

However, in a psychotic outburst he later had the child dismembered and the pieces sent in a box to Cleopatra as a "birthday present" in revenge for his sister-wife's plotting against him.

Within three years of his marriage to Cleopatra II, Potbelly had also raped, then married, her daughter—his niece and stepdaughter—whom he made Cleopatra III and co-regent with her mother. Such incestuous bigamy was unprecedented. Furthermore, the two wives, though mother and daughter, hated each other, each determined that her own children and not her rival's should succeed to the throne. The rivalry only ended with the death of Cleopatra II, quite likely murdered by her daughter.

When revolts broke out, Potbelly massacred the inhabitants of the town of Hermonthis, purged the Alexandrian court of dissidents and banished most of the scholars studying in Alexandria. However, he did succeed in reuniting the old core Ptolemaic kingdom of Egypt, Cyrenaica and Cyprus without Roman interference. Rome, at the time still busy converting Macedonia into a province, was relatively unconcerned about the chaotic antics in Egypt. Nevertheless, around 140 the Senate dispatched a fact-finding mission to the Alexandrian court. Potbelly, whose girth had grown, according to one of the visitors, to "a size and dimension which meant that people could not get their arms around him," gave them a guided tour, waddling around wearing the ivy garland of Dionysus and clothed in an embarrassingly diaphanous purple robe that revealed far too much, "as though he wanted to make a display of what any decent man would try to hide." The Romans congratulated themselves that they had given the Alexandrians a rare experience—"the sight of their king taking a walk." They were lucky to have been spared another sight. Despite his bulk, the king was an active and able performer of a species of obscene dance that, from his reign, would become a tradition at the Ptolemaic court. More pertinently, the Romans reported their astonishment at "the number of inhabitants of Egypt and the natural advantages of the countryside," concluding that "a mighty power could be sustained there if this kingdom ever found capable leaders." There would, however, be no capable leader until the last Cleopatra.

On Potbelly's death in 116, the kingdom descended once more into bloody confusion. He had bequeathed Cyrenaica to his illegitimate son, Ptolemy Apion, and Egypt and Cyprus to Ptolemy IX, his elder son by his niece and second wife, Cleopatra III. She, however, favored their younger son, who did not reciprocate her affection. Instead he used his mother to help him exile his brother to Cyprus and then, after mounting the Egyptian throne as Ptolemy X, had her murdered. In turn, in 89 the garrison of Alexandria ejected him from his kingdom. Rome lent him money for a fleet but he was killed during a sea battle trying to retake Cyprus.

Rome allowed Ptolemy IX to return to Egypt, reuniting it with Cyprus once more, but Cyrenaica soon was gone. Ptolemy Apion had died in 96, leaving his kingdom to the Roman people, though twenty-two years would pass before Rome finally took possession of it. Rome, however, soon resumed her role in determining who should sit on the throne in Alexandria. In 80, the death of Ptolemy IX triggered the familiar pattern of court intriguing, maneuvering and murder. For six months his sister Cleopatra Berenike III, widow of Ptolemy X—and, unlike him, popular with the citizens of Alexandria—ruled the kingdom alone.

However, the arrival in Alexandria of her late husband's son by another woman, Ptolemy XI, who was a protégé of Rome, left her little choice but to do Rome's bidding and marry him. The new king showed his gratitude by murdering his wife and former stepmother after reigning with her for just nineteen days. The Alexandrians had been watching these events with anger and concern. The city's volatile and cosmopolitan population was not opposed to the dynasty in principle but could react violently to events of which it disapproved. A mob surged into the palace, dragged the young king off to the Gymnasium and dismembered him.

After this bloodletting, the Alexandrian court chose two of the three remaining illegitimate children of Ptolemy IX to rule in his place. They married, becoming Ptolemy XII and Cleopatra V, with the title "Divine Lovers of Their Father and One Another." Although his early ancestors had proclaimed the dynasty's divinity, Ptolemy XII became the first king to claim the title of a specific god, calling himself the "New Dionysus." This was somewhat ambitious. His subjects took a less lofty view of their new ruler. Some called him simply "Nothos" (the bastard), others "Auletes" (the piper) because of his love of the soft, velvet notes of the *aulos*, or pipes. Like other Ptolemies, he seems to have been a keen participant in the traditional obscene royal dances and also bisexual. On a stele set up at Philae on the Upper Nile some Egyptian men claimed to have slept with Auletes. However, his greatest distinction would be to father Ptolemaic Egypt's last and most remarkable queen.

CHAPTER 2

Siblings and Sibylline Prophecies

AULETES' HIGH-FLOWN CLAIMS of divinity did not impress Rome, especially since his murdered predecessor had made yet another will appointing the Roman republic his heir. In any case, the Romans were becoming ever more convinced of the innate superiority of their own nation and culture. Even if they respected the works of Greek antiquity, they despised modern Greeks as decadent and lacking in moral fiber—"the most wretched and unruly race," as one influential statesman and moralist had dismissed them. The Romans thought other Eastern peoples even worse. The Senate refused to acknowledge Auletes and his sister as rulers in Alexandria or to endorse their brother, yet another Ptolemy, as king of Cyprus. Meanwhile, a succession of other hopeful Ptolemaic claimants to the throne arrived in Rome brandishing expensive gifts to argue their case, but received no encouragement.

The power struggles that would shortly lead to civil war in Rome meant that every Roman of ambition and influence was determined to keep such a rich prize as Egypt out of the hands of a rival. The result was much scheming and many proposals and counterproposals for what should happen to Egypt—wilder plans even included a scheme to use the country as a place to house the Roman poor—but no action to take advantage of the latest Ptolemaic bequest to seize Egypt. Nevertheless, the precariousness of Egypt's continued independence was brutally demonstrated to Cleopatra's father when, in 64 BC, Pompey the Great conquered the kingdom of the Ptolemies' Seleucid rivals and converted it into the Roman province of Syria. Auletes astutely sent Pompey a token force of cavalry to assist in his "peacekeeping" in neighboring Judaea and threw a feast in Pompey's honor, even if the Roman was not present in person, where a thousand guests quaffed from gold cups changed after every course.

Finally, though, in 59, Auletes obtained a result from all his entreating and bribing of Roman officials. Julius Caesar, who had recently joined Pompey and Crassus in the First Triumvirate, agreed to speak out for Auletes in the Senate in return for six thousand talents—estimated at Egypt's entire revenue for six months. As consul that year, Caesar, helped by Pompey, who no doubt shared in the largesse, pushed through a resolution recognizing the indigent Egyptian king as a "friend and ally" of the Roman people.

Auletes' relief at this legitimization of his rule after twenty years of trying was swiftly extinguished. Just a year later, the Roman tribune Clodius, an aristocrat notorious both for his excesses and for his manipulation of the mob, proposed the formal annexation of Cyprus. The excuse was that its king, Auletes' brother, had aided pirates, and the Senate agreed. The king of Cyprus was offered the position of high priest of Aphrodite at Paphos but chose poison instead. His treasure was shipped back to Rome and paraded through the Forum to the cheers of the crowd. Rage at the loss of the Ptolemies' last overseas possession, contempt for Auletes' flaccid response, and resentment of tax increases to repay the money he had borrowed in Rome to bribe Caesar sparked the Alexandrians to another of their periodic demonstrations of people power and they ejected Auletes from his kingdom.

He fled to the island of Rhodes hoping for an audience with its influential Roman governor, Cato the Younger, to ask assistance in reclaiming his throne. His hopes must have been high as he was ushered into Cato's presence. Had he not just been awarded a "special relationship" with Rome, for which he had paid handsomely? However, the Roman, far from rising to receive him, was squatting. Cato had recently taken a laxative and was, as a consequence, busily evacuating his bowels. The defecating governor dismissively told the flustered Ptolemy to seek a reconciliation with his people. Rome could, or rather would, do little for him. Cato's reception of the Egyptian king, informal to say the least, reflected not only the disdain of this hard-drinking moralist and self-appointed guardian of old Roman values toward foreigners of all sorts and effete foreign kings in particular, but also Rome's indifference to Egypt's problems.

Seemingly impervious to insult, Auletes traveled on to Rome, where, from his lodgings in Pompey's villa in the Alban hills, he embarked on another frantic and undignified round of fawning and bribery. Cut off from Egyptian revenues, he again had to use money he did not possess and borrowed from Roman money-lenders at exorbitant rates of interest. The eleven-year-old Cleopatra may have been with him, observing her father's humiliation at firsthand. An inscription found on a stone epitaph in Athens—and written by command of a "Libyan princess" to honor a lady-in-waiting who had died there—may have been commissioned by Cleopatra when she and her father paused there on their way to Rome. The description "Libyan" was often used to describe the Greek population of North Africa. If Auletes had chosen Cleopatra to accompany him, it suggests a particular closeness to her father, and she would have been a good companion despite her young age—intelligent, inquiring and sharply observant.

Cleopatra was the third of Auletes' six children. The identity of her mother is uncertain but she was probably Auletes' sister and first wife, Cleopatra V, who records suggest died in the year of Cleopatra's birth—perhaps even at her birth—and who had given Auletes two other daughters. Just possibly, Cleopatra's mother was his second wife, about whom nothing, not even her name, is known, who bore him yet another girl, Arsinoe, and then two sons, both named Ptolemy. However, Cleopatra's later and thoroughly reciprocated animosity to this trio suggests that they were not full brothers and sisters. Cleopatra was soon to get her first direct experience of intradynastic rivalry. In Alexandria, Auletes' eldest daughter, her sister, had seized the throne as Cleopatra VI. On her death, his next eldest daughter claimed it as Berenike IV and sought a husband to help her hold it. She found three candidates—two were Seleucid princes, the first of whom died while the marriage negotiations were under way and the second of whom was vetoed by Rome. The third candidate was supposedly related to the Seleucid house but so coarse that the Alexandrians quickly nicknamed him "the salt fishmonger," and within a few days of marrying him Berenike ordered him to be strangled. She subsequently wed a Greek noble named Archelaus.

Meanwhile, the Alexandrians had dispatched an embassy of a hundred men to Italy, led by the philosopher Dio, to defend their action in deposing their pipe-playing monarch. Learning of this, Auletes had some of them murdered as they came ashore in the Bay of Naples. Dio escaped and managed to reach Rome, only to be assassinated soon afterward. The resulting scandal did not help Auletes' case and the despondent king wisely removed himself to the Temple of Artemis in Ephesus, one of the seven wonders of the ancient world, for which, despite his bankrupt condition, he ordered magnificent doors of carved ivory. Here he waited to see what, if anything, Rome might do to help him.

Early in 56 BC, a thunderbolt fizzed from the skies to strike the statue of Jupiter on the Capitol Hill in Rome. Officials hurried to consult the Sibylline Books to discover what this might portend. The Sibylline texts had, it was believed, been brought from the East to Rome by one of her early kings and embodied words of wisdom from the last of the prophetic Sibyls, difficult to translate but infallible if decoded correctly. The originals had been destroyed in a fire in 83 but another set had been assembled from diverse and sometimes dubious sources. The city had a whole coterie of priests and augurs skilled in both decoding and linking prophecies to current dilemmas and, unsurprisingly, the new books grew as respected as the old had been.

Within the volumes' pages was found a pronouncement pinpointing Egypt as the cause of the current divine intervention. It stated that if the king of Egypt sought help, Rome could give him her friendship, but to "succor him with a multitude" would bring terrible misfortune on the city. The message was clear—no armed intervention in Egypt. However, this prompted angry debate in the Senate over who might lead a peaceful embassy to Egypt.

Cicero, a man of modest pedigree who had made himself into Rome's leading lawyer and orator by dint of his justly celebrated talents both for speaking and for self-publicity, applied his finely honed legal mind to break the stalemate. He wrote to his ally and friend Lentulus, the governor of the Roman province of Cilicia in southern Asia Minor, suggesting that he take his army and fleet to Alexandria and install a garrison. Auletes could then safely and independently return to his capital and resume his reign. Such action, Cicero argued, would be entirely consistent with the Sibylline Books. Rome would have given the Egyptian king friendship without supplying "a multitude" literally to accompany him home. (Cicero hoped that he might even be given an official position in Alexandria—a city he was curious to see.)

Aware that Cicero lacked the backing of the Senate in his hairsplitting, Lentulus prevaricated. However, Aulus Gabinius, governor of Syria, was less scrupulous. (Cicero once dismissed him as "a thieving dancing boy in paint and hair curlers.") Ambitious and in sore need of money, Gabinius agreed to restore Auletes in return for ten thousand talents. To raise this enormous sum, the king turned once again to Roman financiers, and to the banker Rabirius in particular, who provided the necessary funds at extortionate rates of interest. In 55, Gabinius marched his men across the desert from Gaza and into Egypt, claiming as his pretext that the Egyptians were encouraging pirates who were damaging Roman trade. His commander of cavalry was the twenty-seven-year-old Mark Antony.

Antony came from an aristocratic and distinguished, albeit impoverished, family. His paternal grandfather had been a noted orator murdered during Rome's civil strife. His father, who had died fighting against pirates when Antony was about eleven, had been a feckless man, according to Sallust "devoid of all cares but those of the moment," and recklessly generous. His strong-minded mother, Julia, was a distant relation of Julius Caesar. Even Antony's enemies admitted that she was a dignified and virtuous woman and it was she who provided the stability in Antony's youth as well as being prominent later amongst his political advisers.

In advance of the main army and at the head of his troopers, Antony rode through the thick, dry drifting sand of the desert and along the edge of sulfurous marshes called by the Egyptians "the Outbreaths of Typhon"—Typho being a monster associated with volcanoes—to storm the Egyptian outpost at Pelusium and open the way to Alexandria. Archelaus resisted bravely until he was killed but his troops put up little fight.

Back on his throne, Auletes settled some scores. One of his first acts was to order the slaying of his daughter Berenike for taking his crown. She was probably strangled in the royal palace, possibly before the eyes of her teenage younger sister Cleopatra. Waves of arrests and executions followed, with anyone suspected of complicity with Berenike killed out of hand. Though obviously traumatic, her sister's death was to Cleopatra's advantage. As the king's eldest surviving daughter, under Ptolemaic tradition she was now in line for the throne—a prospect that with two elder sisters might previously have seemed remote.

Though Antony's stay in Egypt was brief, some claim that during it he first saw and even fell in love with Cleopatra, then fourteen. The second-century historian Appian later wrote, "It is said that he was always very susceptible . . . and that he had been enamored of her long ago when she was still a girl and he was serving as master of horse under Gabinius at Alexandria." This may well be an embroidery of the facts. Appian himself acknowledged his taste for the sensational and for writing about those events "which are most calculated to astonish by their extraordinary nature." But even if Antony did not fall in love with Cleopatra, she must have seen the good-looking young man and heard of his courage at Pelusium. She may also have been struck by his humanity—he successfully interceded with the king for the lives of Egyptians captured at Pelusium and the Alexandrian population would remember him for it when, many years later, he returned to their city as the lover and ally of their queen.

As Cleopatra grew into young adulthood in the royal palace, experiencing a more settled period in her life than she had yet known, she could resume her disrupted education and develop the intellectual powers that even her later detractors would not deny. She was more fortunate than the majority of Egyptian and Macedonian women, most of whom received no formal education. Cleopatra could also hardly have been in a better place than Alexandria. Her ancestor Ptolemy I had founded the great Library of Alexandria and the adjacent Museon, where scholars from across the "civilized world" could live and study for free. *Museon* means "shrine of the Muses" and it had rapidly become the main center of Hellenic learning, supplanting even Athens. In the library scholars edited the first texts of Homer, produced commentaries and divided works up into volumes. The length of the latter was regulated by the optimum length of the papyrus roll—the only writing paper.

The Museon itself was particularly strong in astronomy, mathematics (Euclid worked there) and medicine. Because the Egyptians mummified their dead, they already had a better knowledge of human anatomy than many others. The Greek professors had built on this, probably with the help of condemned criminals supplied by the Ptolemies for vivisection, to understand the nature of the nervous, digestive and vascular systems. They had established that the brain rather than the heart was the seat of intelligence and undertook pioneering surgery including operations to remove bladder stones, cleanse internal abscesses and repair wounds. They had also developed a detailed knowledge of pharmacology and toxicology.

The young Cleopatra could take her pick of tutors from the Museon to pursue her interests, which seem to have been wide-ranging. The tenth-century Arab historian al-Masudi described her as "a princess well versed in the sciences, disposed to the study of philosophy." But as well as her studies she had much else to reflect upon. In particular she could observe at close quarters the conflicting pressures on her father. In fact, Auletes had only four more years to live and they were difficult ones. There was rebellion in the south and his safety in Alexandria was guaranteed only by the Gallic and German legionaries that Gabinius stationed there. With the economy in a desperate state, Auletes debased the country's silver coinage, introduced by Ptolemy I as the country's first currency—under the pharaohs payment had been in kind and coins had been viewed with suspicion. Ptolemy had also established a network of state-controlled banks to manage the flow of funds. Now Auletes reduced the precious metal content in the silver stater, the most common coin, to around a third.

Unable to repay his chief Roman creditor, Rabirius, Auletes appointed him his minister of finance so that he could extort money directly from the populace. It was a shrewd move and the rapacious Rabirius did not last long. Saved from the mob only by taking refuge in Alexandria's jail, he fled back to Rome, where the whole Egyptian adventure had come into disrepute. Some serious flooding of the Tiber, which had caused many deaths and much property damage, had occurred at the time of the invasion and been blamed on Gabinius' disregard of the Sibylline prophecies. Accordingly, both Gabinius and Rabirius were soon put on trial for their freebooting activities in Egypt. Gabinius was exiled but Rabirius acquitted.

In early 51, Auletes, by then well into his fifties and prematurely aged by his troubles and excesses, fell ill. In his will, a copy of which he sent to Rome for safekeeping, he named as his successors the seventeen-year-old Cleopatra, as she must have been anticipating, and the elder of his two sons, the later Ptolemy XIII, who was just ten years old. What actually happened on the king's death sometime in the spring of 51 is, however, obscure. Papyrus documents from those months refer to "the thirtieth year of Auletes which is the first year of Cleopatra," suggesting a period of joint rule between them. Perhaps an ailing Ptolemy wished to make clear to his people that Cleopatra was to be Egypt's next queen. Perhaps Cleopatra kept her father's death a secret until she had secured her position on the throne. Documents as late as July 51 continue to refer to their joint rulership. However, by early August news of the king's death had reached Rome and the reign of Egypt's last queen, Cleopatra VII, had begun.

The new rulers had already been given the titles "Sister- and Brother-Loving" by their father, perhaps more in hope than in expectation. They also took the title Philopater, "Father-Loving."

According to hieroglyphs on a stele set up after her death, early in her reign Cleopatra traveled four hundred miles from Alexandria to the holy shrine at Hermonthis, fourteen miles south of Thebes (Luxor) in Upper Egypt. The reason for her long journey was to participate in the sacred rites of Buchis, the bull. Bull worship had existed in Egypt from the earliest times as a fertility cult and the rites sometimes had a sexual character. At certain times, women were allowed to visit sacred bulls and expose their genitals to them to make themselves fecund. In Cleopatra's time, at least four regions worshipped their own sacred bull. The Apis bull of Memphis, always an ebony black beast with white markings, was the most important, leading a luxurious life pampered by priests. However, the bull Cleopatra had come to venerate—the Buchis bull of Hermonthis—was also deeply revered as the living soul of Amon-Ra, the sun god.

The previous Buchis bull had recently died, its mummified body consigned to a stone sarcophagus in a giant necropolis of dead bulls, the "bucheum." Its replacement, like its predecessor entirely white and with a coat so lustrous it apparently sparkled in the light, was to be ferried in state across the Nile to be installed in its shrine. What more striking way for the living goddess Cleopatra to show herself to her people than to accompany the sacred bull? The inscription records how "the queen, the lady of the two lands, the goddess who loves her father," led it "on to the ship of Amun surrounded by the king's boats. All of the inhabitants of Thebes and Hermonthis along with the priests worshipped the divine animal. As for the queen, everyone was able to see her."*

Cleopatra, it seems, was already aware of the seductive power of spectacle. Like the first Ptolemies, she also appreciated the importance to her people of their ancient religious cults and the explosively emotional nature of their beliefs. When she was ten years old, at a time of tension, a member of a Roman delegation to Alexandria had killed a cat by accident. In Egypt all cats were sacred and, as a writer recorded, "the crowd ran to his house, and neither the

---

*The Egyptians had devised a special method to mummify the sacred bulls. First, to dissolve the internal organs, a turpentine enema was pumped into the body cavity and the anus was blocked with a linen tampon. Once the organs had liquefied, the tampon was removed and the fluid drained out. The process then continued in the usual manner: the body was dried using natron, covered with oils and resins and carefully wrapped. The sacred bulls were then given a royal burial. For a description of human mummification see page 302.

king's representatives who came to ask for clemency for the foreigner nor the fear of Rome were sufficient to save the unfortunate man's life."*

In addition, Cleopatra grasped the economic significance of Egypt's temples. The larger temples were—like the monasteries of medieval Europe—wealthy landowners. They ran industries such as metalworking and linen manufacture. By sponsoring them she was not only aligning herself spiritually with her people but also promoting the nation's wealth.

Perhaps an awareness of her bloodstained heredity and a determination to protect herself from the violent fate that had befallen so many of her forebears caused Cleopatra to assert her independence early in her reign. Certainly, nothing she had witnessed in her young life so far could have given her any confidence that she was safe. She had not known her mother. Her father had been her protector. Without him she was exposed to the plottings of courtiers and the ambitions of her half siblings. The only person on whom she could rely was herself—a lonely and intimidating scenario, but one with no viable alternative.

Documents dated to the first two years of her rule refer to her and her alone. She also minted coins on which only her head appeared. There are no references to her young brother. He should have governed with his sister and, as a minor, been assisted by a council of regents appointed to help him—a eunuch, Pothinus, for administrative and financial matters; Achillas, a military commander to take charge of the armed forces; and Theodotus, a professor of rhetoric from Samos, as his tutor. This regency council should have taken precedence over Cleopatra since, under the Ptolemaic code, kings took precedence over queens. But for a while Cleopatra, still in her teens, apparently succeeded in brushing the council aside, ruling alone without interference—an achievement that says much not only for her determination but also for her youthful self-confidence and ambition.

That ambition was both for herself and for her country. Cleopatra's inheritance was a diminished, depleted kingdom, far removed from the muscular empire of the early Ptolemies. Its continued independence was entirely at Rome's pleasure. Cleopatra had seen her father a supplicant and briber of

---

*Ironically, the Romans popularized the keeping of cats as pets in Europe.

Rome, despised by his people and kept on his throne only by foreign mercenaries. The circumstances had been humiliating. Yet, however she might resent this, she knew her father had survived for more than two decades only because of the Romans. The question of how best to manage the relationship with Rome and exploit it in her favor would become one of her driving preoccupations as queen.

Her first challenge came uncomfortably early when, later in 51, the Roman governor of Syria sent his two sons to Alexandria to order the soldiers stationed there by Gabinius to return to Syria. He needed them to help defend the province against the Parthians but the disgruntled legionaries, who had grown attached to soft Egyptian life, murdered the young men. Fearing Rome might hold her accountable and despite the risk of the remaining Roman soldiery rising against her, Cleopatra did not hesitate. She arrested the assassins and packed them off to Syria in chains.

Cleopatra's actions, though diplomatically astute, provoked a crisis at the Alexandrian court, where she was criticized for kowtowing to Rome. Her situation became yet more difficult when droughts and failing harvests in the third year of her reign began to cause unrest in the countryside, provoking a coup against her at court. Documents issued at around this time under the name of "the King and Queen," and referring to the first year of Ptolemy XIII's reign, show that Cleopatra was no longer sole sovereign but had been forced to accept her young brother—and his regency council—as co-rulers.

At this increasingly precarious time for Cleopatra, Rome's affairs again intruded. In 49, Pompey the Great sent his son Gnaeus to Alexandria to seek Egyptian aid in the civil war that had broken out between himself and Julius Caesar. Help was duly granted—fifty ships, grain and soldiers were dispatched—but the grateful thanks sent to Egypt by Pompey's supporters were addressed only to Ptolemy XIII. Cleopatra had by now been deposed by her brother and fled Alexandria for Upper Egypt.

The details of what actually occurred are sketchy. Caesar wrote that she was expelled by her brother "acting through his relatives and friends." The term "relatives and friends" had a particular meaning in the complex hierarchy of the Ptolemaic court. At the apex were the "Kinsmen," allowed to wear a special headband denoting their status; next came "First Friends," who swept grandly about the court in purple robes, and then "Friends," who also enjoyed special privileges. These individuals constituted the power base at court. Coaxed and bribed by the regency council—Ptolemy XIII himself was too young to take a direct hand, though he seems throughout to have approved of his council's actions—a sufficient number of these courtiers must have turned against Cleopatra, eroding her support and leaving her no alternative but flight.

In 48, Cleopatra left Egypt altogether to take refuge in the Philistine city-state of Ascalon, between Egypt and Syria, where, characteristically defiant and determined to regain what she had lost, she began gathering troops for an invasion—Greeks and Egyptians but also Arabs. Achillas, her brother's commander, also prepared for battle, moving his men into position at Mount Casius, some thirty miles beyond the Egyptian border fortress of Pelusium.

Yet, as would soon become clear to Cleopatra, Rome's civil war, not Egypt's, would decide whether she would resume her place as queen. Caesar had defeated Pompey at the battle of Pharsalus and his vanquished rival had set sail for Egypt hoping to find support. A determined Caesar was not far behind.

PART II

Romulus' Cesspit

CHAPTER 3

The Race for Glory

GAIUS JULIUS CAESAR HAD by his victory at Pharsalus amid the golden cornfields of Thessaly made himself master of the Roman world. In the previous decades he and his equally ambitious rivals such as Pompey and their predecessors had blatantly and successfully twisted the laws of the Roman republic and subverted its constitution to their own ends.

They owed that success to the organic way in which the republic had evolved. The patrician plotters who, in 509 BC, had ejected Rome's last king had substituted a form of government in which each year the male citizens of Rome elected two magistrates, soon to become known as consuls, to run the affairs of the state. Two consuls were appointed not only to share the burden but also so that each could restrain the ambitions of the other. The stipulation of annual elections was designed as another protection against any rising autocrat.

The republic's founders never formulated these new arrangements in a written constitution or any coherent suite of legal documents. Caesar was by no means the first to exploit the flexibility the lack of a written constitution afforded to claim legitimacy for his acts. The city's aristocracy had long felt free to mold and modify the system of government in line with their wishes and best interests while reassuring citizens that they could reconcile any changes with *mos maiorum*, "the tradition of the elders,"—a relatively amorphous but sacrosanct concept.

Over time, the Romans had approved the creation of a number of extra positions, again to be filled by elected officials. Early in the life of the republic, in response to pressure from the common people—the plebs—tribunes had been elected to represent their wishes. The extent and nature of their powers were the subject of heated debate and frequent change. As Rome had grown, other offices had been added, not only to spread the growing workload but also to preserve the checks and balances crucial to the republic's health. Some of these, in particular the position of quaestor, the official responsible for tax collection, and praetor, assistant consul, formed a hierarchy that any aspirant consul had to ascend before he could stand for the top job. The Romans knew the climb as the "race for glory." Both Pompey and Caesar had made the climb but found the glory it afforded insufficient to satiate their ambition. Antony too would struggle to fulfill his aspirations within the limitations imposed by the traditions of the elders.

Rome's power and the extent of the lands she controlled had grown dramatically in the period of the republic's life up to Caesar's birth in July 100.* Within 250 years of the republic's foundation in 509, she had conquered the whole of the Italian peninsula. Her next stride was across the straits of Messina on to the island of Sicily. Here she first came into conflict with Carthaginians. From their capital on the North African coast in what is now Tunisia, the Carthaginians dominated western Mediterranean trade while establishing colonies throughout Sicily. By 227, the Romans had expelled the Carthaginians from Sicily and also from Sardinia and Corsica. But the titanic struggle between the two had just begun. The Carthagians occupied Spain and the silver they mined there soon refilled their war chests for another round in the conflict that became the most complex, in terms of alliances and tactics, in antiquity and probably the most costly in lives and resources.

In 218, Hannibal brought his Carthaginian army, which included thirty-seven war elephants and many thousands of cavalrymen, over the snowy Alpine passes into Italy. Fighting as he went, by August 216 he had reached Apulia, where by a daring, encircling movement on the plains of Cannae he defeated a Roman army of eighty thousand men, killing forty-eight thousand

*According to the Roman calendar the month of Caesar's birth was Quintullus and the year 653, the number of years since legend said that Romulus had founded Rome and become its first king.

of them in a battle so fierce that the rate of killing is estimated at five hundred men a minute. Carthage also invaded Sicily. Rome was at her lowest ebb, releasing debtors and other prisoners to serve in the army, devaluing her currency, desperately seeking allies anywhere she could find them, including in Ptolemaic Egypt, and even sacrificing two Gauls and two Greeks in the middle of the city because the omens seemed to demand it.

Rome slowly fought back. In the critical year of 211, Syracuse, a major Greek city in Sicily allied to the Carthaginians, fell after a long siege in which one of the Alexandria Museon's most famous scholars played a major role. Archimedes was not only a mathematician but also a resident of Syracuse and an excellent engineer. He devised a number of weapons for the city's defense, including a crane with a claw designed to grab the bow of invading ships and a large array of mirrors, probably highly polished brass shields, to channel sunlight into a beam of rays to blind attackers and perhaps even set fire to sails or wooden superstructures. On entering the city the Romans killed Archimedes as he sat at his desk.

The Romans quickly thereafter recovered the rest of Sicily and over the next five years completely vanquished the Carthaginians. Under the harsh terms of the peace treaty Carthage lost her empire and fleet and paid a large indemnity. At the end of one of the most decisive wars in history and one with the most far-reaching implications, the Mediterranean world lay at the feet of Rome. Her victory against the odds owed much to her by now large supplies of manpower, her willingness to adapt to sea warfare and above all Rome's coherence as a society, of which all citizens felt proud and in which all held a stake. The challenge now was to preserve that coherence while embracing and enhancing Rome's superpower status.

Rome's next expansion—at the time when in Egypt Cleopatra's great-grandfather Potbelly was giving rein to his bizarre excesses—took her legions, with Potbelly's formal acquiescence, across the Ionian Sea to Macedonia, homeland of Alexander and the Ptolemies. In a series of wars, Macedonia was defeated, divided and ultimately in 147 absorbed as a Roman province. Meanwhile, other Greek cities had been cajoled and coerced under Roman hegemony, although retaining a veneer of autonomy for a time. In North Africa, the Romans picked a new quarrel with the Carthaginians and after a long siege, followed by a week of hand-to-hand street fighting, in 146 occupied Carthage and leveled it. In the same year, the Romans razed Corinth and removed even the illusion of freedom in Greece. Rome's dominions now spread from Spain in the west to Greece in the east, from the western borders of Egypt in the south to parts of southern France in the north.

Roman society had obviously changed over the years as her possessions grew. The Senate—its name deriving from the Latin word *senex*, meaning "old man" or "elder"—had become the most important political body. With three hundred members appointed for life, the Senate was so arranged that effective control lay in the hands of some twenty patrician families or clans, most of whom traced their descent back to legendary times. One such clan, though not among the most powerful in 100, were the Julians, whose members included Caesar. They claimed descent from Venus via Aeneas, the Trojan hero and the putative ancestor of Romulus.*

Families such as the Julians built power bases through the cultivation of a group of clients whose interests they protected and advanced, in return for their votes and those of a host of subsidiary clients, to secure the election of preferred candidates for the consulate and other posts. (The word for "patron," *patronus*, gave rise to the Italian *padrino*, the term for a Mafia godfather.)

In the latter part of the second century BC, the patrician families slowly divided into two broad groupings. Both proclaimed liberty as their watchword, though they were differentiated as much by their views of how Rome should be ruled, and by whom, as by other differences of policy. The struggle between them would dominate the next century. One grouping, the *optimates* (conservatives or republicans), preferred to retain the status quo whereby the oligarchy ruled collectively more or less in conformity with the amorphous tradition of the elders. The other grouping was the *populares*, or people's party. The people's theoretically broad powers in electing officials and adopting laws in popular assemblies were much reduced by a bloc voting system that rendered patricians more equal than others. Often, therefore, the cultivation of the people by members of the popular party was merely a ploy to break the

---

*Aeneas was also the hero whose desertion of Dido, queen and founder of Carthage, to pursue his own imperial ambitions was said to have caused her suicide—a story much elaborated later by the poet Vergil to the detriment of both Cleopatra and Antony and the benefit of Octavian.

influence of the oligarchy and concentrate power in their own hands, rather than a true effort to empower the masses. Others of the popular party were, however, genuine reformers.

Among the latter were two brothers from the family of the Gracchi. The first, Tiberius, was murdered by a mob of senators and their henchmen after proposing land reforms in favor of the poor. The second, Gaius, tried to stem the corruption of juries and hence to increase the accountability of senators for their misconduct. He also proposed an increase in the scope of Roman citizenship to encompass the Latins, Rome's long-term allies who, like many Italian communities, were becoming increasingly restive at being excluded from the perquisites of the new empire they had helped to found. (Roman citizens were, for example, exempt from direct taxation.) Gaius' proposals aroused violent opposition and in 121 he was forced to commit suicide while numerous of his supporters were executed.

In the last decade of the century, when rebellion broke out in Africa, the Senate gave the command of the Roman army to a general named Marius who, unusually, did not belong to one of the noble families. After securing victory in Africa he defeated Teutonic tribes invading from the north of Italy. He grew so powerful that by 100, the year of Caesar's birth, he was embarking on his sixth consulate. The aristocratic Julian clan had early seen the utility of a political and matrimonial alliance with the rising "new man" or *novus homo*, as those outside the patrician ranks were known—Marius was Caesar's uncle by marriage and the Julians were firmly allied to the popular party.

It is unlikely that Caesar was born by Caesarean section. Although the operation was performed and sometimes saved the child, the mother usually died, and Caesar's mother, Aurelia, lived to be a major influence in his life. The accounts tell us little of Caesar's early years other than that he wrote a poem about Hercules and a tragedy about Oedipus. They do, however, reveal much about the further career of his uncle Marius and the creation of the political tensions that would dominate the remainder of the new century and fashion the backdrop against which the lives—and deaths—of Caesar, Cleopatra and Antony would be played out.

Discontent among the other Italian peoples about their inferior status was undiminished. By 90, rebellions broke out across Italy. Marius and his fellow Roman generals were eventually victorious but the fighting would not have ended so quickly had the Romans not offered citizenship to all people living south of the river Po.

The conflict had thrown up another claimant to power, one of Marius' former junior officers, Lucius Cornelius Sulla. Patrician but poor, he had a large birthmark on his face that the unkind said resembled mulberries with oatmeal sprinkled on top, and had reveled away his early years. Such was his charisma, however, that one of Rome's wealthiest and most celebrated courtesans had left him her fortune. With the backing of this money, he had gone into politics and in 89, fresh from his victories, he stood for and won a consulship. He was almost immediately appointed Rome's commander against Mithridates, king of Pontus, a kingdom bordering the southeastern shores of the Black Sea, who had attacked some of Rome's new Asian possessions.

A successful campaign promised Sulla wealth and fame, but his victory in the consular elections, and in particular his appointment to command in the east, had much displeased his old general, Marius. Though now in his late sixties and more than a little stout, Marius was still both vigorous and ambitious and had had his eye on that potentially lucrative command, judging it to be his by right by virtue of his services to Rome. Embittered, Marius lent his considerable weight to rivals of the conservative Sulla who were, like him, members of the popular party. Tensions between the two quickly spiraled beyond the control of the Senate. Sulla led six legions into Rome and after a few hours of street fighting expelled Marius and his allies. Significantly, this was the first time a Roman leader had broken the traditional ban on armed troops entering the city. Marius fled through Rome's burning streets, eventually to reach Africa. The twelve-year-old Caesar, lying low with his family, was exposed to a valuable lesson—that access to loyal legions was becoming as large a factor in politics as citizens' votes or senatorial approval.

Sulla did his best to rearrange affairs in Rome in favor of his conservative supporters, but he allowed the consular elections for the following year to proceed. One of those elected—Cinna—was no friend to Sulla but all the latter did, before departing to the east and the war against Mithridates, was to make Cinna swear not to disturb his arrangements. On taking his oath, Cinna picked up a stone and hurled it away, asserting vehemently that if he broke his word he should be cast from Rome just as violently as he had thrown the stone.

Swiftly breaking his political promises, Cinna tried to undo Sulla's republican measures and was indeed expelled from Rome. Marius returned from Africa and together with Cinna attacked Rome, capturing the city easily at the end of 87 and allowing their men to plunder, rape and murder at will. Marius' own bodyguard, recruited from runaway slaves, generated such terror that Cinna, who had himself paraded the head of his rival consul on a spike, felt compelled to have them killed as they slept, in the interests of public safety.

Master of Rome once more, but unsure of what to do beyond avenging his grievances, Marius fell prey to nightmares, drank heavily to banish them and died just seventeen days after taking up his seventh consulship. Cinna ruled Rome for nearly three years until messengers brought news that Sulla was victorious in the east and would soon return. Cinna knew better than to expect mercy and decided to take the fight to Sulla in Greece, but his troops mutinied and killed him. Sulla crossed to Brundisium on the southeastern Italian coast and, as he marched north on Rome, two young commanders joined him.

The first was the blond Pompey, then twenty-three years old and far removed from the middle-aged man who more than thirty years later would seek sanctuary in Egypt after his defeat by Caesar at Pharsalus. Plutarch writes that Pompey bore a resemblance to Alexander through "the slight quiff of his hair and the mobility of his features about the eyes"—a resemblance "which contributed quite a bit towards his popularity." He had already won several victories over Sulla's opponents, some by arms and some by words, while marching to join Sulla. So pretty, so precocious and so successful was he that he began to be called, with a hint of irony, "Pompey the Great."

The other commander was the twenty-eight-year-old Marcus Licinius Crassus, the son of a rich patrician whose wealth Marius had seized. He had raised his own private army to support Sulla, achieve vengeance and rebuild his patrimony.

By the end of 82, with the help of these two young leaders, Sulla took possession of Rome and the capital's public places once more ran red with blood. Sulla decreed lists—proscriptions—of public enemies, opponents summarily to be killed and to have their property confiscated. Many names were added at least as much for their wealth as for their deeds. All the republican leaders and their clients profited hugely—Crassus so flagrantly that Sulla felt forced to disclaim his actions.

Crassus and Pompey were two of three men who would, within a few decades, come to dominate Rome. The family of the third—Julius Caesar—had been wedded to the defeated Marius' cause. After Marius' death and probably under the guidance of his widow, Caesar's aunt, and of his own strict but loving mother, Aurelia, now also a widow, Caesar had married Cinna's daughter Cornelia in 84 in an arranged marriage of the kind patrician families found so useful in cementing their web of constantly but subtly changing alliances. A year later she bore him a daughter, Julia. At around this same time Cinna had appointed Caesar a priest of Jupiter.

Romans believed that all important events in life were divinely instigated and that different gods were responsible for particular activities. Perhaps symptomatic of Rome's materialistic society, Roman religion was concerned with success, not with sin or moral judgments. "Jupiter is called best and greatest," Cicero commented, "because he does not make us just or sober or wise but healthy and rich and prosperous." In worship the Romans sought, with the aid of their priests, to appease the gods and to persuade them to look kindly on their activities by offering gifts, pouring libations or, on special occasions, performing animal sacrifices. The Romans had no holy scriptures and like the Greeks, but unlike the Egyptians, their concept of an afterlife was indistinct and shadowy.

In addition to their reliance on the Sibylline Books, the Romans did, however, believe strongly in portents and prodigies of all sorts. Before important events, specially appointed augurs or, in their absence, magistrates and generals looked for signs of the gods' wishes manifested by the pattern of birds' flight (*auspices* originally meant "signs from birds"), the weather or cloud formations. If the signs were unfavorable, meetings or even battles would be postponed. The appearance of comets or of alleged showers of blood, deformed animals or animals acting against their own nature (for example, by devoring their own young) were given automatic credence as omens.

As a priest of Jupiter, Caesar would have been required to perform ceremonies and to inspect the entrails of sacrificed animals to interpret any messages they conveyed for the future. His position allowed him a measure of political power through his ability to manipulate omens. It attracted many privileges but also much regulation. Some rules were bizarre, such as that the priest's home should contain no knots and that his hair could be cut only by a freeman using a bronze knife and the clippings, together with those from his nails, buried in a special place. Others were theoretically more serious, such as a prohibition against holding a magistracy.

Sulla's arrival changed everything for Caesar, even though, fortunately for him, the eighteen-year-old had taken no active part in the opposition. While others were killing themselves to avoid a worse death, Sulla summoned Caesar and offered him amnesty if he divorced Cornelia. Alone among his contemporaries, Caesar refused Sulla's terms and so lost his priestly office, Cornelia's dowry and his family fortune, as well as being compelled to flee Rome. Such a stiff-necked refusal to bow to the authority of others, especially when his honor was at stake, would typify his future career.

Eventually some hard lobbying and even an intervention from the Vestal Virgins secured his rehabilitation.* On bestowing it, Sulla is said to have commented, "Keep him since you so wish, but I would have you know that this young man who is so precious to you will one day overthrow the aristocratic party which you and I have fought so hard to defend. There are many Mariuses in him." He told others to beware of "this youth who wears his toga so loosely girdled." The latter was a reference to a modish, some said effeminate, way of dressing affected by Caesar and some other young bloods of which the conservative Sulla clearly strongly disapproved. Certainly, as the historian Suetonius wrote, "Caesar was something of a dandy, always keeping his head carefully trimmed and shaved; and he has been accused of having certain other hairy parts of his body depilitated with tweezers." He was also tall with a somewhat large mouth and dark, lively eyes.

After his pardon, Caesar wisely took himself abroad, finding a place on the staff of one of Rome's high officials in Asia. Caesar's first mission was to the kingdom of Bithynia on the Black Sea, west of Pontus. Its king, Nicomedes, maintained a luxurious court and was well known for his harem of young men. Nicomedes seems to have taken an immediate fancy to Caesar, who, to the later outrage of Rome, performed the role of cupbearer to Nicomedes at an extravagant banquet. Also according to persistent rumor, reclining on a gold bed

---

*Vesta, keeper of the eternal fire, was one of the most venerated Roman goddesses. Unlike most other deities, she had her own priestesses. The six Vestal Virgins were selected at the age of eight from good families to be raised in chastity to serve the goddess for thirty years. After that time they were free to leave and marry. Before then, if they were convicted of having sexual relations with a man, they were buried alive and their lover whipped to death.

with purple sheets, he became the king's lover—in the words of his later opponents, "the female rival of Bithynia's queen" and "the bottom half of the royal bed." While the Romans and Greeks had no such word as *homosexuality* and relations with youths were accepted and celebrated in verse, the Romans approved only the active role in such relationships for freeborn men. The receptive or pathetic role, which Caesar was said to have assumed with the king, was considered far too submissive for a freedom-loving Roman and to be taken only by foreigners or slaves.*

In 78 came the news that Sulla was dead. He had in 81 revived for himself the office of dictator, abolished at the end of the third century for fear of autocracy. The role, designed for emergencies only, had previously been restricted to a six-month tenure but Sulla had set himself no time frame and used the office to inaugurate a vast number of conservative reforms, among them drastic reductions in the power of the people's representatives—the tribunes—including removing their veto over legislation. He also restricted the freedoms of provincial governors, who were not allowed, without the permission of the Senate, to make war or to lead their legions over their provincial boundaries. However, in 79 and to the amazement of many, Sulla retired into private life, where, once again, he took to riotous drinking and partying in a bid to recapture his youth. Like his old rival Marius, his excesses probably hastened his death, which occurred a few months later. By bringing troops onto Rome's streets, by his murderous proscriptions and by his assumption of dictatorial powers, Sulla had set sinister precedents for the years ahead, both for the fate of the Republic and for the actions of Caesar, Antony and Octavian.

Now seemed a good time to Caesar to return to Rome. Once there, he took his first step into the political limelight by taking up in 77 the case of a group of Greeks against their former governor. Rome had no state prosecutor or formal legal qualifications. Anyone could act on anyone else's behalf and appearing in high-profile legal cases on the popular side was not an unusual way of building a reputation. The governor was certainly unpopular and equally certainly guilty. It therefore says much for the corruption of the Roman courts and juries

---

*According to one academic source, more Roman love poetry is directed toward youths than to girls and women together. There is, however, no love poetry between men.

that Caesar lost this case and a second against another follower of Sulla. But he had done well in his training for the "race for glory." Plutarch sums up what he had already achieved: "In his pleadings his eloquence soon obtained him great credit and he gained no less in the affections of the people by the affability of his manners and address, in which he showed tact and consideration beyond his age; and the open house he kept, the entertainments he gave and the general splendor of his way of life contributed little by little to create and increase his political influence."

CHAPTER 4

"Odi et Amo"

IN 75 CAESAR RETURNED EAST to Rhodes to study rhetoric further under Appolinius Molon, whom Suetonius called "the greatest exponent of the art." However, Mithridates of Pontus interrupted Caesar's studies when, subdued but not fully conquered by Sulla, in 74 he made some exploratory incursions into Roman Asia. Acting for the first but not the last time on his own initiative and entirely without authorization, Caesar took charge of the local militia and repulsed the attacks, thereby gaining much further glory for himself.

Crassus and Pompey too were still on the rise. Pompey, unlike Caesar, had understandably accepted Sulla's suggestion to divorce, since Sulla had offered his stepdaughter as a replacement bride and Pompey was always uncomfortably conscious that his family pedigree was inferior to Rome's best. After Sulla's death, Pompey had led an army to subdue a rebellion in Spain.

While he was away, in the summer of 73 a revolt broke out among gladiators in southern Italy. Such outbreaks were not unusual, but this time, led by a Thracian named Spartacus, the gladiators uniquely formed themselves into disciplined units, drawing further recruits from among runaway slaves. They had rules stipulating that plunder should be shared equally. Sometimes to underline the role reversal they made their Roman prisoners fight as gladiators. At their height, their numbers reached 70,000, some even suggest 120,000, and they defeated several Roman armies, forcing open the road to the Alps and to freedom beyond the Roman frontiers. Why they did not take it but instead turned back into Italy is uncertain, but loot may have been the spur. Crassus sought and was given command against Spartacus and his men. Eventually he trapped them and Spartacus was killed. Crassus crucified each of his prisoners on crosses placed every forty yards or so along a hundred-mile stretch of the Appian Way, Roman Italy's main southern highway.

Pompey returned from Spain at the end of the revolt and with his troops defeated and killed all five thousand men of a breakaway gladiator army, thus stealing some of Crassus' glory and engendering a lasting rivalry. Although Pompey was below the required age of forty, both men were elected consul for the first time—Pompey at thirty-five and Crassus at forty-one. Together they abolished many of Sulla's changes, returning to the tribunes the powers they had previously enjoyed and expelling from the Senate more than a fifth of its members on the grounds that their contributions were worthless.

The twenty-six-year-old Caesar was delighted to be made a member of the College of Pontiffs on his return from Rhodes, succeeding one of his relatives. Unlike his previous priesthood, the lifetime position offered influence and privileges—such as the right to wear a red-striped toga—without serious restrictions. Influence was often exerted and deals done informally and over meals. Around 70, Caesar attended and may have presided as "king of the celebrations" over a dinner to mark the inauguration of a recruit to the priesthood. Unusually, details have been preserved. In addition to the candidate, eleven priests including Caesar and his brother were present. Roman women participated in such dinners and the newcomer's wife and mother-in-law were there too, together with some of the Vestal Virgins. Everyone reclined on ebony couches, the men in two circles and the women in a third.* The diners leaned on their left hand with a cup of wine near their right alongside perfumed oil, perhaps of roses, to anoint their brows. Just as in Egypt, achieving the right ambient aroma was thought essential to conviviality. Dining room floors were often spread with aromatic foliage such as ferns and verbena and scented oils burned.

The dinner menu survives. Among the hors d'oeuvres were sea urchins, raw oysters, mussels, thrushes baked under a thatch of asparagus, clams, loins

---

*Allowing women to recline on couches was a daring (some said decadent) innovation. Previously they had had to sit demurely on stools or chairs.

of wild boar and roe deer and force-fed fowl. The main course included sows' udders, boars' heads, boiled teals, ducks, hares, fish quiches and more.*

The account of the feast does not tell what wines were served but, though relatively abstemious himself, Caesar was a connoisseur who knew the value of wine to draw others into injudicious promises or confessions. At another feast, he astonished his guests because, as Pliny records, "he gave Falerian, Chian, Lesbian and Marmartine—the first time apparently that four types of wine were served [at such an event]."

Pompey's next military command was in 67 against pirates in the Mediterranean, who were becoming a major hazard to Roman trade. Within three months Pompey and his five hundred ships and 120,000 men had swept the pirates from the seas. Unsurprisingly, the next appointment he sought from and was granted by the Senate was in the east against Mithridates, who had followed up the limited incursions, made while Caesar was in Rhodes, with a full-scale invasion of Roman territory.

In his previous campaigns Mithridates had ordered the massacre of some eighty thousand Roman men, women and children and had murdered a captured Roman governor by having his mouth wrenched open and molten gold from a crucible poured down his throat to show that the Roman desire for gold could only be slaked by killing Romans. Despite his setback at the hands of Sulla, Mithridates' forces were strong once more. Nevertheless, Pompey defeated Mithridates in 66 and forced him into exile, where he died three years later. Ever the showman, Pompey appropriated from among Mithridates' possessions a red cloak once said to have been worn by Alexander and in Pompey's view an ideal garment to wear in his own Triumph.

Pompey certainly did much to earn his sobriquet "the Great" during his time in the east, adding Syria and its great capital of Antioch, as well as Pontus,

---

*The Romans relished soft, squishy meats and sows' udders are a frequently mentioned delicacy, as are sows' vulvas and wombs. Plutarch recorded that the best sows' wombs were obtained by jumping on the sow when she was heavily pregnant to bring on a miscarriage. Udders too, he related, were at their finest after this revolting treatment. To consume these delicacies, diners used knife, spoon and mostly fingers (forks were unknown until the fourteenth century AD).

to the Roman provinces. He occupied Jerusalem, where he horrified the temple priests by entering the inner sanctum. Although he eventually withdrew from Jerusalem and Judaea, Roman rule, already establshed on Egypt's western border, was surging ever closer to her eastern one. Of the three great successor states to Alexander's empire—Macedonian, Seleucid and Egyptian—Egypt was now the only one remaining independent. Cleopatra's father, Auletes, though no doubt congratulating himself for the aid he had sent Pompey and sycophantically and publicly toasting his success in Alexandria, must have wondered how much longer that would last.

In Rome, Crassus had continued to finance any emerging leaders who might bolster his faction. Among these was Caesar. Both men gave some initial support to a near-destitute patrician called Catiline. However, in an attempt to win popular support over the heads of the Senate, Catiline began to proclaim wild programs for debt cancellation—an anathema to Crassus as Rome's richest man, though perhaps less so to Caesar, himself heavily in debt. Senators became sufficiently worried that even the most patrician of them supported the new man Cicero against Catiline as one of the two consuls for 63. The gangling, stringy Cicero received the most votes, while the second consular post went to an ally of Crassus, not Catiline.

Also in 63, Crassus backed Caesar for the post of high priest, or pontifex maximus—the top religious office in the state. The appointment, which brought with it a town house in the Forum next to the Vestal Virgins, usually went to an elder statesman. Caesar spent massively on his campaign, both on public shows and on direct bribery of the electorate. According to Suetonius, Caesar told his mother as she kissed him good-bye on the morning of the poll that he owed so much that if he did not return to her as high priest, he would not return at all but have to flee his creditors. To general surprise he won, having demonstrated both his supreme self-confidence and the willingness to stake his future on a single event. Later that year, Caesar was also elected praetor, and at thirty-seven was well on the way to the top himself.*

**Pontifex maximus* means "chief bridge builder"—in early times the chief priest had had responsibility for the all important Tiber Bridge. The title was subsequently appropriated in turn by the Roman emperors and by the Pope.

Catiline stood for consul at the following year's elections but was again defeated. As ambitious as Caesar but less skilled at planning and calculating, he began to plot a rising. Both Caesar and Crassus disclosed to Cicero what they knew of his conspiracy. Further aided by the disclosure of pillow talk by one of the conspirator's mistresses, Cicero denounced Catiline to the Senate, claiming that he intended to set fire to parts of Rome as a distraction and then to murder hostile senators. Catiline fled Rome and was killed after a brief battle in January 62.

Cicero was the hero of the hour and never afterward let the Senate or anybody else he could buttonhole forget that he had saved the Republic. Despite what he himself called his "foolish vanity," Cicero was an astute man. By nature a defender of the republican orthodoxies, he remained suspicious of the radical intentions and personal ambitions of both Caesar and Crassus. In later years he would become Antony's most influential and outspoken critic.

During a debate in the Senate about the fate of the alleged conspirators, who included Antony's stepfather, Caesar first made an enemy of Cato, another key conservative figure in the dramatic period that lay ahead.* Perhaps conscious of his own contacts with Catiline at the time of the plot's infancy, Caesar suggested light sentences for some of the conspirators. The thirty-two-year-old Cato, who despite his relative youth rightly enjoyed a reputation for moral probity and incorruptibility, was a supporter of what he imagined as the stern old republican values and demanded the death sentence. The argument in the Senate grew heated. While Cato was orating, insinuating that Caesar might have been in league with the conspirators, he saw a note being passed to Caesar. Cato suggested to the assembled senators that it was from more undisclosed conspirators and demanded it be handed to him. Reading it, Cato found that it was, in fact, a love letter to Caesar from his mistress, Cato's married half sister Servilia. Cato threw the letter back with the unsophisticated insult "Have it, you drunken idiot"—seemingly the best riposte that Cato, a heavy drinker himself, could muster on the spur of the moment. When the debate closed with victory for Cato, several of his henchmen attacked Caesar. His murder was

---

*Cato was not only the antithesis of Caesar politically. Unlike the dandy Caesar, he deliberately dressed in black rather than the then fashionable purple and, to emphasize his contempt for comfort and luxury, walked everywhere, sometimes barefoot.

averted only by Cicero's intervention, perhaps to his later regret. Cato's enmity, as unbending as his moral certainties, endured.

In 62, Caesar became indirectly involved in one of the great scandals of the Roman republic. Every year the Festival of the Good Goddess was held in the house of one of the magistrates and on this occasion the house chosen was Caesar's. He was forbidden to be present—the celebrations were strictly for women only. Cicero described the Good Goddess as "a mystery beyond the powers of men to know." She was a kind of earth goddess responsible for the female side of life such as the fertility cycle and childbirth. Caesar's second wife, Pompeia, a granddaughter of Sulla whom he had married in 67 following the death a couple of years previously of his first wife, Cornelia, was the hostess, together with his mother, Aurelia. The chief celebrants of the rite were the Vestal Virgins, but most of female high society was present. In defiance of tradition, the young patrician reprobate Clodius infiltrated the gathering.

His scandalous reputation at this time derived not from his being a womanizer who had affairs with married women—such liaisons were, even if disapproved of, common among the elite, where marriages were usually arranged for political ends—but from the report that he had had sexual relations with each of his three married sisters. (The most famous of these sisters was Clodia, about whom another of her lovers, the poet Catullus, wrote the poem "Odi et Amo," "I both hate and love her.") Unlike in Cleopatra's Egypt, in Rome incest was forbidden and considered perverted.

Why Clodius wanted to invade the feast is not clear. Perhaps it was simply bravado and curiosity; perhaps he was having an affair with Pompeia. Whatever the case, he sneaked into the house dressed as a singing woman but was caught loitering in the shadows. The women, as Plutarch puts it, "after covering up the sacred objects . . . drove him out of doors and at once that same night went home and told their husbands."

Conservatives denounced Clodius' behavior as symptomatic of a contemporary decline in moral values and disrespect for tradition. The ambitious Caesar coolly protected his political position by divorcing his wife with the celebrated and enigmatic words "Caesar's wife must be above suspicion" and departed without further comment at the end of his praetorship to take up a governorship in Spain. Cicero was the prosecutor at Clodius' trial. He described in disgust how Clodius, with Crassus' money, bribed the jury. He "settled the whole business, called the jurors to his house, made promises, backed bills or paid cash down . . . some jurors actually received a bonus in the form of assignations with certain ladies or introductions to youths of noble families . . . nevertheless twenty-five jurors had the courage of their convictions . . . As for the other thirty-one, they were more worried about their empty purses than their empty reputations." Though acquitted, Clodius would neither forget nor forgive the witty barbs Cicero aimed at him during the trial and afterward.

Many including both Cato and Crassus were highly apprehensive that on his return from the east Pompey would use the undoubted popularity his successes had brought him to demand for himself new powers and greater rewards. Yet when Pompey returned he acted in accordance with tradition and disbanded his legions. His requests to the Senate were relatively modest—for land to be allocated to his veterans and for ratification en bloc of the administrative arrangements he had made in the east. Pompey divorced his wife, Mucia, a notorious philanderer said to number Caesar among her lovers, and, in an attempt to ingratiate himself with Cato, offered that he and one of his sons would marry Cato's two nieces. Cato refused: "Pompey should know that I will not be outflanked through the bedroom of a young girl." Cato also led the Senate in opposition to Pompey's requests, partly on the procedural grounds that the administrative arrangements should be debated in full and partly simply to underline the Senate's power over any individual citizen, however mighty.

Pompey was nonplussed. His lust was for glory, not for absolute power. At heart he trusted in the Senate and the tradition of the elders and all he wanted was for the senators to show their trust and appreciation of him, his troops and his deeds by meeting his requests without quibbling. Always a poor speaker in the Senate and so politically inept that a contemporary wrote, "He is apt to say one thing and think another but he is usually not clever enough to stop his real aims from showing," he did not know what to do next. Yet within a few months the Senate, at Cato's instigation, had unwisely alienated Crassus and Caesar as well and made Pompey's next step clearer.

Cato opposed a bill put forward by Crassus to secure revisions to the terms under which cronies of the latter had purchased the right to gather (or "farm") the taxes in Asia, since they had clearly overestimated the take and wanted the government to recompense them for their own error. While morally correct, as on so many other occasions Cato could have acted less bluntly to minimize offense, as Cicero realized: "As for our dear friend Cato, the fact remains that with all his patriotism he can be a political liability. He speaks in the Senate as if he were living in Plato's 'Republic' instead of Romulus's cesspit."

Caesar's clash with the Senate occurred when he returned from Spain in 60 to seek the consulship. Because he had won some military victories in what is now Portugal, he had been awarded a Triumph. By tradition, until he celebrated his Triumph a general was still considered under arms, and a general under arms could not enter Rome. The consular elections would take place before his Triumph could be arranged. Caesar therefore sought permission to stand for consul by proxy—a request that his implacable foe Cato took pleasure in persuading the Senate to refuse. Caesar forwent his Triumph to stand for the consulship, which he won handsomely.

Previously, it had been considered almost a law of nature that Crassus and Pompey were irreconcilable rivals but now, each thwarted and slighted by the conservative faction in the Senate led by Cato, they combined forces. It is a measure of Caesar's rapidly rising stature that he promoted this unlikely alliance and joined these two giants of the age in their secret coalition. Soon to be made public, it has become known to historians as the First Triumvirate although it had no legal status. The participants simply agreed to undertake no action detrimental to the others. Nevertheless they, not the Senate, had effective control of Rome.

To cement his place in these new arrangements, Caesar offered the hand of his twenty-four-year-old daughter Julia to Pompey, who accepted with alacrity. Cato condemned Caesar as no better than a pimp to his own daughter, trading her honor for political capital. When Caesar in turn married Calpurnia, the daughter of Piso, the Triumvirate's favored consular candidate for the year after Caesar's tenure of that office, Cato fulminated, "It was intolerable for marriage to be the coin by which leadership of the state was bought and sold and for women to be the means by which men slotted one another into provincial governorships, military commands and the control of resources." Cicero wrote of Caesar's new father-in-law that "talking with him is much the same as holding a discussion with a wooden post in the forum . . . a dull and brutish clod . . . profligate, filthy and intemperate."

With Caesar as consul, a bill was passed granting undeserved rebates to Crassus' tax farmers. Caesar next introduced a law to grant the land his son-in-law Pompey had requested for his veterans. It was opposed, as usual, by Cato and by Caesar's fellow consul for the year, a somewhat ineffectual man called Bibulus, whose election the conservatives had secured by bribery. Caesar, always impatient of dissent, became so enraged by Cato's filibustering tactics in the Senate—a body that had to adjourn its sessions before the early spring sundown—that he foolishly ordered him to be seized and taken off to jail. Several senators made to accompany him, loudly asserting their preference to be in jail with Cato rather than in the Senate with Caesar. Realizing that for the present he had overreached himself, Caesar released Cato.

Determined to have his way, however illegally, in the face of further stalling tactics from both Cato and Bibulus, Caesar with Pompey organized gangs of the latter's veterans who roamed Rome's streets intimidating their opponents whatever their rank. Bibulus had already angered Caesar, issuing edicts describing him as "the queen of Bithynia who once wanted to sleep with a monarch but now wants to be one." When Bibulus tried to postpone another vote on the grounds that he saw inauspicious omens in the sky, Pompey's veterans moved in. They emptied a basketful of dung over Bibulus' head. As he struggled to wipe it off, the veterans smashed the fasces—the bundle of twelve 5-foot-long birch rods tied together with a red leather thong and with an axe in their middle that represented the consular power or *imperium*—and beat up the lictors, his official bodyguards. Recovering himself, Bibulus bared his neck for execution, ready to die and to call down vengeance on Caesar. But Caesar was bent on humiliation, not execution. Bibulus' friends hurried him off, leaving the way clear for Caesar, after this display of brute force, to have the intimidated Senate vote through the land law.

At the end of his consular year, after further political chicanery, Caesar was granted the governorship of Roman (Transalpine) Gaul for an unprecedented five-year period. He had obtained what he wanted—in the words of the contemporary historian Sallust, "a high command, an army and a war in some field where his gifts could shine in all their brightness." Before departing, Caesar struck up an unexpected alliance with Clodius, the man who had disturbed the rites of the Good Goddess.

Clodius had noted the success of Pompey's veterans in forcing through laws in their favor. He gathered his own thugs around him and began to deploy them to further his own political ambitions by intimidating his opponents. The word *fascist* derives from the Roman *fasces* and many have seen parallels between the use of premeditated mob violence by Caesar, Clodius and their contemporaries to subvert weak but legal governments and the actions of

Mussolini and Hitler in the 1920s and 1930s. Such gangs were certainly an increasingly destabilizing factor in the republic's latter days. Caesar secured Clodius' election to a tribuneship further to increase the aspiring demagogue's patronage and influence with the people—both of which he would be sure to use on his own new patron's behalf.*

Within three months and even before Caesar's departure, Clodius forced Cicero into voluntary exile. The orator was not physically a particularly brave man and had been constantly harassed by Clodius' gangs throwing dung and insults and threatening him with trial for irregularities in connection with the execution of the Catiline conspirators. Around this time too, Clodius, with triumviral backing, organized the annexation of the Ptolemaic possession of Cyprus—the act that sparked the Alexandrian mob to chase Auletes from his throne—to replenish Rome's depleted coffers. He also orchestrated the appointment by the cowed Senate of Cato to oversee the annexation as a device to get him out of Rome. Caesar himself, having demonstrated his resolution to secure his own ends however far he needed to go in "persuading" the Senate, soon left for Gaul, where he was to spend, in total, nine years.

The Gauls were brave, volatile men who frequently quarrelled amongst themselves. They were long-haired and moustached, and like their women wore chunky gold or silver armlets. Their southern neighbors mocked them as uncivilized because they wore trousers. Their homeland, Transalpine Gaul, lay, as its name suggests, beyond the Alps, occupying roughly the area of modern-day France and Belgium. In 58 the Romans controlled only a relatively small southeastern portion of this territory.

Caesar's conquest of Gaul, undertaken without the formal authorization of the Senate, is well documented in his own book *De Bello Gallico*. Although it is

---

*Although Roman leaders of the period in practice achieved much by illegitimate and violent means, like many recent dictators—and unlike rulers of medieval times—they almost invariably sought the appearance of legitimacy by standing for office in elections, although electors were too afraid to vote for any other candidate, if indeed other candidates were prepared to stand. Similarly, they took care to have their decisions approved within preexisting but subverted power structures such as the Senate.

designed as political propaganda for himself (it is written in the third person and the name Caesar appears more than 770 times), Caesar was always clear and usually fair, admitting his mistakes and praising the deeds of his juniors. Caesar's clarity is summed up by this advice to other writers: "Avoid an unfamiliar word as a sailor avoids the rocks." However, the format of Roman books would make them anything but clear to modern readers. They were written on papyrus rolls up to thirty feet long and the texts had no punctuation, no paragraphs, no spaces between words and no capital letters.

Caesar's first success was to repulse the Helvetii who invaded the Rhone Valley. He next headed north, marching and fighting through the winter to reach the North Sea. One of his subordinates, Crassus' young son Publius, subdued the west of Gaul, and Caesar gloried in his report to the Senate that he had brought peace and Roman rule to the whole of the country. Back in Rome everyone rejoiced. Cicero, newly returned from exile, led the praise, "Regions and nations unreported to us in books, or in first-hand accounts, or even by rumors, have now been penetrated by our general, our army and the arms of the Roman people."

Auletes, then a humble supplicant in Rome, must have hoped that some of those arms and armies might soon be put at his disposal to help him regain his throne but, as so often in Egypt's relationship with Rome, internal Roman politics once again took precedence over the pleadings of kings. He and Cleopatra would have to wait.

CHAPTER 5

Crossing the Rubicon

IN FACT, it would be another two years before Auletes would be able to buy Rome's military assistance in restoring his kingdom to him. Cicero's return had followed further upheavals in Rome. Pompey had virtually disappeared from public life. Genuinely unsure of what more he wanted to achieve, he retired to seek solace with his young wife, Caesar's daughter Julia, provoking popular mockery that he was just an uxorious, sex-mad old general. Clodius, glorying in his own rising power and Pompey's declining popularity, began to provoke him, at one stage threatening Pompey with the seizure of his mansion and blockading the house.

Like Caesar, Pompey was highly conscious of his *dignitas*—a word that embraces not only our concept of dignity but also those of status, honor and self-esteem. Such a public display of disrespect was entirely too much for him. Goaded into action, he sponsored another tribune, Milo, to recruit gangsters of his own to oppose Clodius. Rome had no police force. The army was not permitted to enter the city. Gang warfare therefore escalated unchecked: "The Tiber was full of bodies, the public sewers choked with them and the blood streaming from the Forum had to be mopped up with sponges." Slowly Pompey began to exert himself. Among his first actions was to secure Caesar's consent to Cicero's return, hence the latter's paean to the Gallic conqueror.

Clodius in turn sought the support of his long-term financier Crassus, who, still keen to keep Pompey in his place, backed him. In consequence, feelings between the two triumvirs became so intense that Pompey told Cicero that Crassus had been behind Clodius' plots all along and wanted to have him killed.

The triumvirate appeared doomed but then, unexpectedly, in spring 56 Crassus and Pompey made peace at a summit meeting brokered by Caesar in Lucca. The upshot was that Crassus and Pompey would become consuls again in 55—the year Antony stormed Pelusium and opened the road for Auletes to return to Alexandria.

It soon emerged what else had been in the reconciliation for Crassus and Pompey, and also for Caesar. After their consulships, Crassus would take a five-year command in Syria and Pompey a similarly lucrative period in Spain. Caesar would get another five years to carry on his work in Gaul. Crassus was intent not just on ruling Syria but, having jealously mocked Pompey's Alexandrian pretensions, now wished to outdo him by conquering the only remaining eastern superpower, the Parthians (the rulers of Persia), before marching further east toward India, just as Alexander had done, heaping the Roman people and, more importantly, himself with glory and loot.

Crassus crossed the Euphrates in the spring of 53 and headed out into the sandy Mesopotamian wastes. Drawn ever onward, deeper into this wilderness, pursuing the shapes of Parthian horsemen on the shimmering horizon, Crassus' splendid legions became increasingly exhausted. Then, not far from a town named Carrhae, the Parthian army materialized through the haze. Attacked by armored heavy cavalry and bewildered by the famous Parthian shot—clouds of arrows fired by mounted archers who wheeled away as they delivered their deadly volleys—the Roman soldiers began to die where they stood in their defensive formations. As the casualties mounted, the lines started to break. The parched legionaries tried to close up into a smaller perimeter, but to no avail. A few, maintaining their discipline, managed eventually to fight their way back to the frontier. Ten thousand became prisoners but twenty thousand died in the gritty desert sands, among them Crassus and his son Publius, who had fought so well with Caesar in Gaul. Crassus' head was taken to the Parthian king, who ordered it to be deployed as a stage prop in a production of Euripides' *Bacchae* that he happened to be watching at the time.

Crassus had failed even to equal his rival Pompey's exploits, let alone those of the legendary Alexander. It would be twenty more years before another Roman triumvir—Antony—crossed into the desert to avenge Crassus and attempt to relive Alexander's dream. This time he would be financed by one of the great Macedonian's distant descendants—Cleopatra.

The triumvirate was now a duumvirate. Soon after the summit in Lucca, Caesar faced a series of rebellions in Gaul, culminating in that led by a chieftain named Vercingetorix. As astute an analyst of what was possible militarily as he was of practical politics, Caesar was as meticulous in his planning as he was neat and elegant in his person. He moved quickly, acted decisively and, undogmatic, was prepared to change his tactics as events unfolded to maintain the pressure on his opponents. Unfazed by having to confront numerically superior forces, he won his legions' hearts by always leading from the front, often on foot, as well as by his commitment to reward them well.

Antony had joined Caesar in Gaul following his success in helping restore Auletes to the Egyptian throne. He was among Caesar's commanders at his last great battle in Gaul at Alesia, near present-day Dijon, where Caesar besieged Vercingetorix in his hilltop fortress. Told by his scouts that a massive relieving army of Gauls was, in turn, about to attack him in the rear, Caesar ordered some of his heavily outnumbered legionaries to about-face and build ramparts at the Roman army's rear to allow the battle to be joined on two sides. Antony was in the thick of the four days of hard fighting. In his *Gallic Wars* Caesar praised his young commander in particular for his calmness and leadership during a nighttime attack by the Gauls, when Antony and another officer skillfully moved legionaries around their defensive perimeter to reinforce weak points and successfully held off the Gauls.

Throughout the battle the red-cloaked Caesar was himself visible everywhere, encouraging his troops until, when he believed his opponents exhausted, he ordered his cavalry to charge. The weight and ferocity of their attack routed his besiegers. Those Gauls who could fled. Those inside the fortress who could not surrendered, including Vercingetorix. Caesar had now finally subdued Gaul, killing, so he calculated, nearly 1.2 million Gauls in battle, to say nothing of the numbers of civilians killed, dispossessed or enslaved with his many prisoners of war. As a result of his efforts, Rome was no longer solely a Mediterranean power. Its legions now also guarded the Atlantic and the North Sea; its merchants and traders had even greater dominions from which to profit.

* * *

While Caesar was facing the Gallic rebels, in Rome the Senate should have been giving thought as to how best to govern the extensive new territories being acquired. Instead, politics in the capital had deteriorated yet further into petty factionalism and corruption, particularly following Crassus' death at Carrhae. Pompey remained uncertain of what he wanted—absolute power or the respect of the Senate. In August 54, his much-loved wife, Julia, died after a miscarriage. When elections were postponed because bribery had become so blatant and universal that the Senate felt compelled to act, some senators turned to Pompey, suggesting that he assume dictatorial power—a proposal that, unsurprisingly, was anathema to Cato.

Cato now put forward as his favored candidate in the much-postponed consular elections Milo, Pompey's former henchman, who had long since fallen from Pompey's favor. Pompey was not amused and neither was Clodius, Milo's long-standing adversary. Clodius, under the guidance of his strong-minded, politically astute wife, Fulvia—who would one day marry Antony and be an equally forceful presence in his life—had, under Caesar's patronage, been attempting to become a mainstream politician. Both outraged and threatened by Milo's candidature, he returned, probably with relish, to his street-fighting past.

Yelling and heavily armed mobs rampaged through Rome's streets once more. Then, in January 52, the two gang leaders and their gangs clashed on the Appian Way. A javelin wounded Clodius in the shoulder, and his supporters carried him bleeding into a neighboring inn. Milo's men rushed in after them, dragged Clodius out and lynched him.

Fulvia, instead of collapsing into paroxysms of grief, had her husband's mangled and naked body retrieved from where it was lying in the street—ironically, next to an altar of the Good Goddess—and coolly orchestrated revenge. First she summoned more of Clodius' supporters from the slums. Then, when they arrived, she exhibited her husband's body to them in the lobby of her house. Carefully and dramatically, she revealed his wounds one by one as the onlookers' indignation rose. The next day, with her encouragement, the mob transported Clodius' corpse to the Senate, where they cremated it using the furniture and papers as makeshift fuel for the pyre, which consumed the Senate building as well as Clodius' remains. Rival gangs fought among the flames.

Every respectable Roman leader was appalled. Even Cato turned to Pompey to rescue the republic from mob rule. Pompey answered the call of duty with alacrity, speedily restoring order, and Milo was exiled. Basking in the glory and respect he had always thought his due, Pompey remarried. He did not accept Caesar's offer of his seventeen-year-old great-niece Octavia—thirty-seven years Pompey's junior and another future wife of Antony—but instead took the hand of the beautiful and highly patrician Cornelia, the young widow of Crassus' son Publius. Pompey was now moving toward the republican faction and away from Caesar and the popular party but, again enraptured by the charms of a young wife, he did not act decisively.

It was Caesar who took the lead by seeking to extend his command in Gaul until he could once more legally stand for the consulship in 48. The hard-line republicans and traditionalists such as Cato opposed the proposal, suspecting that Caesar merely wanted to preserve his armies intact and himself, as an officeholder, immune from prosecution by his enemies for exceeding his authority until after winning the consulship, when, with his veterans at his elbow, he could ram through legislation augmenting his own powers and rewarding his loyal followers. Pompey procrastinated, unwilling to abandon Caesar entirely, but in the end he came down in favor of the Senate, reassuring his new followers grandiloquently that if Caesar intervened militarily, "I only have to stamp my foot and all over Italy legions and cavalry will rise from the ground."

Tensions rose further in what Cicero called "a struggle for personal power at the state's expense" as Caesar maneuvered to bolster his position. Although still in Gaul, he secured a strong man to represent him in Rome: Antony. Under Caesar's patronage, Antony was elected tribune. In the face of the hostility of most of the Senate he displayed not only the physical courage he had shown previously but also a fiery oratory in defending Caesar and virulently attacking Pompey. In January 49, using the powers of the tribunes, restored after Sulla's death, Antony vetoed a Senate bill that ordered Caesar to surrender his command or be outlawed as an enemy of the people. The Senate's response was to eject Antony from their midst and threaten him with death if he returned, as well as to grant Pompey emergency powers. Antony and some other of Caesar's supporters disguised themselves as slaves and, hiding in the backs of carts, fled toward northern Italy, where Caesar, encamped with a single legion, was awaiting the outcome of the Senate vote.

Before Antony could reach him, Caesar heard reports of what had happened in Rome and realized that he had to act decisively, albeit unconstitutionally, if he was to win power or indeed, in all probability, preserve his life. On

January 10, 49, his legion crossed the cold waters of the river Rubicon in the Apennines, which formally marked the boundary between Cisalpine Gaul, one of the provinces Caesar commanded, and Rome. Caesar's laconic comment "Let the dice fly high," made as he gave the order to advance, shows that he knew the gamble he was taking. In marching out of his province in arms toward Rome he was committing treason, breaking one of Sulla's laws that had not been overturned.

Antony joined Caesar at Rimini. Having taken the irrevocable step, Caesar advanced quickly on Rome. The Senate remained suspicious of Pompey and refused to grant him all the freedoms he required to marshal an effective resistance. Thus Pompey took a decision that was sound militarily but disastrous politically. He abandoned Rome, proclaiming that any senator or official who remained was a traitor. Caesar cleverly responded that he, on the other hand, would consider any who were not openly against him as with him.

Pompey retreated swiftly south and, only sixty-five days after Caesar had crossed the Rubicon, Pompey and his troops left Italy for Greece. Pompey was convinced that his best chance of success lay in exploiting the riches and resources of the East, where he had enjoyed so many triumphs and had so many supporters, including, he believed, the Ptolemies. Caesar, who pursued Pompey pell-mell to his departure port of Brundisium and nearly succeeded in blocking the embarkation of the republicans, decided against immediate pursuit since his was the inferior navy. Instead, he determined to cross to Spain to defeat Pompey's supporters in the provinces, where Pompey had so long been absentee governor. Before departing he appointed Antony as his governor in Italy. That he did so demonstrated trust not only in Antony's political and military judgment but also in his loyalty—a trust that was not misplaced.

Caesar soon defeated Pompey's followers and, satisfied that he need no longer fear attack from the rear, returned to Italy. Here too the situation had remained sufficiently calm under Antony's rule for Caesar to feel confident in 48 to cross the Adriatic and face Pompey himself.

This time Caesar entrusted Antony with a military role—to bring five legions of reinforcements across the Adriatic to back up his initial landings. It took Antony three months to get the troops across, because of storms and the activities of the powerful republican navy under Caesar's old foe Bibulus. Caesar's forces were in a perilous situation until Antony and his troops arrived, but once they did, the combined force began to advance. Nevertheless, their first attempt to surround and destroy Pompey's troops, at their main base at Dyrrhachium on what is now the Albanian coast, ended in a serious setback. Caesar himself admitted that Pompey should have won "total victory if only he knew how to be a winner." Undaunted, a few weeks later, in the hot, high summer of 48, Caesar offered battle to Pompey and the squabbling forces of the republic further inland on the plains of Thessaly at Pharsalus.

The republicans had never quite trusted their general, complaining that Pompey still had his own agenda to secure absolute power, was addicted to command and disrespectfully enjoyed treating former consuls and praetors like slaves. Pompey himself did not wish to risk all in a major battle, realizing correctly that he had the resources, including twice as many troops, to withstand a long campaign of attrition better than his opponents. But since, as in Plutarch's words, "he was the kind of man who was swayed by what people thought of him and was ashamed to lose face before his friends, he was forced to change his mind." Pompey gave the order to prepare for battle the next day, August 9, 48. It would be the largest battle ever fought between Romans.

When Caesar saw Pompey's troops begin to deploy he made his own arrangements with his customary speed, decision and tactical awareness. He placed Antony in command on the left. Antony had so distinguished himself previously in the campaign that, according to Plutarch, his reputation "next to Caesar's was the greatest in the army," and Caesar himself thought him his most capable officer. He himself took not the center but the right, with his favored Tenth Legion, opposite where he thought Pompey would be. He realized that he was deficient in cavalry and took what measures he could to counteract this. Knowing that most of Pompey's cavalry were young sprigs of nobility, "young dandies," in his own words, "unused to battles and wounds, bedecked with flowers and long hair" and anxious to protect their handsome faces, not liking "the glint of steel shining in their eyes," he urged his men to thrust not at the cavalrymen's bodies but directly into their faces.

Pompey's inexperienced young cavalry were indeed intimidated by the fierce upward thrust of Caesar's infantry's spears, "turning their heads and covering them with their hands to protect their faces." They soon fled, followed swiftly by the rest of Pompey's forces, whose positions the cavalry men exposed by their flight. When Caesar's victorious legionaries reached the enemy camp they found many signs of fatal complacency—tents crowned with shiny green myrtle leaves ready to celebrate an anticipated victory, silver platters laid out for the victory feast. As so often reported in the history of victorious commanders, Caesar is said to have eaten the meal prepared for Pompey. The latter fled, discarding his insignia of rank and disguising himself as he went.

Caesar was determined to draw the conflict to a speedy conclusion. As he had done throughout the civil war, he ordered clemency to be shown to his captured enemies and, as he had done throughout his military career, the immediate close pursuit of those who were retreating—a task that on this occasion he entrusted to Antony. Walking through the bodies on the battlefield that night (Caesar's estimate was 15,000 Pompeian dead against only 230 of his own men, but later historians put the figures at 6,000 and 1,200 respectively), Caesar is said to have soliloquized in self-justification, "It was all their own doing. Despite all my achievements I, Gaius Caesar, would have been condemned had I not appealed to my army for help."

In reality it had been nothing like as simple. Caesar, Crassus and even Pompey had at times felt themselves sufficiently above the traditions of the elders and indeed Rome's laws to disregard them. Intransigent republicans such as Cato, who was absent from Pharsalus, had resisted any compromises or adaptations to changed circumstances. The strife between the republican and popular parties would not end for some years and even this civil war would continue. The republicans had strong forces still in the east and Africa, and Pompey determined to join them. Stopping only for a tearful reunion with his young wife, Cornelia, he took ship with her and his younger son, Sextus, then in his early teens, for Egypt via Cyprus, accompanied by a small fleet. Some fifty days after Pharsalus, his vessel anchored off the sandbanks and mudflats of the Nile delta.

PART III

Queen of Egypt, Mistress of Rome

CHAPTER 6

Like a Virgin

When he sighted Egypt, Pompey was sure that its rulers would help him—after all, Ptolemy XIII had responded to his request for aid earlier in his struggle against Caesar by sending him men, ships and corn. As a consequence, Pompey's grateful supporters in the Senate had decreed that he should be the young king's guardian as a mark of particular favor to the Egyptian monarch and his supporters. Why should Ptolemy refuse to aid him now? Pompey had his trireme anchored on the bobbing swell within sight of the camp at Mount Casius where Ptolemy's army was preparing to give battle to Cleopatra's forces. From here Pompey dispatched a messenger and confidently awaited an answer.

Pompey's arrival, however, caused consternation to Ptolemy's regency council of Pothinus the eunuch, Achillas the military commander, and Theodotus the king's tutor. According to Plutarch, the last sealed Pompey's fate, arguing that "if they took him in they would have Caesar as their enemy and Pompey as their master, and if they sent him packing they would incur Pompey's anger for expelling him and Caesar's for not holding on to him." The solution, Theodotus insisted, was to kill Pompey. That way Caesar would be grateful and Pompey would no longer be a threat. "And then it is said, he added with a smile, 'Dead men don't bite.' "

And so on September 28, 48, the Egyptians summoned Pompey to his death. The treacherous task was entrusted to Achillas, who with a former

Roman officer called Septimius who had once served under Pompey, a centurion named Salvius and a few henchmen sailed out toward Pompey's vessel. Pompey's companions, anxiously scanning the shore, sensed something was wrong. Why were there no preparations for the magnificent reception that should greet a great Roman general? All they could see, as Plutarch put it, was "a few men sailing towards them in a single fishing-boat." They warned Pompey to put out to sea at once.

While Pompey hesitated, the fishing boat drew nearer. Septimius got unsteadily to his feet and hailed Pompey in Latin as "imperator," "commander." Achillas added his voice, greeting Pompey in Greek and inviting him to board the fishing boat because, he said, the numerous shoals and sandbanks would prevent Pompey's trireme from coming closer in to shore. Pompey's young wife, Cornelia, was already in tears, "weeping in anticipation of his death" as her husband bade her and Sextus good-bye and with two centurions, a freedman called Philippus and a slave clambered down into the fishing boat, whose rowers at once began making for the shore.

The silence was disturbing. Looking closely at the men into whose hands he had entrusted his life, Pompey recognized Septimius as an old comrade in arms but the man simply nodded in brief and curt acknowledgment. Cornelia, watching anxiously from the ship, saw the fishing boat at last reach the shore. Pompey was trying to stand up in the rocking boat, clutching at the hand of his freedman for support, when Septimius ran him through from behind with his sword. Salvius and Achillas also drew their daggers. Pompey collapsed into the bottom of the vessel, where, dragging his toga over his head as the blows fell, he died, according to Plutarch, "with nothing more than a gasp, without saying or doing anything to betray his dignity." It was the day after his fifty-eighth birthday.

While the distraught Cornelia struggled to take in what she had just witnessed, others on the trireme, seeing that ships from Ptolemy's fleet were preparing to sail out and intercept them, hastily weighed anchor and made for the open sea, where a strong wind aided their flight. On shore, Pompey's assassins hacked his head roughly from his body, which they stripped and left "exposed as a ghastly spectacle for anyone to see who wanted to." Philippus remained loyally by the mutilated corpse until, eventually, the crowd of sightseers who had swarmed eagerly around the body grew bored and drifted off. Then he rinsed off the clotting blood with seawater, dressed Pompey's body in one of his own togas and searched the shore for timber to build a funeral pyre for his erstwhile master.

Four days later, on October 2, 48, Caesar sailed into the harbor of Alexandria with four thousand troops and thirty-five warships. If Ptolemy and his council anticipated Caesar's thanks, they were disappointed. Whatever his personal feelings at being rid of his rival—and he must have been relieved—the manner of it shocked him. When Theodotus proudly handed him Pompey's pickled head and heavy gold signet ring with its device of a lion brandishing a sword, Caesar recoiled "as if from a polluted murderer."*

The governing clique around the king watched in growing dismay as the Roman they had assumed would gratefully confirm Ptolemy on the Egyptian throne and consign Cleopatra to exile showed no sign of being so accommodating. Caesar made clear from the start that Pompey's murderers could take nothing for granted, coming ashore with the full dignity of a Roman consul, his lictors bearing the fasces before him as the symbols of his authority. His justification for appearing in official regalia was that the will entrusted to Rome by Cleopatra's father had appointed Cleopatra and Ptolemy as co-rulers of Egypt. With brother and sister on the cusp of war, the will was plainly not being honored, giving him the legal right to intervene.

While Caesar's magisterial attitude was a stroke of good luck for Cleopatra, waiting anxiously beyond Egypt's borders, it galled Alexandria's excitable population. All they saw was an arrogant Roman strutting ashore as if Egypt were already a Roman province. Soldiers and citizens alike began rioting and in the days that followed mobs killed several of Caesar's men strolling unwisely around the city. Caesar began to realize that his own position was precarious. The seasonal north winds gusting boisterously in across the Mediterranean and flecking the seas with foam made it difficult simply to sail away. On the other hand, he had relatively few men to defend him in this volatile, populous, alien city.

Alexandria had once far outshone Caesar's Rome. Arrian, Alexander's ancient biographer, recorded that on his way down the Nile from Memphis, where he

*Dante was so appalled at Ptolemy's behavior toward Pompey that he placed him in the same circle of hell as Cain and Judas.

was crowned pharaoh, Alexander reached a point to the west of the delta and between Lake Mareotis and the sea when "it seemed to him that the site was the very best on which to found a city and it would prosper . . . A longing for the task seized him and he personally established the main points of the city." Legend says that when marking out the foundations, Alexander and his men swiftly ran out of chalk. Instead, they trickled out barley meal from the workmen's food supplies as marker lines. Suddenly "birds infinite in numbers" appeared and devoured the meal. "Even Alexander was greatly disturbed at the omen. However, the seers exhorted him to be of good cheer since the city to be founded here would have most abundant and helpful resources and be a nursing mother for men of every nation."

By the time of Caesar's visit it certainly seemed the seers were correct. Alexandria was still the ancient world's second-largest city after Rome with a population of around half a million, about a sixth of Egypt's total. Rectangular in shape, it was about three miles long and planned on a grid system. One visitor described how "the city is as a whole intersected by streets practicable for horse-riding and chariot-driving and by two that are very wide, around a hundred feet across." Another recalled how "entering by the Gate of the Sun, I was instantly struck by the splendid beauty. I tried to cast my eyes down every street but my gaze was still unsatisfied . . . In one quarter . . . the splendor of the town was cut into squares for there was a row of columns crossed by another as long at right angles." The streets, many of which were shaded by green awnings, were angled to catch the cooling breezes blowing off the Mediterranean. Ancient obelisks and sphinxes brought downstream from Heliopolis, Memphis and other cities of the pharaohs stood in public spaces and dotted the colonnaded streets, giving an exotic and ancient air to the new foundation.

The city's temples, shrines and public buildings were brilliantly colored. From the time of the pharaohs it had become a tradition to leave not a single inch undecorated. Artists had long been pounding lapis lazuli for its rich deep blue, malachite for its subtle green, ochre for its earth colors and charcoal for its dense black. They applied the results to turn carved pillars into palm trees and breathe life into the carved reliefs of kings and queens, gods and goddesses and their spectacular imagined worlds depicted on walls and ceilings.

Alexandria had two main harbors, a western one and a great or eastern harbor. The western harbor was known as the "Harbor of Good Fortune" and had an inner dock built around the entrance to a canal leading to Lake Mareotis and then onward to the Canopic branch of the Nile. The eastern harbor was, according to visitors, divided into subsidiary harbors and numerous quays and was so deep that even the largest ships could berth. The geographer Strabo, writing just after Cleopatra's death, called Alexandria "the greatest emporium in the inhabited world." Among the warehouses full of grain, Egypt's major export, was a great customs house. It also served as a place of noisy trade where the produce of the saffron crocus from Cyrenaica and spices such as cinnamon and pepper, transhipped from Africa, India and beyond, were bought and sold, as were rolls of linen, bags of Egyptian soda—used across the Mediterranean for laundering clothes—and carefully packed crates of engraved Egyptian drinking glasses appreciated by Rome's rich for their fragility.

Heaps of gold-skinned dates from Thebes were considered especially juicy by connoisseurs, while Egyptian gum arabic, made from the acacia thorn, was particularly useful as a fixative for the face paints beloved of Roman matrons. The latter were also interested in the by-product of a more dangerous cargo—crocodiles. The reptiles had first been shipped to Rome in 58 when five were exhibited in a specially built pool with a hippo at one of the regular Roman Games. Subsequently more and more had arrived to be butchered in contests with gladiators. Roman women thought that the creatures' dung would remove facial blemishes and redden their cheeks. Another export for which the demand of Rome's increasing empire was inexhaustible was papyrus to record triumphs, laws and tax takes.

Separating the eastern and western harbors was a causeway nearly three quarters of a mile long pierced by two arches that gave access from one harbor to the other while breaking the force of the prevailing western current and thus providing added protection to the great harbor. At the end of the breakwater was a flat natural island with stout seawalls called Pharos. At its eastern extremity was built the seventh wonder of the ancient world—the lighthouse of Alexandria. Completed in about 283, the Pharos, as it became known, stood for seventeen centuries until after a series of earthquakes it was finally demolished.*

---

*The site is now occupied by Fort Qait Bey. A huge, big-breasted granite figure of a Ptolemaic queen that once stood outside the Pharos was recently removed from the harbor, its once sharp carving smoothed and blunted by the sea.

Coins, drawings and recent underwater archaeology suggest that the lighthouse was probably nearly four hundred feet high—the height of a thirty-five-story building—and surrounded at its lower base by large pink granite sphinxes and tall statues of royal Ptolemaic couples dressed as pharaohs to remind those sailing past that they were entering not only a Macedonian city but the capital of the sovereigns of Egypt.

The lighthouse had three tiers and was approached by a long ramp with vaulted arcades. The first tier was rectangular with windows on all sides giving light to service rooms. The second tier was octagonal and the third cylindrical. Here a series of mirrors, perhaps of burnished brass, would have reflected the sunlight out across the Mediterranean during the day and at night or during overcast days the light of a fire of resinous wood. The rays are said to have been visible for more than thirty miles. The lighthouse was built mostly of the polished white limestone quarried locally. It was reinforced at its base with large blocks of granite, some weighing more than thirty tons; in recent years, underwater investigations suggest that some of these foundation blocks were actually recycled from old obelisks and sphinxes cut to size.* The architect who built the Pharos, Sostrates of Cnidus, reputedly employed a novel ruse to mark the work as his own for posterity. He engraved into the stone of the Pharos an inscription stating that he was the constructor, then plastered this over and engraved into the plaster the name of the ruling Ptolemy, knowing full well that over time the plaster would wear away and his own name would be revealed for all to see.

The royal palace complex also lay along the harbor and contained a private, artificial royal harbor. Each of the Ptolemies had built a palace of their own, leaving those of their predecessors intact. The area had thus expanded over time so that, according to Strabo, the palaces occupied "a quarter or even a third" of the space within the walls that confined the city. Strabo described how "on sailing into the harbor one comes on the left to the royal palaces which have groves and numerous buildings painted in various colours." The palaces too are now sunk below the sea following a series of

---

*The waters around the lighthouse were clearly tricky, even with its presence. Archaeologists have found several shipwrecks nearby.

earthquakes and tidal waves in the fourth and fifth centuries AD. Archaeology has revealed that they and their surrounding gardens were studded with ancient sphinxes and large statues of the gods as well as shrines and works of art. Among the latter were a highly elaborate fountain described in a surviving inscription as made of many kinds of stone, both Greek and Egyptian, and portraying Queen Arsinoe III and sundry nymphs, and a remarkable coiled statue of the city's guardian serpent, the Agathos Daemon, which had reputedly appeared at the time of Alexander's foundation of the city.

Within the palace area also stood the Museon with its covered colonnaded alleys where scholars could pace, think and converse, sheltered from the sun before eating for free in the neighboring refectory. The celebrated library, which by Cleopatra's time contained around seven hundred thousand scrolls, was probably nearby.*

Strabo described how the royal palaces contained the monument known as the Sema, an edifice containing the tombs of the Ptolemies and of Alexander. After Ptolemy I had hijacked the body of Alexander he had interred it in a golden sarcophagus. The latter had been stolen by a later usurping Ptolemy and subsequently replaced with a sarcophagus made of alabaster where Alexander's mummified body remained at the time of Caesar's visit. From the few surviving fragments of descriptions the Sema was a pyramid-like structure with vaults beneath containing the bodies.†

Elsewhere in the city were the Great Theater, the huge colonnaded and porticoed six hundred-foot-long Gymnasium that stood in the center of the city to the south of the royal palaces, and an artificial hill "in the shape of a fir cone" built specifically to give a panoramic view of the great metropolis to residents

---

*Seven hundred thousand scrolls equate to roughly 128,000 books. In contrast, it is estimated that fifteen hundred years later, just before the invention of moveable type, there were only seventy thousand books in the whole of Europe.

†In Christian times St. Mark became another famous Alexandrian corpse when he too was buried in a special tomb, where he remained until, in 828 AD, Venetian merchants famously smuggled him out, insisting to Islamic officials that his body was a shipment of pickled pork, to be buried in the Venetian cathedral that bears his name.

and visitors alike who climbed up the pathway spiraling around it. Outside the city walls was the racetrack or hippodrome.*

The Alexandrians, as all the Egyptians, were highly skilled in waterworks of every kind. The network of canals around Alexandria was sophisticated and led eventually via the Nile and the Bitter Lakes through another narrow canal to a small port on the Red Sea known as Cleopatris, near the modern city of Suez, so that cargoes could traverse the country from the Red Sea to the Mediterranean by water. Alexandrians had also built an intricate system of interconnecting cisterns and aqueducts to supply fresh water since neither the lake nor canal water was fit to drink. Many of the cisterns were underground and their roofs were often supported by several series of thick stone columns.†

Caesar would have heard many languages on the spice-scented quays and in the bustling streets of Alexandria. The Macedonian Greek of the ruling classes vied with other dialects from the Greek islands and mainland and from Syracuse and other Greek settlements around the Mediterranean. The native populations, who congregated to the west of the city, spoke Egyptian; as their Macedonian rulers required, they were a minority in their capital despite increasing immigration from elsewhere in search of work and advancement as Alexandria grew. Roman legates, traders and military advisers conversed in Latin, while Persians, Syrians and Gallic and German mercenaries each used their own tongues.

Much Hebrew was also spoken. Alexandria had a large Jewish population—larger than any other city of the time with the exception of Jerusalem. Of the five "quarters" into which the city was divided, each designated by a letter of the Greek alphabet, the whole of one area (Delta), near the royal palace, and much of another (Beta), were occupied by Jews, and synagogues were scattered throughout the city. During the early days of the Museon, seventy Jew-

---

*The Greeks and Hellenes originally built gymnasia as places of exercise to prepare citizens for the rigors of military service. However, by Cleopatra's time the function had broadened—though exercise remained important, gymnasia were also educational and intellectual centers. In Germany today high schools are still called *Gymnasien*.

†Their existence is revealed today only when some of the columns break, causing the streets above to subside.

ish scholars had been summoned by the Ptolemies to translate the Pentarch into Greek.*

Numerous Jewish people had fled to Alexandria after persecution by the Seleucids. They occupied a wide variety of positions, some in government, some as traders and some as soldiers in the polyglot Egyptian forces. Strabo described how the Jews had a great deal of autonomy: "A large part of the city of Alexandria has been set aside for them. They are presided over by an Ethnarch who governs the race, presides over the law courts and supervises contracts and ordinances just as if he was the supreme magistrate of an independent community."

The newly arrived Caesar installed himself in the luxurious palace complex of the Ptolemies with its airy pavilions and fragrant gardens, quickly announcing his intention to arbitrate between the royal siblings. He ordered Ptolemy to report to him in the royal palace. The young king hurried to Alexandria but left his armies intact on the eastern border—a fact Caesar noted. With him came his treasurer, the eunuch Pothinus, who, loathing and fearing Romans, immediately began to obstruct Caesar's plans, among them exacting from the Egyptians the huge sums of money Caesar insisted he was owed. His claim went back to the lavish borrowings of Cleopatra's father, in particular from the Roman banker Rabirius. After his ignominious flight from Egypt, Rabirius had complained that the king had failed to repay him and Caesar, with an eye to the main chance, had acquired the debt. On Auletes' death, he had agreed to reduce what was owed by around half but now he insisted on being paid the remainder. Despite its political confusion, Egypt was still the world's richest country.

With more energy than common sense, Pothinus made plain that the Romans were not welcome. According to Plutarch, "his words and behavior towards Caesar were often rude and offensive." The grain he sent to feed Caesar's men was old and musty and he "told them to put up with it without complaining, since it was other people's food they were eating." He stirred up the already smarting population by ensuring that Ptolemy's food was served up in crude wooden or chipped pottery dishes, implying that the rapacious

*This translation is known as the Septuagint. It is still regarded as one of the most accurate translations of the Hebrew Bible.

Caesar and his men had grabbed all the household's silver and gold platters for themselves.

As tensions within the palace grew, Cleopatra made her entrance. It is unclear whether Caesar had, as Plutarch suggests, ordered her to Alexandria like her brother or whether, guessing that her physical charms and personal charisma would be her best advocates, she had herself decided to plead her case in person. She would certainly have known of Caesar's susceptibility to women, either by report or, if she had indeed accompanied her father to Rome, by what she had heard and observed there. Caesar, as appropriate for a supposed descendent of Venus, was a man of vigorous sexual appetites. A contemporary dismissed him as every man's woman and every woman's man and indeed, his youthful escapades notwithstanding, he was highly attracted to good-looking women. According to Suetonius, as his troops marched in triumph through the streets of Rome they celebrated his womanizing by singing such verses as:

Home we bring our bald whoremonger;
Romans lock your wives away!
All the bags of gold you lent him
Went his Gallic tarts to pay.

Noting that "his affairs with women are commonly described as numerous and extravagant," Suetonius detailed Caesar's bedding of a succession of well-born Roman women. The woman Caesar apparently loved most was Servilia: "In his first consulship he bought her a pearl worth 60,000 gold pieces. He gave her many presents during the Civil War, as well as knocking down certain valuable estates to her at a public auction for a song. When surprise was expressed at the low price, Cicero made a neat remark: 'It was even cheaper than you think, because a third (tertia) had been discounted.' Servilia, you see, was also suspected at the time of having prostituted her daughter Tertia to Caesar." People also whispered that Caesar was the father of Servilia's son, Marcus Brutus. If true, there was a sad irony to it since Brutus would one day be among his assassins.

Whatever her ultimate intentions, for Cleopatra the task of reaching Caesar was infinitely more difficult and dangerous than for her brother. Ptolemy's forces stood between her and Alexandria, while his navy was blockading the city's harbor. If captured, she would have been killed out of hand and her body quietly disposed of. Cleopatra's solution was to stake everything on one stunningly audacious and theatrical stunt.

She slipped aboard a ship bound for Alexandria and, as it neared the city, transferred into a smaller craft with, as her sole companion, a loyal Greek merchant from Sicily named Apollodorus. In the purpling dusk their tiny vessel slunk into the harbor, where Apollodorus moored in the shadows and prepared to go ashore. He was a carrying a long cylindrical bag of the type used to transport bedclothes or carpets, secured with a leather strap. Somehow he managed to enter the royal palace, find his way to Caesar and deposit his burden at the Roman's feet. Cleopatra extricated herself from the bag, uncoiling in fetching deshabille before the astonished and soon to be enamored Roman.

Their first encounter has fascinated generations. To the Roman poet Lucan, Cleopatra was a corrupt and calculating enchantress: "confiding in her beauty, Cleopatra approaches him, sad without any tears, arrayed for simulated grief as far as is consistent with beauty, as though tearing her dishevelled hair . . . her features aid her entreaties and her unchaste face pleads for her." Her beauty was as fatal and ruinous to those who beheld it as Helen of Troy's and "the hardy breast of Caesar caught the flame . . . in the midst of frenzy and the midst of fury, and in a palace haunted by the shade of Pompey." Lucan blamed Cleopatra, not Caesar, for what happened next: "a night of infamy she passes, the arbitrator being thus corrupted."

Lucan was right in one sense—Cleopatra's sex appeal and power over men is beyond question—but she was probably not conventionally beautiful. Coins, albeit eroded with age, give the best idea of how she actually looked. Those minted in Alexandria and Ascalon early in her reign show a striking young woman with large eyes, full mouth, hooked nose and strong chin. Her abundant hair is drawn back from her face in the braids of the traditional Ptolemaic "melon coiffure"—so called because of the resemblance of the divided braids to the stripes on a melon rind—and finishing in a bun on the nape of her neck. Later coins depict a woman with high cheekbones, strong jaw and even more pronounced nose, whose face looks hawkishly powerful and far removed from the wide-browed, straight-nosed, placid-featured ideal of Roman beauty.

Some coins depict Cleopatra with so-called Venus rings—circles of fat on the neck. Obesity was certainly a characteristic of Cleopatra's dynasty and representations of her ancestors show many were well fleshed. A model of Cleopatra in her late twenties, produced for this book by an expert in archaeological reconstruction using surviving coin images, statues and carvings of her, shows a voluptuously fleshy-faced woman with a broad forehead, hawkish nose, somewhat mannish cast of features, and more than a hint of a double chin, and offers an intriguing alternative vision of a woman more often thought of as lithe and gamine than as Rubenesque.*

Cleopatra had qualities rarer and more compelling than mere prettiness. Plutarch wrote that "according to my sources, her beauty was not of itself absolutely without parallel, not the kind to astonish those who saw her; but her presence exerted an inevitable fascination, and her physical attractions, combined with the persuasive charm of her conversation and the aura she sometimes projected around herself in company did have a certain ability to stimulate others. The sound of her voice was also charming."

Clearly, Cleopatra's erotic appeal was enhanced by an independent, self-reliant spirit and an agile, able mind. Her first language was Greek and this was probably the language in which she addressed Caesar—as an educated Roman, he would have been familiar with the lingua franca of the eastern Mediterranean. Yet Plutarch praised her extraordinary facility "which enabled her to turn her tongue, like a many stringed instrument, to any language she wanted, with the result that it was extremely rare for her to require an interpreter in her meetings with foreigners; usually she could answer their questions herself, whether they were Ethiopians, Troglodytae, Hebrews, Arabs, Syrians, Medes or Parthians. Unlike the previous rulers of her dynasty, she had also troubled to learn Egyptian." In the Roman world intellectual and artistic accomplishments were much appreciated in a woman and thought to add to her attractions. Sallust wrote admiringly of a woman who possessed "intellectual strengths which are by no means laughable: the skill of writing verses, cracking jokes, speaking either modestly or tenderly or saucily—in a word, she had much wit and charm." He could have been writing of Cleopatra as well.

One of Shakespeare's characters observes that there was something of the gypsy about Cleopatra. In more recent times others have suggested that

---

*For details of the process used to build up the model see the appendix.

she had black African blood but there is no evidence of this other than in a symbolic sense of being an outsider in a male- and Roman-dominated world. She was, however, almost certainly dark-haired and olive-skinned. Though some of her early Macedonian forebears had been blond, they came of mixed stock. Also, intermarriage with the Seleucid dynasty had added Persian blood to the Ptolemaic dynasty, while Cleopatra's paternal grandmother, a concubine whose name is unknown, was quite probably Syrian. Some historians believe that Cleopatra's paternal grandmother was, in fact, Egyptian and base their claim that Cleopatra might have been black upon this. There is a precedent—an earlier Ptolemaic king took an Egyptian mistress. However, even if Cleopatra's grandmother was Egyptian it does not follow that she was a black African.

Whatever her complexion, Cleopatra would have known how to make the best of herself. The Ptolemaic queens had long been celebrated for their expertise with perfumes and unguents. An early work on cosmetics has been attributed to Cleopatra and even if she was not its author, she could have been. She certainly would have paid careful attention to her appearance on this first meeting with Caesar, perhaps darkening her eyebrows and eyelids with antimony, adding a translucent luster to her skin with finely ground powders and reddening her lips with the juice of ripe mulberries. Rich musky perfumes would have added to the overall effect. Cleopatra must have seemed the embodiment of the eroticism and exoticism of the East and of glamour beyond royalty—after all, here at Caesar's feet was not only a proud young queen, kin to Alexander the Great, but a living goddess—the representation of Isis on earth.

Cleopatra's bold and imaginative act also appealed to Caesar on another level. He knew all about taking calculated all-or-nothing risks and admired courage in others. In a way, Cleopatra's carpetbag stratagem had been her Rubicon, her opportunity to let the dice fly high. Had it failed she, like him, could have lost everything. Instead she had gambled and won. As Plutarch put it, "This ruse is said to have opened Caesar's eyes to the side of Cleopatra that was far from innocent and to have made him fall for her."

And fall for her he did. The young Egyptian queen and the seasoned Roman general became lovers, probably that very night, as Lucan claims, Cleopatra surrendering her virginity in a calculated act to secure her future. There seems no reason to doubt that she was still a virgin. Nothing suggests she had ever taken lovers and had the young Cleopatra been sexually promiscuous, Roman propagandists would have gratefully and gleefully reported it. At this stage in their relationship Caesar's primary attraction for Cleopatra must have been his ability to help and protect her. Though fit and athletic, he was, at fifty-two, middle-aged. He had also, as his soldiers so raucously sang, lost most of his hair and he resorted to the usual fruitless methods of disguising it. Suetonius reported: "His baldness was a disfigurement which his enemies harped upon, much to his exasperation; but he used to comb the thin strands of hair forward from his poll and of all the honors voted him by the Senate and People, none pleased him so much as the privilege of wearing a laurel wreath on all occasions—he constantly took advantage of it."

As a vain man, Caesar may also have resorted to techniques like those described in the book on cosmetics attributed to Cleopatra, which contained detailed advice for dealing with "falling-off eyelashes or for people going bald all over," enthusing "it is wonderful" before detailing a bizarre lotion: "Of domestic mice burnt, 1 part; of vine-rag burnt, 1 part; of horse's teeth burnt, 1 part; of bear's grease, 1; of deer's marrow, 1; of reed bark, 1. To be pounded when dry, and mixed with lots of honey; then the bear's grease and marrow to be mixed (when melted), the medicine to be put in a brass flask, and the bald part rubbed with it till it sprouts."

Caesar was no doubt a deft lover. Romans had a profound appreciation of good sex as a gift from the gods, a blessing from Venus herself. They believed that both man and woman should derive pleasure from the act, hence Ovid's advice to male lovers:

> Believe me, the pleasure of love is not to be rushed, but gradually elicited by well-tempered delay. When you have found the place where a woman loves to be fondled, don't you be ashamed to touch it any more than she is. You will see her eyes gleaming with a tremulous brightness like the glitter of the sun reflected in clear water. Then she will moan and murmur lovingly, sigh sweetly, and find words that suit her pleasure. But be sure that you don't sail too fast and leave your mistress behind, nor let her complete her course before you. Race to the goal together. Then pleasure is complete, when man and woman lie vanquished side by side.

> This tempo you must keep when you dally freely, and fear does not rush a secret affair. When delay is dangerous, then it is useful to speed ahead with full power, spurring your horse as she comes.*

Cleopatra's ruse had been successful. However, she was not yet safe. Neither, somewhat to his surprise, was her lover.

---

*Curiously though, in contrast to the Greeks, the Romans did not admire the female genitalia. Greek poems eulogized depilated female genitalia that seemed to shine like pearl or alabaster between a woman's soft thighs. By contrast, erotic Roman poets dwelt lovingly on the buttocks, thighs and anuses of youths but wrote with shuddering distaste of the female sexual organs. The attraction of a Roman woman lay in her smooth, unblemished skin, flowing silken hair, small breasts, long legs and rich, sensuous clothing.

CHAPTER 7

The Alexandrian War

When Ptolemy learned the next day that his rival had stolen undetected into Alexandria and had spent the night with Caesar, he rushed out into the streets, ripping his royal diadem from his brow and calling on the people to rise against Cleopatra and her Roman paramour. His histrionics had the desired effect on an already restive and indignant population, and mobs swept toward the palace, carrying Ptolemy with them. Only with the greatest difficulty did Caesar's well-disciplined legionaries hold their nerve, force their way into the crowds, collar the struggling, protesting adolescent and drag him back inside the palace.

Caesar moved quickly, reminding the mob of the late king's will, assuring them with his customary eloquence of his good intentions and declaring that Cleopatra and Ptolemy would rule together. He also decreed that, as stipulated in their father's will, the two should undergo the traditional brother-sister nuptials for form's sake. As a further sweetener to the Egyptians, Caesar restored Cyprus—annexed ten years earlier by Rome—to the dynasty, decreeing that it should be an independent kingdom under the joint rule of Cleopatra's younger half sister, Arsinoe, and her eleven-year-old half brother, yet another Ptolemy.

The rapprochement was marked by a lavish banquet. Lucan bemoaned how "Cleopatra amid great tumult displayed her luxuries, not as yet transferred to the Roman race. The place itself was equal to a Temple, which hardly a more corrupt age could build; and the roofs adorned with fretted ceilings displayed riches, and solid gold concealed the rafters . . . Ivory covers the halls, and backs of Indian tortoises, fastened by the hand, are placed upon the doors, dotted in their spots with plenteous emeralds. Gems shine upon the couches, and the furniture is yellow with jasper; the coverlets glisten, of which the greater part, steeped long in the Tyrian [purple] dye, have imbibed the drug not in one cauldron only. A part shines, embroidered with gold; a part, fiery with cochineal." The attendants were as exotic: "this one has dark hair, another has hair so light that Caesar declares that in no regions of the Rhine has he seen locks so bright; some are of scorched complexion with curly hair . . . Unhappy youths as well, rendered effeminate by the iron and deprived of virility." Their flower-bedecked hair was drenched in costly imported cinnamon "which had not yet diminished its fragrance in foreign air but still carried the scent of its native land, and also with cardamom, freshly and locally harvested."

The centerpiece was Cleopatra herself: "Having immoderately painted up her fatal beauty . . . upon her neck and hair Cleopatra wears treasures and breathes deep beneath her ornaments. Her pale breasts glisten through the Sidonian fabric . . . in which the needle of the workman of the Nile has separated and loosened the warp by stretching out the web."

But Cleopatra would have been realistic enough to recognize that her wealth, even more than her person, was immensely attractive to Caesar. There was a political point behind the ostentation and extravagance of her banquet as well as the spell of spectacle. She plied her Roman guest with delicacies on golden plates and gem-studded bowls brimful with wine. In the heady, drug-like atmosphere, "Caesar learnt how to waste the wealth of the despoiled world."

If Cleopatra had any objections to Caesar's decision about how Egypt was to be ruled, she was too wise to voice them as she continued her seduction of him, but her feelings must have been ambivalent. After all, she was expected to share the throne she regarded as hers with the half brother who had tried to dispense with her. Also, though Cyprus was a traditional heartland of the Ptolemaic empire and, at the dynastic level, she welcomed its return, on the personal one she loathed Arsinoe, who with their younger brother was to rule the island. Caesar too must have had mixed feelings. As would very soon become apparent, he could have made his own position more secure by siding with the king against Cleopatra. Caesar also knew he would be criticized in Rome over Cyprus—proconsular generals, even ones as all-powerful as he, were supposed to acquire Roman territory, not give it away. Yet, as Plutarch suggested, perhaps he could not help himself: "he damaged his reputation and risked his life needlessly for no real reason, and it was just that he was so passionately in love with Cleopatra."

With discontent still simmering in the streets, Caesar kept to the palace, where the four royal siblings, including his new mistress, also bided their time. For a few weeks there was a seeming calm, but in late October 48 Pothinus sent a secret message summoning Ptolemy's army back to Alexandria from the eastern border with orders to attack and dislodge the uninvited Romans from the palace quarter. This was presumably done with the young king's knowledge and consent—though such matters were largely in the hands of his powerful council, everything suggests he joined very willingly in their schemes.

A dismayed Caesar, interrupted in his new love affair, learned that a force of twenty thousand, including two thousand cavalry, was advancing on the city, led by Pompey's chief assassin, Achillas. Knowing that he was vastly outnumbered, Caesar dispatched messengers to Rhodes, Crete, Syria and Asia Minor demanding ships, corn and troops and especially archers and artillery (in the form of catapults). To buy time, he sent two eminent court physicians, both of whom had carried out sensitive missions for Cleopatra's father, as emissaries to Achillas, but the latter contemptuously had them murdered out of hand.

With the Alexandrians eagerly awaiting the arrival of Ptolemy's army, Caesar took the precaution of placing the king under house arrest. Also, accepting that he could never hold the entire city, he fortified the quarter around the royal palace, the adjacent theater and the great library. Soon after, Achillas' forces arrived and launched their attack in what Lucan described as a very un-Roman manner: "weapons rain down on the palace and the household gods tremble. There is no battering ram to breach the walls in one blow and break into the palace, there is no siege engine, nor do flames work for them; rather, the young troops, without any strategy, split up and surround the palace." Caesar's well-disciplined men relatively easily prevented their disorganized enemy from gaining entry, yet Cleopatra and her Roman lover were effectively as much in prison as her half brother. Thus in 48 the Alexandrian War had begun and, as Suetonius wrote, would prove to be "a most difficult campaign, fought during winter within the city-walls of a well-equipped and cunning enemy."

Caesar faced attack by sea as well as by land. In Alexandria's Great Harbor, ships of the royal Egyptian fleet mustered in readiness to assault Caesar's ships, anchored in the palace's private harbor, which they greatly outnumbered. Caesar responded to the apparently hopeless position by ordering his ships to row out to surprise and engage the Egyptian fleet. The shock tactics worked. In fierce hand-to-hand fighting the Romans seized and set fire to many enemy ships. Their pitch-coated wood burned so fiercely that flames whipped up by the wind soon spread to the buildings along the quayside, jumping, in Lucan's words, "from roof to roof like a meteor as it cuts a furrow across the heavens." Here the fires were fed by the dry papyrus of thousands of scrolls waiting to be taken to the great library or to be shipped abroad.*

In the confusion of acrid, choking smoke and searing heat, and with the Alexandrians distracted from the siege of the palace by the need to save their homes, Caesar took a further bold step to secure his safety and that of Cleopatra. Noting that "because of the narrowness of the channel there can be no access by ship to the harbor without the consent of those who hold the Pharos," he dispatched troops by boat to capture the lighthouse at the eastern tip of the island of Pharos. They soon overran it and installed a garrison. It would now be possible for Caesar's much hoped-for reinforcements to enter the harbor and land. Caesar also took advantage of the confusion to throw up further barricades around the palace quarter.

The sudden flight of Cleopatra's young half sister, Arsinoe, however, took the seasoned commander by surprise. Together with her adviser, an ambitious, bellicose eunuch named Ganymedes, the princess managed to reach Achillas and his army. The anti-Roman Arsinoe was more to their taste than the pro-Roman bed partner of Caesar, and they at once proclaimed her queen of Egypt and joint monarch with Ptolemy. This undermined Caesar's position only a

---

*For a long time historians believed that the Library of Alexandria itself was consumed in the flames but although up to forty thousand volumes may have been destroyed in the warehouses, it is now thought that the library itself survived until its destruction during riots in early Christian times. Only one document remains—a papyrus of 235 BC written in Greek discovered in a mummy case in which it had been used as lining. The original is in the National Library of Austria but a facsimile is in the new Library of Alexandria, built some two hundred meters east of where the original library is thought to have stood.

little less than Cleopatra's. Up till then, he could claim the rising was a rebellion against Egypt's rightful king, conveniently, of course, under his protection in the palace, but the proclamation of Arsinoe gave the rising a new legitimacy. However, the infighting so characteristic of the Ptolemaic court came to Caesar's aid. Ganymedes, Achillas and their respective cliques soon began to spar over control of the army. When Pothinus, confined with his protégé Ptolemy in the palace, learned of the feuding, he sent a message to Achillas assuring him of his support and promising to escape from the palace with the king.

This time, thanks to a barber who was, according to Plutarch, "habitually driven by his quite extraordinary cowardice to keep his ear to the ground and poke his nose into everyone's affairs," Caesar learned of the plot in time. He ordered Pothinus' immediate execution, a decision that gave him considerable satisfaction, since he had long suspected the eunuch of plotting his murder. Not long after, Achillas too was dead—murdered on Ganymedes' orders. Ganymedes now took command of the army, assembled a new fleet, flung a tighter cordon around the royal palace and used mechanical waterwheels to pump seawater into the water system feeding the palace area of Alexandria. When Caesar's thirsty troops realized that their drinking water had been contaminated, they panicked, but he calmly ordered them to labor through the night to dig new wells and within a few hours the relieved men tapped into "a great quantity of sweet water."

The sighting off Alexandria, two days later, of the sails of transport ships bringing a Roman legion and supplies from Asia Minor was timely, even though the stubborn contrary wind prevented them from gaining the harbor. Caesar made a dash with his oared naval vessels to meet the transports and, after foiling an Egyptian counterattack during which over a hundred Egyptian ships were lost, took advantage of the softening winds to tow the new arrivals with their cargoes of food and weaponry safely into the royal harbor.

Yet Caesar was still not strong enough to break out, and Ganymedes was profiting from the impasse to strengthen and reequip the Egyptian fleet, tearing down the roofs of colonnades, gymnasia and other public buildings to make oars. In February 47, to frustrate the Egyptians' incessant efforts to set fire to his vessels, Caesar managed to extend his control from the great lighthouse to the entire three-mile-long island of Pharos. However, his attempt the next day to seize the breakwater linking the island to the shore nearly led to his death. He and his men leapt onto the breakwater from their ships and rushed along it to the point where it met the shore. Caesar ordered his troops to construct a barrier here and also to block up the archways beneath the breakwater with stones to prevent Egyptian boats sailing through. They began work but, unseen by them, Egyptian troops had also landed on the breakwater and were advancing swiftly and stealthily behind them. Too late, the sweating Romans realized they were under attack, dropped their spades and grabbed their swords.

Fearing capture, Caesar's own ships began shoving off from the breakwater, leaving him and his men trapped. Some legionaries managed to leap across the widening gulf into the departing Roman vessels; others hurled themselves into the water. The anonymous author of *The Alexandrian War*, probably an officer who was with Caesar, described what happened next: "Caesar yelled words of encouragement, striving to keep his men at their tasks, but when he saw that they were fleeing and that he too was in danger he withdrew to his own vessel." However, "a large number of men followed him and kept forcing their way aboard it," making it impossible to steer the ship or push off from the shore.

At this point, Caesar jumped overboard into the sea. The various accounts of how he saved himself depict him as a superman. Though fifty-two and wearing armor, and despite the fact that he was being attacked by the Egyptians and swamped by the waves, Plutarch reported that he managed to swim with only one arm, in order to save some important papers by holding them above water with the other. Suetonius loyally claimed that, in addition to all his other feats, he "was towing his purple cloak behind him with his teeth, to save this trophy from the Egyptians." Whatever the reality, he managed to reach a ship, from where he sent small craft back to pick up survivors and so saved a considerable number. His own ship, from which he had wisely leapt, had sunk under sheer weight of numbers and most had drowned. In total, Caesar had lost more than eight hundred legionaries, seamen and rowers. The desperate struggle would have been visible to Cleopatra, watching anxiously from the palace walls and for whom Caesar's death would have had terrifying repercussions. Had he been killed, she would have lost not only the new protector on whom she had staked everything but doubtless her own life as well. Sleeping with the enemy would not have been forgiven and her younger siblings would have been delighted to be rid of her.

Ptolemy's supporters judged that this was a good time to persuade Caesar to release their king. According to the author of *The Alexandrian War*, they couched their proposal in dulcet terms: "The whole population, they said, being tired and wearied of Arsinoe, of the delegation of the kingship, and of the utterly remorseless tyranny of Ganymedes, were ready to do the king's bidding; and if, at his insistence, they were to enter into a loyal friendship with Caesar, then no danger would intimidate or prevent the population from submitting." The writer continued, with lofty Roman disdain, that Caesar was not taken in by the tricks of "a deceitful race, always pretending something different from their real intentions." Nevertheless, Caesar decided to let Ptolemy go. Perhaps he and Cleopatra hoped that allowing him to join Arsinoe and Ganymedes would trigger rivalries that would only be to their advantage or that Ptolemy might, as he earnestly promised, order Arsinoe and her advisers to cease the attacks. But after shedding copious tears at parting from Caesar, the duplicitous youth rushed from the palace "like a horse released from the starting gate," no doubt followed equally quickly by members of his entourage.

Ptolemy pushed Arsinoe and Ganymedes aside and took command of the royal forces besieging the palace quarter. However, by early March 47 the bulk of Caesar's long and eagerly awaited reinforcements from Syria and Asia Minor were finally approaching overland. At Ascalon they were joined by Jewish troops from Judaea led by Antipater, father of the future King Herod. Under the overall command of Mithridates of Pergamum, the relief force assaulted and swiftly took the Egyptian frontier stronghold of Pelusium before sweeping on toward Alexandria and a rendezvous with Caesar. To reach the city they had first to cross the branches of the Nile delta. Hoping to check their advance, Ptolemy loaded a large force onto his ships and sailed out of Alexandria through the city's network of waterways to Lake Mareotis and into the Canopic branch of the Nile, along which Mithridates was advancing. Learning of this, Caesar left a small detachment to protect Cleopatra and sailed westward by sea out of Alexandria.

Landing along the coast, Caesar marched rapidly southeast and rendezvoused with the relief force before the Egyptians could come up. Determined to retain the initiative, he turned his attention to the well-defended camp, over the Canopic branch of the Nile, where young King Ptolemy and his advisers were debating their next step. Caesar's legionaries plunged into the warm water or felled trees for makeshift bridges, which they swarmed across. After a stiff fight they eventually took the camp, only to find that the king had fled. However, the ship he had hurriedly boarded sank beneath the weight of panicking men trying to follow their king to safety. Ptolemy drowned. On learning of this, Ganymedes, Arsinoe and the Egyptian army surrendered.

The Alexandrian War was finally over and that night the victorious Caesar hastened back to Alexandria and Cleopatra with his cavalry. He entered through the part of the city formerly held by his enemies, where, as the author of *The Alexandrian War* recorded, "the entire population of townsfolk threw down their arms, abandoned their fortifications . . . and surrendered themselves to him," leaving Caesar "master of Egypt and Alexandria." To prove to the populace that Ptolemy had indeed perished, Caesar ordered the Nile to be dragged until his sodden body was found and then put his golden armor on display.

The dangerous and costly conflict he had just won gave Caesar ample cause to annex Egypt as a Roman province, but he did not. Instead, he confirmed his mistress as queen with, as her co-ruler, her remaining half brother, the twelve-year-old Ptolemy XIV. Cleopatra must also have been gratified that Caesar made her co-ruler with her brother over Cyprus, conferring the island on them as the rulers of Egypt. Cyprus' previous and short-lived queen, the disgraced Arsinoe, was to be sent to Rome to pay the price for her duplicity by trudging as a captive in the procession celebrating Caesar's triumph.

Caesar's actions perhaps reveal something of his feelings for Cleopatra, who, as the author of *The Alexandrian War* states with what with hindsight seems dry economy, "had remained loyal." He is primly silent on the intimate form the Egyptian queen's "loyalty" had taken. Cleopatra was by now pregnant with a child conceived while the danger to herself and Caesar from the Alexandrian mob and the Egyptian army had been at its height. However, though seemingly still infatuated with the Egyptian queen and no doubt flattered by the signs of his virility, Caesar was not so lost to love and what the poet Lucan called "Cleopatra's wicked beauty" that he allowed it to dictate his judgment. His decision was guided above all by the perennial "Egyptian problem" that had so often perplexed Rome—the fact that Egypt was too rich and important to become a province lest, in Suetonius' words, "it might one day be held against his fellow-countrymen by some independent-minded governor-general."

Many would later argue, for motives of their own, that Cleopatra's child was not Caesar's. After all, during his entire life this great lover of women had sired only one acknowledged child, his beloved daughter, Julia, born many years earlier. In twelve years of marriage, his then wife, Calpurnia, had not once conceived. However, while Caesar may have had a low sperm count, it is equally possible that Calpurnia was infertile. Furthermore, that his many well-born Roman mistresses do not appear to have borne him children is also no proof of his infertility. Some would have passed his children off as their husband's; others would have used contraceptive techniques. Though some of these were bizarre—from wearing a cat's liver in a tube on the left foot to carrying part of a lioness' womb in an ivory tube—more sensible and effective methods were available, including blocking the passage to the uterus with concoctions of oil, honey and wool. It was also possible to procure abortions, prompting Ovid's indignant plaint, "Why do you dig out your child with sharp instruments?" Another reason suggested for the relatively low fertility among the Roman elite was the effect of the lead used in the city's water pipes.

Also, if not Caesar, who was the father of the child with whom Cleopatra was swelling visibly? To strengthen her alliance with a protector who she suspected might be incapable of impregnating her, Cleopatra could have taken another, clandestine, lover. Yet the women of the inbred house of Ptolemy were obsessively proud of their lineage and it seems highly unlikely that Cleopatra would have found a man she considered suitable as a Caesar surrogate. It is also implausible that such a careful tactician as Cleopatra would have risked her budding relationship with Caesar by such a trick in the hothouse atmosphere of the palace, where little remained secret for long.

With matters successfully concluded, including access to Egypt's treasure houses to replenish his coffers, Caesar should have left Egypt at once. Though he had appointed Antony his deputy or *magister equitum* (master of the horse) in Italy while he pursued Pompey to Egypt, and knew he could depend on his loyalty, much required his urgent personal attention. Rome's civil war was not yet over. Pompey's supporters were rallying in Africa while, in Asia Minor, King Pharnaces of Pontus was threatening to become as great a menace to Rome as his father, Mithridates, who had taken such pleasure in slaughtering Italian women and children. Instead, using the somewhat lame excuse that the seasonal winds that blew into the harbor mouth continued to make the departure of his fleet difficult, the usually highly disciplined Caesar entirely atypically chose to linger by Cleopatra's side. According to Suetonius, he would feast with his lover until the sun rose over the city to challenge the light of the Pharos.

In the early spring of 47, it seems that Caesar embarked with Cleopatra on a cruise up the Nile. Egyptian royal barges were the stuff of fantasy—sumptuous floating palaces of fragrant cedar and cypress about three hundred feet long, forty-five feet wide and sixty feet high, hung with costly fabrics and sparkling with gems, all supported on twin, catamaran-like hulls. Lying on silken couches and cooled by peacock-feather fans, the lovers could dally as they floated past the rich bright green farmlands along the Nile, Caesar adorned with the wreaths of flowers that were a Ptolemaic fashion.

However, it was more than a pleasure trip. For Cleopatra, there was a strategic purpose in showing herself to the wider Egyptian population beyond Alexandria. Cleopatra was unpopular in her idiosyncratic, cosmopolitan capital, but her relationship with the people of the countryside and especially those of Upper Egypt was warmer. They remembered her homage to the Buchis bull at Hermonthis early in her reign and it was to them that she had first turned for help when forced to flee Alexandria. Now they could see their Isis restored to divine majesty with her powerful Roman ally by her side.

From Caesar's point of view, there was also some political point to this pleasurable river trip—to demonstrate the power of Rome. Appian claims that four hundred ships accompanied the barge. Suetonius states that the plan was to sail to the southernmost part of Egypt, "nearly to Ethiopia," but that, echoing the reluctance of Alexander's troops to advance into India, Caesar's men grew restive and the trip was curtailed. Perhaps the hardened legionaries, hungry for home, wondered what was the point of drifting along the Nile, apart from allowing their leader a scenic sexual interlude—certainly when Caesar finally returned to Rome, his men would sing ribald verses about his enthusiastic couplings with the Egyptian queen. In Rome, Cicero too was wondering where Caesar was, writing, "Caesar seems to be so stuck in Alexandria that he is ashamed even to write about the situation there."

Soon after their return to Alexandria, in late June or early July 47, Caesar at last left Egypt, marching with his troops across the hot deserts into Syria. He was not leaving his heavily pregnant mistress unprotected. To defend her—and to guard Rome's interests—he left behind three legions under the command of a courageous but humbly born officer named Rufio, the son of an emancipated slave. In so doing, Caesar was disregarding the long-established practice whereby only officers who were also senators could command Rome's legions. Yet, mirroring his fears over appointing a governor, Caesar was wary of ceding too much power in Egypt to a potential rival. The son of a former slave was a safer bet.

For the first time since the death of her father, Cleopatra had a protector. Although he would be many miles away from her, he had the power to reach out to her should danger threaten. It is perhaps indicative of her gratitude, her relief and even her love for him that she began building a vast and ostentatiously splendid monument to Caesar—the Caesareum—on the harbor. It must have been a pleasing distraction as she awaited the arrival of the child that would be tangible proof of her alliance with the most powerful man in Rome. An inscription in Memphis suggests that Cleopatra gave birth in early September 47, just a few weeks after Caesar's departure. The child was a son and, with their usual pointed wit, the Alexandrians called him Caesarion, "little Caesar." Cleopatra herself called him Ptolemy Caesar and, even more portentously, an inscription at Hermonthis on the Upper Nile welcomed the baby as "the child of Amon Ra created through the human agency of Julius Caesar." In celebration, Cleopatra ordered the day of his birth to be celebrated as a feast of Isis and also issued new coins in Cyprus. They made no mention of her new husband, Ptolemy XIV. Instead they depicted Cleopatra as Isis suckling her newborn son, the divine child Horus. The reverse side depicted a double cornucopia—an ancient symbol of the Ptolemies signifying a new golden age.*

Cleopatra also ordered bas-reliefs to be carved on the outer walls of the Temple of Hathor, the Egyptian goddess of love, music, joy and fertility,

---

*The date of Caesarion's birth has been much debated. Some have claimed, on the basis of conflicting dates mentioned by Plutarch and dates mentioned in other ancient sources, that Caesarion was not in fact born until shortly after Caesar's death. However, the inscription on the stele from Memphis appears to refer specifically to Caesarion and is widely accepted. (In fact, it gives his date of birth as June 23, 47, but this is because it was probably not inscribed until after the introduction of the new Julian calendar. Under the old calendar still in force in 47, June 23 equates to early September 47.)

founded by Auletes at Dendera. On one side of the hundred-foot rear wall she and Caesarion were depicted on a monumental scale making offerings of burning incense to Hathor and her infant son. The exact date of these carvings is unknown, but the imagery was carefully chosen—Hathor's consort, the triumphant Horus, did not dwell within the same temple. Instead, he lived far away to the south in the temple of Edfu. Once a year, in the Festival of the Beautiful Embrace, an image of Hathor was carried by barge to Edfu. The situation was a neat parallel to Cleopatra's relationship with the absent Caesar. On the other side of the wall, Cleopatra and Caesarion were again depicted, this time making offerings to Isis and her brother-husband Osiris. Cleopatra, shown in the Egyptian style as a slender-bodied, near-naked figure with a protuberant navel, was identifying herself with Hathor and Isis and her son with Horus. The message to her Egyptian subjects was clear: Cleopatra, queen and goddess, had given Egypt—and the Ptolemies—a divine heir.*

---

*Cleopatra also dedicated a temple of birth bearing images of herself and Caesarion at Hermonthis, where, early in her reign, she had worshipped the Buchis bull. It was destroyed in the nineteenth century.

CHAPTER 8

"Veni, Vidi, Vici"

CAESAR'S EMOTIONS ON PARTING from Cleopatra are not recorded but he was immediately preoccupied. According to the author of *The Alexandrian War*, as soon as Caesar reached Syria he learned that "there was much that was bad and unprofitable in the administration at Rome" and that rivalries among the tribunes were producing "dangerous rifts." Caesar, though, did not rush home. Instead, he turned his attention to King Pharnaces of Pontus. Attempting to regain his father's territories, Pharnaces had recently defeated a Roman army sent to stop him and was now inciting other local rulers to rebel. So lightning-quick and easy was Caesar's victory over Pharnaces in Pontus that he could write boastfully to a friend, "Veni, vidi, vici" (I came, I saw, I conquered). He added that it was little wonder that Pompey had built a reputation as a great general if all the eastern enemies he had fought had been of this caliber.

On September 24, 47, Caesar finally landed back in Italy and hurried to Rome to assess the "dangerous rifts" for himself. The problems were formidable—restive, time-served legions eager for disbandment, breakdowns in law and order and economic stagnation. Antony had not performed as well this time as he had during Caesar's absence fighting against Pompey's supporters in Spain.

The thirty-six-year-old Antony had, of course, proved his talents as a military commander early in Egypt and later in Gaul. His men loved him for his courage, judgment and stamina and also for his generosity. Like Caesar, he had an effortless charm and understood how to inspire loyalty and devotion.

Plutarch noted how he had the common touch—the ability to make himself one of the lads: "his swaggering air, his ribald talk, his fondness for carousing in public, sitting down by his men as they ate, or taking his own food standing at the common-mess table made his own troops delight in his company and almost worship him." An imposing physical appearance enhanced his endearingly bluff manner. A handsome bull of a man with wild curls, broad shoulders and muscular thighs, he exuded strength and energy. Cicero would sneeringly deride him as resembling a prizefighter.

Antony could also be a clear-thinking, imaginative, decisive administrator—otherwise Caesar would not have twice left him in charge of Italy in critical times. However, growing quickly bored with the routines of political and administrative life, which held little appeal for him as a natural man of action rather than reflection, Antony had given way with gusto to his sensual, self-indulgent side. Lost in a sybaritic whirl of parties, drinking and lovemaking, his favorite companions had become actors, musicians and courtesans. With ill-placed brio, he had taken to riding about in a chariot drawn by lions in imitation of Bacchus or to taking his favorite actress with him when he visited other cities on official business, reputedly providing her with a retinue larger than he accorded his mother, Julia. Racked by hangovers and bleary-eyed after all-night drinking bouts, he struggled to get out of bed in the morning. On one occasion, after a particularly heavy night, he astonished members of the popular assembly who had summoned him to an early meeting by arriving still worse for wear and throwing up in front of them into a cloak thoughtfully held out for him by one of his friends. When riots broke out in support of attempts by the tribune Dolabella to introduce a decree canceling all debts, a lethargic Antony had at first done nothing, then reacted with unnecessary violence. One reason for his sudden brutality was said to be a growing suspicion that Dolabella was cuckolding him with his wife, Antonia.

Convinced that Antony's had not been a safe pair of hands, Caesar, for the moment at least, dropped him, leaving him without any official role. He had himself elected as consul for the following year, 46, and chose a relative nonentity, Lepidus, whom he thought could be trusted to show no initiative, to be his co-consul and to replace Antony as master of the horse. To sweeten his political supporters, Caesar increased the number of priesthoods and praetorships and appointed his cronies to them. To seduce the populace, he ordered landlords to freeze their rents for a year. He also placed a ban on some of the luxury foods that made up such a key part of the conspicuous consumption envied and despised in equal measure by those unable to afford it. Cicero later complained that having to eat turnips rather than oysters and eels had given him violent diarrhea.

At the same time, Caesar needed money. The civil war was not over and he needed to be able pay his armies to fight for him. After Pharsalus, Cato, one of the most important surviving republicans, had fled to the Roman province of Africa (modern-day Tunisia) and with the help of King Juba of Numidia (northern Algeria) had gathered a large force to continue the fight against Caesar. To raise the necessary funds, Caesar ordered towns across Italy to send gold and took out loans. He also auctioned off the property of those opponents he had not pardoned. Antony was among those who made foolishly high bids, mistakenly convinced that, as Caesar's friends, they would never be expected to pay up. Antony moved into Pompey's luxurious town house, which he had acquired at one of the auctions—according to Plutarch, ransacking and rebuilding it "as if it were not grand enough as it was"—only to be shocked when officials arrived to demand the money he owed for it.

But even with money, Caesar found it hard to raise the army he needed. Many of his experienced legionaries were tired. They wanted to disband and settle into the quiet life on a nice piece of land they believed was their due. Some, including Caesar's beloved Tenth Legion, marched to the Campus Martius, where they asked to be released. Caesar handled them with consummate skill. Addressing them as *quirites*, fellow citizens rather than fellow soldiers, implying they were already free of the army, he agreed to release them. They would receive their promised rewards, he assured them, but only when he returned in triumph from Africa with the new army he would recruit to replace them. This had the anticipated effect—the legionaries, shocked not to be considered indispensable, clamored to accompany the leader whom most of them revered and to share in the glory of his expedition.

That glory was hard won. High winds scattered Caesar's ships as they sailed for Africa from Sicily and, once they had arrived, food soon became scarce. The horses wrinkled their lips at their sparse diet of rinsed seaweed and grass. At the same time, Caesar's adversaries played hit-and-run, avoiding offering battle. However, in April 46 Caesar engaged the Pompeian forces at Thapsus. Some accounts suggest that while he was drawing up his forces Caesar suffered what Plutarch called "one of his usual fits," presumably an epileptic attack. This may explain why, for the only time in Caesar's career, his soldiers attacked before he gave the order. Whatever the case, victory was swift and complete.

News of it reached Cato, left in command of a fortress at Utica on the coast twenty miles from the tumbled ruins of Carthage. Ever since Caesar had forced Pompey out of Italy, the forty-eight-year-old Cato had refused to cut his hair or beard. After Pompey's defeat at Pharsalus, as a mark of mourning, he had eaten sitting, rather than reclining as a Roman should, and had lain down only to sleep.

At dinner, after hearing the news of Thapsus, Cato began to debate philosophy with his friends. The Romans had compensated themselves for the absence of an integrated theology by the contemplation of the sophisticated philosophies of the Greeks, from whose relatively abstract theorizing they derived practical guidance. Two philosophies were prevalent. One was Epicureanism, whose eponymous founder, Epicurus, propounded salvation by common sense and happiness through peace of mind. He dismissed divine providence and the immortality of the soul as illusory. Man should enjoy the world as it is, rejoicing in nature. The universe was limitless. Knowledge was generated through man's inquiring mind and he should strive to understand and enjoy nature's bounty. Remarkably for a man who lived more than two millennia ago, Epicurus emphasized that man should cease depleting the planet's resources through his insatiable greed.

The other was the somewhat somber Stoic philosophy named after the stoa or painted covered passage leading from the Athens marketplace where its originator, Zeno, propounded it. His thesis was that man is a rational being who should lead a virtuous life practicing civic duty, self-discipline and tolerance and respect for others. He should accept and endure whatever fate held in store for him with dignity. In so doing, while conquering himself and his fears, he could take pride in rising spiritually above the vicissitudes of life. Cato was, unsurprisingly, a Stoic, who in the dinnertime conversation that night was adamant that only such a good man could be free. Stoic philosophy predisposed its followers to seek "a good death," even if it was by their own hand, and this was the course Cato determined to follow.

After retiring for the night, Cato stabbed himself in the abdomen. When his son, alerted by the sound of his father's body crashing to the floor and knocking over an abacus, discovered what he had done, he summoned physicians to push his father's protruding intestines back into his body cavity and sew up the wound, but Cato ripped off the dressings. According to Appian, he "opened the suture of the wound, enlarged it with his nails like a wild beast, plunged his fingers into his stomach and tore out his entrails." His final advice to his grieving son was, "In present conditions it is impossible to engage in politics in a manner befitting a Cato, and to engage in them in any other way would be disgraceful." By the time Caesar reached Utica, Cato was already in his grave, a potent martyr for the austere old republican values, as he had intended. Just before his death he had said, "I am not willing to be indebted to the tyrant for his illegal actions. He is acting contrary to the laws when he pardons men as if he were their master when he has no sovereignty over them."

In late July 46, Caesar, decked with the laurels of victory, marched back into Rome. The Senate was apprehensive. The followers of the traditions of the elders could only hope that, like Sulla, he would swiftly renounce his powers after rewarding his friends, thus leaving their unwritten constitution basically unchanged. It cannot have encouraged them that at around this time Caesar sent messengers to Egypt summoning Cleopatra to join him. The publicly proclaimed purpose of Cleopatra's visit was to reaffirm the bonds between Egypt and Rome but the prospect of the Egyptian queen's arrival must have stoked senatorial concern that Caesar might be seeking autocratic power in Rome similar to that which Cleopatra wielded in Egypt.

Caesar's true motives for sending for Cleopatra are as intriguing as they are opaque. He was far too wise not to have realized that there was no political imperative for Cleopatra's presence and indeed some downside to it. Perhaps his action had something to do with his own self-image. With her would come Caesarion—reassuring confirmation that, though middle-aged, Caesar was virile and vigorous. He would also have been curious to see his only son, by then nearly a year old.

In addition, the thought of his royal mistress witnessing his pomp and power must have been highly appealing. Even before he had marched back into Rome, the Senate had awarded him unique privileges in order to appease his ambition. He was to be dictator for the next ten years—an unprecedented period—and have the right to nominate magistrates. He was also to be prefect of morals, a new position that caused some sniggering but would allow him to censor and control his opponents. The *supplicatio*, the traditional festival of prayers and thanksgiving to honor a victor, was to last forty days compared with the fifteen that had celebrated Caesar's successes in Gaul in 57, and his triumphal chariot was to be placed before the statue of Jupiter on the Capitol, together with a bronze statue of Caesar, bestriding a globe to symbolize his mastery of the world. The inscription would hail him as a demigod.

The Senate also awarded Caesar his Triumphs. Between September 20 and October 1 Caesar held four great parades marking his victories over Gaul, Egypt, Pontus and Africa. The processions, each lasting a day, began in the Campus Martius and ended before the Temple of Jupiter. Here Caesar ascended the hundred steps, passed through the great bronze gates and sacrificed white bulls before laying his laurels in the lap of the god. The marveling crowds were shielded from the autumn sun by silken awnings extending all the way up to the Capitol. Among the impressive trophies and gorgeous treasures carried by the marching columns were signs boasting of the number of battles fought and enemies killed. The tally was fifty battles and between one million and two million slain, excluding his fellow Roman citizens. Caesar, wearing a rippling purple toga, rode in his triumphal chariot pulled by three white horses. His face was painted with red lead in tribute to Jupiter, who had made Rome great and whose representative Caesar was. His balding head was wreathed in laurels and in his hand he grasped an eagle-headed scepter. Lest in these moments of glory he forget his mortality, as was traditional, a slave holding a golden wreath above his head whispered repeatedly in his red-tinted ear, "Remember you are human."

In the procession celebrating Caesar's victory in the Alexandrian War, mock flames rose from a model of the phallic Pharos lighthouse borne through the streets as Caesar's men belted out raucous songs celebrating their leader's sexual feats in Egypt. The crowds roared their approval at pictures portraying the bloody deaths of Pothinus and Achillas, but their greatest interest was in the pathetic figure of Cleopatra's half sister, Arsinoe, stumbling along in chains with the other prisoners at the head of the procession. Prisoners were usually executed immediately after a Triumph. Vercingetorix, who had been kept caged for six years after his capture, had been executed immediately after the Gallic Triumph. However, the sight of the young princess roused the pity of the Roman crowd. Caesar read the people's mood and spared her the strangling that was the traditional fate of conquered rulers. He permitted Arsinoe to leave Rome and, like her father, Auletes, before her, to seek sanctuary in the vast white marble temple of Artemis at Ephesus, whose fine ivory doors had been installed by her father.

As he had when he displayed Arsinoe, Caesar also misjudged when, as part of his African Triumph, he arranged for a float depicting Cato's suicide to be drawn through the streets. It was usually considered bad taste to gloat over the defeat of fellow Romans, but Caesar's justification was that Cato and those who had fought with him had been mere mercenary lackeys of King Juba. Their deaths, he argued, had been the just deserts of collaborators. The people of Rome wept openly at the representation of Cato's lonely end, stoically ripping out his own guts. The infant son of the dead King Juba, another Juba, was also carried in the African procession and, as a child, was spared. Plutarch observed that "it was a highly fortunate captivity for him, since instead of being an uncultured Numidian, he came to be counted among the most learned writers of Greece."*

Among the many celebrations that Caesar arranged to accompany his Triumphs were five days of wild-animal shows. Such shows, which almost inevitably culminated in a hunt, or rather slaughter, of the exhibits, had a long history but had become ever more spectacular in the past few decades. Lions, ostriches (known for some reason to the wits in the audience as sea sparrows) and leopards (known as African mice) had been exhibited for some time as, of course, had bulls, bears and stags. More recent imports were hippopotamuses and crocodiles.† But Caesar, like his predecessors, strove to dream up ever more novel displays. Some of his spectaculars were achieved by sheer numbers—on one occasion he loosed four hundred snarling lions. He also delighted the crowds by producing creatures entirely new to them, being the first to import a giraffe, probably from Egypt. Another novelty was Thessalian bullfighting, where mounted riders chased the bull until the beast was so exhausted the riders could leap from their saddles, grip the bull's horns and, in theory at least, with a quick twist break the bull's neck.

Elephants had been shown for nearly a quarter of a century, and Romans felt very sympathetic toward them. At Pompey's games in 55, some had escaped into the crowd and the spectators, excited by both pity for the beasts and

---

*In later years he would marry the daughter of Cleopatra and Antony.

†Later, Nero had polar bears chasing seals.

fear for their own safety, had shaken their fists at Pompey. Cicero had written that there was "a feeling that the monsters had something human about them." Rather than pitting elephants against other elephants or bulls, as was customary, Caesar fitted them with "castles," presumably like howdahs, from which men fought as part of two contending armies in a mock battle involving five hundred infantry, thirty cavalry and twenty elephants. The battle was enacted in the Circus Maximus, from which, according to Suetonius, Caesar removed the central barrier around which the chariots ran to allow the camps to be pitched facing each other.

Another of Caesar's innovations was a dramatic naval battle staged in a large pool on the Campus Martius in a swampy area near the Tiber where four thousand oarsmen and two thousand costumed warriors—gladiators and condemned prisoners—bloodily reenacted a naval battle. The games bored Caesar himself and, at the climax of a later spectacular, he was observed in his box pointedly attending to his government papers rather than watching. However, the crowds took a different view. According to Suetonius, "Such huge numbers of visitors flocked to these shows from all directions that many of them had to sleep in tents pitched along the streets or roads, or on rooftops; and often the pressure of the crowd crushed people to death. The victims included two senators."

Some young men of the patrician classes even took part in the horse-riding events at the games, racing each other in the Circus Maximus. Each rode a pair of horses roped together, vaulting from one to the other at the end of every lap.* Not content with providing spectacular shows, Caesar feasted so many citizens as part of the celebrations that he had to provide twenty thousand couches.

Yet just as interesting to the people of Rome as these lavish festivities was the arrival in their city of the exotic queen of Egypt with her retinue of eunuchs and slaves, baby son, Caesarion, and thirteen-year-old brother-husband, Ptolemy. The exact timing of Cleopatra's arrival is unclear. She may have missed the Alexandrian Triumph and Arsinoe's public humiliation, and in any

---

*They rode bareback and, of course, without stirrups, which were not used in Europe until 750 years later.

event, however violent her hostility to her half sister, it hardly would have been seemly for her to watch Arsinoe's disgrace in person or, indeed, a Roman Triumph celebrating the defeat of her countrymen, albeit her enemies. A greater disappointment may have been Caesar's decision to spare her sister—as long as Arsinoe was alive she was a potential risk to Cleopatra and her son. Cleopatra would later look to Antony to free her of that danger.

In Rome, Cleopatra, her husband and their respective entourages were installed in mansions in the beautiful gardens of Caesar's estate on the right bank of the Tiber. In the warmth of an Italian summer, less shatteringly hot than in her own more easterly capital, Cleopatra must have been hoping that this interlude would strengthen the emotional bonds between herself and Caesar. As she would have known, he was not a faithful man, and his opportunities for sexual encounters, even with queens, were legion. His affair with the beautiful Eunoe, queen of Mauretania, was the subject of common gossip and he had almost certainly been sleeping with her during his African campaign. But now it was Cleopatra with her diaphanous garments, rich jewels, compelling sexuality and agile intellect who could fill Caesar's horizon and drive thoughts of other women from his mind.

Her armory of course included the child he had not yet seen—the boy whose paternity became the subject of avid speculation among Rome's chattering classes. Caesar did not publicly acknowledge the boy as his own, though Antony would later claim that he had done so in private, but Cleopatra's choice of name for him was a blatant statement to the world that he did nothing to deny. Perhaps she also hoped to become pregnant by Caesar again and give birth this time in Rome. The thoughts of Caesar's childless wife of thirteen years, Calpurnia, living in their town house, about the arrival of the Egyptian queen and her son are unrecorded but can be guessed.

CHAPTER 9

"*Slave of the Times*"

POLITICIANS ON THEIR WAY UP—or indeed on their way down—crowded the mansion where Cleopatra held court, hoping to persuade her to use her influence with Caesar on their behalf. To ingratiate themselves with her they had to force themselves to put aside their traditional Roman contempt for royalty and the luxury of the East. Cleopatra, however, seems to have felt sufficiently confident in her relationship with Caesar to see no need to solicit the support of important Romans. The Senate had soon dutifully and obediently ratified a treaty endorsing Cleopatra and her half brother as friends and allies of the Roman people.

The power and ability to snub were enjoyable for a proud woman whose father had been a laughingstock in Rome, forced to go cap in hand to moneylenders. Among those offended by Cleopatra's hauteur was Cicero, who had not taken an active part in the civil war but remained one of the most influential conservative figures now that the fight was once more being fought with words, not swords. "I hate the Queen," he later wrote in a letter to his friend Atticus. "Her arrogance, when she was living across the Tiber in the gardens . . . I cannot recall without profound bitterness." Yet even he acknowledged her erudition. She offered to obtain him some books from Alexandria, causing him to reflect that, despite the scandalous stories circulating about her in Rome, "her promises were all things that had to do with learning, and not derogatory to my dignity, so I could have mentioned them even in a public speech." If politicians incurred Cleopatra's contempt, she was generous to singers and musicians for creating the sophisticated, cultured ambience she was used to and appreciated in Alexandria.

Whether Antony visited Cleopatra's salon in the fragrant gardens along the Tiber is unknown. He had anyway recently remarried. Having thrown out the wife—his cousin Antonia—he suspected of cuckolding him with Dolabella, he had wed Fulvia, widow of the murdered tribune Clodius, whose bloodstained body she had so astutely and theatrically revealed to the mob.

After Clodius, Fulvia had married Curio, who, like Clodius, Antony and Fulvia herself, had once been a member of Rome's fast young set. According to Cicero and others, he had also once been Antony's lover. "No boy bought for the sake of lust was ever so much in the power of his master as you were in Curio's," wrote Cicero of Antony. Yet Curio had been equally besotted and had even offered to stand surety for Antony's huge debts. Desperate to end an affair that had become the scandal of Rome, Curio's father, who had repeatedly had Antony thrown out of his house, on Cicero's advice bought Antony off, settling his debts himself, provided that the two young men parted.

Curio had been killed fighting for Caesar in Africa. Antony seemed to Fulvia a suitable—and malleable—replacement. So ambitious that Plutarch described how "a private citizen was beneath her notice—she wanted to rule magistrates and give advice to generals," she schooled Antony carefully, restrained his excesses and encouraged him to be more single-minded in his pursuit of power than was his natural wont. When, in later years, Cleopatra took Antony as her lover, she "owed Fulvia the fee for teaching Antony to submit to a woman, since she took him over after he had been tamed and trained from the outset to obey women."

Though some hoped to profit personally from Cleopatra's influence over Caesar, others pondered the implications of his infatuation with her. In particular they noted Caesar's ambitious plans for the remodeling of Rome. Was he trying to fashion a new Alexandria on the Tiber?

Rome, unlike Alexandria, was an unplanned city, which had grown organically. At the time of Cleopatra's visit it lacked the grandeur, grace and elegance of her own capital. Before the visitor reached the city itself, he passed the shantytowns where country people, lured to the city by free grain and constant amusements, had their dwellings. He also passed the great necropolises, where the ashes of the richer Romans were buried after their ceremonial cremations, since tradition prohibited burials within the city boundaries. Many of the necropolises were covered with graffiti either extolling or vilifying politicians. These crumbling tombs provided excellent cover for muggers and shelter for poor prostitutes, "those filthy sluts who conceal their trade in tombs." The bodies of the poor were simply taken out of the city by night and tossed with all the other rubbish into huge pits near the Esquiline Gate. Here foraging animals, such as the wild gray wolves of Italy who reputedly suckled Romulus and Remus, disinterred them, gnawing the flesh and leaving piles of bones strewn along the roadside.

Rome itself was still built entirely on the east bank of the Tiber, but on the west bank were the premises of a mass of smoky, smelly industries banned from the city proper, partly because of their noxious fumes, partly because of the risk of fire. Among them were the making of matches, glassblowing and metalworking as well as tanning. The last relied on the copious use of human urine brought from the city in overflowing vats, which the tanners and fullers had positioned at convenient locations to attract those either too lazy to seek out the public toilets or too poor to pay the trifling fee they demanded.

After passing by the Campus Martius, the open space along the banks of the Tiber outside the walls that was used for large meetings and other public events, the visitor entered the city through one of the main gates in the walls. He was immediately confronted by a maze of rubbish-littered streets and alleys so narrow and winding that Caesar had introduced a law prohibiting wagons being driven along them during daytime; all porterage had to be on the backs of men or animals. If he needed to look for landmarks, perhaps on one of the seven hills, each between 100 and 150 feet high, around which everyone knew the city was constructed, the visitor's line of sight was often blocked by the tenement buildings known as *insulae* or islands where most of Rome's population, approaching a million people, lived. These five- or six-story tenement buildings cut off much of the sunlight from the narrow streets, usually had shops on the bottom floor, and were poorly and flimsily constructed, prone to fire and entirely without sanitation or running water. So many people simply emptied chamber pots from the upper stories on to the heads of passers-by that a law had to be introduced regulating how much compensation those doused could claim. The wealthy Crassus had been one of the most unscrupulous developers of such tenements. Cicero still was. In a letter to Atticus he lamented that "two of my shops have collapsed and others are showing cracks so that even the mice moved elsewhere, to say nothing of the tenants." But then he cheered up, reporting that he had "a building scheme underway which should turn this loss into a source of profit."

Of the seven hills, the Capitol Hill was reserved for the gods and topped by the Temple of Jupiter. The smartest private addresses were on the Palatine Hill, where Cicero himself lived, though even here lack of space meant the gardens were small.* The Aventine Hill, opposite the Palatine, had a more mixed and bohemian population. In the broad valley between the two hills was the Circus Maximus—the oldest entertainment venue in Rome, supposedly first used for chariot racing in the time of the kings. Over the years, it acquired first wooden stands and then, in 329 BC, starting stalls for the chariots. Charioteers raced under the colors of factions such as the red or the white. Attendance could reach 250,000, still the largest crowd recorded at a sporting stadium. Circulating vendors kept the partisans well supplied with food and, in particular, drink. They roared each faction on and placed bets on the outcome.

The charioteer was a striking figure in his tunic in team colors, holding a long whip and a knife in his hand. The latter was used to cut the traces if he crashed, the only way he could save himself. Once the race started, he would lean out almost horizontally over his galloping horses. Four was the most common number but some races even involved chariots with ten horses. Races were over seven miles in distance and usually lasted a quarter of an hour. The trickiest moments were the tight turns, where the driver needed to seize the inside position, slow his team enough to make the turn and deny opponents any gap to squeeze through. Another of the driver's skills was to crowd opposing chariots into one another in the hope of causing collisions, which were indeed frequent. There were rumors of charioteers being bribed to hold back their horses or of horses being doped by rivals. The races were particularly popular with the young since men and women were allowed to sit together and share the excitement, unlike in the theater and amphitheater, where they were segregated.

On the other side of the Palatine Hill, between it and the Capitol, was the Forum, the center of Rome's political life, from where not only Rome but the whole of the Roman world was ruled. The Forum itself was paved with stone, was rectangular in shape and measured about 600 feet by 230 feet. Law

---

*Our word *palace* derives from the grand buildings on the Palatine.

cases were conducted outdoors in the Forum, whatever the weather. Although there was a Senate house, meetings of the Senate also took place in various of the buildings and temples grouped around the Forum and elsewhere. To the north was the assembly ground, where politicians addressed the people from a platform decorated with ships' prows captured in a long-ago sea battle. The platform was given the name *rostra*, the plural of the Latin word for a ship's prow.*

To the southeast, the dwellings of the Vestal Virgins and of the chief priest, the pontifex maximus, at this time Caesar himself, were close together near the Temple of Vesta. Nearby, too, was a remnant of the past nearly as old as the reed shepherd's hut said to be the birthplace of Romulus and Remus and still preserved amid the opulence of the Palatine. This was the palace of Rome's former kings. Increasingly dwarfed by the surrounding buildings, it housed the official archives and calendar.

To the east of the Forum, in a valley between three other of Rome's hills, was Suburia, where the Julian clan had its ancestral home and where Caesar himself had been born. Suburia was now an entertainment district, succinctly summed up by the poet Martial as a "seething, wakeful and clamorous" place where "hot chickpeas cost just a small coin, just like sex." Here young bloods ate at fast-food stalls selling goat stew, sausages and bass "caught between the Tiber's two bridges." (This was not a particularly sanitary location since this was where the city's great sewer, the Cloaca Maxima—still visible to this day on the riverbank and big enough for a man and a cart to drive through—discharged into the Tiber.) Later, one of the many fast women leaning from windows or sitting in bars and brothels might catch their eye. Some of the least expensive and most practical worked from what one visitor called "an alcove with a price list."

Caesar's ambition was to change the face of Rome and create a city fit to be the capital of the world. He opened the first quarries at Carrara to produce marble for his projects and shipped in other materials from far and wide. His recollections of the broad, graceful thoroughfares of Alexandria lined with porticoes and statues undoubtedly influenced the plans he had been nurturing

*The singular is *rostrum*, hence our English word.

for some time. In particular, he planned to remodel the old Forum and create a grand new precinct in the very heart of Rome to be known as the Julian Forum.

Caesar's new Forum was a long, open rectangle surrounded by porticoed colonnades and shops but, most significantly, at one of the short ends of the rectangle, Caesar constructed a temple to Venus the Mother (Genetrix), from whom he claimed divine descent. In making this dedication, he was fulfilling his vow to raise a sacred place to the goddess if she granted him victory over Pompey. However, near to the image of Venus herself, Caesar placed a magnificent gilt-bronze statue of his own living goddess—Cleopatra. Though the Ptolemies had long placed their images alongside their gods, in Rome such a step was unprecedented. That the honor had been given not to a Roman but to a foreigner and a woman caused shock, outrage and heightened speculation about Caesar's intentions toward the Egyptian queen.

Caesar's motives were probably mixed. He would have been mindful of the association of Venus with Isis and of Cleopatra's claim to divine status as a reincarnation of the latter. Also, though there could have been no political imperative behind his placing of her statue in the temple and it did not change her official status, it allowed him to demonstrate to the people of Rome her importance to him personally as his lover and as the mother of his only son. This veneration of the child's mother also seems clear confirmation that the child was indeed his, especially if recent research suggesting that the statue also incorporated a young Caesarion held on his mother's shoulder is correct. A marble head of Cleopatra believed to date from between 40 and 30 and to be based on her statue in the Temple of Venus was discovered in the eighteenth century. Although the body on which the head is placed is not the original, indentations in the marble below Cleopatra's left eye and just below the left corner of her mouth are consistent with where the fingers of Caesarion's left hand would have rested had she been holding him on her right shoulder.*

---

*Today the marble head is in the Vatican Museum. Interestingly, a limestone statue of a woman of the Ptolemaic era holding a child on her shoulder in exactly this manner has been recovered from Aboukir Bay and is now on display in the National Museum of Alexandria.

As Suetonius recorded, Caesar wanted all his projects to be "the biggest." He planned a huge new theater to eclipse that built by Pompey in 55 when, using riches acquired in his eastern campaigns, Pompey had raised a stone theater on the Campus Martius. By placing a temple on the western rim he had cleverly bypassed a law banning stone as a construction material for places of entertainment. The prohibition seemingly derived from the lofty view that secular theaters were immoral places invented by Greeks and, if to be tolerated in Rome, should be made of less permanent material such as wood. Pompey's theater complex, then the biggest in the world, was more than a thousand feet long and seated some seventeen thousand. Its revolutionary design became a template for future theaters, including the Coliseum a hundred years later. Unlike previous theaters, which were based on Greek precedents and dug into hillsides, Pompey used the Roman invention of concrete. His theater was freestanding and set on a foundation of barrel vaults ideal for providing access to the auditorium and stage. The seats rose in tiers above the vaults. Behind the stage was a large colonnaded courtyard, inside one of the halls of which stood a statue of Pompey surrounded by representations of the fourteen nations he had conquered. This hall was sometimes used for meetings of the Senate and would be on the ides of March just two years later. Caesar intended to build his own theater just west of the Capitol itself and began purchasing and clearing land, tearing down existing houses and temples.

Some of Caesar's works were clearly influenced by what he had seen in Cleopatra's Egypt. In 46, a hundred years after the Romans had razed Corinth, Caesar decided to refound the city by disposing of some of Rome's surplus population there. The Egyptians' ability to build canals linking branches of the Nile delta and Lake Mareotis had so impressed Caesar that, as part of the Corinth project, he launched a search for a feasible route between the Ionian and Aegean seas. Centuries later this resulted in the Corinth canal. On Cleopatra's advice, Caesar probably made use of Egyptian geographers in his schemes to improve the canal system around Rome and, indeed, to drain the nearby Pontine Marshes, a project abandoned at his death and not eventually achieved until Mussolini's time.

Cleopatra's presence in Rome and Caesar's experiences in Egypt also had a profound intellectual impact on Roman society and culture. His admiration for the Library of Alexandria inspired Caesar to establish a great library of Rome that, by bringing together the whole of Greek and Roman literature and knowledge, would outdo Alexandria and make Rome the cultural as well as political center of the world. Unlike the canals, this project was completed shortly after Caesar's death.

Caesar's discussions with Cleopatra and the professors who studied in the Museon and the Library of Alexandria also inspired his reform of the calendar. The first of the great Alexandrian astronomers was Aristarchus. Around 270, using a modified sundial to determine the height and course of the sun and the angle at which the sun shone on the moon, he had deduced that the sun was far from the earth. He also postulated that the earth circled the sun—a theory rejected by earthcentric astronomers for another eighteen centuries.

A few decades later, another of Alexandria's astronomers estimated the circumference of the earth within 250 miles and calculated within a tenth of a degree the tilting of the arc of the earth's rotation that gives us our seasons. About eighty years before Caesar's visit to Alexandria, Hipparchus, working in the Museon, produced a catalog of the stars, with estimates of the distances between them. By studying when solstices occurred over a period of years, he validated the general accuracy of the Egyptian calendar, which was based on the sun and divided the year into 365 days, and estimated the length of the solar year within six minutes of the true figure of 365 days, five hours and forty-nine minutes.

The Roman calendar, by contrast, had developed from a lunar calendar and counted years from Romulus' founding of the city. The Romans had at frequent intervals added extra days into their calendar, which had 355 days (divided initially into ten but soon into twelve months), to try to bring their calendar back into line with the seasons, which, of course, derived from the progress of the sun. However, by 46 the Roman calendar had drifted more than two months ahead of the seasons.

Guided by Sosigenes, a celebrated astronomer from the Museon, whom Caesar may have met during his time in Alexandria in 48 and 47 and who had come to Rome either as part of Cleopatra's entourage or at Caesar's direct request, Caesar determined on a once-and-for-all adjustment to align the Roman calendar with the solar year. He therefore introduced a calendar that had 365 days divided into twelve months, as at present, with an extra day in February every fourth year to keep the calendar in balance. (Such a calendar had been introduced into Egypt by Ptolemy III in 238, but the addition of the extra day every fourth year had not always been adhered to.)

Caesar's calendar made January rather than March the first month of the year, but he retained the old names of the months, which meant that several—such as September, October and November—contained the wrong numeral in their title. However, the Senate soon changed that of Quintullus, the month of Caesar's birth, to Julius (July) in his honor. The Romans did not have the concept of weeks or weekends, and Caesar did not change the division of the month, which was defined by particular days such as the kalends, the first of the month (and the origin of our word *calendar*); the ides, which fell in the middle of the month, either on the thirteenth or fifteenth depending on whether the month was a long or a short one; and the nones, the ninth day before the ides. Other days did not have particular names but were positioned by reference to their being before or after the named days. Certain days were specified in the calendar as lucky and others as unlucky. The Roman day did have twenty-four hours, but only at the equinox was each hour of equal length. Daylight was divided into twelve hours and darkness into another twelve, so that the length of an hour of daylight (and of night) differed from month to month. To tell the time, people used public sundials and water clocks, these last adjusted to fit the current season of the year.

To get the calendar back on track, Caesar added two months to the year 46, making it 445 days long and what Caesar called "the last year of confusions." Confusion there certainly was in relation to commercial contracts, and a Roman governor in Gaul increased the annual taxes due for that year because it had extra days. Conservatives or traditionalists disparaged the change, which was promulgated across the Roman world by edict, as they did any of Caesar's reforms, on this occasion suggesting that Caesar was not content with ruling the earth but wanted to rule the stars. When told that a particular constellation would be visible next morning, Cicero commented sourly, "Yes, in accordance with Caesar's edict."

However, as would soon become clear, Caesar could control neither the heavens nor his own bright star. Despite all Caesar's power he was still, as Cicero pointed out, "the slave of the times."

CHAPTER 10

The Ides of March

IN THE WINTER OF 46, Caesar was forced to leave Rome and Cleopatra. Pompey's two sons—young Sextus, who had witnessed his father's murder off the shores of Egypt, and his much older brother, Gnaeus—had raised thirteen legions in Spain, including seasoned veterans from Pharsalus and the African campaign, which Caesar's legates had been unable to defeat. It was, as Plutarch wrote, an extremely dangerous situation. So swift was Caesar's departure that he had no time to oversee elections to fill the key political offices for the following year. To defer the problem until his return, he had himself elected sole consul for 45.

Appian relates how Caesar made the long journey from Rome in just twenty-seven days. As he bounced about in a springless carriage he composed a lengthy poem entitled, appropriately enough, "The Journey," but now lost. On March 17, 45, at the battle of Munda, east of modern Seville, he defeated the Pompeian forces, but only after fierce fighting, during which the fifty-four-year-old Caesar dismounted, grabbed a shield and shamed his faltering troops by rushing at the enemy. He later told his supporters that although he had often fought for victory, this was the first time he had fought for his life. Sextus managed to escape, but a few days after the battle his elder brother, Gnaeus, was caught and killed, ending the rising. Caesar, who had usually been merciful during the civil war, punished the rebels without mercy—executing them in droves and ordering their heads, including that of Gnaeus, to be displayed on spikes. Perhaps hot blood and a consciousness of the closeness of the conflict hardened his heart, together with a desire to signal that no further risings would be tolerated.

Cleopatra's movements during this time are unclear. Cicero, writing in 44, seems to suggest that some while earlier she had left Caesar's estate. She might have taken the opportunity to return briefly to Alexandria to reassure herself that all was well there. However, she would have known that King Bogud of Mauretania was once again assisting Caesar, just as he had in North Africa, and that with him would be Eunoe. Cleopatra therefore would not have wished to absent herself from Rome for long. Far better to remain and be ready to greet the returning conqueror and remind him of all he had been missing.

Antony did not wait for Caesar's return to congratulate him. Anxious to regain Caesar's favor, he hurried off to join him in southern Gaul and was delighted by Caesar's response. His old patron conspicuously honored him, choosing him as his traveling companion in preference even to his young great-nephew, Octavian.* Ill health had prevented Octavian from accompanying Caesar when he left for Spain, but after recovering sufficiently he had followed after him, surviving shipwreck and enemy-infested roads to reach him. Being displaced from Caesar's carriage by Antony and relegated to traveling in the chariot behind must have seemed a poor reward.

Curiously, during the long, bumpy journey back to Italy, though the two men talked of many things, comfortable in their reestablished amity, Antony failed to mention that an old drinking friend, Gaius Trebonius, had hinted of a plot to murder Caesar. He had been sounding Antony out to see whether he might wish to join it. Antony had firmly refused but did not see fit, as he lolled by Caesar's side, to warn him of the plotting that in a few months would claim his life. Perhaps for the moment he was hedging his bets. Perhaps he did not wish to incriminate a friend.

Weakened by the campaign and the epileptic fits that were becoming ever more frequent, Caesar decided not to return at once to Rome. Instead, he went to his country estates southeast of Rome, where Cleopatra may have joined him. While he convalesced he wrote his will, to be given into the care of the Vestal

*Octavian's actual name was Gaius Octavius and he later became Gaius Julius Caesar and even later the emperor Augustus, but to save confusion he is referred to here as Octavian.

Virgins. It named Octavian as his main heir. On Caesar's death he was to receive most of Caesar's huge wealth and become his adopted son. The document, kept private for the present, made no reference either to Caesarion or to Cleopatra but could hardly have done so since the law prevented Roman citizens—even dictators—from naming foreigners as their heirs. However, according to Suetonius, Caesar "provided for the possibility of a son subsequently born to himself" by designating guardians for the child. Cleopatra must have been the mother he had in mind. Ironically, those he appointed to protect any future child were to be among his own assassins.

News of Caesar's final triumph over his republican enemies had already prompted the Senate to load him with fresh honors and titles. He was awarded the right to wear his triumphal robe at all public gatherings. Like Cleopatra, his statue was to be erected in a temple—in Caesar's case that of Quirinus, the divine form of Rome's mythical founder, Romulus. The inscription was to read, "To the undefeated god." Another statue of Caesar was erected on the Capitol next to those of the kings, while his ivory effigy was to be carried in the procession of gods that preceded the games. The Senate also handed him complete military and financial control over Rome and appointed him consul for ten years.

In early October 45, restored to health, Caesar marched in glory into his capital. This time the Triumph lauding his Spanish victories made no pretense he had conquered anyone other than dissident and treacherous Romans. It concluded with a feast for the entire population of Rome, not once but twice. In a gesture designed to whip up popular adulation, Caesar dismissed the first repast as too meager and ordered it to be repeated four days later with "more succulent provender." However, his grandiose gesture increased rather than stifled people's unease, and it is indicative that he could not see this. The greater the honors heaped on Caesar, the more isolated he was becoming and thus the more faulty his judgment. Unlike the citizens of Alexandria, Romans were not conditioned to living gods. To many, Caesar appeared to have forgotten the warning words whispered by the slave in his ear during his Triumphs: "Remember you are human."

Unsurprisingly, resentment focused on the continued presence by Caesar's side of his Egyptian mistress, whose statue gleamed portentously within the temple of Venus. While Romans were indulgent, even admiring, of their leaders' sexual peccadilloes while on campaign, back in Rome it was a different matter. Sex was seen as diminishing physical prowess—the week before a fight, gladiators' penises were fitted with an apparatus of metal bolts to prevent them ejaculating and diluting their strength. Additionally, sexual overindulgence, indeed any kind of overindulgence or lack of self-control, was viewed as a character defect. Caesar was condemned, not admired, for succumbing to Cleopatra's sexual magnetism. If a man could not govern his own appetites, how could he govern other people?

Some, though, saw Cleopatra as something far more dangerous than just Caesar's mistress. To them she epitomized an unwholesome, alien, royal and despotic influence on republican Rome. Stories spread that the besotted Caesar intended to shift his capital to Alexandria—even that he planned to marry Cleopatra. Suetonius related that a tribune, Helvius Cinna, "admitted to several persons that he had a bill drawn up in due form, which Caesar had ordered him to propose to the people in his own absence, making it lawful for Caesar to marry what wives he wished, and as many as he wished, for the purpose of begetting [legitimate] children." The accusation was probably fabricated but the very fact that such stories gained credence shows the suspicion and resentment toward the Egyptian queen, for if Caesar wished to take another wife, surely it would be Cleopatra.

Caesar, though, was thoroughly preoccupied with what he intended to be the most glorious and ambitious campaign of his career—crushing the Parthian Empire. Rome had not yet avenged the Parthians' humiliating defeat of Crassus at Carrhae in 53, and their horsemen were now menacing Rome's eastern provinces, raiding into Syria. The Parthians were originally seminomads from the southeastern shores of the Caspian Sea. In the decades following Alexander's defeat of the Persians they had increased their territories to include Mesopotamia, and by this time their empire extended from the borders of Roman Syria in the west to the Indus in the east, and to the south embraced much of Persia, giving them a dominant position across the eastern trade routes. The conquest of Parthia would therefore be an immense undertaking in which the support of Rome's allies—especially the wealthy Cleopatra—in providing money, ships and men would be essential. However, the rewards would be commensurately great.

It is impossible to know what was in Cleopatra's mind during her time in Rome, but her detractors were probably right to fear her intentions. In Alexandria she had deliberately bound herself to the Roman world's most powerful man to secure her personal position. Now in Rome she perhaps began to glimpse an important, even central role for her kingdom in what might follow. For Cleopatra, the future in early 44 must have seemed ripe with possibilities. Like Caesar, she was capable of thinking on a grand scale, innovatively pushing forward the boundaries of the practicable. If Caesar conquered Parthia, he would be leader of the Mediterranean world's only remaining superpower. What could he then not do for those he owed—and, indeed, for those he loved? And what better heir to this great empire than a boy with the blood of Alexander's people and also of Caesar in his veins, her beloved Caesarion?

The date set for Caesar's departure from Rome for the Parthian campaign was March 18, 44, and, as the winter months passed, Cleopatra was probably also planning her own return to Egypt, from where she could directly oversee the Egyptian aid to be sent to Caesar. She would also be closer to Caesar and able speedily to join him and share in his expected triumphs.

Others were less enthusiastic about Caesar's eastern adventure, which he himself estimated would take three to four years to accomplish. Although the campaign would remove him from Rome, they knew that during his absence he would appoint compliant cronies to rule on his behalf. Caesar's powers to dictate how Rome would be governed seemed removed by only a hair's breadth from those of a king. When the custodians of the Sibylline Books conveniently "discovered" a prophecy that "only a king can conquer the Parthians," this fed the rumors that Caesar intended to use the Parthian campaign as a springboard to kingship.

So did Caesar's behavior, which was becoming increasingly autocratic. His arrogant attitude was no doubt influenced by his belief that the Senate needed to be subjected to his strong, executive direction in order for the empire to be ruled effectively—and by the increasing impatience and intolerance of an aging man with many plans and little time for the constitutional process and the tedious business of conciliating opponents for whom he had long felt only contempt. Also, one of the driving forces behind his career had always been his consciousness of his *dignitas* and the respect to which he felt himself entitled. Perhaps he felt that by now his achievements were such that he and his actions were beyond question or scrutiny.

When, without warning, Caesar resigned as consul and named two supporters as consuls for the remainder of 45, it caused great offense. He seemed to be treating the consulship as a mere gift for services rendered rather than a serious office held on behalf of the people. He also extended eligibility for citizenship to more parts of the empire and increased the number of senators from six hundred to nine hundred to enable him to reward his supporters and friends. The new senators included a number of freedmen, even Gauls. While these actions wisely reflected the growing diversity of the Roman empire and gave a greater stake in Rome's success to those living in her provinces, Roman traditionalists joked about senators wearing trousers who were such strangers to Rome they could not find their way to the Senate house. To them Caesar's reforms seemed a gesture of contempt toward Rome's ancient institutions and their own treasured privileges.*

Whatever the senators' private fears, in public, as if uncertain what else to do, they continued hectically heaping honors upon Caesar, declaring his birthday a public holiday and conferring on him the right to sit on a golden chair in the Senate and wear the golden wreath of the ancient Etruscan monarchs. Caesar had already taken to appearing in the high red boots of the Alban kings. In addition, the Senate sycophantically agreed that Caesar was to have his own shrine and his own priest—Antony—and, on his death, was to become Divus Julius (Julius the god). Most significantly of all, Caesar was appointed dictator perpetuus (dictator for life), an honor he accepted in February 44 after only a little hesitation. His head now appeared on Roman coins—the first time any living Roman had been so honored and dangerously close, in the eyes of some, to the personality cult surrounding royal rulers such as Cleopatra in Egypt.

All that was lacking was the title of king. The previous month, when a man had hailed Caesar as Rex, he had replied that no, he was Caesar. However, when the tribunes had the man arrested, Caesar punished them, not the man. A few days after Caesar had become dictator for life, he presided from his gilded chair on the speaker's rostrum over the feast of the Lupercalia. This was an ancient spring fertility ritual. First, priests sacrificed a dog and some goats. Then the goats were skinned and well-born young men wound the skins around their otherwise naked bodies and, glistening with oil, ran through the streets lightly

---

*Caesar also offered citizenship to individuals or groups of individuals with skills needed to keep Rome running—for example, any foreign doctor willing to work in Rome.

striking women with strips of the fresh hairy goat hide to make them fertile or, if pregnant, to ensure a safe and easy delivery.

As consul for 44, Antony was participating. Even though at thirty-eight he was beyond his first youth, he was still proud of his physique. Clad only in his bloody goatskin loincloth, he ran up to the platform in the Forum where Caesar was seated on his golden throne and wearing his golden wreath. Several times he tried to place a laurel-decked diadem on Caesar's head. Whether Caesar knew in advance of Antony's gesture is unclear. What is certain is that there was no responding roar of enthusiasm from the crowd. Instead, "a groan echoed all round the Forum." According to Plutarch, "The amazing thing was that, although they were already, for all practical purposes, under the rule of a king, they rejected the title, as if it represented the loss of freedom." Caesar firmly declined the diadem and ordered it to be sent to the Capitol and dedicated to Jupiter, Rome's only king.

Despite this public act of self-denial, many still suspected Caesar of aiming at the ultimate prize and of having contrived the whole thing with Antony to test public reaction. Cicero later asked, "Where did this diadem come from?" and claimed that "it was a premeditated crime prepared in advance." Caesar's behavior seemed to bear this out. In one notable outburst he shouted that the republic "was nothing—a mere name without form or substance." He added that Sulla had been a dunce to resign his dictatorship.

Despite the fact that Caesar had pardoned both Brutus, Cato's nephew and Caesar's rumored son, and Cassius, a former officer of Pompey the Great after Pharsalus and had even made them praetors for 44, they had lost faith that he would ever restore the republic inaugurated by the coup of Brutus' ancestor, Lucius Brutus, against Tarquin. They believed that Caesar made policy in private with his advisers and cronies and then, rather than discuss it with his peers in the Senate as tradition demanded, cut out the Senate and went directly to the people and to his soldiers to secure backing for his decisions. Both thought Caesar's death would lead to the restoration of the Senate's supremacy. Wanting to make a clean sweep, Cassius had argued for the deaths not only of the dictator but of his deputy in the dictatorship, his master of the horse, Lepidus, of Antony and a host of others. Brutus, however, insisted that their target was one man only—Caesar. The day they chose was March 15, three days before Caesar was due to depart on his Parthian campaign. The place, perhaps symbolically, was to be a meeting of the Senate, the institution whose powers Caesar had so diminished. The assassins pondered inviting Cicero to join the plot but decided he was too old, timorous and, above all, indiscreet to be of any use.

Caesar perhaps had some intimation that Brutus and Cassius were his foes. According to Plutarch, when someone warned him that Antony and Dolabella were subversives, he replied, "I'm not afraid of these fleshy, long-haired men, so much as those pale, lean ones," that is, Cassius and Brutus. But, contemptuous of danger and confident no one would wish to risk reigniting civil war by killing him, Caesar ignored a rash of graffiti scrawled on public monuments. Among them were the words "If only you were alive now" daubed on a statue of Brutus' king-ousting ancestor, and the following verse scribbled on Caesar's own statue:

Brutus was elected consul
When he sent the kings away;
Caesar sent the consuls packing,
Caesar is our king today.

Caesar had dismissed his two-thousand-strong guard and was moving openly about the city, almost as if tempting fate. Anxious friends urged him to appoint a new bodyguard, but he ignored them. He would rather die, he said, than spend his life anticipating death. When the augur Spurinna predicted that Caesar would meet his doom on the ides, which fell on March 15, Caesar shrugged this off as well.

On the night of March 14 Lepidus invited him to dinner. The two men are said to have discussed what manner of death was preferable, and Caesar's choice was a death that came swiftly and without warning. The next day, Caesar woke feeling groggy and ill and reluctant to attend the meeting of the Senate he had called, which was to take place in Pompey's great stone theater. Calpurnia, unnerved by a night of terrifying dreams in which she cradled Caesar's murdered body in her arms, begged him to stay at home. Caesar offered sacrifice, and the diviners' unfavorable reading of the omens provided by the sacrificed animal's entrails added to his unease. He decided to send Antony to the meeting of the Senate in his place. However, Decimus Brutus, one of the plotters, opportunely happened to call at Caesar's house and laughingly derided the diviners and managed to persuade Caesar to change his mind.

Just before noon, Caesar was borne by litter to Pompey's theater, where the Senate was awaiting him in an assembly hall. As he climbed down, a Greek scholar who had learned something of the plot pushed forward to thrust a scroll into his hand, crying out, "Read this one yourself, Caesar, and read it soon. The matters it mentions are urgent and concern you personally." The insistence in the man's voice convinced Caesar to keep hold of the scroll instead of passing it as usual to his servant, but he did not unroll it. Seeing Spurinna standing by the entrance to Pompey's theater where the Senate would meet, Caesar remarked sarcastically that the ides of March had come. The augur replied, "Yes, they have come, but they have not yet gone."

While Gaius Trebonius, the man who almost a year earlier had attempted to draw him into the conspiracy, detained Antony on a pretext, Caesar entered the building. The senators rose to greet him as he made his way to his chair beneath the statue of his rival Pompey, which he himself had ordered to be reerected. Some of the sixty conspirators were ranged behind it. Others now pushed through the ranks of senators, as if eager to present a petition to him. When Caesar waved them away, one of the supposed petitioners grabbed at Caesar's toga with both hands. This was the agreed signal for the attack. Caesar turned the first blade, that of Casca, aside before it could penetrate deep into his throat, but the other conspirators closed around, each determined to deliver the dagger blow they had promised. Their knives thrust into his body until finally Caesar, bleeding copiously from twenty-three stab wounds, crumpled at Pompey's feet. He pulled his bloodstained purple toga over himself to hide his dying moments from the round-eyed senators watching in horrified disbelief. Suetonius wrote that "Caesar uttered no word after the first blow . . . although some say that when he saw Brutus about to strike he reproached him in Greek with, 'You too, my son!' "

The bloodstained assassins tumbled half crazed from Pompey's theater and, running across the Campus Martius, entered the city and ran onward to the Forum shouting, "Liberty!" Waving his dripping dagger in the air, Brutus declared the tyrant dead and wished long life to the republic. But there were no answering cheers. Instead, as the news spread, panicking people tripped over one another in their hurry to get home and barricade their doors against the chaos they feared was about to burst over them. For Cleopatra, it was a terrible moment. She and her son had lost their protector. All she could do now was try to save their lives.

PART IV
Isis Alone

CHAPTER 11

"Flight of the Queen"

IMMEDIATELY AFTER CAESAR'S MURDER, Antony fled, according to some, disguised in the nondescript garments of a slave. He took refuge first in a friend's house and then in his own—the grand mansion on the Palatine that had once been Pompey's and for which Caesar had made Antony pay in full—which he barricaded. In the uneasy hours that followed he must have wondered, like Cleopatra, whether the assassins would also come for him. But as the hours passed, he began to take heart, especially when a messenger sent by "the Liberators," as the assassins were styling themselves, brought word that they wished to treat with Antony. Rome, they insisted, must not be plunged into further bloodshed. Lepidus, Caesar's master of horse, who commanded the only troops in Rome, also contacted Antony. He had marched his legion to the Campus Martius and, in the gray dawn light of March 16, had seized the Temple of Ops, Rome's treasury, and occupied the Forum. Lepidus was demanding immediate vengeance on Caesar's killers.

Antony would have sensed, as he discussed his plans with his wife, Fulvia, that this was his moment. If he acted quickly, he could take control, becoming the leader of Rome rather than playing the loyal supporting role. Given his present position, restraint, not chaos, would best serve his ends. Needing to get his hands on the levers of power with as little fuss as possible, he made his way to Caesar's house, where the stiffening corpse now lay, and asked Calpurnia to hand over Caesar's papers and the huge sums of money in their house, which the grief-stricken widow did without demur. Next, Antony sent a message to

Lepidus urging him to hold back from military action and promising him the post of pontifex maximus if he did so. Then, by dint of his authority as the surviving consul and thus the highest officer of state, he summoned the Senate to meet the following morning, March 17, in the Temple of Tellus, close to his house.

When the senators arrived they found the temple ringed by Lepidus' troops. Antony needed all his skill to control the debate in a nervy Senate, many of whose members sympathized with the Liberators, who did not themselves dare attend. Their attempted appeals to the populace had met with a sullen response and, isolated and apprehensive, they remained on the Capitol, protected by the battle-scarred gladiators they had hired to defend them. Their fate, as they knew, depended on what their supporters in the Senate could achieve. Some senators argued that Caesar's murderers should be feted and rewarded as public benefactors. Others, taking courage, insisted that Caesar had been a tyrant, all of whose acts should be annulled. Antony cannily pointed out that the majority of those present owed their positions to ordinances of Caesar and asked whether they were really proposing to renounce their appointments.

Self-interest won the day. New elections would be expensive and the results uncertain. Even Cicero, whose sympathies lay with the conspirators, recognized that, for the present, there was no alternative and reluctantly supported Antony. The senators hastily confirmed Caesar's acts, accomplished or in gestation, as being "for the good of the state." This gave Antony carte blanche to bring forward all manner of schemes that Caesar had been planning—or so he claimed. He could also, in the months ahead, nominate anyone he wished to official positions, blandly maintaining that he was only fulfilling the dead Caesar's wishes. Wits called the new appointees *charonides*—men who owed their power to Charon, ferryman of the underworld, who it appeared was now, on his return journey, conveying the dead Caesar's wishes to Antony, his living representative.

Somewhat paradoxically, given the legitimacy they had just conferred on Caesar, at Cicero's urging the senators also immediately agreed on an amnesty for Caesar's assassins. They would not be prosecuted and no inquiry would be held into the murder. For the moment this suited Antony. In the vacuum following Caesar's death he needed to achieve some kind of political equilibrium in order to maintain his authority as consul and, with the help of the politically attuned Fulvia, begin to sound out new allies and confirm existing ones. The Liberators were invited to come down from the Capitol while Antony and Lepidus sent their own children to the hill as hostages. A formal public reconciliation followed, after which Antony and Lepidus played host to Caesar's murderers at dinner. Clearly any vengeance for Caesar was to be a dish consumed cold. Dio Cassius described a tense evening during which "Antony asked Cassius, 'Have you perchance a dagger under your arm even now?' To which he answered: 'Yes, and a big one, if you too should desire to make yourself tyrant.' "

That same day, March 17, Caesar's will was read out in Antony's house, and Cleopatra and the world learned that it contained no reference to her or to their son, Caesarion. Most disturbing to Cleopatra were the intentions of the heir Caesar had named, Octavian. He would never look favorably on a child who, though Caesar had not acknowledged him publicly, was almost universally believed to be his son and blatantly and brazenly bore his name.

Cleopatra's mind must have been in turmoil. At the flash of the assassins' knives, she had lost both her main emotional bulwark and her political support. She and her son were alone in a hostile and uncertain environment whose political systems were alien to her own and where she had been seen as a pernicious influence on the murdered leader. She would have known that with Caesar dead, Antony was, in theory at least, the most powerful man in Rome. Perhaps in those first difficult days she contemplated turning to him, recalling his courage and compassion after his triumph at Pelusium, when he had counseled moderation, not murder, to her vengeful father, Auletes. Yet she would not have known whether she could trust him entirely.

Emotionally, Cleopatra needed time to mourn and to reflect on her feelings for Caesar. A clever, gifted man endowed with the glamour and charisma of great power, he was not only the father of her child but perhaps also a father figure, supplanting the memory of the weak and pleading pipe player Auletes. Though she had engineered her liaison with him, she no doubt felt affection, passion, even love for him. Letters written to Cicero by his friend Atticus suggest the close bonds between them—they had attended fashionable parties together and were regarded as a couple.

Like so many mistresses through history, Cleopatra did not attend her lover's funeral. On March 20, five days after his murder and with the Senate's agreement, Antony, who had a ready appreciation of theater and its power over the popular imagination, staged a public funeral for Caesar. This was a far cry from the fate Brutus had originally planned—the late dictator's still-warm body being impaled on the executioner's hook, dragged swiftly to the Tiber and tossed into the water like that of a common criminal. Antony's stated plan was to bear Caesar's corpse on an ivory funeral couch draped with purple and gold cloth through the Forum to the Campus Martius, where he would be cremated on a vast pyre by the tomb of his daughter, Julia. Antony carefully orchestrated the procession, hiring musicians and masked, wailing professional mourners to walk in it, clad in the robes Caesar had worn at his Triumphs. When it reached the Forum the cortege paused before the speaker's platform and the ivory couch was set down. Here, in front of the couch, Antony, in the absence of any close male relative, delivered the *laudatio* or eulogy.

Shakespeare's Antony begins by declaring that praising Caesar is not his business. The real Antony did praise Caesar and very cleverly. A herald solemnly read a list of all the decrees passed by the Senate and people of Rome in Caesar's honor and intoned the oath of loyalty sworn to him by every senator. Next he related every war and battle won by Caesar, all the prisoners, kings among them, and all the rich booty he had brought to Rome. When the herald finished this rehearsal of greatness Antony mounted the rostrum to address the hushed crowd. He played his audience expertly. Voice cracking, he reminded them what manner of man Rome had lost, exhibiting the bloodstained toga Caesar had been wearing when he was assassinated.

A wax effigy of Caesar, which had probably been concealed behind or within the draped couch, was then produced and hoisted high above the crowd. Operated by a mechanical device, it slowly rotated to reveal the all too realistic simulations of every one of the twenty-three livid wounds hacked into Caesar's body. The crowd erupted in grief and anger, tearing down anything wooden it could find to build an impromptu pyre for the dead leader. Wailing women tossed in their bracelets and necklaces. As the flames crackled and burned, angry mobs sought out the houses of the plotters and were restrained only with difficulty from burning them to the ground. A tribune unfortunate enough to share the name of Cinna with one of the assassins was mistaken for him and ripped apart. The mob paraded his head through the streets on the point of a spear before it realized its error. Eight years previously Fulvia had, by displaying the wounds of her dead husband, Clodius, to the mob, provoked a surge of emotion that led to the Senate house being consumed as Clodius' funeral pyre. Now her new husband's oratory and display of Caesar's body led to the reconstructed building going up in flames once more.

Antony had succeeded magnificently in mobilizing the loyalty of the people to the dead Caesar. In the process he demonstrated the power of the late dictator's name and established himself, at least for the present, as the leader of the pro-Caesarean party. The moral victory that Brutus and Cassius had believed was theirs had been plucked from them. Antony had also shown himself strong, decisive and capable of maintaining order, if anyone could. He had mastered the crisis, but what to do next was more difficult. He was perhaps uncertain, like Pompey before him, of what he wanted to achieve politically—whether autocracy or some form of republican government. Significantly, Antony's next move, within just a few weeks of Caesar's death, was to take the highly symbolic measure of bringing before the Senate a motion abolishing the dictatorship for good. This may have indicated no more than a consciousness of the need to conciliate the more moderate republicans, but perhaps more likely it indicated a disinclination to aim for sole power, at least for the present. Yet his relationship with the republicans and others would undergo many twists over the next few months as he pragmatically sought to preserve and enhance his position.

While Antony was lauded for his good sense and moderation, the streets of Rome were no longer safe for Brutus and Cassius, and by mid-April they and many of their fellow conspirators thought it only prudent to withdraw to their country estates. A dyspeptic and depressed Cicero lambasted them for having "the spirit of men but the common sense of boys." The bookish, high-principled Brutus and his associates had courageously removed the dictator but devised no strategy for dismantling his apparatus of power and obliterating his regime. If the conspirators had thought about it at all, they had naïvely assumed that with Caesar dead, the old republican system would simply resurrect itself of its own accord. This was, in Cicero's view, "absurd." "Freedom has been restored and yet the republic has not," he raged. In particular, he blamed the conspirators for not having seized the initiative and convened the Senate themselves immediately after murdering Caesar instead of allowing Antony time to react and use his position as consul to take control. Cicero fumed that had he had his way, Antony would have been killed as well, leaving both Senate and Caesarians more obviously leaderless.

Cicero too decided to leave Rome, heading to the purer air of the Bay of Naples to wait on events. His despair at the political situation added to recent turmoil within his family and deep personal grief. In early 45 Tullia, the daughter to whom he had been so devoted that enemies accused him of incest with her, had died in childbirth. Perhaps Cicero saw her death as punishment for having divorced his wife of more than thirty years—a woman who, in a society in which only 50 percent of people reached adulthood, only 30 percent forty years of age and a mere 13 percent sixty, would achieve the remarkable feat of living to 103—in favor of one of his nubile and rich young wards, Publilia. The marriage had taken place mere weeks before Tullia's death. When teased for wedding such a young girl, the sixty-one-year-old Cicero had leerily responded, "She'll be a woman tomorrow." In his anguish at his daughter's death and Publilia's apparent lack of sympathy, Cicero had sent his new wife back to her family and asked his friends to prevent either the girl or her family from seeking him out while he arranged a divorce. Now, a year later, moving between his assorted villas overlooking seas just beginning to grow warmer in the early spring sunshine, he contemplated the shipwreck of his political fortunes and the loss of the republic he held so dear and whose arcane procedures he was so adept at manipulating. His response was not to acquiesce in its fall but rather a newfound steely resolve to use any means possible to prevent this.

By this time, Cleopatra had also decided that her most prudent course would be to quit Rome and take Caesarion back to safety in Egypt. In mid-April, a month after Caesar's murder, Cicero was writing dismissively to his friend Atticus, "I see nothing to object to in the flight of the queen." The term the hostile Cicero used to describe her exit from Rome was *flight*, a word implying panic, which probably belies the calculation behind her decision. Three weeks later, after lamenting the miscarriage suffered by Tertia, Cassius' wife and Brutus' half sister—all too probably induced by the stress of Caesar's murder at the hands of the two men closest to her—Cicero added somewhat mysteriously, "I am hoping it is true about the queen and that Caesar." This seems to be a reference to some misfortune that had befallen Cleopatra and Caesarion on their journey back to Egypt. Perhaps reports had reached Rome suggesting that they might be dead. Though not short of things to talk about, Rome was clearly abuzz with a story or scandal about Cleopatra that refused to go away. On May 17 Cicero noted that the rumor about the queen was finally dying down, but a week later he was still embroiled in speculation, writing again, "I am hoping it is true about the queen."*

Whatever Cicero may have hoped, papyrus documents show that by late July 44 Cleopatra, Caesarion and her brother-husband Ptolemy XIV were safely back in Egypt. About a month later, Cleopatra's fifteen-year-old co-ruler was dead. The historian Josephus, writing in the first century AD, believed Cleopatra had poisoned Ptolemy and he was probably correct. Cleopatra was as accomplished as any Roman at seizing the moment and perhaps even more cold-bloodedly ruthless. Paramount in her mind, now that she had lost her Roman supporter, was the need to safeguard her own position and that of her son, Caesarion. Her half brother would have seen the child, as he grew older, as a rival. The traumatic events of her girlhood at the Alexandrian court, especially her sister's murder at the hands of Auletes, could hardly have demonstrated more clearly that, individually, the Ptolemies had most to fear from those nearest to them. Only a few years thereafter, her elder half brother had attempted to eject her from the throne. Sharing power with him had only given rise to factionalism and was in any case probably not best suited to her nature. As Josephus wrote of her character, "If she lacked one single thing that she desired, she imagined that she lacked everything." And if Cleopatra did kill her brother, she was following a long tradition. Plutarch, writing with lofty disapproval, thought such activities an inherent characteristic of the Hellenic dynasties: "With regard to the assassination of siblings, it was a well-established habit . . . as widely used as were the propositions of Euclid by mathematicians, it was legitimized by the kings, in order to guarantee their security."

Even if she was not the direct agent of her brother's death, Cleopatra would not have agonized long over it. She could now elevate her son to the throne beside her. He was far too young to question her or to take any part in decision making. Like all parents, she would have believed that her relationship with her

*Historian Michael Grant believed that Cicero's reference to Tertia's miscarriage immediately before mentioning Cleopatra in his letter is significant. This positioning, he suggested, might imply that Cicero had learned that Cleopatra had also miscarried a child and that Cicero's reference to "that Caesar" means not Caesarion but a new child conceived by Cleopatra while in Rome. However, there is no evidence either to disprove or to substantiate this idea.

child would avoid previous familial mistakes. Like all mothers, she wanted both to protect Caesarion and to see him succeed. Her ambition for him and for his security and that of her dynasty would henceforth become a major driving force. For obvious reasons, as their joint reign began, she abandoned her previous title of Philadelphus, "brother-loving." Caesarion, ruling as Ptolemy XV Caesar, was called Theos Philopater Philometer, "God Who Loves His Father and Mother." The adored father, as Cleopatra wished to state clearly to the world—and doubtless to Octavian in particular—was Julius Caesar. Her son allied Egypt with Rome, East with West, a geopolitical claim no other familial union would be able to make until she and Antony became lovers.

To drive that message home to her people, Cleopatra milked the symbolism of her identification with Isis. The goddess was a potent image in people's minds—the embodiment of the power of the moon, of the sea and the Nile, of the underworld and of the life beyond. The earliest surviving Greek or Roman account of the myth of Isis is Plutarch's. He wrote of how Isis and her twin brother, Osiris, the offspring of sky and earth, fell in love while still in the womb. Their uterine bond was absolute. When Osiris was later murdered and dismembered into fourteen parts by his envious brother, Seth, a distraught but devoted Isis managed to find all the pieces except one—the phallus. Using magic in place of the missing sexual organ, Isis managed to become pregnant and give birth to a son, Horus, who was not only Osiris' child but a reincarnation of the god himself. After the ides of March, Cleopatra could use the imagery of Isis to present the murdered Caesar as Osiris and Caesarion as Horus, his divine and undisputed son.

To honor her dead lover further, the grieving Cleopatra commissioned a carved bust of Caesar to be placed in the still-incomplete Caesareum. A surviving head of green diabase stone, quarried only in Egypt, may well be that image. It shows a man with thinning hair and crow's feet but an intent and masterful gaze.*

If anything had induced Cleopatra to leave Rome quickly—if not in a panic, as Cicero sneeringly alleged—it was probably the news that the eighteen-year-old Octavian was on his way to Rome to claim his inheritance. Octavian had

---

*Today the head is in Berlin.

been born in 63, at the time of the Catiline conspiracy. The son of a wealthy *novus homo*, the first of his family to reach the Senate, who had died when Octavian was only four, he had grown up with the knowledge that his route to power would depend as heavily on patronage as on his own abilities. He had already acquired the skill of self-publicity. According to Suetonius, at his coming-of-age ceremony, "the seams of the senatorial gown which Caesar had allowed him to wear split and it fell at his feet." Bystanders might have interpreted this as an evil portent but Octavian seized the moment to declare, "I shall have the whole senatorial dignity beneath my feet." Whether made on the spot or invented with his advisers sometime afterward, this priggish statement from one so young would have been deeply impressive to Roman ears.

It was Octavian's great good fortune that his mother, Atia, was Caesar's niece, making him one of Caesar's closest male relatives. Young as he was, he had already striven to cultivate this relationship. His determination, despite shipwreck and illness, to join his great-uncle on campaign in Spain in 45 had greatly pleased and impressed Caesar. That year Caesar had asked the Senate to raise Octavian's family to patrician rank. (The patricians were the descendants of Rome's ancient nobility. The number of acknowledged patrician families had remained unaltered since 450, but Caesar had gained the right to nominate new members to their ranks.)

Busts of the young Octavian depict a fine-boned face, slighty protuberant ears, a long neck and light, slender shoulders very different from those of the muscular, bull-necked Antony. Octavian was probably no more than five feet six or seven inches tall, according to Suetonius—short by Roman standards. Suetonius added that, "one did not realize how small a man he was, until someone tall stood close to him." Though generally negligent about his appearance, Octavian was sensitive about his height and had his footgear made with "rather thick soles to make him look taller." His body was dotted with birthmarks, which his flatterers in later years proclaimed were configured like the constellation of the Great Bear. He also apparently suffered from gallstones all his life and had "a weakness in his left hip, thigh and leg, which occasionally gave him the suspicion of a limp." This perhaps explains why "he loathed people who were dwarfish or in any way deformed, regarding them as freaks of nature and bringers of bad luck." His red-blond hair was curly and unkempt and, in later years, to save time, he "would have two or three barbers working hurriedly on it together."

Immediately on learning of Caesar's death—Atia wrote to him on the very evening of the murder—Octavian left Apollonia in Macedonia, where he had been training with Caesar's troops for the Parthian campaign and, in his spare time, studying Greek literature. Though his mother urged him to come at once, she also warned him to be cautious. He slipped across the Adriatic, landing on a deserted beach south of Brundisium. After sending members of his retinue ahead to check that all was well, he made his way to the town where, to an earsplitting welcome from the garrison, he learned for the first time that he had become Caesar's adopted son and heir to both his name and his fortune.

Yet Octavian allowed neither the crowd's adulation nor the news of his inheritance to go to his head. Only the omnipresent blotches on his skin, which modern doctors suggest were produced by nervous eczema, betrayed his anxieties. He mastered any youthful impulse to dash straight to Rome. Instead, showing the same cool ability for political analysis and calculation that would one day make him emperor, he decided first to call on Cicero and other influential republicans, who had removed themselves from the capital until things quieted down, to assess their feelings toward him. Cicero did not give him a particularly warm welcome. He had loathed Caesar and was glad he was dead. He had no wish to entertain the ambitious great-nephew with the piercing gray-eyed gaze whom Caesar had been grooming since he was sixteen. "I cannot see how he can have his heart in the right place," Cicero wrote, and made his feelings clear, refusing to address his visitor as "Gaius Julius Caesar," as Octavian now wished to be called. Nevertheless, such was his vanity that, despite himself, Cicero found Octavian's deference gratifying, writing, "The young man is quite devoted to me."

Cicero was entirely wrong. To Octavian, he was an arrogant, cantankerous but potentially useful old man who probably had been complicit in Caesar's murder. Visiting him had simply been prudent. Cicero had also misread Octavian as an inexperienced youth who would probably get his comeuppance in Rome, where there would be plenty of ambitious men to challenge the dictator's heir. He had not discerned Octavian's diamond-hard determination, belied as it was by the slender, almost puny body. As the historian Velleius Paterculus later put it, the self-contained Octavian was a man who "spurned mortal advice and preferred to aim at dangerous eminence rather than at safe obscurity." To that extent, he was not so different from Cleopatra. She could have chosen "safe obscurity" rather than unrolling from a carpet at Caesar's feet.

Octavian did not receive the comeuppance Cicero had anticipated. Knowing the excitement and interest it would cause, he planned his arrival in Rome in late April 44 with care. To avoid any seeming arrogance or presumption, he separated from most of his followers and entered the city with only a few attendants. Yet, according to Suetonius, his arrival in Rome did not go unmarked—a shimmering, rainbow-like halo ringed the sun, though the skies were clear. Many took it as an omen from the gods of great things to come.*

Octavian had intentionally chosen to arrive while Antony was away attending to the resettlement of large groups of Caesar's veterans in Campania. As soon as Antony marched back into Rome, Octavian requested an interview. The young man's arrival put Antony in a quandary. Until now Antony had been the acknowledged leader of the Caesarians but also had managed to hold the Senate. He had achieved a delicate balance, but if Octavian began to press for vengeance against Caesar's murderers, maintaining that equilibrium would become impossible. If he openly supported Octavian, he risked alienating much of the Senate and, of course, the Liberators and their factions, while if he refused, he would anger Caesar's friends and veterans. Antony therefore must have reasoned that he needed metaphorically to play for time, both to think and to assess his potential rival. He did so clumsily, at their first meeting literally keeping Octavian waiting in an anteroom. When he was finally ushered in, Antony was blunt and dismissive and, when Octavian asked him to hand over Caesar's papers and money, downright unhelpful. Falling back on technicalities, he argued that Octavian's adoption as Caesar's son had not yet been formalized and that separating out Caesar's money from public funds would take time.

Off to a bad start, the relationship between the two men, who should have had much in common, would soon get much worse. On a personal level, Antony was probably suspicious of the motives of the young Octavian and jealous of him. Caesar had named Antony, his most trusted commander, as one of several secondary heirs, while Octavian had inherited nearly everything. Antony's resentment of Octavian may explain why he soon began a propaganda campaign against Octavian to denigrate his lineage and diminish

---

*In fact, the phenomenon probably originated from the presence in the atmosphere of dust from a recent eruption of Mount Etna.

his dignity. He alleged that one of his great-grandfathers "had been only a freedman, a ropemaker . . . and his grandfather a money-changer." Another great-grandfather, Antony sneered, had kept a bakehouse and a perfumery. Antony would also deploy the usual Roman smear tactics of accusing Octavian of playing the passive role in a homosexual relationship, alleging that "Julius Caesar made him submit to unnatural practices as the price of adoption." Antony's brother, not to be outdone in accusations of unmanliness, claimed that Octavian "used to soften the hairs on his legs by singeing them with red-hot walnut shells." A desire to diminish Octavian's unique relationship to Caesar and thus his status may also explain why, if Suetonius is correct, Antony told the Senate "that Caesar had, in fact, acknowledged Caesarion's paternity."

Yet for the moment, the quiet-spoken albeit insistent Octavian seemed a less immediate threat than did Caesar's murderers and certain to support any move against them. Antony was particularly worried what would happen when the Liberators took command of the provinces and the armies assigned to them before Caesar's death, fearing that they might use them as power bases to gather forces and money for a move on Rome. One of them, Decimus Brutus, was already in Cisalpine Gaul and thus in control of the key northern gateway into Italy. In early June, Antony managed, through a vote in the popular assembly, to strip him of the province and have himself appointed governor in his place for the next five years. This angered the Senate, who thought it their right to control provincial appointments and jealously guarded this prerogative. Antony also pressured the Senate into giving Brutus and Cassius special commissions to oversee Rome's corn supplies from Asia and Sicily rather than their assigned provinces. This was exile under another name. The two men were left angered and humiliated but could not decide how to assert themselves. Cicero at around this time went to an inconclusive council of war attended by Cassius, Brutus and their wives at which Brutus' mother, Servilia, played a key role. Her promise to use her still considerable influence at least to get the corn commissions revoked was one of the few actions agreed upon. Cicero wondered why he had bothered to go, commenting, "I found the ship breaking up, or rather already wrecked. No plan, no thought, no method."

Octavian, however, did have method and probably a greater certainty about his long-term goals than any other of the Roman leaders. He began to build alliances and to pressure and undermine Antony, who, he claimed with justice, was obstructing the legislation that would ratify his adoption by Caesar. He also claimed that Antony had helped himself to money belonging either to himself, as Caesar's heir, or to the Roman treasury and now would not, or could not, free the money to honor Caesar's bequests. In July, Octavian staged lavish games in his adoptive father's honor and used the occasion to fulfill Caesar's legacy to the people of Rome, stipulated in his will, of three hundred sesterces a man. Octavian made abundantly clear to the public that he was paying this from his own purse, although he may in fact have used some of the contents of Caesar's war chest for the Parthian campaign, which he was said to have seized on his way to Rome. He also attempted to display the golden throne and wreath that the Senate had granted Caesar. Seemingly anxious to avoid a confrontation between the Caesarian and anti-Caesarian factions by Octavian's glorifying of Caesar, Antony refused to allow even this, causing the crowds to bellow their disapproval.

Popular anger against Antony mounted when, for seven evenings in a row, a bright comet flared in the sky to the north, as if symbolizing the spirit of the divine Caesar elevated to heaven.* To ensure people did not forget the portent, Octavian ordered a flaming star to be placed on the forehead of Caesar's statue. "You, boy, you owe everything to your name," Antony taunted Octavian. But the boy was quietly outflanking the man in the propaganda war to which Roman politics had descended, making every use of his name to stake his claim to be Caesar's political as well as personal heir.

Whatever the two protagonists said in public, it must have been obvious to them both that they coveted the same thing—to succeed Julius Caesar as the most powerful man in Rome. Each may have had his own ideas about how such power should be deployed and it also must have been obvious that a confrontation was not far away.

Perhaps influenced by Servilia's behind-the-scenes lobbying and with Octavian becoming ever more aggressive, Antony decided to conciliate the Liberators. He may well have recognized that, in any contest for the leadership of the hard-line Caesarians alone, he would be likely to lose out to Octavian and that therefore his best chance of success lay in capturing the middle ground.

*The records of contemporaneous Chinese astronomers confirm that there was indeed a comet at this time.

Accordingly, to find somewhere they could go with honor but where they would pose little threat to stability, in late July Antony convinced the Senate to award Brutus the governorship of Crete and Cassius the governorship of Cyrenaica. He addressed the Senate with such silkily conciliatory words that, learning of them, Cicero abandoned a proposed journey to Athens to visit his son, who was studying there. Instead he turned his steps back toward Rome, hoping but perhaps not expecting to find a less aggressively autocratic Antony acknowledging the authority of the Senate.

However, Antony's conciliatory tactics, by giving his critics courage to speak out, backfired. When the Senate met on August 1, Caesar's father-in-law, Piso, who had once offered to mediate between Caesar and Pompey, lambasted Antony for dictatorial behavior and fraudulent use of Caesar's papers. Suspecting the hand of Brutus and Cassius behind the attack, Antony tossed aside the velvet glove and, in an instant reversal of tactics, immediately issued a consular edict threatening Brutus and Cassius with force for reneging on various official responsibilities. He also wrote them an aggressive letter. Their reply of August 4 was equally mettlesome. "We are amazed that you are so little able to control your animosity that you reproach us with the death of Caesar," they said self-righteously before themselves issuing an implicit threat by noting that Caesar had not lived long once he began to play the king. By late August 44 both Brutus and Cassius had abandoned Italy, not for the provinces they had been allocated but for Macedonia and Syria.

Cicero reached Rome in time to attend a Senate meeting called by Antony on September 1 and was cheered by the crowds as he entered the city. One of Antony's purposes in summoning the Senate was to propose a special day to honor Julius Caesar each year, an overt bid to woo the pro-Caesarean party and anathema to Cicero. Weary from his journey and wanting time to assess the situation, the sixty-two-year-old stayed away from the Senate. Interpreting his absence as a slight to his dignity, Antony threatened to pull Cicero's house down and did not attend the Senate himself the following day. Cicero, however, did and launched the first of a series of increasingly vitriolic attacks on Antony, which he nicknamed the "Philippics."*

---

*Cicero named the Philippics after the Athenian Demosthenes' denunciations of Philip of Macedonia, Alexander's father, as the enemy of the freedom of the Greek states.

To the old statesman, any means of attack was valid. Antony had become to him as great a menace to the republic and its traditions of senatorial authority as any Catiline or Caesar. Cicero used the Philippics to detail Antony's supposed sexual depravities, calling him "a public whore" and raking up his affair with Curio, in which he alleged Antony had been the shameful, passive partner. His assault embraced Fulvia, whom he portrayed as a malignant influence, just as she had been on his old enemy, her previous husband, Clodius. "Life is not merely a matter of breathing," he lectured an uncertain Senate. "The slave has no true life. All other nations are capable of enduring servitude—but our city is not." Liberty, he insisted, was worth dying for. Lathering himself into self-righteous indignation, he pilloried Antony as a drunken, vomiting, womanizing wastrel who, hell-bent on his own glory, continued to abuse the constitution and the Senate.

Antony withdrew to his villa in the country to consider his response. On September 19 he marched into the Senate, "not to speak but as usual spew up his words," as Cicero sneered to Cassius. Cicero himself was not there to hear Antony's accusations of how, when Cicero was consul, he had put citizens to death without trial after the Catiline conspiracy, including Antony's own stepfather, and had set Caesar and Pompey at one another's throats.

Cicero bided his time. He knew that what people feared most was a bloodbath and that Antony's strength was that he offered stability to a Rome still dazed by events and demoralized by memories of civil war. Cicero needed to find an alternative figurehead, and his gaze fell on the slender, sharp-eyed young man whom several months earlier he had snubbed—Octavian. Over the next few months the two would become allies of expedience. Octavian would conveniently forget, for the time being at least, that Cicero had celebrated Caesar's murder, while the elder statesman would flatter himself that, whatever Octavian's unfortunate forebears, he was an intelligent, impressionable young man who could be molded in a more republican image, a man infinitely better than that "gladiator looking for a massacre," as he had derided Antony.

Caesar's heir was by now locked in a tribal dance with Antony as complex as any internal power struggles of the Ptolemies. Alarmed by Antony's breach with the Senate and his growing hostility toward Octavian, Antony's officers pleaded with him to avoid an open break. He responded by staging a public reconciliation with Octavian on the Capitol. But just two days later came sensational news of a plot orchestrated by Octavian to murder Antony. Octavian probably correctly vigorously protested his innocence and claimed it was all a conspiracy to discredit him. Nevertheless, on October 9, claiming his life was at risk, Antony departed for Brundisium with Fulvia to greet the four legions he had summoned home from Macedonia to enable him to oust Decimus Brutus from Cisalpine Gaul. As his officers feared, he was becoming isolated and hence vulnerable to his enemies.

Cicero, who was among the first, most vindictive and influential of these, accused Antony of planning first to bribe the legions and then to bring them to Rome "to subjugate us." Octavian, though, was the one doing the bribing, sending agents to Brundisium equipped with propaganda leaflets intended to vilify Antony and buy the legionaries over to him. He also traveled around Campania with carts brimming with money, recruiting his own troops. This was entirely illegal, since he did so without the Senate's authority, but Octavian's lavish offers of more than two years' pay up front soon attracted three thousand eager volunteers from the colonies of Caesar's veterans.

Antony, meanwhile, was having a hard time in Brundisium with the legionaries newly arrived from Macedonia. Soldiers throughout this period rightly sensed they had more to gain in terms of payments, pensions and plunder from a single strong man than from the diffuse rule of the Senate, but they were becoming increasingly dissatisfied with Antony in the role of a strong, independent leader. Why had he weakly allowed their beloved Caesar's assassins to go free? they demanded. And, less nobly, why was the bounty he was offering them so much less than what Octavian was promising his recruits? So dangerous was the situation that Antony had lists of the dissenters drawn up and ordered those whose names were randomly selected from amongst them by lot to be battered to death in front of himself and Fulvia. So close was she standing that blood spattered her face. Having, as he thought, quelled the mutiny, Antony sent three legions north and hurried back to Rome with the remaining legion, the elite "Larks," to take firm control of the city and then to deal with Octavian and his illegal army by whatever means necessary.

Learning of Antony's advance, Octavian was sufficiently alarmed to send repeated and urgent messages to Cicero asking what to do, even offering to lead the republicans in a war against Antony. After some agonizing, Cicero stilled any doubts he had about his ability to control Octavian and advised him to take his men to Rome as fast as possible, believing, as he wrote to a friend, he would "have the city rabble behind him and respectable opinion too if he convinces them of his sincerity." Octavian reached the city before Antony, on November 10, and camped on the Campus Martius outside its walls. Here he addressed his forces, damning Antony while lauding his adoptive father, Caesar. However, his veteran recruits had marched to Rome under the impression they were to fight against the Liberators. Antony, they protested, had been loyal to Caesar, just as he had been to the soldiers he commanded. Appian related how some, disillusioned and upset, "asked if they could return to their homes." Helpless to stop his new army from breaking up, Octavian watched as at least two thirds of his force melted away. In despair, he withdrew the remnants north.

Antony arrived with his Larks several days later. Delighted that Octavian had put himself so clearly in the wrong by flouting the law and bringing the forces he had raised illegally to Rome, he ordered the Senate to meet on November 24, declaring that any senator who was absent would be considered a traitor. He heaped more verbal ordure on Octavian's head. Caesar's heir was, he said, provincial, effete and the descendant of manual laborers—all deep insults to a Roman of his time and class. Antony even contemplated trying to declare Octavian an enemy of the state, but while he pondered whether he would win sufficient support for this drastic step, alarming reports reached him that two of his Macedonian legions, including the veteran Martian legion still smarting from Antony's treatment of them at Brundisium, had deserted to Octavian, seeing him as the more likely to avenge Caesar and reward them well. Thus they readjusted the balance of power once again.

Accordingly, Antony decided to set off for Cisalpine Gaul to dislodge Decimus Brutus. Once in control of this strategically important province, he reasoned, he could retrench and deal with his other enemies. Before leaving, on November 28 Antony again summoned the Senate, this time to what was a highly irregular evening meeting, at which he reallocated the provinces between his supporters. A number of senators and wealthy citizens, unnerved by Octavian's recent illegal and bellicose acts, so reminiscent of Caesar at his most dictatorial, swore their allegiance to Antony and bade him a reluctant farewell as he marched north. According to Appian, "He got a splendid send-off."

The news filtering through to Cleopatra during those months must have been as confused and fragmented as the situation itself. For the moment, with the three-year-old Caesarion by her side on the throne as Ptolemy XV Caesar, she could concentrate only on strengthening her hold on the country. The fact that no serious unrest seems to have occurred during her absence in Rome suggests that her authority had not been challenged and that her officials had governed well.

Cleopatra was fortunate to have inherited a centralized, sophisticated and efficient system of land management, which had survived down the centuries since the time of Ptolemy I and provided stability. Officials graded all agricultural land according to its productivity. The choicest land was allocated to the crown, then leased back to the peasants under strict rules about which crops to cultivate, when to sow, when to reap, how much to hand over to the government as rent and how much seed corn to retain. The headman of each village supervised the farmers, reporting to a hierarchy of Greek and Macedonian officials, at whose apex was Cleopatra—the country's greatest farmer, industrialist and merchant.

These arrangements ensured an annual stream of grain into the royal granaries. After supplying the needs of the population, Cleopatra, who held the monopoly in grain production and sale, could dispose of surpluses on the world market. Her other monopolies included olive oil (a vital commodity used in everything from food production to skin care and lighting), salt, perfume, the brewing of beer, and the tall, triangular-stemmed and feathery papyrus that grew in dense, bright green thickets in the swamplands of the Nile delta.

"No one has the right to do what he wishes," an early Ptolemaic decree had informed Egypt's citizens, "but everything is organized for the best." However, Rome's new conflicts would not leave Egypt and its well-regulated administration untroubled for much longer and Cleopatra would once again be forced to take sides.

CHAPTER 12

Ruler of the East

STORMING INTO NORTHERN ITALY—Cisalpine Gaul—which Decimus Brutus, insisting that he was upholding the rights of the Senate and the people of Rome, was refusing to relinquish, Antony besieged him in Mutina (Modena) and began pounding the town with boulders flung from his *ballista* (siege catapults), which used torsion energy to throw missiles long distances.* One particular kind was known as the "wild ass" because of its kickback. He was anxious for a quick victory since, on January 1, his own consulship would end and he suspected that his enemies were likely to persuade the pusillanimous Senate to send to Decimus' aid the new consuls, Hirtius and Pansa, both former generals of Caesar's but now inclining to the republican cause. Indeed, by early December, Cicero was back in Rome and urging war against Antony. He was also openly and lavishly praising Octavian, calling him by his adoptive name of Caesar in public for the first time.

By now Octavian had the support of five legions and also archers, cavalry and even some elephant units. Unleashing some of his finest oratory, Cicero cajoled the Senate into raising Octavian to the rank of senator and conferring on him the right to command an army, thus legalizing his leadership of the troops he had originally raised from the veteran colonies to march on Rome. Together with the consuls Hirtius and Pansa, the Senate commanded Octavian

---

**Ballista* gives us our word *ballistic*.

to go to the aid of Decimus Brutus. It was a strange mission—Caesar's adoptive son succoring one of Caesar's murderers against Caesar's most seasoned and trusted lieutenant—but for the moment this does not appear to have troubled Cicero, who had his mind set on the elimination of Antony. As for Octavian, for the moment he was prepared to temporize.

To Antony, Octavian's actions must have signaled just how far he was prepared to go to achieve his ambitions. Antony's friends, still struggling to avert a war, convinced the vacillating Senate to dispatch ambassadors to Antony, but this proved futile. The ambassadors' arrival did not distract him for one moment from his bombardment. In a determined mood, he rejected their demands that he withdraw south across the Rubicon—the border of Cisalpine Gaul—but keep at least two hundred miles from Rome and submit to the Senate. Instead he issued his own unrealistic counterdemands. These included the recall of Brutus and Cassius from their eastern commands, confirmation of the legality of his and Caesar's actions (including his own seizure of funds after Caesar's murder), the grant to him of the province of Transalpine Gaul for five years and rewards for his legionaries.

Reeling at the hubris of Antony's ultimatum, or at least pretending to, Cicero urged the Senate to declare a state of war and denounce Antony as a public enemy. However, Antony's determined mother, Julia, and wife, Fulvia, donning mourning garments, lobbied the senators on his behalf. As a result, more moderate voices arguing for the declaration of a "state of emergency," not a war, once again prevailed. Though Antony's demands were refused, he was not yet outlawed, and his siege of Mutina continued. Furthermore, his allies in the Senate tried to engineer another embassy to Antony. Cicero was to be one of the ambassadors, but his sudden withdrawal sabotaged the mission, as he no doubt intended. With Octavian and Hirtius already in position near Mutina, the war that Cicero was trying so passionately to promote moved closer.

In late March the Senate dispatched a further four legions, this time of new recruits, north under Pansa to join Octavian and Hirtius. Learning of this, Antony decided to intercept them en route and on April 14 ambushed them as they passed through a village. Unknown to him, the inexperienced recruits had been joined by more seasoned soldiers—the Martian Legion which had defected from him. The struggle, on boggy ground, was bloody and protracted. According to Appian, the legionaries fought with determination in a grim silence punctuated only by the clash of weapons and human groans. Each side suffered heavy losses. A javelin struck Pansa in the side and mortally wounded him. Antony eventually emerged the victor. However, as his forces returned to camp weary and sweat-soaked but singing songs of victory, they were ambushed in turn by fresh waves of troops sent by Hirtius. Only with difficulty did Antony manage to extract his men and withdraw to safety as night fell. He left behind on the battlefield two legionary eagles and sixty standards, as well as many of his veteran men. During the night Antony sent search parties to rescue as many as he could. Appian described how the rescuers "set the survivors on their own horses, swapping places with some, and lifting others up beside them or encouraging them to cling to the horses' tails and run along with them."

On the brink of capturing Mutina, whose inhabitants were starving, Antony was not inclined to give in and raise the siege, but six days later, on April 21, Hirtius and Octavian infiltrated his camp while Decimus Brutus led a sally out of the besieged town. In the ensuing confused struggle, Octavian, who had reputedly hidden away during the previous battle, is said to have carried one of the legionary eagles after its bearer fell, and Hirtius was killed in the fighting around Antony's tent. Antony's men eventually recaptured their camp and forced Decimus Brutus' men back into Mutina. But recognizing he could not take the town while being constantly harassed from the rear, Antony decided to withdraw over the chill passes of the Apennines. His hope was to join forces with Lepidus, who the previous year had taken up his post as governor of the provinces of Narbonese Gaul (Provence) and Nearer Spain and was currently in southern Gaul with seven legions—provided, of course, that Lepidus was still loyal to him.

According to Plutarch, "Antony's nature was to excel in difficult circumstances" and in the retreat he showed his finest qualities. "Antony was an incredible example to his men: for all his extravagant and indulgent lifestyle, he did not hesitate to drink stagnant water and eat wild fruits and roots . . . tree-bark was eaten." As the cold and hungry men crossed the mountains, they and their leader "ate animals which had never before been tasted by man."*

---

*Shakespeare changed "stagnant water" to "stale of horses" when he cribbed this account from Plutarch, showing his masterly touch at heightening dramatic imagery.

When news of the second battle at Mutina reached Rome on April 26, the Senate finally felt sufficiently secure in its ascendancy to declare Antony and his supporters public enemies and to order Decimus Brutus, to whom they awarded a Triumph, to hunt them down. Cicero was now at his most politically influential since the time of the Catiline conspiracy. At his behest, the Senate also confirmed Cassius and Brutus in the provinces of Syria and Macedonia that they had seized and gave them authority over all the other governors in the east. However, amid the general rejoicing and self-congratulation, the Senate failed to award any significant honors to Octavian. Though Cicero had argued for the relatively minor distinction of an *ovatio* for him, he probably thought it timely to bring Caesar's young heir, whom just a few weeks earlier he had been extolling as "this heaven-sent boy," to heel. A pun, a witticism of a perhaps overconfident Cicero, caused much mirth among his friends: "*laudandum, ornandum, tollendum*"—"Octavian must be praised, honored and extolled"—but the last word also means "removed."

This joke, which was swiftly reported to Octavian, would prove unwise. The situation was polarizing, and Octavian was about to reassess his options and, after a careful calculation of the risks, make his choices. On one side were Cassius and Brutus, the murderers of Octavian's adoptive father, who as every day passed were being given luster and legitimacy by an increasingly conservative, anti-Caesarean Senate urged on by Cicero. Between them they had seventeen legions. On the other side were the basically pro-Caesarean forces of Antony, with whom, personal rivalry apart, Octavian had far more political affinity and whose military skill he would need to defeat the considerable forces of Cassius and Brutus. Octavian, with the glory of Caesar's name behind him, and Antony, with his military strength and experience, should, he reasoned, be a powerful combination.

Octavian therefore judged that his own status had been sufficiently raised and that of Antony sufficiently diminished by the previous round of fighting to make any future alliance between them one of equals, and refused either to pursue Antony himself or give aid to others sent to annihilate him. He also profited from the deaths of the two consuls, Hirtius and Pansa, to enhance his position. Discarding Cicero as Cicero had assumed he could discard him, Octavian arranged in July 43 for four hundred of his centurions to march to the Senate to demand the consulship for him. When the Senate prevaricated, a company commander named Cornelius threw back his cloak, put his hand on his sword hilt and brazenly cried, "If you do not make him consul, this will." Opposition ceased. On August 19, still only nineteen, Octavian entered Rome as the youngest consul ever, his disregard for the Senate now as clear as that of his adoptive father. According to some, at his first taking of the auspices, twelve vultures circled in the hot skies above—the same number that had appeared to Rome's founder, Romulus.

Octavian used his new powers to have himself formally recognized as Caesar's heir and to demand vengeance on his murderers. Soon after, he set off north again with his legions to find Antony. In his absence, his docile cousin Pedius, selected to be his co-consul, persuaded the cowed Senate to rescind its condemnation of Antony as an enemy of the state. The stage was artfully set for the grand reconciliation of the two Caesarean leaders.

Meanwhile, in Gaul, Antony had located Lepidus, whom Cicero and the Senate had been attempting to win over with ever more spectacular inducements. Instead, or so accounts relate, having found Lepidus' camp, Antony just wandered in, a wild-haired, bearded and smiling figure, to be saluted by Lepidus' men, who recognized him immediately. Moments later, amid the cheers of the legionaries, he and Lepidus embraced. Lepidus wrote nonchalantly to the Senate that his soldiers had forced his hand. Decimus Brutus' position was now hopeless. His armies swiftly deserted him and Antony's men hunted him down and killed him.

Lepidus now brokered a meeting between Antony and Octavian, which took place around the end of October on an island in the Lavino River near Bononia (Bologna). It was staged with the care of a gathering of Mafia chiefs. Antony and Octavian approached from opposite sides of the river, each with five legions. Having scoured the island to ensure there were no lurking assassins, Lepidus, the go-between, waved his cloak to signify that all was well. Each man then crossed to the island with a bodyguard of three hundred. Before sitting down in full view of their men to begin negotiations, each gave the others body searches to check for concealed weapons. Two days later, the three told their jubilant troops that they had reached agreement. They would be *viri rei publicae constituendae* (three men responsible for restoring the government of the republic), with consular powers for five years. Historians would call this the Second Triumvirate. It was, to all intents and purposes, another dictatorship.

With the eastern half of the empire largely in the hands of their adversaries, the three triumvirs carved up Rome's western empire between them "as if,"

Plutarch wrote, "it were an ancestral estate." Antony was to have Cisalpine and Transalpine Gaul, Octavian received Africa, Sicily, Sardinia and Corsica, and Lepidus—who was to remain as consul in Rome while Antony and Octavian made war on Cassius and Brutus—was to retain Narbonese Gaul and to acquire, in addition to his existing province of Nearer Spain, the remainder of Spain. To reward their veteran soldiers, on whom their future success depended, the triumvirs agreed to appropriate private land from some of Italy's richest towns and redistribute it once final victory was theirs.

The troops greeted the news with roars of support. They also cheered the news that, to confirm their new bonds, Octavian had given up the woman he had been engaged to wed and would instead marry Clodia, Antony's stepdaughter, the scarcely pubescent child of Clodius and Fulvia. What they were not yet told was that, like Sulla thirty-nine years earlier, the triumvirs had drawn up lists of opponents to be punished—"proscribed"—for their role in Caesar's murder. Anyone so proscribed would have no option but to flee Italy or face death, and all his property would be forfeit to the state. Prominent on the list, at Antony's insistence, was Cicero. Although revenge on their enemies would be sweet, a major purpose was to raise money for the forthcoming war in the east to smash Brutus and Cassius and establish their own preeminence beyond dispute. In consequence, as Appian noted, many unfortunates were outlawed solely "on account of their wealth."

The triumvirs dispatched a band of executioners in advance to deal with seventeen key men on the list, including Cicero, and followed with their legions to Rome, which they entered separately on three successive days. A nervous Senate had no choice but to endorse the dictatorial powers the three men had already grabbed for themselves and in so doing sanctioned its own demise as a meaningful political entity. Panic spread through the city as the lists of the proscribed—perhaps as many as three hundred senators and three thousand of Rome's wealthiest and most prominent citizens—were made public. Large rewards awaited those prepared to "become hunting dogs for the murderers for the sake of the rewards," as Appian put it. The head of any of the proscribed brought a reward of twenty-five thousand denarii if brought in by a free man and ten thousand denarii if brought by a slave.

Appian described the desperate plight of the fugitives: "Some descended into wells, others into filthy sewers. Some took refuge in chimneys. Others crouched in the deepest silence under the thick-set tiles of their roofs. Some were not less fearful of their wives and ill-disposed children than of the murderers." Some unfaithful but influential wives took advantage of the witch hunt to have their husbands' names added to the list to be rid of them. Other women, however, offered Antony sex in return for their husbands' lives.

Fulvia used the situation to settle some scores. Appian wrote of a man named Rufus who "possessed a handsome house near that of Fulvia, the wife of Antony, which she had wanted to buy, but he would not sell it, and although he now offered it to her as a free gift, he was proscribed. His head was brought to Antony, who said it did not concern him and sent it to his wife." According to Appian, the murders even extended to orphan children "on account of their wealth. One of these, who was going to school, was killed, together with the attendant, who threw his arms around the boy and would not give him up."

There were many such scenes of great courage. Appian praised the fidelity "of wives, of children, of brothers, of slaves who rescued the proscribed or . . . died with them when they did not succeed in their designs. Some even killed themselves on the bodies of the slain." He described how one man "was concealed by his wife, who communicated the secret to only one female slave. Having been betrayed by the latter, she followed her husband's head as it was carried away, crying out, 'I sheltered him; those who give shelter are to share the punishment.' As nobody killed her or informed on her, she came to the triumvirs and accused herself before them. Being moved by her love for her husband, they pretended not to see her. So she starved herself to death." Antony's elderly republican uncle Lucius Caesar, whom Antony had agreed to place on the list to please Octavian since he had supported Caesar's murderers and as a quid pro quo for Cicero, was saved by Antony's own mother, Julia, who interposed herself between the old man and the soldiers who came to murder him.

Cicero did not escape. As with Louis XVI trying to flee the mobs of revolutionary France, his indecision proved fatal. He had fled to sea from Astura in a small boat in the hope of escaping down the coast but, retching with seasickness, had ordered the boatman to make once more for land. Disembarking, Cicero had tottered on foot northward again toward Rome but, reaching the Appian Way, halted. Fearing he would be recognized and arrested on this thronging highway, he turned back toward Astura, where he spent a dreadful night tormented by "terrible thoughts and desperate plans." His attendants persuaded the hesitant, nervous orator to take to sea again and sail south to his villa at Caieta near Formiae.

Here Cicero stayed, hoping the madness would pass him by, but a search party flushed him out. He tried to escape by litter but pursuing soldiers caught up with him in a wood. Cicero had once written, "What gladiator of ordinary merit has ever uttered a groan or changed countenance? Who of them has disgraced himself, I will not say on his feet, but who has disgraced himself in his fall? Who after falling has drawn in his neck when ordered to suffer the fatal stroke?" Now, accepting his own fall, the haggard, unshaven old man unflinchingly stretched his own wrinkled neck to the soldiers' blades and paid the price of his outspoken Philippics against Antony. His head and hands were nailed to the rostra, the speaker's platform before the Senate house where he had delivered so many speeches. Fulvia, wife to Clodius as well as to Antony and with a double dose of vengeance to extract, apparently spat in his blood-smeared face and, yanking out his once voluble tongue, impaled it with a hairpin.

Fulvia was less than sympathetic to the plight of some fourteen hundred wealthy Roman women whose relatives had been proscribed and who were themselves being taxed to fill the triumvirs' coffers. Led by Hortensia, daughter of the famous orator Hortensius, they forced their way into the Forum: "You have already deprived us of our fathers, our sons, our husbands, and our brothers . . . but if in addition you take away our property you will reduce us to a condition unsuitable to our birth, our way of life, and our female nature," Hortensia argued. "Why do we share in the punishments when we did not participate in the crimes?" With the crowd shouting their support, the triumvirs gave ground, reducing the number of women subject to the tax to four hundred. Using the money they had sequestered, they now concentrated their efforts on planning to take the fight to Brutus and Cassius in their eastern exile.

Despite the rapprochement between Antony and Octavian, to the queen of Egypt, anxiously monitoring events from a distance, it must have seemed far from clear who would triumph in the forthcoming showdown. The architects of Caesar's assassination had prospered. Brutus had been consolidating his position in Asia, while in Syria Cassius had defeated Dolabella, sent as governor to wrest back control of the province. Both Cassius and Dolabella had appealed to Cleopatra, who had had to decide the safest course for herself and Caesarion.

Cleopatra's natural affinity was of course with those seeking to avenge Caesar's death and, after careful thought, she had encouraged the legions left by Caesar in Alexandria to go to Dolabella's aid. However, at some point they had defected to Cassius. Hopelessly outnumbered, in July 43, the month when Octavian's soldiers had demanded the consulship for him, Dolabella took refuge in the seaport of Laodicea and, when Cassius bribed the town's commanders to throw open the gates, ordered his slave to decapitate him.

The aid she had sent Dolabella had left Cleopatra exposed to reprisals by Cassius, and her position was weakening. Her governor in Cyprus had also gone over to Cassius, sending him ships to bolster his fleet, while in Ephesus Cleopatra's younger half sister and rival, Arsinoe, was planning a comeback. In the Temple of Artemis, the high priest was already hailing her as Egypt's new queen.

There seemed every danger that, eager for Egypt's wealth, Cassius would move into Egypt, plunder its treasuries himself and depose Cleopatra in favor of the more compliant Arsinoe. If that happened, who knew what the fate of Caesarion would be? Cassius had killed the father. Why should he spare the son? At one of the most perilous moments of Cleopatra's short reign, she was fortunate that Brutus asked Cassius to hurry to Smyrna for a council of war. By the end of 43 Cassius had arrived in Asia Minor.

The reason for this urgent consultation was the news that Antony and Octavian, having buried their differences, were moving against them. To build up their own forces, Cassius increased his already heavy demands on the eastern kingdoms for money and men but, mindful of who was by far the richest ruler in the east, renewed his demands on Cleopatra in particular. Once again she must have agonized. Cassius and Brutus were closer geographically than Antony and Octavian. Defying them was risky. But yet again Cleopatra decided to link her fate to Antony and Octavian. An important factor was the triumvirs' decision to sanction Caesarion's right to sit beside her on the throne of Egypt as a reward for her previous help to Dolabella. The passing of such a decree, as they astutely deduced, was exactly the way to appeal to Cleopatra, both as mother and as dynast.

Cleopatra informed Cassius, with perfect truth, that the Nile had failed to rise to its usual bountiful level and that the harvest that year had been poor. Desperate for food, some Egyptians were binding themselves to others as servants for many years—a device to bypass the law forbidding free people to sell themselves into slavery. One woman engaged herself as a servant for ninety-nine years. There had also been an outbreak of plague. In the Museon in

Alexandria, one of Cleopatra's personal physicians, Dioscurides Phacas, tracked the spread of the disease. In the world's first medical treatise, he documented the plague's terrible course, from the swollen lymphatic glands to the black, evil-smelling, suppurating boils of the victims. With her own people suffering so badly, Cleopatra argued that she could spare no men or food for Cassius. He, however, was skeptical of such excuses. When he learned that Antony and Octavian were massing their troops at Brundisium ready for ferrying across the Adriatic to Macedonia, he dispatched one of his admirals to the southern point of the Peloponnese with a fleet of sixty ships, a legion of men and orders to intercept any ships that Cleopatra might try to send to the aid of Antony and Octavian.

Indeed, not only had Cleopatra, despite her apparent economic distress, managed to build and equip a fleet in the shadow of the Pharos in Alexandria but, in one of the bold, theatrical gestures at which she was so gifted, she was planning to do what no queen of the East had done since the fifth century, when Queen Artemesia of Halicarnassus led a squadron of ships to assist her Persian ally Xerxes against the Greeks at Salamis: to be the admiral of her own navy. She would lead it to support the triumvirs.* Only the weather defeated Cleopatra. Storms beat back her ships long before they met any challenge from Cassius. Many were wrecked, some of their broken hulls drifting northward to be washed up on the beaches of Greece. Cleopatra herself, laid low with seasickness aboard her flagship, managed to regain Alexandria. She at once began preparing a second fleet but events were moving so swiftly that by the time it was ready the battle between Caesar's avengers and Caesar's murderers was over.

Even without Egyptian aid, the Caesarean forces had dodged the enemy squadrons sent against them by Cassius and Brutus and landed safely in Macedonia. Here Octavian fell ill, apparently with dropsy—a disease in which watery fluid collects in body tissue. While he remained behind to recover, Antony marched their twenty-eight legions over the mountains to take up position near the town of Philippi and await the arrival of the enemy forces.

*According to Herodotus, Artemesia unsuccessfully urged Xerxes not to fight at Salamis. She herself fought bravely in the battle until his defeat and then escaped by sinking a ship in her way, causing Xerxes to remark, "My men have become women and my women men."

ndstone relief, south wall, Temple of Hathor, Dendera. Cleopatra offers incense behind Caesarion, who depicted as a pharaoh.

Above: Julius Caesar, a bust possibly commissioned by Cleopatra for the Caesareum in Alexandria.

Above: Octavian, later the Empero
Augustus

Right: Octavia, wife of Antony and sister of Octavian.

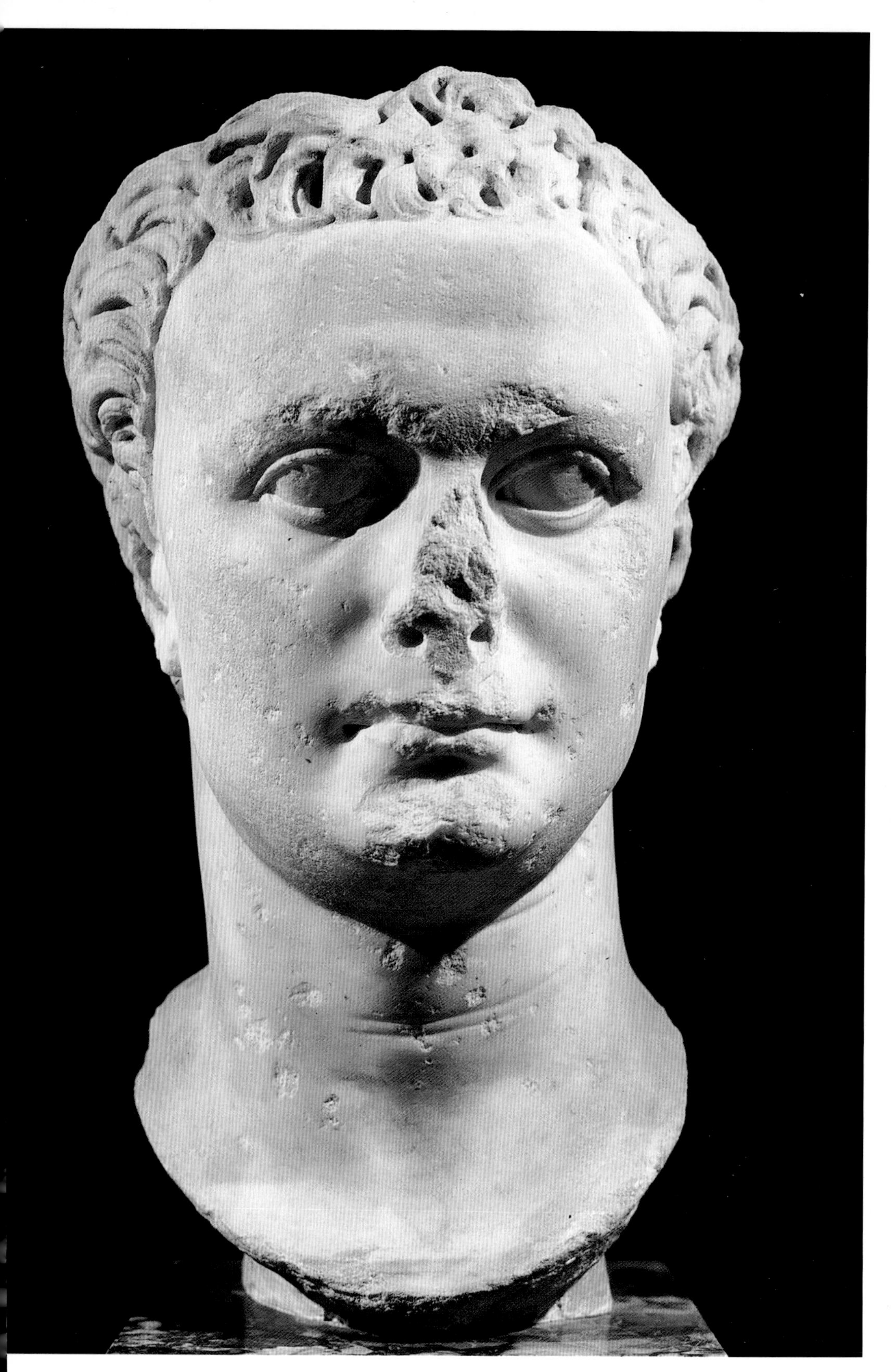

Mark Antony (Marcus Antonius).

The so-called Pompey's Pillar on the site of the Serapeum in Alexandria.

Left: Stone falcon protecting a young prince said to be Caesarion, Temple of Horus, Edfu.

Above: Reconstructed panorama of Alexandria showing the harbors and the Pharos lighthouse.

Below: Armlet depicting the goddess Nut.

Model of Cleopatra based on contemporary images, created for this book by Dr. Martin Weaver. It shows how Cleopatra may really have looked as compared with later, more iconic images that contributed to the Cleopatra myth.

Roman oil lamp with obscene depiction of Cleopatra sitting on a phallus, from the first century AD.

Cleopatra holding her pearl earring, by Giambattista Tiepolo, 1740s.

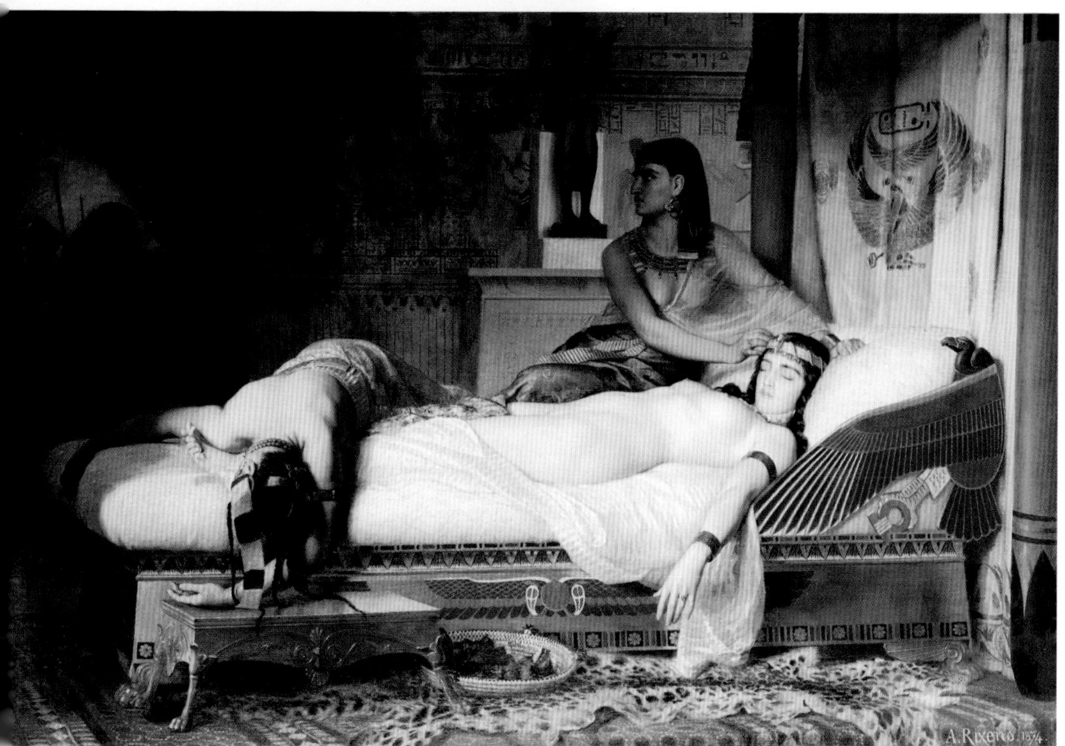

eath of Cleopatra, Jean-André Rixens, 1874.

Theda Bara as Cleopatra, 1917.

The most famous screen Cleopatra and Antony—Elizabeth Taylor and Richard Burton, 1963.

Antony had with him some of the most tried and trusted legions, many of whom had previously served Julius Caesar and who had long been eager to avenge his death.

Caesar's uncle Marius had reformed the legions more than fifty years earlier, making the army into a professional one subject to rigorous discipline and drill, rather than a citizen militia. He had stopped the practice of disbanding legions at the end of each campaign and given them numbers and emblems, in particular the legions' eagle. Made of silver and gold and mounted on a long pole, it was carried by a standard-bearer who had a special lion-skin headdress, and it served as a rallying point to be defended to the death. Its capture was a lasting disgrace. At full strength, which was rare, each legion consisted of some six thousand men split into ten cohorts of six hundred men each. Each cohort had its own symbol—for example, a golden hand—and contained six centuries of one hundred men, each led by that backbone of the Roman army, the centurion—a career soldier distinguished from the ordinary legionary by the transverse crest on his helmet.

Another of Marius' changes had been to make the legions more mobile and less vulnerable by reducing the baggage train. He made the legionary carry more of his own food and equipment, including sixteen days' rations, a cooking pot and two stakes as a contribution to the palisade thrown round the camp for protection. All this gear, the legionaries joked, turned them into "Marius' mules." Burdened with such a heavy pack, weighing some sixty pounds, the legionary was subject to frequent training runs with full kit, like modern soldiers.

A legionary's weapons were the sword and the spear. The sword had a double cutting edge and a stabbing point. The spears—six-foot-long javelins—were designed so that the soft iron of their neck would bend on impact, thus preventing the spear from being thrown back if it missed its target and hit the ground, and also making it more difficult to pull from a wound if it did not. Unlike most armies of the time and for a long time afterward (until the seventeenth century, in fact), the Roman legionary had a standard uniform—a leather jerkin over which he wore chain-mail armor. (The latter was soon to be displaced by a leather or metal breastplate.) His bronze helmet had protective cheek pieces and was pear-shaped, rising to a lead-weighted topknot surmounted by the crest. His shield was oval and slightly cylindrical, to curve around and protect his body. It was made of leather-covered wood with a metal boss. The legionary went bare-legged but on his feet wore sturdy leather sandals, lacing up above and around his ankles and with their soles studded with iron nails.

Brutus and Cassius did not rush to battle, preferring to leave the Caesarean forces to run short of supplies and patience. Instead, after attempting to ensure the loyalty of their legions, of which they were much less certain than Antony was of his, by payments to each man of fifteen hundred denarii, they carefully drew up their troops in a strong position on high ground west of Philippi—Brutus' troops on the right flank were protected by mountains and Cassius', on the left, abutted marshland. Antony decided to confront his enemies head-on and boldly encamped his own troops in the plain beneath the high ground where his opponents sat. To remedy his inferior position, he had his men rapidly throw up a series of towers and fortifications. During this period, determined to share in what he hoped would be a glorious victory, Octavian joined Antony as soon as he felt strong enough, but he would remain physically below par throughout the campaign.

Still confident in their ability to wear down their opponents by cutting off their supplies, Brutus and Cassius made no move. Frustrated by his failure to draw them into battle, in October 43 Antony formulated a plan secretly to build a causeway through the marshes to outflank them. Drawing his main army into battle formation to deflect his enemies' attention by suggesting that a frontal attack was imminent, Antony ordered others of his men to work under the cover of the high reeds to construct the causeway. To do so they piled up embankments of earth and stone and used timber to bridge the deepest parts of the squelching marsh. After ten days of this work, Antony succeeded in getting a body of his men across the causeway and led them in an attack on the perimeter of Cassius' fortification. The weight of their charge swiftly put Cassius' men to flight and they fell back on their camp proper. However, Antony's legionaries smashed through the gates, despite showers of missiles from the defenders above. Soon the camp was Antony's, and Cassius fled up the hill toward Brutus' position. Because of the confusion of battle and the all-pervasive clouds of dust obscuring the plain, Cassius, who in any case had poor sight, thought that he saw signs that Brutus too had been defeated. Without waiting for confirmation, a despairing Cassius killed himself, according to Plutarch with the very dagger he had used against Caesar. However, far from dead, Brutus had, in fact, taken advantage of the engagement to capture Octavian's camp. Caesar's heir was not there. According to some, he had taken refuge deep in the marshes.

The result of the battle had been inconclusive and Brutus' army still had the better position and better supplies. Indeed, the same day as the battle at Philippi, the Liberators' navy had destroyed a convoy bringing two more legions as well as provisions to Antony and Octavian. However, Cassius' death had unsettled the republican forces. There were desertions among some of the contingents of their eastern allies. Growing impatient, just like Pompey's men before Pharsalus, the majority clamored for action and revenge. Antony did his best to provoke his opponents further by regularly leading out his troops in battle array and having them yell alternately at Brutus' men accusations of cowardice and offers of bribes if they would desert.

A cultured and relatively gentle man with limited military experience, Brutus could no longer restrain his forces, and just three weeks after the first encounter, the second and decisive battle of Philippi was joined at three o'clock in the afternoon. After a bloody hand-to-hand struggle of Roman against Roman, the Caesarean troops finally overcame their ideological foes. Brutus retreated to the mountains. There, after realizing that he had no more than four legions left to call upon, Shakespeare's "noblest Roman of them all" chose suicide. Plutarch described how, after shaking hands with his remaining officers, "he placed the tip of his drawn sword on his chest, and with the help of a friend's strong arm, they say, plunged the sword in."

Antony ordered the body to be covered with a purple cloak and cremated but, according to Suetonius, Octavian later ordered Brutus' head to be hacked off and sent to Rome to be hurled at the feet of Caesar's statue. Suetonius also related how when a father and son begged for their lives, Octavian coldly invited them to draw lots. Instead, the father chose to give his life for his son, who was so distressed that he at once committed suicide. Octavian watched both men die and his callous conduct so disgusted other prisoners that as they were led off in chains "they courteously saluted Antony as their conqueror, but abused Octavian with the most obscene epithets." Among the defeated dead was Cato's son, who, with the stubborn courage of his father, had refused to retreat and was killed where he stood. According to Plutarch, his wife, Porcia, who was also Brutus' sister, determined on suicide when news of their deaths reached Rome. Evading the friends who were keeping watch on her, she seized a glowing coal from a brazier and swallowed it.

Philippi was Antony's victory. Again he had proved his military skill and leadership while Octavian, still in frail health, had played only a minor role, as Antony very well knew. In later years the tall, muscular Antony would deride Octavian as "a puny creature in body" who "has never by his own efforts won a victory in any important battle by land or sea. Indeed at Philippi, in the very same battle in which he and I fought as allies, it was I who conquered and he who was defeated." Nevertheless, recognizing that they still needed each other, the two men redistributed Rome's provinces between them. Lepidus, far away in Rome and much less powerful than either, was the loser. Antony and Octavian suspected him of plotting with Sextus Pompey, the surviving son of Pompey the Great, who was waging a successful maritime war from his base on Sicily and disrupting Rome's grain supply, while being demonized as a pirate for his actions.

Accordingly, consulting no one, least of all the Senate, they imperiously divided Lepidus' provinces between them and allotted him Africa. Octavian took Spain, while Antony, as the dominant partner, was to have the whole of Gaul beyond the Alps, though he agreed that, as Caesar had intended, Cisalpine Gaul should be absorbed into Roman Italy, which would be held in common. Antony also took command of the provinces east of the Adriatic—Macedonia, Greece, Asia, Cyrenaica, Syria and Bithynia. This also made him guardian of Rome's client kingdoms to the east, of which by far the most important in practice was Cleopatra's Egypt, even if it nominally still enjoyed full independence. Above all, Antony hoped to use his new position to carry out Caesar's plan of conquering the Parthians.

In late 42 Antony departed on the road that would lead him to Cleopatra. He spent the winter months in Athens, touring the sights and enjoying the honors lavished respectfully upon him. He tactfully ignored the fact that two winters earlier, statues of Brutus and Cassius had been everywhere on display. With the arrival of spring, Antony sailed east. In Ephesus, women dressed as bacchantes, and men and boys clad as satyrs and Pans hailed him as the new Dionysus, the bringer of joy, and conducted him riotously through the streets.* Plutarch wrote, "The city was filled with ivy, thyrsi, harps, reed-pipes and wind-pipes." Antony doubtless loved it. Octavian could call himself the

*The Greek god Dionysus was known to the Romans as Bacchus.

son of a god, but better by far to be an actual god, especially one associated with glorious triumphs in the east, lauded and adored. Antony made several magnanimous gestures to the city that had given him such a wild reception, including extending the rights of the Temple of Artemis to grant asylum. Whether he encountered Arsinoe, still in sanctuary there and no doubt regretting her collusion with the governor of Cyprus against Antony and Octavian, is not recorded.*

Antony was happy to reward Ephesus and other cities that had suffered at Cassius' hands, but he badly needed money to pay off the veterans and for his forthcoming campaign against Parthia. He therefore summoned the local rulers of the region to a meeting in Ephesus. It was an order few dared disobey. According to Plutarch, "Kings beat a path to his door, while their wives, rivals in generosity and beauty, let themselves be seduced by him."

Antony enjoyed the flattery, but not sufficiently to be entirely forgiving. While graciously accepting the rulers' explanations that they had supported his enemies only under duress, he smilingly told them that he and Octavian had 170,000 soldiers to pay off. To help meet the debt, he demanded the same sum they had paid Cassius: ten years' taxes in a year. When the shocked rulers, already bled dry by the republicans, stuttered that they could never find the money, Antony relented only a little, remitting one year's taxation and extending the payment period to two years.

Leaving Ephesus, Antony visited several important client kingdoms of Rome in Asia Minor. He was aware that if his Parthian campaign was to succeed, he needed stability at his rear in Rome's satellite states along the eastern borders. He therefore paid particular attention to a dynastic dispute in Cappadocia, a kingdom important because its ruler also controlled parts of Armenia and hence the frontier with the Euphrates. According to some, however, of even greater interest to Antony were the charms of Glaphyra, a beautiful Cappadocian princess with whom he probably had an affair.

Antony was every bit as susceptible to women as Caesar had been, perhaps more so. Plutarch thought:

---

*To further enhance his divine status, Octavian apparently claimed that his mother, Atia, had been ravished by Apollo in the form of a snake nine months before giving birth to him and had been left with a permanent mark on her stomach from the snake's fangs.

> His weakness for the opposite sex showed an attractive side of his character, and even won him the sympathy of many people, for he often helped others in their love affairs and always accepted with good humor the jokes they made about his own . . . Well versed in the art of putting the best possible face on disreputable actions, he never feared the audit of his copulations, but let nature have her way, and left behind him the foundations of many families.

He was about to encounter another royal ruler ready to let nature have her way in pursuit of her goals and who would dominate the rest of his life.

PART V

Taming Heracles

CHAPTER 13

Mighty Aphrodite

IN THE EARLY SUMMER OF 41, Antony arrived in Tarsus, future birthplace of St. Paul, on the river Cydnus in what today is southern Turkey. Pompey had made it the prosperous capital of the new Roman province of Cilicia but Antony found a city impoverished by Cassius' tax demands. Appian described how "being pressed for payment with violence by Cassius' soldiers, the people first sold all their public property and next they coined all the sacred articles used in religious processions and the temple offerings into money. When this was still not sufficient, the magistrates sold free persons into slavery, first girls and boys, afterward women and miserable old men, who brought a very small price, and finally young men."

Antony ordered any remaining citizens still enslaved to be freed, then turned his attention to one important ruler who had yet to account for her conduct during the recent civil war. Antony dispatched the clever, smooth-tongued Quintus Dellius to Alexandria to summon Egypt's queen and Caesar's former mistress to appear before him in Tarsus.

Cleopatra must have been relieved by the defeat of Brutus and Cassius at Philippi. She also must have been pleased that Antony, whom she knew, rather than Caesar's heir Octavian—an unknown quantity and potential threat to Caesarion—had emerged as the Roman Empire's new leader in the east. Although there was a threat implicit in Antony's summons, Dellius soothed any fears she might have had. Plutarch related that "as soon as Dellius, Antony's messenger, saw what she looked like and observed her eloquence and subtle intelligence, he realized that the idea of harming such a woman would never occur to Antony . . . and he allayed her worries about Antony, describing him as the most agreeable and kind leader in the world."

Even without Dellius' reassurances, Cleopatra was probably not unduly worried. She could readily defend her actions and point to the help she had tried to provide to Antony and Octavian. She was probably already looking beyond self-justification, assessing how to turn her meeting with Antony to her long-term advantage. Dellius, it seems, was her willing accomplice. Guessing that "she would come to occupy a very important place in his [Antony's] life," Dellius "set about ingratiating himself with the Egyptian and encouraging her to come to Cilicia dressed up in all her finery . . . Since she believed Dellius . . . she readily expected to bring Antony to her feet."

Eight years earlier, when she had been less experienced, Cleopatra had conquered Caesar. Now she was twenty-nine years old. She would be going to Antony, in Plutarch's words, "at the age when the beauty of a woman is at its most dazzling and her intellectual powers are at their peak. So she equipped herself with plenty of gifts and money, and the kind of splendid paraphernalia one would expect someone in her exalted position from a prosperous kingdom, to take. Above all, however, she went there relying on herself and on the magical arts and charms of her person."

Plutarch was critical of Cleopatra, depicting her as a cold-blooded siren who as well as seducing Caesar had bedded Gnaeus, son of Pompey the Great, an accusation for which there is no supporting evidence. Yet his conclusion that Cleopatra intended to dazzle and "vanquish" Antony was probably entirely correct. With her gift for spotting a good opportunity, she planned her campaign with as much care and calculation as her former lover Caesar had planned his military ventures, assessing her target's vulnerabilities, one of which, she knew, was a predilection for beautiful, flamboyant women.

Cleopatra had also noted Antony's enthusiastic reception in the East as the "new Dionysus." This title had once been accorded her own father, Auletes, and was deeply intertwined with the Ptolemies since Dionysus was their legendary ancestor and an especial patron of the royal house of Egypt. One Ptolemaic king even had the god's ivy leaves tattooed on his body. Cleopatra's ancestor Ptolemy II had introduced a lavish festival, the Ptolemaia, held every four years. Accounts of one festival describe a riotous procession that took two days to pass through the broad streets of Alexandria. The high point was a fifteen-foot vine-and-ivy-decked statue of Dionysus in a robe of purple and gold drawn by 180 sweating, heaving men. Behind him, on another cart, sixty men dressed as satyrs trampled grapes in a vast wine press in time to the piping of flutes while a further cart bore a straining, overflowing wineskin stitched from leopard skins and holding twenty-six thousand gallons, ready to be dispensed to the clamorous spectators. All three were followed by a 150-foot long golden penis embellished with a three-foot-wide starburst at its tip to emphasize the priapic aspect of the god.

Dionysus, who was closely identified with Osiris, was not simply the god of wine and joyous physical abandon whose diaphanously clad followers indulged in wild sexual rites but a deity of deep mystical significance. He was worshipped as brave and benevolent and his manifold virtues were closely associated with Alexander the Great, whose triumphs in the east were often depicted as an inspired Dionysian progress and whose golden image was also carried in the procession.

As well as playing at being Dionysus, Antony also deliberately evoked his own supposed divine ancestor, the hero-god Heracles, who was believed to feast at Dionysus' table. The image of the muscular, lion-skin-clad strongman overcoming obstacle after obstacle chimed with Antony's growing vision of himself. Plutarch painted a convincing picture of a man who modeled himself on a heroic deity:

> There was a noble dignity about Antony's appearance. His beard was well-grown, his forehead broad, his nose aquiline, and these features combined to give him a bold and masculine look, which is found in the statues and portraits of Heracles. In fact there was an ancient tradition that the blood of the Heracleidae ran in Antony's family, and Antony liked to believe that his own physique lent force to the legend. He also deliberately cultivated it in his choice of dress, for whenever he was going to appear before a large crowd of people, he wore his tunic belted low over his hips, a large sword at his side, and a heavy cloak.*

If Antony wished to play the god, Cleopatra was more than equipped to outdo him in the divinity stakes. Not only was she regarded by her people as a

---

*Though Heracles' mother was mortal, his father was Zeus and he came to be worshipped as a demigod.

living goddess, the personification of Isis, but the Ptolemies claimed Heracles as well as Dionysus as an ancestor. The mother of Ptolemy I was supposedly a direct descendant of Heracles.

To arouse Antony's interest and heighten his expectations, Cleopatra did not rush to obey his summons but took her time. Plutarch related that "although she received many letters from both Antony and his friends demanding her presence," she treated them with scorn. In addition to being determined to show Antony she was an independent ruler and her own mistress, there was another motive for Cleopatra's delay: she genuinely needed time to prepare. In an age when the great majority of the population in Alexandria or Rome was illiterate, spectacle was the medium for communicating with the masses. Just as Caesar's magnificent Triumphs celebrating Rome's mastery of the world had wrung roars of approval from near-hysterical crowds, so Cleopatra intended to create a pageant of royal wealth and divine beauty that would not be easily forgotten. Thus she chose her own moment to depart with her royal barge and its accompanying escort of ships across the Mediterranean for Tarsus.

Plutarch lusciously described how Cleopatra made the final twelve miles of her journey up the river Cydnus to Tarsus:

> She came sailing in a barge with a poop of gold, its purple sails billowing in the wind, while her rowers caressed the water with oars of silver which dipped in time to the music of the flute, accompanied by pipes and lutes. Cleopatra herself reclined beneath a canopy spangled with gold, dressed in the character of Aphrodite as we see her in paintings, while on either side to complete the picture stood boys costumed as Cupids who cooled her with their fans. Instead of a crew the barge was lined with the most beautiful of her waiting-women attired as Nereids and Graces, some at the rudders, others at the tackle of the sails, and all the while an indescribably rich scent, exhaled from countless incense burners, was wafted from the vessel to the river-banks. Great crowds accompanied this royal progress, some of them following the queen on both sides of the river from its very mouth . . . And the word spread on every side that Aphrodite had come to revel with Dionysus, for the happiness of Asia.

The imagery suited Cleopatra perfectly. Aphrodite, born from the shimmering waves of the sea, was not only a counterpart to the divine Isis, whose living reincarnation she claimed to be, but, like her Roman equivalent Venus, the goddess of sexual pleasure and patroness of the sexually passionate wife. Furthermore, Tarsus had been known for four centuries as the place where the goddess of love had encountered and made love with Dionysus, divine ruler of the east. What better way to signal her intentions than to arrive as Aphrodite made flesh?

Antony, at whom this sensual assault was principally aimed, was, as no doubt intended, left feeling and looking rather foolish. He had been seated at the public tribunal in the marketplace ready to receive his royal visitor but she had not disembarked and come to him as he had anticipated his status—his *dignitas*—required. Instead, as frenzied excitement surged through the city at the arrival of the Egyptian queen, the crowds hurried off to the riverbank to see the amazing sight for themselves, leaving Antony alone with a few guards and attendants. Somewhat nonplussed, he sent Cleopatra an invitation to dine with him that night but, unwilling either to surrender the initiative or to break the spell she had cast, she bade him instead come to her aboard her royal barge. Also her barge was her own territory—in a subtle, clever way she was reversing Antony's summons to her and making Antony come to Egypt.

Feasting is an age-old metaphor for sexual pleasure as well as its frequent precursor in practice. Cleopatra had prepared a scene to arouse and tantalize. Antony was greeted by a spectacular sight. With the care of a film director, Cleopatra had arranged an "amazing multitude of lights." Plutarch wrote of "so many lights hanging on display all over the place, and ordered and disposed at such angles to one another and in such intricate arrangements—some forming squares, others circles—that the sight was one of rare delight and remarkable beauty." Purple tapestries shot through with silver and gold gleamed on the walls. Soft, silken dining couches awaited the Roman guests, the tables before them spread with golden drinking vessels and dishes crusted with precious jewels. Antony the triumvir was reduced to the uncertainty of a naïve boy, stammering his amazement at such opulence. Cleopatra apologized that in the time available she had been unable to make more suitable arrangements for his reception. Next time, she promised, she would provide better. In the meantime she nonchalantly made him a present of everything used at the feast—couches, goblets and all.

The following night, Antony dined again with Cleopatra on her barge in the heady incense-laden air that was an Egyptian specialty. Egyptian perfumes had been celebrated since the days of the pharaohs for their intensity and also their subtlety. Helen of Troy was said to have been trained in their use in

Egypt. As Cleopatra had promised, the magnificence of the previous night's banquet was eclipsed. As well as being given everything they had used during the banquet, the principal guests were presented with Arab horses with gold trappings and borne home on litters with lithe Ethiopian boys, flaming torches in their hand, running lightly ahead through the dark streets of Tarsus.

The next day, Cleopatra agreed to dine with Antony as his guest. The forty-year-old general "desperately wanted to outdo the brilliance and thoroughness of her preparations but he was outdone and defeated on both counts by her. He was the first to make fun of his meagre offerings." It must have amused her to see the great general abashed and embarrassed by what Plutarch calls a "rustic awkwardness." Cleopatra read Antony's character with ease, quickly deducing how to appeal to him. His jokes revealed to her that "there was a wide streak of the coarse soldier in him. So she adopted this same manner towards him . . . in an unrestrained and brazen fashion." The disapproving Plutarch also lamented that Cleopatra unlocked latent vice in Antony. "For a man such as Antony there could be nothing worse than the onset of his love for Cleopatra. It awoke a number of feelings that had previously been lying quietly buried within him, stirred them up into a frenzy, and obliterated and destroyed the last vestiges of goodness, the final redeeming features that were still holding out in his nature."

Appian believed that Antony succumbed to Cleopatra's charms "at first sight." "Antony was," he wrote, "amazed at her wit as well as her good looks, and became her captive as though he were a young man, although he was forty years of age. It is said that he was always very susceptible in this way." Appian also believed, with the benefit of hindsight, that "this passion brought ruin upon them and upon all Egypt besides." Whether Cleopatra and Antony's affair indeed began in Tarsus is unclear but seems very probable. Like Caesar, Antony saw himself as a great lover. He was certainly a great womanizer who enjoyed sex.

On the fourth night, Cleopatra entertained Antony in a saloon on her barge whose floors were strewn with drifts of fragrant rose petals eighteen inches deep. Some ancient writers claim that to further impress Antony with her wealth, if any more demonstrations were needed, Cleopatra wagered that she could spend an almost unimaginable sum—10 million sesterces—on a single meal. Antony, who loved a bet, accepted eagerly and waited to see what new extravagances she would conjure. The banquet duly took place but though again extremely lavish, one of Antony's companions calculated that it could not have cost anywhere near the obscene sum promised by the Egyptian queen.

A smiling Cleopatra waved a hand and a small table was set before her. Upon it was placed a single goblet. She then removed one of the two huge, glistening pearls she was wearing in her ears and held it up for all to see. Pearls were immensely valuable in the ancient world. Pliny the Elder wrote that "the topmost rank among all things of price is held by pearls." The company readily agreed that Cleopatra's translucent gem was worth more than the outstanding sum. Cleopatra at once tossed the pearl into the goblet, which, unknown to Antony, she had ordered filled with vinegar. The pearl disintegrated and she drank the contents of the goblet, swallowing the expensive draught under the astonished gaze of her lover. She then reached for her other earring to consign it to the same fate, but her guests assured her she had already won the wager and so the second pearl was saved.

This story of the dissolving pearl seems pure fiction—pearls do not instantly disintegrate in vinegar or anything else quaffable.* But the fact that the tale was so widely related and readily believed shows a reputation for wanton extravagance that must have had some substance. In fact, Cleopatra would remain associated with the power and opulence of pearls. In the sixteenth century Rabelais punningly invented a role for her in the afterlife as an onion seller in Hell—the word *onion* coming from the Latin *unio*, meaning "an enormous pearl."

Cleopatra's extravagant playacting clearly touched an answering chord in Antony. The historian Socrates of Rhodes related how not long after these encounters while in Athens Antony "prepared a very superb scaffold to spread over the theatre, covered with green wood such as is seen in the caves sacred to Bacchus; and from this scaffold he suspended drums and fawn-skins and then sat there with his friends getting drunk . . . and after that he ordered himself to be proclaimed as Bacchus throughout all the cities in that region."

---

*An American academic proved in a series of experiments in the 1950s that whole pearls do not dissolve. He suggested that just perhaps the story was based on Cleopatra's using ground pearls (effectively lime) in wine as an expensive antacid to counteract the effects of all the feasting. Others have suggested she may have swallowed the pearl whole knowing that later she or one of her attendants could retrieve it from her feces.

Yet amidst the revelry and pageantry and passion there was hard business to attend to. As she had doubtless anticipated, Cleopatra had little difficulty convincing Antony that she had resisted the threats of his enemies and done nothing to help them. She pointed out that she had sailed in person with her fleet from Alexandria, intending to aid Antony and Octavian against Brutus and Cassius, and had been prevented only by a sudden storm. She had also attempted to send legions from Egypt to help Dolabella in Syria. It was hardly her fault that they had defected to the enemy.

Antony was anyway far more interested in Cleopatra's future help than her past behavior. His desired model for governing the east, at least for the present while he dealt with Parthia, was no different from that of his Roman predecessors. Like Pompey and Caesar, he wished Rome's eastern empire to consist of a core of pacific, prosperous provinces administered directly by Rome. Their safety and security would be guaranteed by a buffer zone of surrounding client kingdoms whose rulers understood the rewards of loyalty to Rome—and the risks of disloyalty. Within this tidy, Romanized world Antony intended Cleopatra's Egypt to continue to occupy her traditional place. Under the Ptolemies the country had, of course, long been an ally of Rome. Her wealth, strategic importance and judicious wooing of Rome at the right moments had retained for Egypt a unique position with continuing independence beyond that of any ordinary client state.

Antony hardly can have believed Cleopatra would do anything to prejudice this. However, over and above Cleopatra's acquiescence in his plans for the east, Antony wanted her specific assistance. His forthcoming campaign against the Parthians would, as he well knew, be costly and difficult. He would need a secure source of supplies for his legionaries, which the wealthy Egyptian queen could supply.

From Cleopatra's perspective, to find herself so integral and important to Antony's plans was ideal and enabled her to achieve some immediate ambitions of her own. She demanded the death of her half sister Arsinoe, spared from execution five years earlier by Caesar, self-righteously pointing out that while she herself had been blameless, her sibling very likely had aided Brutus and Cassius. Her accusations were enough to have Arsinoe dragged out from her refuge in the Temple of Artemis at Ephesus by centurions sent by Antony and killed. Arsinoe's execution meant that four of Cleopatra's five siblings had met a violent end—two at her direct instigation. Cleopatra also sought the death of the high priest of Artemis on the grounds that he had recognized Arsinoe as queen of Egypt but, though Antony was quite happy to acquiesce, when a delegation arrived from Ephesus to plead for the priest's life Cleopatra decided to let him live, probably for reasons of political expediency.

She was not, however, so merciful to the former governor of Cyprus, who had supported Arsinoe and sent ships to Cassius. His death was essential to underline that she had not been complicit in his acts. Neither did she show compassion to a young man who appeared in the city of Aradus claiming to be Cleopatra's erstwhile husband-brother Ptolemy XIII, supposedly drowned in the Nile in his gleaming golden armor while fleeing Caesar. Antony obliged, ordering both men to be executed. He also confirmed Caesar's gift to her of Cyprus.

All this was highly satisfactory to Cleopatra. Even more so was Antony's agreement, before they parted, to visit her in Egypt.

CHAPTER 14

"Give It to Fulvia"

ANTONY WAS NOT LONG in following Cleopatra. He paused briefly in Syria, where he appointed one of Caesar's former generals as the province's new governor. He also settled matters in neighboring Judaea, confirming Hyrcanus, who with his minister Antipater had aided Caesar in Egypt in 47, as ruler. Antony also confirmed Antipater's sons, Phasael and Herod, as Hyrcanus' viceroys in Jerusalem and Galilee with the princely rank of tetrarch, despite the fact that after Caesar's death they had aided Cassius during the civil war, albeit, as they said, under duress. Their appointments were made in the teeth of violent opposition from the Maccabees, also known as Hasmonaeans—a powerful faction in Judaea. The name Maccabee, probably meaning "the hammer," was the appellation of Judas, who in 168 with his brothers had launched a guerrilla war against the occupying Seleucids. In 142 the Seleucid garrison had finally been expelled from Jerusalem, leaving the Jews to be ruled by the hereditary Hasmonaean high priests, the dynasty to which Hyrcanus belonged.

Although Hyrcanus supported Phasael and Herod, many Hasmonaeans distrusted them because they were from Idumaea, a district south of Jerusalem and Bethlehem whose inhabitants had been forcibly converted to Judaism toward the end of the second century during a period of Jewish expansion and who were not considered proper Jews by the orthodox. Even worse in their eyes, Phasael and Herod's mother was not Jewish but an aristocratic Arab and thus, since Judaism was a matrilineal religion, the two men were not Jewish at all.

Antony ignored the protests and in the autumn of 41 sailed eagerly on to Alexandria and into the arms of his new mistress. Cleopatra, according to Appian, gave him "a magnificent reception." Unlike Caesar, who had immediately aroused the animosity of the Alexandrians by entering their city with all the pomp of a Roman consul, with lictors bearing the fasces before him and marching columns of helmeted and armed legionaries, Antony came softly, "without the insignia of his office." He adopted "the habit and mode of life of a private person, either because he was in a foreign jurisdiction, in a city under royal sway, or because he regarded his wintering as a festal occasion." Consequently, the Alexandrians for their part welcomed Antony as an honored guest who had come at the explicit invitation of their queen. He had already shown during his tour of the east that he admired the Hellenic world and, as he walked their streets, the citizens noted with approval that he had abandoned Roman garb for "the square-cut garment of the Greeks" and white Attic sandals.

During the winter of 41 to 40, Cleopatra created a fantasy world for Antony, where his every whim was granted and every day brought new surprises. Plutarch deplored Antony's "many follies," bemoaning how Cleopatra "abducted Antony so successfully . . . that he was carried off by her to Alexandria where he indulged in the pastimes and pleasures of a young man of leisure, and spent and squandered on luxuries that commodity called the most costly in the world, namely time." Cleopatra, he alleged, always found "some fresh pleasure and delight to apply whether he was feeling serious or frivolous and so she kept up his training relentlessly without leaving him alone either by night or by day." She was constantly with him, whether he was "playing dice, drinking, and hunting; she watched him while he trained with his weapons."

According to Plutarch, Cleopatra and Antony "formed a kind of club called the Society of Inimitable Livers, and every day one of them had to entertain the rest." This magic circle of exquisite bon viveurs "spent incredible, disproportionate amounts of money." A doctor living in Alexandria at the time, who was invited to visit the royal kitchens by one of the cooks, later regaled Plutarch's grandfather with tales of prodigality almost beyond belief.

> He was surreptitiously brought into the kitchen and when he saw all the food, including eight wild boars roasting on spits, he expressed his surprise at the number of guests whom he imagined were going to be entertained. The cook just laughed and said that there were not going to be

> many for dinner, only about twelve, but that every dish which was served had to be perfect and it only took an instant's delay for something to spoil. He explained that Antony might call for food immediately a party began and then a short while later postpone it and ask for a cup of wine instead, or become distracted by a discussion. Therefore, he said, they prepared many meals, not just one, since they could never guess when the exact moment was going to be.

Roasted boars apart, the food at the feasts of the Inimitables can best be imagined from our limited knowledge of Egyptian delicacies and from descriptions of lavish Roman banquets. Pâté de foie gras was probably on the menu. The Egyptians had been the first to appreciate it, sending fattened geese to the Spartans in around 400. The Romans too had swiftly acquired the taste, with detailed recipes surviving from the first century BC for how best to "cram" a goose. Other delicacies might have been the flesh and in particular tongues of flamingos from the Nile; snails, which the Romans were the first to breed for the table; and dormice. The latter, our field mice, were bred in captivity from Greek times to the Middle Ages. The Romans kept them in the dark in large jars and fattened them on walnuts, figs and chestnuts. When the dormice were plump they were roasted, often glazed with honey and sometimes scattered with poppy seeds. Cleopatra and Antony may have tried roasted ostrich, whose range then extended to North Africa, but cooks struggled to render it tender enough, although the brains were relished, as, it seems, were those of other exotic birds, such as peacocks and parrots. Such use of only a small part of an animal or fowl was another way of demonstrating prodigality.

Along with sows' udders, elephants' trunks and camels' heels were consumed—the last said, on somewhat unreliable evidence, to have been a favorite of Cleopatra's. Other tricks were to build delicacies into fantastic centerpieces themed on concepts such as the signs of the zodiac or the shield of Minerva, or indeed to sculpt one animal by bringing together bits of others. One satirist suggested that a skillful cook could even make a dish of pork look like a fattened goose garnished with fish and different kinds of birds. There would also have been plenty of flaky pastry, copied from the Arab filo pastry, to top the pies.

The Romans were accomplished marinaders and sauciers. Octavian's favorite poet, Horace, thought a chicken drowned to death in wine had a particularly good flavor. (The hen, originally from India, was first recorded in Europe in the sixth century BC.) Antony would have relished such dishes, as well as other more conventional sauces. Among the most popular was a clear fish sauce made by fermenting salt and fish for up to three months. Sanguine garum was an expensive and stronger version made from a particular kind of tuna's blood. Other sauces included a bright yellow concoction made from mustard (grown, like fenugreek and cumin, in Egypt) and a very popular one based on a herb called siliphum from Egypt's neighbor Cyrenaica.* The Romans and Egyptians also enjoyed using fruit sauces to produce a sweet-and-sour taste, serving slices of veal, for example, in a sauce of raisins, honey, pepper, onions, wine vinegar and herbs.

Less exotically, fish from the Nile and, of course, vegetables grown along its banks would have been served. The Egyptians enjoyed fibrous papyrus stalks, crisp lotus roots, lentils and garlic.† Their preferred use of the homely cabbage was as a hangover cure.

Although the Romans knew the technique of distilling, neither they nor the Egyptians drank spirits. Egyptian beer had been brewed since pharaonic times and had an excellent reputation but was probably not grand enough to serve to the Inimitables. Their bejeweled goblets would, however, have brimmed with wine. The Egyptians had been producing named wines and labeling vintages from at least the time of Tutankhamen (1327) onward. Hostile Roman poets were certain that Cleopatra so much enjoyed wine from the area around Lake Mareotis that she was usually fuddled with it. Reports reached Rome that on Cleopatra's ring was an amethyst engraved with the figure of Methe, the goddess of drunkenness who follows in the wake of Dionysus, and this was gleefully interpreted as proof of decadent dipsomania. In fact, the symbolism was

---

*Unfortunately, for some reason siliphum disappeared from the market in the middle of the first century AD and no one nowadays is quite sure what plant it was.

†A century later, the cook Epicurus celebrated the Egyptian bottle gourd in the following recipe for gourd Alexandrian fashion. Drain a boiled gourd, season with salt and arrange in a dish. Crush pepper, cumin, coriander seed, fresh mint and asafoetida root. Moisten with vinegar. Add caryota date and pine kernel; crush. Blend with honey, vinegar, fish sauce, concentrated grape juice and oil. Pour the whole over the gourd. Bring to a boil, season with pepper and serve.

more complex and perhaps to the Roman mind more disgraceful. The amethyst was the stone of sobriety, so what the carving of Methe actually symbolized was "sober drunkenness"—the overwhelming ecstasy or "drunkenness without wine" that possessed the female followers of Dionysus.

Cleopatra needed to be as fantastic and fascinating as the heady, intoxicating atmosphere in which she cocooned Antony. Plutarch described her predilection for dressing "in the robe which is sacred to Isis." If the depiction of the goddess by the writer Apuleius in the second century AD is accurate, Cleopatra, as Isis, must have dazzled Antony. Isis wore her hair falling "in tapering ringlets on her lovely neck" and "crowned with an intricate chaplet in which was woven every kind of flower. Just above her brow shone a round disc, like a mirror, or like the bright face of the moon." The uraeus, the Egyptian cobra sacred to the god Amun-Ra and a feature also of the royal Egyptian crown, reared on each side to support the disc, "with ears of corn bristling beside them."* Heavy pendant earrings of gold set with gems—lapis lazuli and turquoise, perhaps, or deep red garnet—and rings and armlets of golden wire artfully twisted into the coiled bodies of serpents would have added to the effect.

Isis' "many-colored robe was of finest linen; part was glistening white, part crocus-yellow, part glowing red and along the entire hem a woven border of flowers and fruit." The dramatic effect was heightened by "the deep black luster" of a mantle slung across the body from "the right hip to the left shoulder, where it was caught in a knot resembling the boss of a shield; but part of it hung in innumerable folds, the tasselled fringe quivering. It was embroidered with glittering stars on the hem and everywhere else and in the middle beamed a full and fiery moon." Isis' dramatically particolored robe symbolized her all-embracing power, "concerned with matter which becomes everything and receives everything, light and darkness, day and night, fire and water, life and death."

Cleopatra intended to be everything to Antony—to fill his days and satisfy his nights to the exclusion of all else. She was no longer bent on mere seduction. That had been achieved at Tarsus, and the speed with which Antony had followed her to Alexandria was proof of its success. What mattered now

*The ancient Egyptians also found a practical use for the cobra, fashioning condoms from its skin.

was to bind Antony to her as the best means of protecting herself and her country.

Compared with Antony, Cleopatra was sexually inexperienced. She had had only one previous lover compared with Antony's probable hundreds. Yet the Ptolemies must have imbibed something of the sexual attitudes of the people they ruled. The ancient Egyptians had, like the Romans, regarded sex as infinitely pleasurable and nothing to be ashamed of. Many Egyptian words were associated with the sex organs, while more than twenty expressions described making love. A famous erotic papyrus in the Egyptian Museum in Turin shows a cartoon-like sequence of sexual activities between a woman and an extraordinarily well-endowed middle-aged man.

Unused to privacy, the Egyptians took nakedness for granted. All bodily functions were performed publicly, except in the very highest circles. Since people were so used to nudity, they did not find bare flesh especially erotic. Far more arousing to a man was the sight of a woman in a clinging, semitransparent robe, nipples or navel protruding through the thin fabric, as depicted in many carvings, not least of Cleopatra herself at Dendera.

She and Antony were clearly well suited physically but, ever a shrewd judge of character, she would have studied Antony carefully, working out how to make herself indispensable to him at every level. She spiced the sensuality of their relationship with slapstick, encouraging Antony's love of schoolboy practical jokes—"childish nonsense," Plutarch grumbled. Cleopatra would "dress as a serving-girl, because Antony used to do his best to make himself look like a slave," and together they roamed the nighttime streets of Alexandria. Antony liked to stand "at the doors and windows of ordinary folk and mock the people inside." Unsurprisingly, this "would constantly earn him a volley of scorn and not infrequently blows too before he returned home, despite the fact that most people suspected who he was."

While on a fishing trip amongst the tall reeds of Lake Mareotis, Antony complained to Cleopatra that he was having little luck. Subsequently he secretly persuaded one of the fishermen accompanying them to swim down and attach one of the fish that had already been caught to his hook. According to Plutarch, "He hauled in two or three fish on this basis but he did not fool the Egyptian queen. She pretended to be impressed and to admire her lover's skill but told her friends all about it and invited them to come along the next day . . . When Antony had cast his line she told one of her own slaves to swim over to his hook first and to stick on to it a salted herring . . . Antony thought he had caught something and pulled it in, to everyone's great amusement, of course. 'Imperator,' she said, 'hand your rod over . . . Your prey is cities, kingdoms and continents.' "

According to Plutarch, "the Alexandrians loved the way Antony played the fool and joined in his games . . . They liked him and said that he adopted the mask of tragedy for the Romans, but the mask of comedy for them." He alleged that "Cleopatra did not restrict her flattery to Plato's four categories, but employed many more forms of it." Plato defined the four categories in his *Gorgias*, where he invited the reader to compare the false, flattering arts of sophistry, rhetoric, pastry cooking and cosmetics with the "genuine" arts of lawgiving, justice, medicine and gymnastics. Plato believed morality to be the essential basis of human existence and in *Gorgias* was challenging those whose first priority—as Plutarch was accusing Cleopatra—was the pursuit of pleasure.

But if much of what Cleopatra did to fascinate Antony was conscious and contrived, as in this early stage of their relationship it must have been, it could not have been so successful had it not touched something deep in them both. They shared a hunger for life. Excess was for both Cleopatra and Antony a natural, joyful expression of that hunger—whether making love night and day, feasting on impossible rarities, giving each other fabulous gifts or just playing the fool. Their appetites were well matched, their ambitions on a similarly grand scale, and instinctively they responded to one another. Nobody else would ever be as close to either of them as they would become to the other, although the mutual realization of that truth still lay some way in the future.

During those riotous winter months in her palace overlooking the harbor Cleopatra became pregnant, just as she must have hoped would happen. Yet if she thought this would detain her lover longer by her side, it was not to be. Antony had probably intended to leave Egypt and Cleopatra in the spring of 40, to allow him time to deal with the remaining eastern client kings—a task he had neglected in his rush to Alexandria—before embarking on his Parthian venture. However, the Parthians, with their armored cavalry and swift mounted archers, had seized the initiative, launching an ambitious two-pronged invasion of Rome's territories. In late February, messengers brought news that Pacorus, son of the Parthian king Orodes, had invaded Syria, killing its Roman governor as he tried to flee. He had seized Jerusalem and deposed Hyrcanus from the throne of Judaea, installing Hyrcanus' nephew Antigonus in his place as a puppet. Herod had fled for safety with the women of his family to the fortress of Masada in the dry, dusty mountains by the Dead Sea. At the same time, a former Roman republican now in the pay of the Parthians, Quintus Labienus, was pushing deep into the Roman province of Asia at the head of a strong force.

Shaken from the long, languorous dream of the past few months, or as Plutarch less sympathetically put it, "like a man struggling to wake up after a drunken night," Antony tried to rally himself. After a hasty leave-taking from the pregnant Cleopatra he sailed to Tyre, one of the few Phoenician ports that had not yet succumbed to the Parthians. Here further ill tidings awaited him. A number of Rome's client kings had thrown in their lot with the Parthians and some of his own troops in Syria had also defected.

Yet messengers from Italy delivered even worse news. Antony's formidable wife, Fulvia, and his younger brother, Lucius Antonius, had instigated a revolt against Octavian and been utterly defeated. Fulvia was fleeing eastward to her husband. Antony received what Plutarch called "a miserable letter" from her. Any thought of continuing north to deal with the marauding Parthians was put aside. Instead, Antony headed back toward Italy to salvage what he could.

Lucius Antonius was, according to the hostile historian Velleius Paterculus, "a partaker of his brother's vices, but destitute of the virtues that the latter sometimes showed." As consul for 41, he had opportunistically seized on Octavian's difficulties in resettling the veterans as he and Antony had promised to do after Philippi. Finding enough good land was always going to be a contentious task and, to the dismay of the inhabitants, Octavian had confiscated territory in eighteen Italian cities. Seeing a chance to damage and diminish Octavian, Lucius Antonius had begun raising objections. Octavian, he alleged, was usurping Antony's position by settling his men in his absence. Even worse, he was giving all the best land to his own veterans.

Fulvia, who had remained in Rome while Antony went east, had initially opposed her brother-in-law, arguing wisely that this was an inopportune moment to foment discord. However, Lucius convinced her otherwise, dangling before her an image of a Rome governed by Antony, with her as a powerful influence behind him. Now she became an active participant in a campaign to discredit and, if possible, oust Octavian. She allowed Lucius to present her and

Antony's children to Antony's legionaries. In an emotional address, Lucius urged the soldiers to gaze on their wronged leader's family. He implored them not to forget their commander, who, though absent in the east, had been the true victor of Philippi.

Irritated by these maneuvers but uncertain whether Antony himself might be behind them, Octavian reacted cautiously. He refrained from criticizing his fellow triumvir. Instead, he reserved his criticism for Antony's wife and brother, claiming that they were trying for their own ends to prevent him from fulfilling the agreement he had reached with Antony. He also took the opportunity to repudiate Fulvia's daughter Clodia, whom he had married after Philippi as part of his reconciliation with Antony. He sent the teenager back, assuring Fulvia cheerfully that she was still "*intacta*." It was a terrible insult and one that a woman such as Fulvia, who had used Cicero's tongue as a pincushion, was unlikely to forgive.

Yet at the same time, Octavian tried to contain the situation by permitting Antony's own agents to oversee the land settlements. Thus wrongfooted, Lucius Antonius shifted his ground completely. He decided to exploit the anger of the thousands thrown off their land by Octavian, who was continuing his veterans' resettlement program regardless of their protests. A recent calculation suggests that about a quarter of the land in Italy changed hands during the proscriptions and evictions. Among the families affected was that of the poet Vergil, whose estates were seized. In one of his poems he distills the pained cry of the victims:

A godless soldier has my cherished fields,
A savage has my land: such profit yields
Our civil war. For them we work our land!
Yes, plant your pears—to fill another's hand.

The economic problems caused by the eviction of so many landowners and farmers were worsened by the activities of Pompey the Great's younger son, Sextus, who from his Sicilian base was again harassing Roman shipping and cutting off grain supplies. In desperation, the dispossessed converged on Rome, according to Appian, "in crowds, young and old, women and children, to the forum and the temples, uttering lamentations, saying that they had done no wrong for which they, Italians, should be driven from their fields and their hearthstones, like people conquered in war." In the Senate, Octavian attempted to introduce measures to alleviate some of the suffering but the rioting crowds surging through Rome's streets had lost faith in him.

At the same time, the legionaries began to doubt his intentions. An ugly incident occurred when Octavian arrived late at the Campus Martius, where a division of land to veterans was to take place. As the soldiers' grumbling grew louder and angrier, a centurion rebuked them. Octavian, he claimed, had been delayed by illness and would soon be among them. But "they first jeered at him as a sycophant. Then as the excitement waxed hot on both sides, they reviled him, threw stones at him and pursued him when he fled." Finally, they killed the centurion, tossing his body onto the road along which Octavian was due to pass. Hearing what had happened, Octavian's advisers warned him not to go to the Campus Martius, but "he went forward, thinking that their madness would be augmented if he did not come." The dead centurion's blood-soaked body was still lying in the dust when he arrived. Realizing the volatility of the situation, Octavian wisely forbore from punishing the killers. Instead, he announced that he would leave them to "their own guilty consciences and the condemnation of their comrades" and withdrew.

Profiting from the deep despair and rising resentment, Lucius Antonius began raising an army and preparing to take on Octavian in the field. Octavian too began gathering forces, and both men helped themselves to temple treasures to fund the coming fight. Soldiers on each side, fearful of a renewed civil war, tried to broker a reconciliation, arranging a conference between Lucius and Octavian at Teanum. The two leaders met but, though a compromise of sorts was reached, nothing important was acted upon. Before long, Lucius and Fulvia fled to Praeneste, a stronghold east of Rome, making a great noise that they were in fear of their lives from Octavian. Again, anxious legionaries tried to head off a conflict, arranging a further meeting at Gabii, a town between Rome and Praeneste, but Lucius failed to turn up, while his agent produced a letter that he claimed had been written by Antony and which gave the green light to war.

Lucius' next step was to march on Rome. Pushing aside Lepidus, the third triumvir, who put up only a feeble resistance, he briefly occupied the city. To the cheers of many senators, soldiers and members of the popular assembly, Lucius promised that his brother Antony would renounce his powers as triumvir and assume those of consul. He was, in effect, announcing the restoration of the Roman republic. However, losing his nerve, Lucius soon headed north, hoping to join forces with Antony's generals, whom Fulvia had summoned from Gaul—but, divided by rivalries of their own, uncertain of Antony's wishes and distrustful of Lucius and Fulvia, they did not come.

Outmaneuvered by Octavian's forces, Lucius and his supporters, including a number of Antony's Italian-based commanders and their legionaries, withdrew into the ancient Etruscan rock fortress of Perusia (Perugia) north of Rome, where Octavian laid siege to them. A relentless blockade followed during which Octavian's forces girdled Perusia with a rampart seven miles in circumference containing fifteen hundred wooden siege towers.

Octavian focused his ire and his irony on Fulvia. After all, what better way to make Antony look ridiculous? The poet Martial preserved some lines of an obscene epigram by Octavian taunting Fulvia over Antony's affair with Glaphyra of Cappadocia and accusing her of waging war with Octavian as a surrogate for sex. They include:

Glaphyra's fucked by Antony. Fulvia, therefore, claims
a balancing fuck from me. I hate such games.
She cries either let's fuck or fight!
Doesn't she know my prick is dearer to me than life. Let trumpets sound.

Slingshots recovered from the site show the depths of verbal vitriol to which the besiegers resorted and their hatred of Antony's masterful and ambitious wife in particular. "Give it to Fulvia" was lewdly inscribed on one and "I am aiming at Fulvia's cunt" on another.

The besieged within Perusia responded with slingshots inscribed with slogans such as "Greetings, Octavian, you suck prick" and "Octavian has a limp dick." Soon, however, they began to starve. Lucius ordered the bodies of those who died of hunger to be buried, not burned, so that no smoke from funeral pyres should reveal his plight to Octavian. By late February 40, with no sign of any forces marching to his relief and after a final, desperate, unavailing sortie, Lucius surrendered Perusia.

Octavian ordered Perusia to be sacked but, before his victorious troops could rampage through its narrow streets, the city burned down, possibly after a citizen deliberately set fire to his house before killing himself. Octavian spared Lucius, not from compassion but because he judged it would be ill-advised to slay Antony's brother. Instead, he made Lucius governor of Spain, where he died not long after. Octavian also shrewdly allowed Antony's own soldiers to go free but executed all the members of Perusia's city council except for one man who, as a juror in Rome, had voted to condemn Caesar's murderers. Suetonius reported the belief of some writers that Octavian chose three hundred prisoners of equestrian or senatorial rank and offered them as human sacrifices on the ides of March at the altar to the divine god Julius Caesar in Rome, and Dio Cassius reported similar rumors. Yet, although early in his career Octavian showed he could be brutal, there is no hard evidence, such as the names of the dead, to support the allegations.

Fulvia, meanwhile, fled eastward with her children to find Antony. Perhaps jealousy of Cleopatra had incited her to reckless acts. She must have seen Cleopatra in Rome and known her to be a formidable rival. Now in her midforties, Fulvia also knew her husband's susceptibility to younger, beautiful women—especially those endowed with the glamour of royalty. Appian alleged that Fulvia believed that "as long as Italy remained at peace Antony would stay with Cleopatra, but that if war should break out there he would come back speedily." Therefore, "moved by a woman's jealousy," Fulvia had incited Antony's brother to rebellion. Plutarch also thought sexual politics were at work, asserting that Antony learned from friends "that Fulvia had been the cause of the war, being by nature restless, meddling and headstrong, and hoping to tear Antony away from Cleopatra by stirring up commotion in Italy."

Yet Fulvia was an experienced, sophisticated woman interested, above all, in power. If she was jealous of Cleopatra, it was not so much on a sexual level as on a political one. The Egyptian queen, in her scented, silk-hung palace in Alexandria, was distracting Antony from the business of governing and conquering. That winter of 41 to 40, it must have seemed as if Cleopatra had bewitched Antony. As Appian wrote, in Alexandria Antony had "laid aside the cares and duties of a general" and on falling under the Egyptian queen's spell "Antony's interest in public affairs began to dwindle." Drugged with pleasure and excess, Antony had become oblivious to the real world. Some of his veterans had actually sought him out in Alexandria and tried to warn him of the crisis brewing in Italy, but he had ignored them. All this would have been deeply aggravating to a woman of Fulvia's temperament, who had known Antony since his wild youth and hence knew his vulnerability to distracting temptations of the sort dangled by Cleopatra.

Fulvia probably believed that by supporting Lucius' attempted coup she was being a loyal wife, saving Antony from himself, jolting him out of an inertia that in Roman eyes was one of the great vices of the East. In intervening actively on her present husband's behalf, she was doing no more than she had when she sought vengeance for the murder of Clodius, rousing the crowds by showing his wounds. She was in some ways following in a long tradition of powerful Roman matrons including Servilia—Brutus' mother and Caesar's onetime mistress—and Caesar's mother, Aurelia. But she was also breaking with convention. Despite the considerable freedom of well-born Roman women, there was still a belief that they should exercise their influence behind the scenes. By taking the initiative so publicly and in such a violent fashion—and, most importantly, because she failed—Fulvia, like Cleopatra in later years, laid herself open to attack and misrepresentation not only by contemporaries but also by later writers. Dio Cassius called Fulvia, not Lucius, the true inspirer of the uprising, alleging that, unlike any other Roman woman, she took a direct hand in military matters: "She girded herself with a sword, gave the passwords to the soldiers and often made speeches haranguing them." Paterculus sneered that she "had nothing of the woman in her except her sex" and "was creating general confusion by armed violence."

Antony probably shared the latter sentiment. Landing in Athens to be reunited with the crestfallen, distraught Fulvia, he learned at firsthand how she and his brother had deliberately destroyed his relationship with Octavian. He became furiously angry. Some would allege that he must have known what they were doing and was angered only by their failure, but there seems little logic to this. While he might have planned for the coup to take place during his time in the east, this would have been an obviously flawed strategy. Without the charismatic commander beloved by officers and soldiers alike present in person to lead it, any coup would have been unlikely to succeed.

Antony also found another of the strong-minded women in his life—his intelligent and politically astute mother, Julia—waiting for him in Athens. Now in her sixties, Julia had fled to Sextus Pompey in Sicily. After hurried negotiations, she had set off once more, this time to meet her son. With her she had brought two envoys from Sextus instructed to offer Antony an alliance with their leader. Antony, however, still shocked by the speed of events and his wife and brother's inept interfering, was reluctant to take a step that would lead to an inevitable breach with Octavian. Instead he told the envoys that if Octavian was still adhering to the agreement reached after Philippi, he would do his utmost to reconcile Octavian and Sextus. Only if Octavian had renounced their pact would he ally himself with Sextus. Then, angrily denouncing Fulvia and his brother for the stupidity of their actions and refusing even to bid his wife good-bye, Antony left for Italy.

Fulvia, broken by events and ailing, was thus brutally abandoned to mourn her folly. The pregnant Cleopatra, watching from the sidelines, was forced once again to await the result of a Roman power struggle that would have profound implications for her future.

CHAPTER 15

Single Mother

IN THE SUMMER OF 40 Antony arrived off Brundisium with his advance guard, no longer the unquestionably dominant partner in the business of governing Rome. Octavian had grown considerably stronger in the eighteen months since Philippi. Not only had he convincingly crushed Lucius but, earlier that year, in a deliberate breach of the agreement between the triumvirs, he had taken advantage of the sudden death of Antony's legate in Gaul, Calenus, to bully his inexperienced son into handing over the province and its eleven legions. According to Appian, the young man was so terrified he "delivered everything over to Octavian without a fight." Octavian had also begun publicly calling himself "son of the god," in reference to his deified adoptive father, Julius Caesar.

Antony, though, had just acquired an important new ally in the fiercely republican Domitius Enobarbus, the seasoned warrior portrayed by Shakespeare as Antony's loyal officer and devoted friend. Enobarbus had earlier supported Cassius and Brutus and taken charge of their fleet but after the fall of Perusia had been persuaded to give Antony his allegiance.* In dramatic scenes off the Adriatic coast, Enobarbus' great fleet had swooped down on Antony's as if he meant to attack but at the last moment he had swung his flagship broadside

---

*Enobarbus is the form of the name used by Shakespeare and here. The precise classical transliteration is Ahenobarbus, meaning "bronze beard."

to the ram on the prow of Antony's ship in token of submission. Enobarbus was neither the first nor the last die-hard republican to join Antony in preference to Octavian. That so many did so indicates a belief that Antony's intentions were less autocratic than those of his fellow triumvir.

The appearance of Enobarbus' and Antony's combined fleets off Brundisium caused the troops stationed there by Octavian to panic. They blocked the crescent-shaped harbor to deny entry to Antony's ships and barred the town against him. This was probably without Octavian's knowledge but, whatever the case, they had no right to do so. Antony was still a triumvir with all the authority that conferred. Interpreting the soldiers' actions as a sign that the war he had not wanted with Octavian had begun, Antony sailed further along the coast, disembarked his advance guard and, moving on Brundisium, laid siege to it.

By now, the maverick Sextus Pompey had also thrown in his lot, at least for the present, with Antony. This was a blow to Octavian, who, fearing just such a development, had tried to neutralize the troublesome Sextus through the time-honored Roman tactic of a matrimonial alliance. In the aftermath of the siege of Perusia, Octavian had, to general ribald mirth, proposed to and been accepted by Scribonia, a twice-married woman at least ten years his senior whose brother was Sextus' father-in-law. No doubt laughing along with everyone else at Octavian's nakedly cynical maneuverings, Sextus had immediately pursued an alliance with Antony.

Octavian hurriedly dispatched his erstwhile school friend Marcus Agrippa, who would be his lifelong supporter, from Rome to Brundisium with orders to raise the siege. As he marched, Agrippa recruited more troops from among the recently disbanded veterans he encountered along the way. The men joined readily enough because they mistakenly thought their target was to be Sextus Pompey. When they learned that they were instead marching against Antony, under whom they had so recently defeated Caesar's murderers at Philippi, many turned around and went home. Once again, the weary, wary veterans were demonstrating their disinclination for civil war. As Octavian followed in Agrippa's wake to Brundisium, his veterans too made their views plain—nothing less than a permanent settlement between the triumvirs, they insisted, would satisfy them.

Reaching Brundisium, Octavian found that Antony had thrown ditches and palisades across the prong of land leading to the peninsula on which the city lay. It would be impossible to relieve Brundisium from the landward side. Yet for all the strength of his position, Antony was caught between Octavian's ever-growing forces and Brundisium's high walls. Unless he could take the fortress and harbor quickly, the legions he had summoned from Macedonia would be unable to land unopposed. Instead they would have to disembark further along the coast, fighting their way onto the beaches.

All this was food for reflection, as was his knowledge that his new ally Sextus was volatile and unreliable. So too was the news that reached him of the death near Corinth in Greece of Fulvia, who, Appian wrote, "had become a willing victim of disease on account of Antony's anger." Antony could now place all blame for the rebellion against Octavian on the shoulders of a forceful, ambitious and conveniently defunct wife. How much grief Antony felt at Fulvia's loss is debatable. They had known each other since their youth, but the close bonds between them had loosened even before the recent fiasco. Though Antony had once depended on Fulvia, his reliance on her emotionally and politically had declined, otherwise he would have taken her east with him. Instead, he had reveled alone in his unprecedented new powers and godlike position. The "new Dionysus," as he imagined himself, felt no need of a bossy middle-aged Roman matron by his side, however astute she was.

To survive politically and stabilize the Roman world, Antony was prepared to compromise. A mutual friend with well-honed diplomatic skills, Nerva, agreed to act as go-between between Antony and Octavian. With both men anxious to achieve a peaceful solution, Nerva's primary problem was to find a way in which neither would lose face. At his artful suggestion, Octavian wrote not to Antony but to his mother, Julia, who had sailed with him from Greece. Octavian assured her that he had not ordered the Brundisium garrison to bar her son's ships from the harbor. The men had acted on their own initiative. He also reproached her for having fled from him to Sextus, assuring her she had never been in danger from him and that he would always treat her honorably.

These honeyed words proved sweet enough. A conciliating Antony sent Enobarbus off to be governor of Bithynia, ordered Sextus to withdraw to Sicily and, in early October 40, concluded the Pact of Brundisium with Octavian. The watching soldiers roared their approval as the two men embraced, but Antony was probably less transported. Though the triumvirate was to continue and Italy was to remain common ground, leaving Antony full rights to recruit there, the pact obliged him to yield his territorial rights in the west to Octavian. In other words, Antony had lost Gaul for good. The line dividing their respective lands would run through Scodra (Scutari) in modern Albania. It formed a true border in terms of geography, culture and language. Everything to the Greek-speaking Hellenized east would be Antony's, everything to the Latin-speaking Romanized west Octavian's. The province of Africa was to remain under the ineffectual third triumvir, Lepidus.

It was a disappointing, even somewhat humiliating outcome for the victor of Philippi, who had lost Gaul while gaining nothing that he had not had before. Yet Antony had learned through the twists of the civil war to be a pragmatist. The outcome, as he well knew, could have been worse, and he was at least free to resume his plans for the invasion and subjugation of mighty Parthia, which, if he succeeded, would make him unassailable.

That same autumn in Alexandria Cleopatra gave birth to Antony's twins—a girl and a boy. Following Ptolemaic tradition, she named her daughter Cleopatra, but given that its literal meaning is "glory of her father," there was perhaps an implied message here for Antony. She called the boy Alexander in honor both of her own relation Alexander the Great and of her lover's ambitions to become the new Alexander. Just as with the birth of her first child, the Roman father was not there to admire and exult in his offspring.

News of the Pact of Brundisium probably filtered through to Cleopatra as she recovered from the birth. She was relying for much of her information on an Egyptian astrologer she had infiltrated into Antony's household. With two new children to scheme and plan for, she would have pondered the pact's implications carefully. Politically, the most important point was that Antony remained in control of the east. Though she would have preferred Antony to obliterate his young rival, the situation was better than she might have feared when Antony had rushed back to Italy to confront Octavian.

On a personal level, though, the possible consequences of the pact were more complex. Any hopes that her lover would soon return to her and resume their "inimitable" days and nights were quickly dashed. Cleopatra learned that he had also agreed at Brundisium that, to cement their relationship, he and Octavian should be allied through marriage. With Fulvia dead, as Plutarch wrote, Antony was "generally held to be a widower . . . since although he made no attempt to deny his relationship with Cleopatra, he refused to call her his wife." He was thus free to marry Octavian's beautiful, recently widowed older sister—already the mother of three young children and around the same age as Cleopatra herself.

Images of Octavia suggest a classic Roman beauty with slender neck, straight nose and regular features. Writers, both in her lifetime and later, lauded her as the model of a virtuous Roman wife, with none of the unwomanly stridency and personal ambition of Fulvia or oriental wiles of Cleopatra. Plutarch wrote of her "dignity and intelligence, as well as her great beauty" and, in a recognition of the potent influence women could exert behind the scenes in Roman politics, of how men hoped "she would prove to be the savior and moderator of all Rome's affairs." The glowing depictions of Octavia were at least partly fashioned by propaganda, which depicted her as a veritable Griselda, too cloyingly patient and good to be true. Yet facts suggest Octavia was indeed astute and conciliating as well as patient, gentle and kind—in fact, the antithesis of the martial, managing Fulvia. She would need all these qualities during her marriage to Antony. She must have known her new husband was—in Plutarch's words—"a lover, drinker, warrior, giver, spender" and above all "outrageous." But Antony was now, at forty-three, on the threshold of middle age and perhaps ready for a life of greater gravitas and domestic calm.

How much Octavia knew of Cleopatra can only be guessed. She had agreed to fulfill one of the primary roles of aristocratic Roman women—to be fodder in the marriage market to benefit the ambitions of her male relations and to further the greater glory of her family.

In Rome, news of the impending marriage was received with delight, as it signaled that war had been averted. The Senate marked its approval by waiving the law stipulating that widows could not remarry within ten months of the death of their husband. Since Romans believed babies were born between seven to ten months after conception, this was intended to remove all doubt about the paternity of any child that was born.

Antony and Octavia married in early November 40—a month that, unlike May or early June, was considered auspicious for weddings. The ceremony was always the same, regardless of whether it was a first marriage or not. Octavia's female relations gathered in her house to dress her in a simple white tunic secured at the waist by a girdle fastened in a double knot, which Antony would later have to unfasten. Using the head of a spear, they divided Octavia's hair into six bunches, which they secured with ribbons. Finally, they draped her with a saffron cloak and placed a flame-colored veil over her head, topped with a wreath of verbena and sweet marjoram. When she was ready, Antony arrived and a sacrifice was made to the gods. As soon as the entrails had been examined and the auspices judged favorable, Antony took Octavia's right hand in his and the pair exchanged vows before the assembled witnesses, who affixed their seal to the marriage contract while the guests with one voice exclaimed "*feliciter*" (congratulations).

After the wedding feast, Antony enacted the age-old charade of abducting his bride, dragging a seemingly reluctant Octavia from the arms of her family. Then, to a chorus of obscene remarks and jokes, Antony led her in rowdy procession, preceded by flute players and torch bearers, to his house. Arriving before the door, Octavia performed the ritual of decorating it with lengths of wool and smearing it with oil and lard. To avoid any possibility that his new bride might inauspiciously trip on entering her new home, Antony then carried her over the threshold, which was spread with white cloth and branches of greenery. After Antony had offered her fire and water, one of Octavia's three bridesmaids led her to the scented nuptial couch, where, as the bridal party withdrew, she lay down and Antony began to undress his new wife.

The early days of such a high-profile arranged marriage were a very different existence from the wild hedonism of the Inimitable Livers. Not only the Roman people but each spouse had much to gain by making their relationship succeed. Plutarch thought Antony wished to obliterate his idyll with Cleopatra from his memory, writing, "His rational mind was resisting his love for the Egyptian." To celebrate his Roman marriage, Antony struck golden coins depicting his new bride. With her frank, open gaze and hair curling softly on her neck, Octavia looked everything a well-born Roman lady should and the antithesis of the Egyptian voluptuary who had ensnared him.

Octavia's new home was Pompey's former mansion on the Palatine Hill—a house of suitably aristocratic splendor. A Roman architect enthused that for people of great rank, "we must provide princely vestibules, lofty halls and spacious gardens, plantations and broad avenues finished in a majestic manner. Further there must be libraries and basilicas of similar grace, and as magnificent as the equivalent public structures, because in such palaces public deliberations as well as private trials and judgments are often performed."

Guests were shown into a large, rectangular and open reception hall or atrium. It had a pool to collect rainwater at its center, and along the sides were ancestral statues and wall cupboards containing wax death masks of male ancestors—the Roman equivalent of family portraits. The masks were taken out for family funeral processions to be worn by actors who dressed in the full insignia of the defunct dignitaries they were impersonating and rode in chariots before the litter bearing the deceased. Ornate public rooms lined with marble and decorated with mosaics and frescoes opened off the atrium, while the family's private apartments were toward the back of the house, arranged around the garden.

Respectable Roman life was an orderly one of prudence, restraint and duty. Romans were early risers. Perhaps consequently there was little luxury in the bedchamber. Furniture there was minimal—usually just the couch that gave the room its name (the *cubiculum*), a chest to store clothes and a chair. Mosaics depict sumptuous-looking bronze couches with ivory feet but, compared with the soft beds of the East, they were not all that comfortable, with their sprung base of rope interwoven with webbing on which was placed a mattress and a bolster that served as a pillow. Like the rest of the house, bedrooms were kept warm in winter by portable charcoal braziers and by hot air centrally produced by a furnace in the basement and circulated through a network of ducts.

Roman men did not undress to go to bed, removing only their cloak and toga and keeping the rest of their clothes on. These comprised a loincloth knotted around the waist and a simple tunic of two widths of linen or wool sewn together to make a shirt that was pulled over the head and fastened around the waist with a belt. Different social classes wore different types of tunic—a soldier's military tunic, as favored by Antony, was shorter than a civilian's, while those of Roman senators had vertical purple stripes. If, like Octavian, a man felt the winter cold, he might wear several tunics.

After a simple breakfast of water, fruit, fresh bread and honey, the Roman male prepared for the day. Though he cleaned his teeth in the morning with a bicarbonate of soda mixture, he preferred to bathe in early afternoon, either at the public baths or, if an important man like Antony, in his own small baths at home. Antony would have had a slave especially trained as a barber to shave him. The Romans did not have soap and so the barber used only razor and water, making the whole process a painful one and cuts so frequent that, according to Pliny the Elder, a special plaster made of spiderwebs soaked in oil and vinegar was devised to stanch them.

The poet Martial lists having to wear the heavy, expensive and voluminous toga only rarely as one of the keys to a good life, along with good health and inherited wealth. Nevertheless, the toga had a symbolic significance—only freeborn Romans could wear it. The garment had evolved from the cloak and took its name from *tegere* (to cover). Spun from soft wool, the toga worn by the ordinary Roman was an unbleached brown but senior officials edged their togas with a broad purple band and triumphant generals wore purple togas bordered with gold. (The purple dye came from seashells.)

The toga comprised a semicircle of cloth with a diameter of up to eighteen feet. About six and a half feet of the straight edge was draped over the left shoulder, across the back, under the right arm, over the chest and then over the left shoulder again, and the folds arranged so that the curved edge formed the garment's hem. The toga had no fastening, requiring the wearer to keep his left arm crooked to keep the draperies in place.

As aristocrats, Octavia and Antony probably slept apart so their own slaves could tend them. Roman women also kept their underclothes on at night—loincloths, a form of brassiere and a long tunic. They too bathed in the afternoon. Their daytime outer garment was the long, flowing stola, nipped in at the waist by a belt and colored using a variety of dyes—the saffron crocus for yellow, woad for blue, madder for red, oak gallnuts for black and salt of tartar for white. The dresses of women such as Octavia were richly embroidered, often with gold thread, which, like their elaborate jewelry, caught the light.

Octavia would have employed a special slave—her *ornatrix*—to dress her hair and help with her makeup. Hairstyles in this period were relatively simple compared with later imperial tastes. Octavia wore her hair in a soft topknot—the *nodus*—from which a thin braid, drawn back along a central parting, joined two side braids in a smooth knot on the nape of her neck, a style she invented and which set a fashion in Rome. Makeup, though, was elaborate. The *ornatrix* first used lanolin—the grease from unwashed sheep's wool—as a foundation and then applied white chalk powder to Octavia's forehead and arms, red ochre to her cheeks and black charcoal to her eyebrows and eyelids. A heady perfume completed her toilette. When she was ready to go out, Octavia draped a shawl, the *palla*, over her shoulders, securing it with a *fibula*—a brooch that was both shaped and functioned like a safety pin, though infinitely more decorative. A cloth called a *mappa*, which she could use to dab off dust and perspiration, dangled from her wrist. Slaves held parasols over her to protect her from the sun and fanned flies away.

Yet Octavia's life was more than the comfortable routine of the wealthy, well-connected and fashionable Roman matron. As she settled into her new life as wife to one of the two most powerful men in Rome and sister to the other, she had done as much as anyone to restore peace and stability. However, her role as peace broker between a power-hungry brother and an ambitious husband was far from over.

CHAPTER 16

"The Awful Calamity"

IN ROME THE HEARTFELT relief that civil war had been averted inspired the thirty-one-year-old Vergil to compose his famous Fourth Eclogue. Underscored by a plaintive yearning for peace and plenty, it predicted the arrival of a savior-child who would preside over a time of universal goodwill among men:

Now comes the crowning age foretold in the Sibyl's songs,
A great new cycle, bred of time, begins again.
Now virginal Justice and the golden age return,
Now its first-born is sent down from lofty heaven.
With the birth of this boy, the generation of iron will pass,
And a generation of gold will inherit all the world.

Vergil was vague about the identity of the child's parents. Possibly he was referring to Octavian and his aging bride, since Scribonia was pregnant, though the ludicrous aspects of the marriage make this unlikely. Far more plausible is that Vergil meant Antony and Octavia, who were soon expecting a child.

News of Octavia's pregnancy would have been deeply worrying to Cleopatra and threatening to her twins by Antony, whom he had not yet seen. With Antony apparently content with his new wife and position in Rome and showing no sign of wishing to return to her, the outlook must have seemed bleak. Yet throughout her life Cleopatra, as a successful ruler, had learned the art of patience. Unlike her elder sisters, she had not overtly plotted for her father's throne. When Antony had summoned her to Tarsus, she had not rushed to obey. Even such apparently impetuous acts as throwing herself at Caesar's feet had been the result of careful calculation. She must have known that, however difficult, her best chance lay in waiting, knowing that before long her ambitious lover would return east to pursue his campaign against Parthia and, to do so, he would need Egypt's wealth. She never seems to have considered abandoning her relationship with Antony or, indeed, her country's close ties with Rome.

And Cleopatra had immediate problems of her own. With her lover and supposed protector absent and apparently distracted from the affairs of the east, she had to safeguard her own position on the Egyptian throne. This meant being on the lookout for internal dissent—there had been periodic outbreaks of nationalist feeling against the Ptolemies for most of their three-hundred-year reign. It also meant managing her country's economy, the base of her power, prudently and carefully. As a result of the damage done to Egypt's economy by her father's debts, earlier in her reign Cleopatra had been forced to debase the country's silver currency yet further. However, she had since revived the production of bronze in her mint in Alexandria and become the first Ptolemy to introduce separate denominations within Egypt's bronze coinage and to establish a standard system of bronze weights to restore people's confidence in the purchasing power of their coins. As a result of Cleopatra's innovative reforms, her citizens calculated the worth of their coins by the denominations marked on them, rather than by the value of the metal of which they were composed.

Cleopatra also wished to ensure that Egyptian agriculture—source of so much of her wealth—was prospering. She knew that nothing was so likely to cause civil discontent as shortages of grain or overexploitation of the workforce by greedy, grafting officials. A decree of April 41 reveals her close scrutiny of what was happening. Learning that local administrators were imposing unreasonable burdens on holders of estates outside Alexandria and hence on their peasants, she declared herself "exceedingly indignant." Citing her "hatred of evil" and determination to halt abuses, she ordered the excessive demands to stop:

> Nor shall their goods be destrained for such contributions, nor shall any new tax be required of them, but when they have once paid the essential

dues, in kind or in money, for corn-land and for vine-land, which have regularly in the past been assigned to the royal treasury, they shall not be molested for anything further, on any pretext whatsoever.

Evidence suggests that such decrees, written down by scribes, would have been authorized by Cleopatra's addition of the single word *ginesthoi* (let it be so).

At the same time, Cleopatra had to navigate through complex regional politics—in particular those of neighboring Judaea. In 40, displaced by the Parthians, the thirty-two-year-old Herod had hastened to Alexandria to seek Cleopatra's help. He could not be entirely certain of his reception. His ambition was to regain the remainder of his territories intact from the Parthian invaders and the usurping Antigonus and his followers. However, Judaea had once been part of the Ptolemaic empire and Cleopatra, as he rightly suspected, nurtured hopes of someday regaining it.

For the moment, though, Cleopatra and Herod, as staunch allies of Rome, shared a common interest—first to contain and then to repulse the fanatically anti-Roman Parthians, who, if not stopped, might threaten the very borders of Egypt. According to Josephus, Cleopatra received Herod with great splendor and even offered him a command in her own army, perhaps as a way of keeping some control over him. However, still grieving over news that his brother Phasael had committed suicide in a Parthian prison cell, Herod was determined to go to Rome to beg for aid in regaining his lost lands. After some hesitation Cleopatra agreed to provide him with a ship to take him as far as Rhodes, where he could obtain other transport to take him on to Rome.

Cleopatra must have soon regretted her generosity. Arriving in Rome in the autumn of 40, not long after the Pact of Brundisium, Herod persuaded the triumvirs to convince the Senate not only to appoint him ruler of Judaea in place of Hyrcanus, now a captive of the Parthians, but also to award him the title of king of the Jews, an honor previously denied to Hyrcanus. In addition, Herod was awarded substantial territorial additions north of Jerusalem and a coastal strip to the southwest that probably included the port of Gaza, terminus of the Arabian spice route. Most unwelcome of all to Cleopatra was that, unsolicited, several of Antony's supporters had spoken up for Herod in the Senate. In her eyes, their desire for a renewed and strong Judaea was more than a device to counter the Parthians—it was a signal that Rome did not wish Egypt to be the only power in the region. Yet once again, Cleopatra knew she could do little but wait for more propitious times to push her own claims.

Josephus recorded that Herod had been warned he would find Italy "very tumultuous and in great disorder," which he did. The Pact of Brundisium had not ushered in Vergil's "golden age." Rome's citizens were hungry and angrily demanding bread—a situation for which Sextus Pompey was largely to blame. Affronted to have received nothing concrete out of the Pact of Brundisium and by Antony's apparent disinclination to act on his promise to try to reconcile him with Octavian, he had resumed his disruption of Rome's grain supplies, attacking ports and shipping and seizing Sardinia and Corsica to add to his Sicilian strongholds. When Octavian and Antony, raised taxes on slaves and inheritances to pay for troops to fight Sextus, rioting mobs took to the streets to protest. Reports of Octavian's lavish parties and feasts so angered people that they surrounded and began to stone him in the Forum. His life was saved by Antony, who, hearing of his predicament, quickly assembled troops to attack the protestors and himself bravely pushed through the mêlée to snatch the injured Octavian to safety—a clear indication of his loyalty to Octavian at this time.

With Sextus' rampaging growing ever more blatant and ever more damaging to the authority of the triumvirs, Antony urged Octavian to seek a meeting with him. The encounter took place in somewhat bizarre circumstances in the spring of 39. The setting was Misenum at the northern end of the Bay of Naples, where so many of the Roman elite had built their luxurious holiday villas. Fearful of treachery, Antony and Octavian would not trust themselves to a shipboard meeting, and Sextus would not accept one on land. Sextus ordered the erection of two platforms supported on wooden piles a little way offshore and near the harbor mole and calculated their positioning to the inch. The platforms were near enough for men to be able to hear one another but too far apart for an assassin to leap between them. Antony and Octavian climbed onto the platform nearest the shore where their troops were waiting, while Sextus occupied the seaward perch close to his flagship.

Sextus' demands were ambitious—he wanted nothing less than to join the triumvirate. When the existing triumvirs refused, the strange conference adjourned while Sextus consulted his wife, Julia—Scribonia's niece—and his mother, Mucia, who begged him to moderate his demands. Back on his platform with the warm waters of the Mediterranean lapping around him, Sextus shouted across to Octavian and Antony fresh ultimata, which the triumvirs finally accepted. In return for a huge payment, Sextus would cease raiding shipping and ensure that Rome received her grain. He was also to be consul for 38, to be left in control of Sicily, Sardinia and Corsica and to acquire the Peloponnese, which Antony agreed to hand over. Sextus also won concessions for his followers, including the many republican exiles who had fled to him and who were now to be allowed to return home and receive partial compensation for their estates. Only those who had been complicit in Caesar's death were excluded. The agreement was signed, sealed and dispatched for safekeeping to the Vestal Virgins in Rome.

To celebrate, Sextus invited Antony and Octavian to dine aboard his magnificent flagship, an invitation the two men now felt sufficiently confident to accept. Before dinner, Sextus resentfully chided Antony that this vessel was "the only family home Pompey has left," a rebuke for Antony's having appropriated the mansion of Pompey the Great on Rome's Palatine Hill. Plutarch went on that at the height of the party, when, in typical male fashion, "jokes about Antony and Cleopatra were flying thick and fast" as the wine flowed, one of Sextus' commanders whispered to him in an undertone, "Shall I cut the ship's cables and make you master of Rome, not just Sicily and Sardinia?" In other words, once out to sea, they could murder the triumvirs. Sextus thought for a moment in silence then replied, "You ought to have done it without telling me about it beforehand. For now, let's be satisfied with things as they are. It's not my way to break a promise."

It was perhaps Sextus' last and best chance, as his treaty with the triumvirs did not endure long. Disgruntled that Antony, with Octavian's connivance, was denying him tribute from the Peloponnese, which he believed was his, Sextus resumed his blockade of Rome's grain. Captured pirates who confessed under torture that they were in Sextus' pay gave Octavian every justification to resume hostilities.

Octavian also took advantage of the situation to get rid of his wife, Sextus' relation. On the very day that Scribonia gave birth to their daughter Julia, Octavian divorced her because, or so he said, "I could not bear the way she nagged at me." Octavian's brutal act in fact had less to do with either Scribonia's failings or Sextus' renewed hostility than with a consuming new passion. The object of the hot and urgent desires of the usually cool and restrained

Octavian was a young married woman, the beautiful nineteen-year-old Livia Drusilla of the ancient house of the Claudii, his future empress and, as Suetonius believed, "the one woman whom he truly loved until his death." Her patrician husband was the staunchly republican Tiberius Claudius Nero, with whom she had escaped after the fall of Perusia, where he had fought on Antony's brother's side. After surviving a terrifying series of adventures, he was one of the exiles permitted to return to Rome following the pact with Sextus. Livia herself was at the time heavily pregnant—some claimed, probably incorrectly, with Octavian's child—and already had a two-year-old son, Tiberius. However, none of this—husband, child, pregnancy—mattered to Octavian, who was determined to have her.

Some accounts, including that of the historian Tacitus, suggest that Octavian virtually abducted Livia from her husband's house. Nevertheless, anxious to retain at least some semblance of propriety, Octavian sought advice from the priests on the delicate matter of how soon he could marry a woman pregnant at the time of her divorce. Faced with an unprecedented situation, the priests agreed the marriage could take place as soon as the child was born. In January 38, just three days after giving birth to her second son, Drusus, Livia duly married Octavian, given away by her complaisant former husband. To Octavian's great disappointment, though their marriage would last fifty years, she would never bear him a child. Unlike those of Antony and Tiberius Claudius Nero, none of Octavian's descendants would be emperors.

Antony and Octavia were not at the wedding. In the autumn of 39, shortly after Octavia had given birth to a daughter, Antonia, they had sailed together for Athens so that Antony could prepare for his Parthian campaign. Plutarch claimed that Cleopatra's astrologer, still attached to Antony's household, had advised him to go: "Either as a favor to Cleopatra, or because he wanted to tell the truth, he spoke frankly to Antony and told him that despite his great brilliance . . . he was being eclipsed by Octavian and he advised him to put as much distance as possible between himself and the young man." If Cleopatra had had a hand in urging Antony eastward, it did her little immediate good: Antony made no attempt to contact her.

Whatever Cleopatra may have hoped, Antony, it seems, was still enjoying the novelty of a quiet domestic life with Octavia. Athens suited them both. Octavia liked conversing with Athens' philosophers, while Antony, a longtime admirer of the Hellenic world, relished the more relaxed atmosphere. Just as he had done in Alexandria, he put aside his Roman garb for a Greek tunic and white shoes. Appian wrote, "He took his meals in the Greek fashion, passed his leisure time with the Greeks and enjoyed their festivals in company with Octavia with whom he was very much in love, being by nature excessively fond of women." Their marriage was honored by a sacred marriage between Antony and the goddess of the city, Athena, with whom the Athenians associated Octavia. Both were hailed as "beneficent gods."

As well as a cultured, pleasant place, Athens was also Antony's military headquarters. His plan was for his generals to drive the Parthians from the territories they had occupied in Asia Minor, Syria and Judaea while he reserved the glorious conquest of Parthia for himself. The campaign was, in fact, already well under way even before Antony reached Athens. Earlier in 39, his skillful commander Publius Ventidius, a veteran of Caesar's campaigns and an ally of Antony since his darkest hour after Mutina, had defeated the Roman renegade Labienus and the Parthians under his command in the Taurus mountains. The next step was to conquer Armenia.

However, in 38 Antony's program was disrupted by a request for assistance from Octavian, who was again confronting Sextus Pompey. Though he would have preferred to crush Sextus himself and take the credit, Octavian had reluctantly concluded he needed Antony's help. Antony duly sailed from Athens to Brundisium, only to find that Octavian was not there. Angered by the younger man's apparent disrespect and by no means keen to become embroiled again in a distracting war with Sextus when all his thoughts were on Parthia, Antony sailed back to Athens, leaving only a brusque message that Octavian was on no account to break their pact with Sextus. Octavian, in turn, claimed that Antony should have waited for him and continued with his preparations for war.

Good news soon made Antony forget his irritation with Octavian when, in June 38, messengers brought word that Ventidius had vanquished Pacorus, son of the Parthian king, near Antioch and sliced off his head. The Parthians had made the fatal error of deploying their heavy cavalry, the mail-clad cataphracts, rather than their swift-moving, devastating mounted archers. Although the bulk of Pacorus' troops had escaped over the Euphrates, this and his defeat of Labienus' Parthians were the first occasions on which Roman forces had defeated those of Parthia. Ventidius made slower progress in subduing a neighboring renegade king, some said because he had been bribed to do so. Antony supplanted him and took personal command. He did, however, allow Ventidius to return to Rome for the Triumph already voted to him by the Roman people for his previous success. The Triumph, the first ever celebrated over Parthia, had the very useful side effect of shedding reflected glory on Antony and reminding Rome of his campaigns in the east on its behalf.

Antony quickly seized Samosata, the capital on the Euphrates of the renegade king. While he was there, Herod, who had been enjoying little military success, arrived to beg his help in dislodging the Parthian-backed Antigonus in Judaea. Antony agreed and appointed his supporter Sosius to command the expedition. Sosius in turn allowed Herod to go ahead with a vanguard of two legions—a rare example of Roman forces being placed under the command of a foreigner. With them, Herod defeated Antigonus' troops at Jericho and then invested Jerusalem, where he was soon joined by Sosius and his larger Roman force.

However, Antony's plans for Parthia were about to be disrupted yet again by Octavian, who had ignored his strictures and launched an ill-considered attack on Sextus in Sicily. In a series of disastrous actions, which underlined his lack of ability as a commander, Octavian had lost many of his ships to Sextus' superior seamanship and much of the remainder to bad weather. Confronted by what Appian described as a sea "full of sails, spars and men, living and dead," he had been forced to call off the campaign, leaving a jubilantly swaggering Sextus to proclaim himself "son of Neptune." In desperation, Octavian had recalled Agrippa, whom he had made governor of Gaul, to oversee the construction of a huge new fleet and, in Suetonius' words, to get them "into fighting condition"—a task that included training thirty thousand freed slaves in oarsmanship.

Octavian also asked again for Antony's help, and in the early summer of 37, Antony and Octavia, pregnant once more, arrived off Brundisium with a fleet of three hundred ships. To Antony's rage, in what must have seemed a repetition of events a year earlier, he found Octavian had once more failed to keep the rendezvous. Reluctant simply to depart again, he sailed southwest around the heel of Italy to the Gulf of Tarentum, from where he sent messages to Octavian that, despite his snubs, he remained ready to join loyally in the attack on Sextus and awaited an explanation of his brother-in-law's bizarre and disrespectful behavior.

The reality was that, with his new fleet in good shape, Octavian had recovered his nerve. He had decided he no longer needed Antony and, reluctant as ever to share power or glory, regretted summoning him. He also wondered why Antony had arrived with such a large force and suspected some ulterior motive. He tried to fob Antony off with excuses that must have sounded ridiculous even to his own ears, but the nervous thoughts running through Octavian's ever active, always questioning mind must have been obvious. Antony may also have reflected that, in a sense, Octavian was right to be wary—he did have another motive for returning to Italy, which had nothing to do with Sextus. It concerned his need for troops for the Parthian campaign and the fact that, in contravention of the Pact of Brundisium, Octavian had been obstructing his efforts to recruit in Italy. Antony knew that he could do little to compel Octavian to comply with the Pact, but he hoped that by helping defeat Sextus he would be able to take over some of his considerable forces and at the same time convince Octavian to loan him further troops.

In an attempt to reassure Octavian, Antony dispatched Octavia from Tarentum on a mission to her brother. She faced a difficult task. Her brother criticized Antony for not waiting for him at Brundisium the previous year, ignoring the fact that he was the one who had failed to keep the rendezvous. He also accused Antony of seeking an alliance with their fellow triumvir, Lepidus, against him. Octavia did her best to soothe Octavian, reassuring him that the only reason Antony and Lepidus had been in touch was to discuss a possible marriage between their children. Plutarch, who admired Octavia as a peacemaker and harmonizer in contrast to the divisive scheming of Cleopatra, claims she pleaded with her brother "not to connive at her downfall from a state of perfect happiness to one of complete misery," for "if matters degenerate and war breaks out [between you], there is no telling which of you is destined to win and which to lose, but in either case my lot will be wretched."

Her eloquence apparently moved Octavian. However, he also knew expedience dictated that now, while Sextus was still a threat, was no time to break with Antony, however much he might have yearned to do so. Therefore he agreed to meet him on the banks of the estuary of the river Taras near Tarentum. With his massive fleet bobbing at anchor, Antony drew up his troops on one side of the river and waited. Octavian arrived late, but Antony, no doubt urged by Octavia, lingered until his brother-in-law at last appeared, with his troops and entourage, including the poets Horace and Vergil, on the other bank. The scene was farcical rather than dignified. Each leader climbed into a small boat and had himself rowed out into midstream. There, under the eyes of all their troops, they debated which of them should cross to the other's side. Eventually, Antony gave way to Octavian's argument that he wished to visit his sister. Symbolically taking no bodyguard with him, Octavian spent that night in Antony's camp and the result was yet another compact—the Treaty of Tarentum.

The treaty provided for the triumvirate, whose formal life span had lapsed at the end of 38, though no one had wished to point out this inconvenient fact, to be renewed for five years, until the end of 33. It formally recorded Antony's support for the war against Sextus. It also provided for Antony immediately to hand over "a hundred bronze-rammed warships" and twenty further vessels to supplement Octavian's navy, in exchange for twenty thousand Italian troops—four legions—to be provided by Octavian at some future date for the Parthian campaign.

Antony was, despite his previous experience, once more taking a great deal on trust. Indeed, Octavian would only supply 10 percent of the troops he had promised and only after a delay of two years. Perhaps Octavia suspected something of this, which was why she coaxed her brother into giving her husband a thousand picked men immediately in return for an additional ten ships. The pact was sealed by the betrothal of Antony's son by Fulvia, the nine-year-old Antyllus, to Octavian's two-year-old daughter, Julia. Coins depicting the conjoined heads of Antony and Octavian and sometimes that of Antony alone facing Octavia were minted to celebrate the peace she had brokered. Such coins as these were a novelty for Rome, but not in the Hellenic world, where Isis and Serapis, as well as kings and queens, were often depicted thus, particularly when the aim was to emphasize the harmony between them.

Given what was about to happen, Octavia's intervention may also have been prompted by fears for her marriage. In the autumn of 37, she and Antony sailed once more for the east, but at Corcyra (Corfu) her husband ordered her to return to her brother in Italy. The excuse he gave was that this would be safer for her, their daughter and their unborn child than accompanying him on his Parthian campaign. Octavia dutifully obeyed and returned first to Athens and then back to Rome.

Though Antony's action in sending her home was not unusual—Roman commanders on campaign routinely left their wives behind—it was telling that he waited until Corfu. Antony might have hoped his marriage to Octavia would protect him from Octavian's neurotic suspicions and expedient and disrespectful disregard of promises, and perhaps he blamed her for them. Or perhaps he was growing preoccupied with the military challenges ahead and feared distraction. Or perhaps something—or someone—else was to blame. Plutarch had no doubt: "The awful calamity which had been dormant for a long time, his love for Cleopatra, which seemed to have been charmed away and lulled to sleep by better notions, blazed up again with renewed power the nearer he approached Syria."

Before long, Octavia had no further cause to wonder. News reached her and all of Rome that Antony had summoned Cleopatra to Antioch. Their affair had resumed with a passion undiminished, perhaps even heightened, by the years they had spent apart, and Octavia's marriage of barely three years was over in all but name.

PART VI

Gods of the East

CHAPTER 17

Sun and Moon

THE LARGE CITY OF ANTIOCH in northern Syria was a good choice for a military command center. As Antony waited for Cleopatra to join him, he planned the political reordering of the east that was an essential precursor of his campaign against Parthia. The eastern Mediterranean and Asia Minor had to be securely under his control before he could safely march out with his legions. Egypt was central to his plans, and Antony's summoning of the mistress he had not seen for nearly four years had at least as much to do with politics as with passion. He had for obvious reasons been unable to summon her to Rome as Caesar had done. Yet on several occasions he had been close enough to have engineered a diversion to Alexandria and still had made no effort to see her—a fact that would not have escaped her. While he could not have doubted that, despite his neglect, Cleopatra was still his political ally, like any man who extracts himself from a highly charged, sexually engrossing extramarital affair, he must have felt a certain awkwardness about the coming reunion and the reactions of his former lover.

Unlike Cleopatra's tardy, teasing response to Antony's summons to Tarsus in 41, this time she responded quickly. Antony's abandonment of her had not made the thirty-three-year-old queen either bitter or unduly sentimental. Even if she longed for his return to share her bed and support her in her lonely autocratic role, she was wise enough to know that his reason for wishing to see her that winter was above all strategic. She could also reflect that she was in a different league from the other regional rulers whom he was wooing. She was no parvenu adventurer or grateful princeling but the descendant of an ancient line. Her kingdom—rich, stable and with a long and proven history of loyalty to Rome—was easily the most important to Antony's plans. If she was clever, she could drive a hard bargain politically.

On the personal level, Cleopatra knew that she and Antony were compatible. She had charm, intelligence and charisma and she also had some emotional ammunition. Octavia had given Antony a daughter but she had borne him a son. Though she easily could have chosen to leave them behind, she disembarked at Antioch with the young twins, Alexander and Cleopatra, whom Antony had never seen. Between three and four years old, they would have been an appealing sight and an effective reminder of the bonds that had once bound the Inimitable Livers.

Whether sentiment, lust or political expedience was the prime catalyst, Cleopatra and Antony very quickly resumed their affair. On Antony's side, the speed and completeness with which he returned to Cleopatra's arms suggest that he had reached a watershed. He was yielding with relief, indeed relish, to a life that suited him far better than that of Rome. He was once again the "new Dionysus" with, as his consort, no demure Roman matron but the powerful queen of the east.

Antony himself now added to the Egyptian queen's powers. Within a few weeks—probably by the close of 37—Cleopatra had coaxed enormous concessions from her once more fervent lover. In the Levant, Antony gave her a string of wealthy coastal cities along the Syrian coast, where only the ports of Tyre and Sidon remained independent. Further inland, Cleopatra acquired the kingdom of Ituraea, whose ruler Antony had executed for colluding with the Parthians. South of Ituraea, Cleopatra took control of some of the Decapolis—meaning "ten cities"—along what is today the border between Israel and Jordan. Along the southeastern coast of Asia Minor, Cleopatra gained territories in Cilicia, including two important harbor towns.

Cleopatra also wanted lands in Judaea that were key to the trade route between Syria and the Persian Gulf, which was a potential rival to Egypt's lucrative trading links via the Nile and the Red Sea. Herod had only recently regained his kingdom when, thanks to Sosius, he had finally defeated Antigonus and taken Jerusalem. Sosius had dispatched Antigonus in chains to Antony, who had had him executed. Herod, meanwhile, had preserved the city and its temple from looting by buying off the Roman soldiery with lavish bribes. Perhaps Cleopatra felt that now was a good time to target Herod, still shakily establishing himself and loathed by many of the Hasmonaean faction.

However, on this Antony dug in his heels. Just as Cleopatra had feared when she learned that the Senate had agreed to make Herod its king, a strong, independent Judaea was integral to Antony's strategy and he refused to deliver the kingdom up to her. It was not in her nature to give up, though. So relentless were her claims that Antony sought to appease her by forcing Herod to renounce most of his coastline so that the only port left to him was Gaza. This gave Cleopatra almost the entire seaboard from Egypt to the far north of modern Lebanon. Antony also made Herod hand over his valuable plantations of date palms and balsam near Jericho, some fifteen miles from Jerusalem. Herod's palm groves—nicknamed "hangover palms" for the potency of the wine pressed from the luscious dates—were the finest in the ancient world, while his two balsam groves produced the so-called balm of Gilead, sold at enormous profit for both perfume and medicine. Cleopatra allowed Herod to lease back his groves, but only in return for an immense annual rent.

Finally, Cleopatra made gains at the expense of Malchus, king of the Nabataean Arabs, whose lands ran south along the Red Sea and southwestward to the Gulf of Aqaba and the Sinai Peninsula and included the stronghold of Petra.* In particular, she acquired territory on the southern end of the Dead Sea, where the Nabataeans harvested the bitumen or asphalt that collected on the surface of the salty water and had a variety of profitable uses, from mortar and medicine to insecticides and embalming dead bodies. As with Herod's date palms and balsam, Cleopatra was happy to lease the bitumen deposits back to the original owners. To placate the dangerous and covetous queen, and also to give himself scope to interfere in the affairs of his Arab neighbors, Herod offered to gather the moneys on the Egyptian queen's behalf—an offer she gladly accepted. Not only was this an effortless way of collecting revenue, but there was a good chance that Herod and the Nabataean king might fall out over it, which could only be to her advantage.

Herod's concessions to Cleopatra did not lessen her antipathy to him as a rival influence on Antony nor her wish to erode his state. Indeed, she soon

---

*Meaning "rock" in Greek, Petra was an apt name for the rose-red city carved into rock and entered by a narrow defile.

revealed her continuing hostility by intervening in Judaean affairs. In the spring of 37, shortly before the capture of Jerusalem, Herod had married the beautiful, highly strung Mariamme, a princess of the Hasmonaean (Maccabee) dynasty he had replaced. The Hasmonaeans, as descendants of an ancient priestly line, had combined the role of ruler with the important post of high priest. Hyrcanus, Mariamme's grandfather, had been high priest until the usurping Antigonus had deposed him and, according to Josephus, savagely "cut off Hyrcanus's ears" to prevent him ever holding the office again, since the law required high priests to be "complete and without blemish." The Parthians had subsequently released Hyrcanus, who had returned to Judaea but could not of course resume his duties. Herod, as an Idumaean with no venerable priestly forebears, lacked the necessary pedigree for the post, leaving Mariamme's sixteen-year-old brother, Aristobolus, apparently as beautiful as his sister, as the obvious choice. Herod, however, feared giving his brother-in-law so much influence and, citing his young years as an excuse, appointed another man.

This gave Cleopatra her opportunity. The mother of Aristobolus and Mariamme, Alexandra, who was Hyrcanus' daughter, was a longtime friend of Cleopatra's. Angered by Herod's treatment of her son, in late 37 this forceful and formidable woman entrusted a message pleading for help to a musician, who duly carried it to Cleopatra in Antioch. She in turn interceded with Antony, who ordered Herod to depose his candidate and appoint Aristobolus in his place. Herod had no choice but to obey.

Despite the irritant of Judaea, Cleopatra must have been delighted by the extent of Antony's gifts, which far exceeded his concessions when, four years earlier, she had sailed upriver to Tarsus in her gilded barge. Antony had, in Plutarch's words, presented her "with no slight or trivial addition to her possessions." The net effect of his new concessions was almost completely to restore the great Egyptian empire of the early Ptolemies. Papyrus records and coins minted around this time in Syria reveal that an exultant Cleopatra recalculated the start of her joint rule with Caesarion to begin in the year 37–36 as if everything before this had been a mere overture.

Antony's acknowledgement of their children was another bonus for Cleopatra. At Antioch the twins were honored with highly symbolic additional names. The little boy was named Alexander Helios and the girl Cleopatra Selene. In Greek eyes, Helios the sun and Selene the moon were themselves twins and close associates of Victory. In the Greek world, people associated the sun with the dawning of a golden age when east and west would dwell in harmony, and Romans too ascribed a special significance to it, as shown in Vergil's Fourth Eclogue. After his victory at Philippi in 42, Antony had issued coins bearing the image of a blazing sun. Now, to mark the designation of his young son Alexander as Helios, Antony ordered fresh coins depicting the glory of the sun's rays, as if he and Cleopatra were about to usher in a shining new age. The golden child who would heal the world would be their son, not any future son of Antony and Octavia's, as Vergil had perhaps been suggesting. The choice of "moon" for little Cleopatra implied that, like her mother, she was an earthly representation of Isis, goddess of the moon. The imagery was also a studied swipe at Parthia, whose king claimed the title "Brother of the Sun and Moon." By appropriating the names, Antony was showing his contempt for the pretensions of his enemy.

Cleopatra awarded herself a new title in celebration of her new lands. The Syrian cities of which she was now overlord hailed her as Thea Neotera or "Youngest Goddess," another reminder that she was Isis incarnate, divine mother, ever youthful, ever giving. Silver coins minted in Antioch around this time portray her as strong-jawed, hawk-nosed, powerful in an almost masculine sense, and her image was complemented on the other side of the coin by an equally commanding depiction of Antony. The message was clear: this was an alliance almost of equals in which the military might of Rome would be bolstered by Egyptian wealth.

Opinion in Rome was, predictably enough, outraged. Some of Cleopatra's new possessions had previously been administered by Rome, so Antony was effectively handing Roman territory to Egypt. Plutarch believed that

> what was particularly infuriating about the honors he conferred on Cleopatra was the shame of it all. And he only highlighted the scandal by acknowledging the twin children she had borne him whom he . . . surnamed respectively Sun and Moon. But he was good at glossing over disgraces, and so he used to say that the greatness of the Roman empire manifested itself not in what Romans took but in what they gave, and that if one had noble blood it should be spread by begetting heirs from many sovereigns . . . he used to claim that his own ancestor was fathered by Heracles, a man who did not rely on just a single womb for the

continuation of his line, and was not cowed by laws which tried to regulate conception but followed his natural inclinations.

However, after Antioch, Antony became a one-woman man. Not even his critics' propaganda suggested Antony had any other lover than Cleopatra thereafter. But even if, with the benefit of hindsight, Antioch was a tipping point in the relationship between Cleopatra and Antony, when they began to commit their destinies, both personal and political, to each other, Antony's gifts to Cleopatra were not the mindless acts of a man wallowing in sensuality or even in a love deepened and renewed. He had not, as his critics later suggested, lost all self-control and sense of duty—sins unforgivable in Roman eyes. Instead, his actions reflected practical politics. Although, unlike his other major allies, Cleopatra was not expected to provide contingents of soldiers, she had a major role in the forthcoming struggle against Parthia—not only to provide a large proportion of the necessary funds but also to build, equip and man a navy for him. The squadrons Antony had yielded to Octavian under the Treaty of Tarentum had depleted his forces and her help with replacements was essential. Many of Cleopatra's new lands were richly forested with groves of oak and forests of cedar. There would be no shortage of timber for the Egyptian-built fleet that Antony intended should patrol the eastern Mediterranean on his behalf while he was fighting in Parthia.

Antony's expansion of Egypt and bolstering of its resources was also part of his wider strategy. Just as he had been intending before Fulvia and his brother had rebelled against Octavian and disrupted his plans, he still wished to remodel the east into a coherent core of provinces to be directly administered by Rome and protected by a buffer zone of loyal kingdoms. Egypt with her enhanced possessions would, as in the past, enjoy the special status justified by her long and loyal relationship with Rome. Antony intended the other kingdoms to be ruled by Hellenic Asian monarchs of his own choosing. In some cases he selected able men with no dynastic connections with the lands they were to govern and whose loyalty would therefore be to him, such as Amyntas in the central kingdom of Galatia and Polemo in Pontus to the northeast. In addition, Antony awarded Cappadocia, to the southeast, bordering Parthia on the Euphrates, to Archelaus, son of the beautiful Cappadocian princess Glaphyra, with whom Antony had once had an affair. In Judaea, Antony knew he could rely on Herod, who owed his position entirely to Rome.

As Antony negotiated alliances and contributions of troops with Asian rulers, he recognized that success against Parthia would make Rome beyond doubt the most powerful state in the known world and—equally beyond doubt—himself the most powerful Roman, entirely eclipsing Octavian. Crassus would be avenged and his legionary eagles recovered, and the road to India and beyond would lie open to Antony as it had previously only to Alexander.

In working out his campaign strategy, Antony could study the invasion plans Caesar had assembled just before his death while reviewing the lessons of Crassus' catastrophic defeat. He decided that, unlike the unfortunate Crassus, he would not invade Parthia directly from Syria by marching east into the deserts of northern Mesopotamia, where his infantry could be picked off by the more mobile mounted Parthians. Instead, he would attack from the north by circling through the lands of Artavasdes, king of Armenia, whom he had cajoled by force into an alliance. He would then turn down past Lake Van and the towering 16,750-foot-high Mount Ararat into the lands of Parthia's staunch ally Media, whose king was also, confusingly, named Artavasdes, and thence into Parthia. This route would, initially at least, give his troops the protection of more broken and mountainous country less suited to the Parthian horsemen.

Antony also hoped to profit from Parthia's internal problems. The Parthian king Orodes, distraught at the death of his son Pacorus at Roman hands, had named his next son, Phraates, as his heir. Unwilling to wait, Phraates had promptly murdered his father and more than thirty of his brothers and other close relations to take the throne. In the resulting chaos, a group of important Parthian noblemen had defected to Antony, including Monaeses, governor-general of Parthia's western frontier. Antony rewarded him with a substantial stretch of land in Roman Syria. All seemed to augur well for a successful campaign.

After ordering Canidius Crassus, his most senior and able general, to begin further preparatory campaigns in the Caucasus, Antony left Antioch with Cleopatra and some of his legions in the spring of 36. However, by the time they reached Zeugma on the Euphrates, Cleopatra had discovered that she was again pregnant. No doubt reluctantly, the queen, who numbered both Parthian and Median among the many languages she spoke, accepted Antony's instruction to return home. She would have much preferred to accompany the momentous expedition, participating as an allied leader and sharing in the spoils, in much the same way as her ancestor Ptolemy had accompanied Alexander. She would also have wanted to remain by Antony's side to keep herself and not Octavia in the forefront of his mind and affections and to ensure that when the campaign ended he returned to his family in Alexandria—not to the one in Rome.

Antony and his legions marched northeast up the Euphrates to Carona (modern Ezerum), where he rendezvoused with Canidius Crassus and the troops of his allies. Antony's army comprised sixty thousand Roman legionaries, ten thousand cavalry from Roman Spain and Gaul and an allied contingent of some thirty thousand, among whom the largest component, nearly half, was supplied and led by Antony's new ally, Artavasdes of Armenia. To satisfy the logistical needs of such an army in hostile territory, Antony had also procured a large supply convoy. Knowing that there was little good timber available on his chosen route to fabricate them, he assembled in advance a strong siege train of battering rams, catapults and other heavy equipment to assault the fortified towns of Media and Parthia. The battering rams were iron-capped tree trunks that swung on iron chains from large frames and could be propelled by brute manpower into the masonry and gates of enemy towns. Plutarch, who is said to have used for this part of his history a lost account of the campaign by Dellius, one of Antony's leading generals and the man who had summoned Cleopatra to Tarsus, wrote that one of the battering rams was as long as eighty feet and that the whole siege train needed three hundred wagons to transport it.

Midsummer had passed before Antony led his army out from Ezerum, rumor of whose size and magnificence had already, according to Plutarch, terrified even the Indians living beyond Bactria and made the whole of Asia tremble. Antony's first objective was to capture the Median capital of Phraaspa, possibly for use as a winter base from which he could launch his final assault on Parthia the following spring, once the cold and snow had departed.* However, like many Roman generals before and after operating outside lands they knew well, Antony seems to have taken insufficient account of the terrain he would en-

---

*The Medes are generally regarded as the ancestors of today's Kurdish people. The location of Phraaspa is a matter of some academic dispute. The generally accepted suggestion is Qaleh-i-Zobak, now in northwest Iran.

counter and the vast distances he would have to cover. He miscalculated how long it would take to get to Phraaspa and in particular how cumbersome and slow his extensive siege train would prove to be over the upland country. Impatient to make progress, Antony took a fatal decision to divide his forces. He himself led the major body forward more quickly, leaving the siege train to follow at its own pace under the protection of two understrength legions commanded by the general Statinius and a contingent of troops from Pontus led by their newly appointed king, Polemo.

When Antony's main body of men arrived beneath the walls of Phraaspa, the city refused to surrender, and Antony, bereft of his siege equipment, was compelled to set his men to constructing a great earth rampart by the wall from which they could fire down into the city. In the meantime, Phraates, the Parthian ruler, had heard that Antony had left his siege train to follow behind and immediately ordered a force of fifty thousand mounted archers to encircle and attack it. They were led by Monaeses, whose allegiance to Antony had proved short-lived and probably had been a deceptive ruse from the start. The Parthians were using compound bows that could outdistance the simpler Roman bows and gave their arrows such velocity that they could penetrate the legionaries' armor. Deprived of any ability to maneuver to confront their enemy by the need to protect their lumbering, heavy equipment, Antony's forces were soon overwhelmed. Statinius was killed, Polemo and many others were captured, the siege equipment was burned, and the Parthians acquired more Roman standards. Antony's reluctant ally, the Armenian king Artavasdes, gave up on the Roman cause at this point, according to Plutarch, and decamped back to Armenia, taking all his men with him, further damaging the morale of Antony's remaining forces, who, with his desertion, perhaps already numbered scarcely more than three quarters of those who had set out.

No sooner had Artavasdes departed than the Parthians themselves appeared at Phraaspa "flushed with their success" and taunting the Romans as they galloped around their position. Antony, strong in a crisis, decided that to leave his men inactive would only further damage their morale and so he took out a strong force, including all his remaining cavalry, ostensibly on a foraging expedition but in fact in a bid to entice the Parthians into a pitched battle. As usual, the Parthians kept their distance, firing arrows from the safety of their saddles as they circled the Roman columns. Suddenly Antony gave the order for his own cavalry to charge. Yelling and screaming, they plunged into the

Parthian ranks before they could disperse and were soon followed into the heaving mêlée by Antony's battle-hardened legionaries. The shock of their combined assault unnerved the Parthians and put them to flight. Antony sent his men in pursuit but did not succeed in inflicting serious casualties or taking many prisoners.

Almost as soon as he returned to Phraaspa and the siege, the Parthian horsemen were back, again harassing his camp and relentlessly firing their arrows from a distance. Next, a sortie by the Medes from their city panicked the Roman legionaries on the artificial mound Antony had ordered to be built overlooking the wall. They fled ignominiously back to the main camp. Determined to maintain discipline, Antony inflicted decimation on those who fled, dividing them into groups of ten and then executing one of their number chosen by lot.*

As the siege wore on, the circling Parthian horsemen began to shout overtures for a truce. Fearing the onset of winter, Antony agreed to negotiations.† His starting demand was for the return of Roman eagles and any surviving prisoners lost at Carrhae and elsewhere. However, Phraates refused this concession and Antony had to content himself with the promise of safe passage out of the country. The Parthians did not even keep this promise and harried the retreating Roman columns constantly.

Antony once more showed his great courage and leadership in adversity. Rallying his men, he insisted that they keep in formation, with the infantry marching in hollow squares protected by javelin throwers and slingers and, beyond that, by a screen of cavalry who were instructed to keep close order and not to be enticed into pursuing apparently fleeing Parthian horsemen. Plutarch records how Antony won the loyalty of his men:

> All whatever their rank or fame would have sacrificed their lives for Antony. They surpassed the behavior of ancient Romans. Among the many reasons for this were Antony's high birth, his eloquence, his straightforward manner, his prodigious generosity, his sense of humor and his geniality. By the

---

**Decim* is the Latin word for "ten."

†Winter is both harsh—temperatures can fall below −22° Fahrenheit (−30° Celsius) and also starts early (late October) in these uplands.

way he shared in the distress and difficulties of the ill and the unfortunate, granting them as best he could whatever they wanted, he made even the wounded and the sick as eager to serve him as those who were well and strong.

Despite all their bravery, Antony's men still suffered heavy losses on their retreat along a shorter and even more mountainous route shown to them by a local guide. However, their discipline endured. On one occasion they saved themselves and their comrades by forming the famous Roman *testudo* (tortoise) formation for protection as they descended one of the jagged, barren and steep hills common in the area with the Parthians firing down on them from above. Plutarch described how:

> The Roman shield-bearers wheeled around and enclosed the lightly armored troops within their ranks, dropping down on one knee and holding out their shields as a defensive barrier. The men behind then held their shields over the heads of the first rank while the third rank did the same for the second rank. The resulting shape looks very like a roof and is the surest protection against arrows, which merely glanced off it. The Parthians however mistook the Romans falling on to one knee as a sign of exhaustion and so dropped their bows, grabbed their javelins and rushed to join battle at close quarters. But the Romans suddenly leapt to their feet roaring their battle cry and lunged forward with their spears, killing the front ranks of the Parthians and putting all the rest to flight.

Nevertheless, starvation weakened the men, who turned to eating roots, some of which proved so poisonous as to provoke diarrhea, vomiting, delirium and then death. Only once on their harrowing twenty-seven-day retreat, as they neared one of the final barriers to their crossing back into Armenia, the river Araxes, did their discipline fail. Antony had ordered a night march to avoid a Parthian assault of which he had been warned. During the march the Romans seem to have given way to panic. Perhaps unsettled at some rumor of attack, they lost all cohesion and floundered in the dark, turning violently on one another, plundering their own baggage wagons and even stealing Antony's drinking vessels. Antony contemplated the necessity for suicide, summoning one of his bodyguards and making him swear that on his command he would run him through "and cut off his head to prevent the enemy capturing him alive or recognizing him in death."

However, rising, as usual, to a practical crisis, Antony mastered any despair he felt and took the sensible decision to halt the march and make camp. This eventually led to the restoration of order and calm. The feel of the cool breeze from the river on their cheeks reassured the troops of its proximity. The next day, once more in good order, they crossed. The watching Parthian horsemen made a show of unstringing their bows—a sign that they would pursue them no further.

Once back in Armenia, Antony reviewed the ragged ranks of his troops to find that, in addition to the desertion of all Artavasdes' contingent, he had lost some twenty-five thousand men, half through illness and disease. Much as he and his men might have wanted to, Antony was in no position to punish the Armenian king for his desertion but had to be friendly toward him to secure rations and safe passage.

As soon as he could, Antony seems to have sent a message to Cleopatra asking her to join him and to bring supplies before ordering his legions to continue their retreat back through Syria to the Mediterranean coast. It was deep, cold winter and there were incessant snowstorms, and eight thousand more of his men fell on the march. When Antony finally completed his retreat from Phraaspa, which modern historians have likened to Napoleon's 1812 retreat from Moscow, he had showed great leadership but, just like Napoleon, had sacrificed his best troops and lost his best chance for world domination.

Also like Napoleon, once certain his troops were safe from further attack, Antony himself had hurried ahead to assess the consequences of failure and plan for the future. He arrived at the small port of Leuke Come (White Village), on the Syrian coast, to which he had summoned Cleopatra. However, released from the day-to-day rigors of command, he seems to have collapsed, losing his resolution and wandering around aimlessly longing for Cleopatra's arrival. Plutarch wrote: "He missed her terribly . . . Before long he devoted his time to drinking himself into a stupor, although he could not recline at the table for long before leaping to his feet in the middle of a drinking session to go to look for Cleopatra's coming."

Plutarch was wrong in ascribing Antony's distress solely to an overwhelming desire to be reunited with Cleopatra, which, he alleged, had also led him, "as if he had been drugged or bewitched," to rush the Parthian campaign.

However, Antony no doubt yearned for her arrival, not only for the fresh resources she would bring and the strategic advice her astute brain could provide, but also for her emotional consolation and support at a time when his grand ambitions had been shattered.

He was even more in need of her comfort and reassurance when news reached him that while he had been retreating in defeat and despair, Octavian had finally succeeded in crushing Sextus Pompey. After a series of humiliating naval defeats earlier that year that had left Octavian almost suicidally depressed, on September 3, 36, his navy, trained and led by Agrippa, had vanquished Sextus at the battle of Naulochus off the Sicilian coast. Sextus had fled to Asia Minor and Octavian was enjoying the prestige of military success that had so long eluded him.

Octavian had also used the situation, without any consultation with Antony, to get rid of Lepidus. He had summoned the triumvir and his legions from Africa to assist in the assault on Sextus. Lepidus had invaded Sicily from the west and, following Sextus' defeat at sea, had pushed eastward to take and sack Messina. By this point, eight of Sextus' legions had surrendered to him. With a combined force of twenty-two legions, Lepidus, so long kept on the margins by Octavian and Antony, made an ill-judged attempt to claim Sicily for himself. Octavian's response was to enter his camp with only a handful of men, whereupon Lepidus' legionaries at once went over to him. A contemptuous Octavian spared the groveling Lepidus his life but dismissed him from the triumvirate, took over his fertile, corn-producing province of Africa and sent him into ignoble exile in a seaside resort south of Rome. It was an ominous clearing of the decks.

CHAPTER 18

"Theatrical, Overdone and Anti-Roman"

SINCE PARTING FROM ANTONY on the banks of the Euphrates, Cleopatra's journey back to Alexandria had not been uneventful. After enjoying a stately progress through some of her recently acquired new territories, she had decided to visit Herod in Judaea. Though the niceties were doubtless preserved on the surface, he must have loathed the arrival of the woman who had stripped him of his profitable groves of balsam and date palms. He must also have suspected her motives. Josephus alleged that during her stay in the Antonia palace in Jerusalem, the Egyptian queen tried to seduce Herod, for reasons either sexual or political. Basing his accusations on Herod's own memoirs, recorded by Nicolaus (a scholar from Damascus who, at the time of Cleopatra's visit to Herod, was tutor to her children but who later became Herod's adviser and supporter), Josephus described her visit:

> When she was there, and was very often with Herod, she endeavored to have criminal conversation with the king: nor did she affect secrecy in the indulgence of each sort of pleasures; and perhaps she had in some measure a passion of love to him, or rather, what is most probable, she laid a treacherous snare for him, by aiming to obtain such adulterous conversation from him.

Josephus continued that Herod

> had a great while borne no good will to Cleopatra, knowing that she was a woman irksome to all; and at that time he thought her particularly worthy of his hatred, if this attempt proceeded out of lust . . . and called a council of his friends to consult with them whether he should not kill her, now he had her in his power . . . and that this very thing would be much for the advantage of Antony himself since she would certainly not be faithful to him.

His friends, Josephus claims, dissuaded him from such a rash and bloody act on the grounds that Antony would never forgive him, though it would be for his own good. Instead, Herod "treated Cleopatra kindly, and made her presents, and conducted her on her way to Egypt."

The claims of attempted seduction are puzzling, especially as Cleopatra was pregnant. She had everything to lose and nothing to gain by such a liaison, which could not have been kept secret from Antony. If true, the only credible explanation would be that suggested by Josephus—that she wanted to induce Herod to make an open pass at her, which she could repulse and use to discredit him with Antony. The whole story is probably without foundation. Herod's account in his memoirs of what happened, written long after Cleopatra's visit, was no doubt intended to curry favor with Octavian and to play to the lascivious, devious image of Cleopatra he had created. Cleopatra's motive in traveling to Egypt was perhaps to visit her friend Alexandra, Herod's mother-in-law. She may also have wanted to enjoy a gloat over the concessions she had wrung from Herod. Most likely of all, as a shrewd businesswoman, she wished to check that he was indeed paying her the agreed fees for renting back his plantations from her as well as collecting all the moneys owed her by the Nabataeans for leasing back their bitumen deposits. Cleopatra with an abacus seems far more likely than Cleopatra burning with deceitful ardor. The idea that Herod wanted her dead would have been little surprise to her. Equally certainly, she would have known he would not dare assassinate her.

And so Cleopatra returned safely to her capital, where she duly gave birth to her second son by Antony, whom she named Ptolemy Philadelphus, after the great Ptolemy II, who had become king of Egypt almost exactly 250 years earlier and done so much to secure the future of the dynasty. It was in Alexandria that the message from Antony in Armenia reached her. Though she must have been glad that he had turned to her, she did not respond especially quickly to his summons. She needed time to raise the money and supplies he had requested, and perhaps she also wanted time to think. Her lover's campaign had obviously been a disaster and in her mind, just as in Antony's, must have been the question of how best to retrieve the situation.

In early January 35 Cleopatra arrived at White Village for her rendezvous with the anxious Antony, bringing funds to pay his troops and warm winter clothing. According to Plutarch, rumors spread that she had not brought enough money and that, to save face, her besotted lover was distributing his own cash in her name, but this hardly seems likely. Cleopatra did not lack funds and would not have been so niggardly toward the man on whom her future hopes depended.

Perhaps another of Cleopatra's contributions was to assist Antony first in composing himself and then in preparing dispatches to Rome claiming great success. The basis for his claim was that he had not actually been defeated in any engagement in which he had taken personal command. Octavian, who was not yet ready for an open breach and now had his own victories to boast of, colluded in the fiction. At his urging, the Senate hailed Antony's incursion into Media as a victory and gave thanks to the gods. But Octavian had another motive too. If Antony had indeed been victorious in the east, then he could be expected to raise troops there. There would be no need for him to insist on his right to recruit in Italy. This gave Octavian an excellent justification for continuing to renege on his commitment at Tarentum to send Antony twenty thousand soldiers. Another good excuse was that Octavian himself was about to go to war against the troublesomely aggressive tribes that were attacking along the empire's northeastern frontiers from their mountainous strongholds in Illyricum on the east of the Adriatic. He therefore needed troops himself.

Subtle as he was, Octavian even devised a way of turning Antony's need for support to his own advantage. When he was still in Syria in the spring of 35, Antony heard that Octavia, who the previous year had given birth to their second daughter, had left Rome and was on her way to him with two thousand soldiers, seventy ships, supplies and clothing. It was obvious that, whatever Octavia's personal intentions—and she may well have wanted to take help to her husband—Octavian was cynically using her. Her "mercy mission" not only allowed Octavian to maintain that he was dutifully assisting his fellow triumvir, although the scale of the help was derisory—a mere 10 percent of the men Antony was actually owed and ships that he had neither requested nor needed—but was also a trap. If Antony spurned Octavia, he would lose influence and respect in Rome, while if he received her, it would prejudice his relationship with the wealthy Cleopatra. The snare, though so obviously laid, was difficult for Antony to evade.

This was also a pivotal moment for Cleopatra. Plutarch claimed that she "realized that Octavia was coming to take her on at close quarters" and

> therefore made a great pretence of passionate love for Antony. She allowed her body to waste away on a meagre diet, put on a look of rapture whenever he came near, and when he went away looked melancholy and forlorn. She contrived it so that he often saw her weeping, but then she would quickly wipe away the tears as if she did not want Antony to notice them . . . Flatterers also worked hard on her behalf. They reproached Antony for being so hard-hearted and insensitive that he was destroying the woman who was utterly devoted to him and him alone. They said that although Octavia enjoyed the name of his wife, it was a political marriage, arranged by her brother; Cleopatra, however, a queen with countless subjects, was called Antony's mistress, and yet she did not reject the name or scorn it, as long as she could see him and live with him. But if she were driven away, they said, she would not survive the shock.

Such histrionics seem implausible, not because Cleopatra was not capable of them but because she did not need them. In a sense, Antony had already made his choice when he sent the pregnant Octavia back to Rome and summoned Cleopatra to Antioch. His dependence on Cleopatra and in particular on her practical support was stronger than ever. That was why he had rushed to get messages to her after his defeat in his Parthian campaign. Skilled student of human nature and survivor that she was, Cleopatra must have understood what lay behind Octavian's maneuverings. He was making preparations to attack Antony through his love for her. Without as yet making any direct comment, he was encouraging the populace to see Octavia as the path of Roman virtue to which Antony should return, while she, Cleopatra, was to be seen as an unwholesome influence, seducing Antony from his duty.

But Cleopatra could afford to feel confident in Antony. Apart from his very evident attachment to her, Antony was not a man easily blackmailed. Furthermore, with the whole of the eastern empire under his command and his hopes of a victory over Parthia battered but still alive, he remained a powerful man. Why should he kowtow to his ambitious, mischief-making brother-in-law? Cleopatra's confidence proved well founded when he wrote to Octavia ordering her to send on the troops, ships and supplies but to return to Rome herself. These blunt instructions reached her in Athens, and she obeyed her husband.

As Antony must have known he would, Octavian indeed tried to inflame public feeling against himself and Cleopatra, still not by any public pronouncement but by quietly suggesting to his sister that she leave Antony's house. Octavia, however, refused. According to Plutarch, her behavior bordered on the saintly:

> She even begged Octavian, if it was not too late and he had not already decided for other reasons to go to war with Antony, to make nothing of her situation. After all, she said, it would be terrible if the two greatest commanders in the world plunged Rome into civil war, one because he loved a woman and the other out of protectiveness. And her actions only showed how much she meant these words. She lived in Antony's house as if he were there and cared not only for their children, but also his children by Fulvia.

Yet Plutarch believed, probably correctly, that by so doing she was inadvertently wounding her husband, making him "hated for wronging such a good woman." Octavian further milked the propaganda advantage by declaring Octavia *sacrosanctitas* (inviolable)—the status enjoyed by the Vestal Virgins and the most exalted position a Roman woman could attain.

Cleopatra did not allow Roman politics and posturing to distract her from her personal political objectives. During the early months of 35, she tried to destabilize and further undermine Herod. Her excuse was the murder of Judaea's young and handsome high priest Aristobolus, whom Herod had so reluctantly appointed barely a year earlier. He had drowned during a swimming party in Jericho. Herod claimed the young man's death had been an accident and gave him a magnificent funeral. However, Aristobolus' mother, Alexandra, was convinced that during all the splashing and merriment, strong hands had held her son beneath the water on Herod's orders. She wrote to her friend Cleopatra demanding vengeance and found a willing advocate. Indeed, just a few months earlier Cleopatra had been urging Alexandra and her son to flee to Alexandria. They had tried to smuggle themselves aboard a ship concealed in coffins but at the last moment had been discovered. Their attempted escape had endeared neither son nor mother to Herod, although, fearing Cleopatra's influence with Antony, he had not dared punish them openly.

At Cleopatra's insistence, Antony now summoned Herod to Laodicea in Syria to account to him for the death of Aristobolus. According to Josephus, after hearing Herod's account, Antony did not meet all of Cleopatra's expectations. Instead of punishing Herod, he declared that "it was not good to require an account of a king of his government, for at this rate he could be no king at all; those who had given him authority ought to permit him to use it." Antony did, however, force Herod to give Cleopatra as a "gift" the port of Gaza in Idumaea—a concession that left the Judaean king landlocked and even more resentful of the woman who continued to intrigue against him. Hopeful of obtaining the remainder of Idumaea, Cleopatra tried to prompt a rebellion there against Herod by inciting the governor, Costabarus, to rise. Herod discovered the plot in time but, again afraid of Cleopatra's influence with Antony, did not punish Costabarus or the other rebel leaders.

By the late spring of 35, Antony had left his forces in their winter quarters in Syria and returned with Cleopatra to Alexandria to gather funds and provisions for a renewed assault on Parthia. But before he could concentrate on his Parthian campaign, he faced yet another distraction. After fleeing to Asia Minor the previous autumn following his defeat by Octavian, the ever wily, ambitious and resentful Sextus Pompey had seized a town, raised three legions and, after an unconvincing attempt to ally himself with Antony, begun colluding with the Parthians. Knowing it would be unwise to launch a renewed campaign against Parthia with Sextus on the loose in his rear, Antony dispatched one of his commanders, Titius, with a large force to deal with him. The errant Sextus was finally captured and sent to Titius, who executed him, possibly without Antony's knowledge or consent.

While publicly commending his fellow triumvir for his firm action, Octavian still found a way to discomfit him. He encouraged the Senate not only to honor both him and Antony by erecting their statues in the Forum and the Temple of Concord but also, as Dio Cassius related, to allow them the privilege of being permitted to feast in the temple with their wives and children.

This was a useful device for reminding the Roman populace that while Octavian was married to the patrician Livia, Antony had abandoned his Roman wife, preferring to cavort with an alien queen.

Though he had been absent for four years, Antony was still popular in Rome. Perhaps he considered returning between campaigns to remind his followers there, especially those in the Senate, of his qualities as a commander and of his need to be able to recruit and to settle his veterans in Italy. To avoid any awkwardness with Octavian, he could have timed his visit so that he arrived after his brother-in-law had departed across the Adriatic on his Illyricum campaign. Yet he could hardly have avoided Octavia and their two daughters—one of whom, of course, he had never even seen. Perhaps the potential for personal embarrassment outweighed other, bigger imperatives. Perhaps Antony wished for no further delay in planning his new Parthian campaign. Perhaps Cleopatra, mindful that once before in their relationship Rome had proved a powerful distraction, urged him forcefully not to go. Perhaps he did not wish to leave his lover's side. Whatever the case, he would never see Rome or his fine house on the Palatine again.

The problem of Sextus had made any major campaigning in 35 impracticable. However, events appeared to have fallen neatly in Antony's favor. Artavasdes of Media had quarreled with Phraates of Parthia over the loot seized from Antony's baggage trains. So enraged was Artavasdes that he sent Antony's client and ally King Polemo, whom he had captured during the Parthian campaign, as his envoy to Alexandria, offering Antony his heavy cavalry and mounted archers for a fresh invasion of Parthia. Antony was delighted since, as Plutarch related, he believed that the only thing that had hindered his defeat of the Parthians was that "he had gone there with too few cavalry and archers . . . and so it was in a very confident frame of mind that he began to prepare to return inland through Armenia, rendezvous with the Mede and then go to war."

Antony also made overtures to the other Artavasdes, king of Armenia, by suggesting that the five-year-old Alexander Helios be betrothed to Artavasdes' daughter and inviting the Armenian monarch to visit him in Alexandria. Suspecting a plot to take both himself and his daughter hostage, Artavasdes failed to reply. Antony would later allege that Octavian had secretly persuaded him to refuse his offer.

In the spring of 34, the snubbed Antony set out to conquer Armenia as a prelude to his renewed attack on Parthia. He advanced up to the gates of its capital, Artaxata, sitting below snowy Mount Ararat and not far from the modern-day Armenian capital of Yerevan. Little is known of the campaign except that Antony induced Artavasdes to come to his camp, where he demanded the king surrender his treasuries and his fortresses. Whatever Artavasdes may have wished, his army refused to agree and promptly put his son Artaxes on the throne in his place. The Roman legions quickly crushed the Armenian forces, causing Artaxes to seek sanctuary with the Parthians while Antony sent Artavasdes, bound with chains of silver, with his wife, two younger sons and a large amount of Armenian treasure to Alexandria and annexed Armenia. Leaving the able Canidius Crassus behind to garrison and organize the administration of Armenia into a Roman province and handing some territory to the Median king, whose daughter, Iotape, his only child, it was now agreed would be betrothed to Alexander Helios, Antony set out for Egypt preparatory to renewing his Parthian campaign the following year. He was about to demonstrate dramatically and publicly the strength of his ties to Cleopatra and their children.

In the autumn of 34 Antony rode in triumph into Alexandria. The captive king of Armenia, Artavasdes, weighed down by his silver chains, staggered as best he could before Antony's chariot. Antony himself, in saffron robes, garlanded with ivy beneath a golden crown, wearing long high-heeled boots and brandishing the *thyrsos*—the ivy-wreathed wand tipped with a pine cone that was a symbol of Dionysus—had chosen to present himself to the Egyptians as that deity made flesh rather than as a conquering soldier of Rome. The imagery was of the great god of the east about to meet his goddess. Long lines of marching legionaries followed Antony's chariot along the city's wide, colonnaded streets, together with swaying, wooden-wheeled wagons loaded with booty, including, it is said, at least one solid-gold statue that the Armenians had not been able to hide.*

---

*Armenian histories recount how the local population preserved one large golden statue coveted by Antony to present to Cleopatra by cutting it to pieces and hiding the sections separately.

Cleopatra, "seated in the midst of the populace upon a platform plated with silver and upon a gilded chair," according to Dio Cassius, waited ready to receive Antony's gifts, together with the miserable Artavasdes and his family. Despite "much coercion" and "much ill-treatment," the Armenian refused to prostrate himself before her and, instead of acknowledging her titles and supremacy, addressed her simply by her name. In spite of this defiance, his life and the lives of his family were spared, and they were sent into confinement as prisoners of state.

A few days later, Antony gave the Alexandrians a yet more remarkable and significant spectacle. The setting was one of the city's most splendid buildings, the great Gymnasium, which stood in the center of the city adjoining the agora, the city's meeting place and market. Antony had ordered golden thrones for himself and Cleopatra to be placed upon a silver stage, with smaller thrones at a slightly lower level for their children. Before a packed, expectant crowd, Antony rose to his feet. First, he confirmed Cleopatra as queen of Egypt, Cyprus and her possessions in Syria and decreed that henceforward she would be known as the "Queen of Kings." Next, Antony confirmed the thirteen-year-old Caesarion as joint ruler of Egypt with his mother and awarded him the title "King of Kings." Yet more significantly, Dio Cassius related that Antony proclaimed Cleopatra to have been "in very truth the wife" and Caesarion "the son of the former Caesar"—in other words, Caesarion was Caesar's legitimate son. All the measures he was taking, Antony asserted, were "for Caesar's sake."

Turning to his own children by Cleopatra, Antony announced that the six-year-old Alexander Helios was to be king of Armenia in place of Artavasdes and overlord of Media and all the lands east of the Euphrates "as far as India"—vast territories that, of course, included Parthia. His twin, Cleopatra Selene, received Cyrenaica, while the two-year-old toddler Ptolemy Philadelphus acquired Egyptian possessions in Syria and Cilicia and was appointed overlord of all lands westward from the Euphrates to the Hellespont.

Plutarch related that while making this announcement, Antony "brought his sons forward for all to see," impressively attired in the garb of their new lands. Alexander was kitted out in Median clothes with, on his young head, the regal tiara—a turban-like cap topped with a waving peacock's feather. Ptolemy was dressed like a tiny Macedonian king, in military boots, purple cavalryman's cloak, a woolen or goat-hair Macedonian bonnet and a royal diadem. This was, as Plutarch noted, the style of dress "adopted by all the kings since Alexander the Great." After the no doubt somewhat shy and puzzled small children had formally saluted their parents, as they left the stage Alexander was given a guard of honor in Armenian dress and Ptolemy one of soldiers in Macedonian costume.

Cleopatra clearly gave careful thought to her own appearance at this great moment in her life. Plutarch described how she appeared before her people as Isis incarnate. Of the many faces of the goddess, Cleopatra was probably on this occasion evoking the image of Isis the great mother, in recognition of the honors lavished on her children. She may also have been wearing the grand headdress, the triple uraeus, in which three hooded cobras reared from the headband above her forehead and which, as statues of the period reveal, she had adopted as her personal insignia. A double uraeus—two rearing cobras—had long signified the Egyptian monarch's rule over Upper and Lower Egypt. Cleopatra's bold adoption of a third serpent could have been used by her to signify various things at various stages of her reign—for example, to mark her acquisition of lands once ruled by the rival Seleucid dynasty. Now it could have taken on an additional significance, recognizing her rule over her three sons as "Queen of Kings."

The glamour and glitz of the Donations of Alexandria—as the ceremony came to be known—were signs that the balance in the partnership between the couple had swung yet further Cleopatra's way. Antony's failure in Parthia had badly damaged his hopes of becoming the Roman Alexander. Despite his modest triumph in Armenia, events had left him increasingly dependent on Cleopatra and thus increasingly sympathetic to her Hellenic concept of monarchy. The ceremony of the Donations was to her benefit rather than Antony's and can only have been at her prompting as a demonstration of their personal and political commitment.

In practice, the Donations were more form than substance, making little difference to how the various territories would be administered. Many of the lands so portentously conferred on her and her children by Antony already belonged to Cleopatra. Of the remainder, Alexander Helios' hopes of actually governing Media depended on his future father-in-law, the current king of Media, while Armenia was, in fact, under the firm governance of Roman legions and Parthia had yet to be conquered. Of Alexander's other acquisitions as overlord many, like those of his younger brother, Ptolemy Philadelphus, already had rulers, some of whom were Antony's clients and could not be expected to be delighted at this turn of events.

The political importance of the Donations to Cleopatra was the potent underlying message conveyed to her people and those of the neighboring lands. Antony was establishing a new hierarchy of power in the east. Until then, client kings such as Amyntas, Polemo, Herod and others had given him their allegiance direct, not in his own right but as the representative of Rome. By making Alexander Helios and Ptolemy Philadelphus their overlords he was implying that the client kings would owe their loyalty first to Cleopatra, the "Queen of Kings," and only thence to distant Rome. Furthermore, by declaring Alexander Helios overlord of Parthia, Antony was indicating that, when the war of conquest in due course resumed, Parthia too would be subject first to Hellenized Egypt and then to Rome. Cleopatra could present herself and her kingdom as being exalted to a status only a little beneath that of Rome itself.

Another important subtext of the Donations of Alexandria concerned Caesarion. Antony's confirmation of him as co-ruler of the Egyptian empire with his mother was, of course, no surprise. Cleopatra had marked him out from birth as heir to the Ptolemaic empire, ensuring that his image was prominently displayed to her Egyptian subjects.*

The truly satisfying part of Antony's pronouncements about Caesarion for Cleopatra was therefore his public reaffirmation of the boy as Caesar's legitimate son. This was a direct challenge to Octavian. Caesarion was, as everyone knew, not legitimate in any conventional sense—Caesar had been married to Calpurnia at the time of his birth and Roman law did not countenance bigamy. Even had Caesar not been married, Roman law did not recognize the marriage of any Roman citizen, even those as powerful as Caesar or Antony himself, to a foreigner. The children of all such unions were illegitimate and could not inherit. This was rather different from the situation in the Egyptian royal family, where there were several precedents for illegitimate offspring to inherit the throne, particularly in the absence of any legitimate heir. But, encouraged by Cleopatra, Antony was brushing this aside, perhaps on the basis that the union

---

*At the entrance to the great Temple of Horus at Edfu, one of a pair of large black granite falcons stands protectively over a young prince believed to be Caesarion between the ages of eight and eleven.

between Caesar and Cleopatra had been a union of gods and therefore above such banalities as marriage ceremonies. In the words of Dio Cassius, Antony wished to remind the world that Octavian "was only an adopted and not a real son" of Julius Caesar and that Caesarion had a better claim on the loyalties of Caesar's Roman followers. Antony also may have wished to suggest a similar type of legitimacy for his own children by Cleopatra.

The silver coins issued by Antony to mark his Armenian victory and the Donations of Alexandria and depicting both himself and Cleopatra, one on each side, mark her ascendancy. Though she is somewhat unflatteringly portrayed, with thin lips, a long and beaky nose, a sharp chin and a slight frown, this was perhaps not the point. The stark image conveyed an uncompromising power and authority. The encircling description, "To Cleopatra, queen of kings and her sons who are kings," proclaims her newly acquired status. It was an unprecedented honor. Until this time, only two other women had been represented on Roman coins—both Roman and both Antony's wives, Fulvia and Octavia. While this shows Antony's unusual and disarming propensity to admit and, indeed, celebrate his consorts' important place in his political life, neither woman had been named. Conversely, the coin records no new honors or titles for Antony—the only member of the "family" whose status remained unchanged, formally at least, at the Donations of Alexandria. Though atop the new power structure he had created, he remained a triumvir of Rome. The simple inscription running around his forceful profile reads simply, "Antony, after the conquest of Armenia."

To Octavian in Rome, however, the situation must have appeared menacing. He suspected Antony of intending to lay claim to the empire in the west through Caesarion and to a vast empire in the east through Cleopatra and their children, with himself as supreme overlord. But Octavian's own position had meanwhile been strengthening. His campaigns in Illyricum had been successful—he had subdued the tribes that had been energetically raiding northern Italy and plundering along the eastern shores of the Adriatic, seized their strongholds and thus secured the northeast approaches to Italy. These victories allowed him to demonstrate that he as well as Antony was capable of defeating foreigners. He had also shown his personal willingness to fight. A stone missile that struck him on the knee and crippled him for several days made useful propaganda for him. In addition, the Illyricum campaigns had allowed him to train and battle-harden an army, ready for whatever new demands he might make of it.

And now his rival had played right into his hands. The news of Antony's Armenian celebrations had caused considerable resentment in Rome. According to Plutarch, what Romans found "particularly offensive" was that, to please his mistress, "he gratified the Egyptians with the noble and solemn ceremonies proper to his homeland," rather than dedicating the spoils of war to Jupiter in his temple on the Capitol in Rome. On a less lofty level, Antony had denied his fellow citizens the revels and feasting that were a traditional part of a Roman Triumph, giving the sweets of victory instead to the Alexandrians. Then, within days, Antony had compounded his sins by mounting what Plutarch called the "theatrical, overdone and anti-Roman" Donations of Alexandria, scattering Roman possessions among his mistress and children as if such decisions were matters of little consequence about which he need only follow the whims of Cleopatra and not consult the Senate and people of Rome. What better proof did Octavian need to maintain that Antony had "gone native"—a situation no decent Roman should tolerate?

CHAPTER 19

"A Woman of Egypt"

ON JANUARY 1, 33, Octavian rebuked Antony openly in public for the first time. To do so he used the customary New Year debate in the Senate about the state of the republic. Speaking, as he invariably did, from a prepared text, "to avoid either his memory betraying him or wasting his time in learning the speech," on this occasion he restricted himself to savaging Antony's management of affairs in the east. However, building on the groundwork he had previously subtly laid, he soon broadened his propaganda offensive to encompass Antony's character, his treatment of Octavia and, in particular, his alleged subservience to Cleopatra and its disastrous consequences for Rome.

Parts of Antony's reply have been preserved. In response to Octavian's claims about his relationship with Cleopatra he wrote, "What has changed for you? Is it because I have sex with the queen? Is she my wife? Do you think it a new affair? Didn't I start it nine years ago?" Detecting a whiff of hypocrisy, he went on, "Do you only sleep with Livia? I congratulate you if when you read this letter you haven't fucked Tertulla or Terentilla or Ruffila or Salvia Titisenia. What does it matter where I stuff my erection?" As for a charge by Octavian that he had falsely recognized Caesarion as Caesar's son, he dismissed it with the simple comment that Caesar himself had done so.

Turning to more weighty political matters, Antony reproached Octavian for his failure, after his success against Sextus Pompey, to keep his promise to return the ships he had borrowed from Antony and for his broken commitment to send Antony twenty thousand troops for his Parthian and Armenian campaigns. Very belatedly he complained that Octavian had deposed Lepidus without consultation and had expropriated all his territories for himself. He had also failed to make proper provision for Antony's veterans in Italy. Antony therefore claimed half of all the territories and revenue Octavian had seized and demanded that half the troops Octavian had recently recruited be sent to him in the east. His remonstrations dispatched, Antony returned to Armenia, where he still had hopes of resurrecting his campaign against the Parthians.

Octavian's reply was brisk and to the point. Antony could have half of Octavian's conquests when Antony gave him half of Armenia. Lepidus had been justly deposed. As for Antony's complaints about his veterans, they were entirely unjustified. Surely, Octavian suggested disingenuously, Antony could settle them in Parthia and Media, which he had so recently conquered?

Each man continued to sling accusations at the other. Many centuries before the phrase "*qui s'excuse s'accuse*" was coined, Antony wrote a whole pamphlet to refute allegations of his drunkenness, while Octavian likewise commissioned one to explain why Caesar could not be the father of Caesarion and hence, in the eyes of some, the proper heir to Caesar. (Disappointingly, both documents are now lost.) Perhaps concerned about the impression that reports about the self-indulgence of the Club of the Inimitables had made, Antony alleged that Octavian, dressed as a god like all the other participants, had presided "at a feast of the divine twelve" remarkable not only for debauchery but also for gluttony. All this had taken place at a time of food shortage—presumably during Sextus' maritime blockade of Italy—which led the Roman population to shout the next day, "The gods have gobbled all the grain."

Antony went on to pillory Octavian's sexual appetites. He and his supporters revived earlier allegations that as a youth Octavian had allowed Caesar to sodomize him. They claimed that nowadays, despite Octavian's buttoned-up public persona, his friends pimped for him, behaving "like the slave dealer Toransius in arranging his amusements. They would strip married women and mature girls naked and inspect them as if they were for sale." Antony also reminded everyone of the scandal of Octavian's overhasty betrothal to Livia while she was heavily pregnant with her former husband's child and recounted another story of how Octavian had hauled an ex-consul's wife from her dining room into the bedroom before her husband's eyes, subsequently returning her blushing and disheveled. Switching his attack, Antony accused Octavian of cowardice at Philippi and elsewhere, alleging that it was Agrippa who had beaten Sextus and the pirates while Octavian lay petrified on the deck, not even capable of giving the order to engage.

By the late summer of 33, with conflict seeming increasingly probable, Antony ordered his senior general, Canidius Crassus, to curtail his preparations for further campaigns against Parthia and to bring his sixteen legions to Antony's new winter base near Ephesus. Here Cleopatra joined him, bringing with her money, two hundred ships and other resources to bolster his forces. Antony yet again showered his ally and lover with presents, including the contents of the library at Pergamon and many other looted works of art, all designed to beautify Alexandria.

Despite his prolonged absence from Rome, Antony still had a numerous and loyal band of supporters there, some of whom were former staunch republicans, others allies of many years' standing. Two of them, Enobarbus and Sosius, were due to become consuls for 32. With an eye to their winning further support for him in the Senate, Antony wrote to them a full justification of his actions in the east, including the Donations of Alexandria. Just like Pompey so many years earlier, he asked that the Senate formally ratify them. He also clearly stated that he would lay down his triumviral powers if Octavian did so too. It is a measure of just how badly Rome had received the news of the Donations that even the two consuls, supporters of Antony as they were, decided not to publish the justification Antony had given for them or to seek their ratification.

However, in February 32, Sosius addressed the Senate in favor of Antony while attacking Octavian virulently. Octavian, who had wisely absented himself from Rome at the time of Sosius' speech, soon returned with his troops and entered the Senate, showing his now customary disregard for senatorial traditions and contempt for its current membership. He came not alone but with a large and threatening group of bodyguards and a coterie of allies all concealing weapons beneath their clothing. Interrupting the day's business, Octavian marched up to where the two consuls were seated and placed himself between them. From this position he harangued the Senate, informing its members that he would bring to its next meeting documentary proof of Antony's misdeeds quite sufficient for the senators to condemn him out of hand as a traitor. Octavian then stalked out, followed by his phalanx of bodyguards. The threat to any senator so unwise as not to collaborate in Octavian's condemnation of Antony was all too clear. Sosius, Enobarbus and about three hundred of the one-thousand-strong Senate did not stay around long enough for Octavian to appear a second time but packed their bags and fled to Antony at Ephesus.

Octavian let them go and offered any others who wished the opportunity to follow. He was conscious, perhaps, that clemency had been key to Caesar's civil war campaign and also that he had gone quite some way toward purging Rome of his opponents. He knew too that since many of the departed were remnants of the republican faction, they would be likely to exacerbate tensions in Antony's camp, where die-hard republicans already coexisted uneasily with allied kings, the supporters of Cleopatra and Antony's pan-Hellenism and, most of all, with Cleopatra herself.

If the latter was indeed in his mind, Octavian was soon proved right. Antony welcomed his new supporters and, mindful that the adherence of the year's two consuls gave his faction an appearance of legality, convened a Senate in exile to debate the course of the forthcoming political and military campaigns. In these debates Enobarbus, who continued to hope for some reconciliation between the two sides, played a prominent role. Alone among Antony's supporters and as befitted a nephew of the stiff-necked Cato, he refused to address Cleopatra by her new title of "Queen of Kings" or even as "Queen," calling her simply Cleopatra. Her attempts to ingratiate herself with him by naming a town in Cilicia after him probably only confirmed his suspicion of her egotism and despotism. At around this time Enobarbus seems to have convinced Antony that his cause would best be served if he ordered Cleopatra to return to Egypt to see out the forthcoming hostilities there. However, Canidius Crassus spoke in her defense, arguing:

> that it was wrong to exclude a woman who had contributed so much towards his war effort and secondly that he would regret lowering the morale of the Egyptians who made up much of his navy, besides Canidius certainly could not see that Cleopatra was the intellectual inferior of any of the allied kings. She had governed a vast kingdom all on her own for many years and she had also been with Antony for a long time and had learned to manage important matters.

Plutarch claims that Cleopatra had bribed Canidius Crassus to speak on her behalf, concerned, not unreasonably, that in her absence a further peace settlement might be pieced together that would disadvantage her personally and politically, by Antony being reconciled with Octavia as well as Octavian. Whether bribed or not—at about this time he did acquire lands and privileges in Egypt, as attested by a surviving royal decree—Canidius' arguments were logical. Antony listened to them as well as, no doubt, Cleopatra's private entreaties and relented. Nevertheless, Cleopatra's presence would continue to symbolize the deep division among Antony's supporters and serve as a focus for the discontent of the republicans.

While at Ephesus, Antony continued to assemble his armies. He had at his disposal not only seventy-five thousand legionaries, more than half of whom Canidius Crassus had marched the fourteen hundred miles from Armenia to join him, but also the troops of his client rulers, who numbered around twenty-five thousand infantry and, importantly, twelve thousand cavalry. One of Antony's most loyal client kings was not, however, present. Herod had gathered a body of troops and "carefully furnished them with all necessities and designed them as auxiliaries for Antony," only to be ordered by Antony not to lead them to him. Instead he was asked to use them to bring to heel the king of the Nabataean Arabs, who had failed to maintain the rent payments for the bitumen deposits that Herod had been supposed to collect on Cleopatra's behalf. Josephus wrote that Antony's order was issued at the pleading of Cleopatra, who saw it "to her advantage that these two kings should do one another as great mischief as possible." Cleopatra also dispatched a contingent of her own troops from Egypt to monitor what was going on around the Red Sea. According to Herod, they only got in his way, as no doubt intended, thus preventing him winning a too clear-cut victory.

In the spring of 32, Antony and his military advisers determined that the ground for any conflict between themselves and Octavian's forces should be Greece, just as it had been for the battle between Caesar and Pompey and Antony and Octavian themselves against the Liberators. Greece was the frontier state between the Hellenic east and Rome and offered reasonable scope for supply and military maneuver, as well as a launch pad for any invasion of Italy once Octavian had been defeated.

Plutarch and others suggested that by moving to Greece in 32, Antony lost his opportunity for an immediate invasion of Italy with the numerically superior forces he then had. This, however, overlooks some key points. Antony's army was not yet fully assembled and trained. There were few landing points in Italy and all were well defended. And most importantly, if Antony brought with him his eastern levies and Cleopatra, an undefeated Octavian could easily have presented himself as the savior of Italy, rallying the population to repulse an alien horde. Yet if Antony had left Cleopatra and the others behind, his numerical superiority would have been lost.

While their armies were boarding their mostly Egyptian transport vessels for the voyage to southern Greece, Antony first made the very much shorter voyage from Ephesus with Cleopatra to the island of Samos. Here they stayed for less than a month, mainly to stage a lavish festival of theater and music. According to Plutarch:

> Every practitioner of the arts sacred to Dionysus had been compelled to congregate on Samos and while all around almost the whole inhabited world was filled with sighs and groans a single island resounded day after day with the music of pipes and lyres while theaters were crowded and choruses competed with each other. Every city sent an ox for a communal sacrifice and kings vied with one another in the parties they threw and the gifts they gave. As a result people began to ask "if their preparations for war are treated as an occasion for such extravagant festivities how will Antony and Cleopatra celebrate their victories?"

This was precisely the impression they had wished to create. They designed the festivities to reaffirm their associations with Dionysus and Isis and also to echo similar events organized by Cleopatra's predecessor Alexander before he went to war. At the end of the celebrations both Cleopatra and Antony embarked for Athens, but not before presenting the artists with property in the city of Prirene as a reward for their participation.

The couple passed the summer in Athens, where Antony and Octavia had previously spent some of the happier days of their married life and Octavia had become a great favorite of the Athenians and honored patron of their city. Antony, as well as Cleopatra, must have been uneasily conscious of this. He therefore set about raising Cleopatra's status, leading an Athenian delegation to Cleopatra to present her with a decree awarding her a whole variety of privileges. Cleopatra reciprocated with a series of extravagant festivals to celebrate her newfound relationship with the city. In return, the

Athenians erected a statue of Cleopatra bedecked in the robes of Isis on the Acropolis itself.

Then, around the end of May, Antony gave Cleopatra the gift she must have wanted the most. He took the profoundly symbolic step of formally divorcing Octavia, even going so far as to have his agents evict her from his house on the Palatine in Rome. Octavia, as she seems to have done throughout, behaved well. Plutarch adds, "She left with all Antony's children except for the eldest of Fulvia's sons who was with his father and they say that she was in tears, upset by the idea that people might regard her as one of the causes of war."

Antony's actions would have pleased Cleopatra politically as well as giving her the emotional reassurance that she was indeed the only woman in his life. Any reconciliation with Octavian that might threaten their eastern plans was becoming ever more unlikely. The divorce, unsurprisingly, increased Cleopatra's confidence and perhaps also her hauteur. According to Plutarch, she treated two former consuls, Plancus and his nephew Titius, who had spoken out against her staying with the headquarters, so insolently that they deserted to Octavian. There was probably behind their action more calculation over who would be the most likely victor than this report of Plutarch suggests. Plancus had previously been quite willing to forget his consular dignity and be painted blue, dance, and fawn in other unbecoming ways before Cleopatra. Even historians favorable to Octavian saw him as "diseased with desertion."

The two ex-consuls certainly would have brought news to Rome of the dissension that surrounded Cleopatra's position in Antony's camp. They may also have told Octavian that Antony had entrusted his will to the care of the Vestal Virgins in Rome. Octavian knew that the Roman people and their legions were tired of civil wars and had welcomed his declaration in 36, after his victory over Sextus Pompey, that they were at an end. Furthermore, Antony was respected as Caesar's trusted lieutenant and avenger. Therefore, if Octavian wished to gain the support of the country to move against Antony he needed to show that Cleopatra had so besotted him that he was a mere puppet in her scheming foreign hands. The news of his divorce from Octavia would certainly help, but Octavian believed that judicious use—or misuse—of Antony's will might aid his efforts. Therefore he seized the document from the sacred care of the Vestals, illegally entering their temple to do so. He did not publish the will but carefully marked it up, then convened the Senate and read to them what he claimed were extracts, some of which at least he may have fabricated.

The passages he quoted reiterated Antony's claim that Caesarion was Caesar's son and detailed legacies to his own children by Cleopatra. But, most important and most suspect, Octavian reported that Antony had given instructions that, even if he died in Rome, his body should be ceremonially escorted through the Forum and then sent to Cleopatra in Egypt for burial in Alexandria. Octavian used the latter provision to emphasize that Antony's heart now metaphorically lay in Alexandria, as it would do physically in death, and to give credence to the rumors circulating that if Antony was victorious, he and Cleopatra would move the empire's capital to that city.

Octavian could contrast Antony's love for Alexandria with his own efforts and those of his supporters to beautify Rome and to improve its public facilities. They had restored public buildings, built public parks, repaired the ancient sewers and constructed the first new aqueducts in generations, as well as new bathhouses. At least for a while, use of the latter was made free, as was the olive oil used to cleanse the skin.

From the content of the surviving propaganda exchanges, from the work produced by Octavian's court poets such as Horace, Propertius and Vergil shortly after Antony's defeat and from the writings of the ancient historians, it is clear that Octavian now concentrated his propaganda fire on Cleopatra. He encouraged the Roman people to see the coming conflict as one in which, according to one of his historians, he and Cleopatra would fight respectively "one to save and one to ruin the world."

Octavian's first step had to be to show that Antony was indeed entirely subservient to Cleopatra and had thus abandoned even the last shred of the dignity and sense of duty that were the birthright of every Roman. To this end, one of Octavian's propagandists circulated stories that Antony had publicly massaged Cleopatra's feet, placing himself in an obviously subordinate position. He also alleged that in the middle of hearing legal pleas from his seat on the podium, Antony had received billets-doux from Cleopatra scratched on tablets of onyx and crystal and had read them immediately.

Additionally, on one occasion, while listening to a speech by a highly respected Roman, Antony had suddenly seen Cleopatra passing by in a litter and had leapt to his feet, quitting the court in midsession to accompany her while clinging to the litter. He was in any case said regularly to follow behind Cleopatra's litter on foot among the company of her eunuchs.* Other writers described how Antony became "the Egyptian woman's slave and devoted his time to his passion for her, causing him to do many outrageous things." Sometimes Cleopatra was credited with bewitching Antony so that he became "a slave to passion and the sorcery of Cleopatra."

Octavian's propaganda purported to show how, under Cleopatra's influence, Antony had been led into the self-indulgence that was such a serious and disabling vice in Roman eyes and "degenerated into a monster." Egyptian court life had so corrupted him that he had assumed the trappings of royalty, another ready trigger for Roman disdain, by appearing in a purple jeweled robe with a golden scepter; all he had needed was "a crown to make him a king dallying with a queen." Others went so far as to say Antony had become so effete as to use a golden chamber pot, "an enormity of which even Cleopatra would have been ashamed," and, equally decadently, a mosquito net, something that no hardy Roman should ever contemplate. Octavian even criticized Antony's florid speechmaking, suggesting he was a madman for wanting "to be admired rather than understood" and for bringing into "our language the wordy and meaningless gush of Asiatic orators."

Octavian summed up his view of Antony:

> Who would not weep when he sees and hears what Antony has become, leaving behind his ancestral customs and embracing foreign and barbaric ones . . . giving away islands and parts of continents as if he were lord of the whole earth . . . It is impossible for anyone who indulges in a life of royal luxury and pampers himself as a woman to conceive a manly thought or do a manly deed since it cannot but follow that a man's whole being is modelled by the habits of his daily life. Let no one consider him a Roman but rather an Egyptian.

---

*Castration was forbidden in Italy. Consequently, to the Romans eunuchs were always a subject of prurient interest and an easy and tantalizing signpost to the decadence of the East.

Having established Antony as a mere feeble tool of the Egyptian queen, Octavian demonized her both as a foreigner and as a woman who had got above her feminine station. He proclaimed:

> We Romans are the rulers of the greatest and best parts of the world and yet we find ourselves spurned and trampled upon by a woman of Egypt . . . Would we not utterly dishonor ourselves if, surpassing all other nations in valor, we then meekly endured the insults of this rabble, the natives of Alexandria and of Egypt . . . they worship reptiles and beasts as gods, they embalm their bodies to make them appear immortal, they are most forward in effrontery but most backward in courage. Worst of all they are not ruled by a man but are the slaves of a woman. Who would not groan at hearing that Roman knights and senators grovel before her like eunuchs?

Octavian's racism drew on well-established prejudices. Romans had long felt themselves superior to others, as Cato's lavatorial reception of Cleopatra's father, Auletes, had shown. Egyptians were routinely stigmatized as treacherous. In the history of Caesar's Alexandrian war, written a few years previously, Cleopatra's brother Ptolemy XIII was described as crying crocodile tears "so as to live up to the character of his countrymen because he was well trained in wiles . . . no one can doubt this breed is most apt to be treacherous." Dio Cassius had Octavian maintain that Egyptians, and Alexandrians in particular, while putting on a bold front, were utterly useless as warriors. Another author bolstered this canard, long established even then, by suggesting the hot sun drained the courage from southern peoples such as the Egyptians.

Misogynism was another easy totem to excite the crowd. Just as Fulvia's behavior had been put down to sexual frustration, so Octavian and his propagandists condemned Cleopatra's domination of Antony as unnatural. They alleged that, in her thrall, "he plays the woman and has worn himself out with lust." Cleopatra was at fault for using her wiles on Antony, not Antony for, Adam-like, succumbing to them. Cleopatra's "unchastity cost Rome dear." Writings and illustrations of the period often compare Antony under Cleopatra's rule to his hero Heracles under the thumb of Omphale, queen of Lydia. Plutarch captured this thread of Octavian's propaganda when he wrote, "Antony like Heracles in paintings where Omphale is seen removing his club and stripping off his lionskin was frequently disarmed by Cleopatra, subdued by her spells and persuaded to let slip from his hands great tasks and necessary campaigns only to roam and disport with her on the seashores by the Nile."

Octavian was implicitly encouraging his soldiers to suppress Cleopatra to ensure that no woman made herself the equal of a man, nudging them to think what this might mean in more domestic contexts. Cleopatra was both a head of state and a commander in chief, positions to which no Roman woman could aspire, despite the political influence some wielded behind the scenes. In Octavian's eyes, in proclaiming Cleopatra "Queen of Kings," Antony was simultaneously disregarding not one but two Roman tenets—those of men's superiority to women and the immorality of monarchy. In portraying Cleopatra and the east as a real threat to Rome, Octavian suggested that she and Antony wished to rule Italy, that her favorite oath was "as surely as I shall dispense justice on the Capitol" and that she regularly boasted that she and her eunuchs would dine on the Capitol, Rome's most sacred place. He could use Antony's insistence on Caesarion's paternity to suggest that the two wished to found a ruling Roman–Egyptian dynasty. However, he had to be careful not to prompt questions as to why, if Cleopatra was such a witch, his adoptive father had not only been seduced by her but invited her to Rome and placed her statue in one of the city's holy temples, where it still remained.

In conjuring this eastern menace, Octavian was able to call on any number of anti-Roman prophecies of considerable age. One such, that of the so-called mad praetor, known to have circulated for at least a century, foretold how a mighty army would come from the east to enslave Rome. Others, related to the Sibylline prophecies, were frankly millennial and apocalyptic and spoke of a woman's rule, after which would come damnation:

And then the whole wide world would be ruled by a Woman's hand
and obey her in everything,
and when the Widow shall queen the whole wide world
and into the sea divine have the gold and silver hurled
and into the water have hurled the bronzen swords of men,
those creatures of a day, all the world's elements then
shall be widowed, and God, who dwells in the heavens
shall roll up the sky like a scroll.
And on earth divine and on the sea the multitudinous sky

shall fall, while cataracts of wild fire from on high,
ceaseless pour. The earth he'll burn, the sea he'll burn with his curse.

The widow was equated by Octavian and his supporters with Cleopatra. Yet other prophecies spoke bloodily of eastern revenge on Rome. It is symbolic of Antony's divided camp that, while Cleopatra could have used such prophecies to unite the east, disgruntled and oppressed as it was by Roman taxation and arrogance, any reference to them would have completely undermined Antony's position in Rome and lost him all senatorial or republican support.

While this torrent of propaganda may have engulfed some of the waverers in Italy and convinced them that in fighting against Cleopatra they would be fighting to protect the Roman way of life, others remained more concerned with practical, parochial matters. Octavian was desperate for funds. First he compelled freedmen to pay a tax of one eighth of their capital assets. When this failed to yield enough, he imposed a kind of income tax of some 25 percent on the free population, including those same unfortunate freedmen.* Unsurprisingly, the Italian public grew resentful—a resentment that sporadically boiled over into rioting and arson, quickly suppressed by Octavian's troops.

As part of his pretense of unity, Octavian induced the population to take an oath of loyalty to him, later boasting that "the whole of Italy of its own free will swore loyalty to me, and asked me to take charge of the war that I won at Actium. The provinces of the Gauls, the Spains, Africa, Sicily and Sardinia swore in the same way." Surviving records do not reveal how the idea of the oath was instigated or promulgated or indeed relate its formal wording, although, clearly and tellingly, it referred to personal loyalty to Octavian, not to the Senate or other apparatus of the Roman republic. However much Octavian's propagandists railed against Antony's pretensions to monarchy, Rome was pledging loyalty to another autocrat. The shrewd political skill underlying the oath was that to refuse to make such a relatively anodyne pledge would single out a man for special surveillance if not immediate attention.

---

*The Roman citizens' exemption from direct taxation had long since disappeared to pay for the costly upheavals of the civil wars.

Even discounting the inevitable bias of the histories, it is hard not to see Octavian as setting the agenda throughout this period and Antony reacting to it. Antony, in turn, tried to bolster his diverse coalition by administering oaths of his own to his supporters and allies. Cut off from Rome, he had recruited many of his legions from the east by offering the men Roman citizenship, with its advantages such as immunity from torture and the right to trial in Rome—a right taken advantage of by Saint Paul a century later. Now, to reinforce the legions' status, Antony had minted a series of silver and gold coins—enough to celebrate each of his thirty legions, his bodyguard and his scout unit individually. Each coin displayed the appropriate eagle, standards and name or number on one side, while the other showed a warship from Antony's fleet.

Despite the mutual oath swearing, there were still those who hoped for reconciliation. Some of Antony's friends in Italy, sensing that the damage that Octavian's propaganda against Cleopatra was doing was being aggravated by her presence at the heart of Antony's headquarters, sent an envoy to Antony. Named Gaius Geminius, the envoy's remit was to urge Antony again to dismiss Cleopatra from his presence and to focus more effort on outmaneuvering Octavian's attempt to isolate him politically. Plutarch recounted what happened:

> Geminius sailed to Greece but Cleopatra suspected him of acting in Octavia's interests so at dinner he became the constant butt of jokes and was insulted by being allocated the least prestigious couches. He put up with everything, waiting for an opportunity to have a meeting with Antony. Eventually he was told to deliver his message in the middle of supper. He said that most of the discussion he had come for required a clear head but that drunk or sober there was one thing he knew—that all would be well if Cleopatra were sent back to Egypt. Antony lost his temper and Cleopatra said, "Geminius, you have done well to confess the truth without it being tortured from you."

A few days later Geminius returned to Rome.

With the collapse of such final mediation efforts, Octavian used his dominance of the rump of the Senate to at last have Antony deprived of his triumviral status and of the consulship he was due to assume in 31. War became inevitable. Even so, Octavian chose not to declare war on Antony, just on

Cleopatra alone. In doing so he made the war one ostensibly against a foreign opponent and not a civil war. At the same time, he shrewdly had the Senate pass a resolution "that Antony's adherents would be pardoned and commended if they deserted him."

To underline the solemnity and nationalism of his declaration of "a just war" (*justum bellum*), Octavian revived a long-obsolete ceremony for the purpose. Accompanied by his followers, who had symbolically fastened on their military cloaks, he himself marched from the temple of the goddess of war, Bellona, the sister of Mars, brandishing a spear dripping the blood of a sacrificial animal, to the Campus Martius, Rome's old military assembly ground, where, facing east in the direction of his enemy, Egypt, he flung it quivering into the ground.*

*Octavian disregarded one particular element of the traditional process for the declaration of a just war—the requirement to attempt to negotiate a peaceful settlement before war could be declared.

CHAPTER 20

The Battle of Actium

As the campaign began Antony, with his powerful forces and the economic, military and political backing of Cleopatra and his allies in the east, as well as his still substantial support in Rome among exiled republicans, had as good a chance of emerging victorious as Octavian. In the autumn of 32, with Cleopatra at his side, Antony transferred his headquarters from Athens to make a winter base at the city of Patras. Strategically situated at the head of the Gulf of Corinth, this city was at the middle of the string of naval bases Antony had established from Corfu in the north to the coast, of North Africa in the south in order to protect his supply routes. Command of the sea would be key to the forthcoming struggle. It would allow the domination of the Ionian coast, where Octavian would need to land if he wished to come to grips with Antony and Cleopatra's forces in Greece.

However, for reasons never satisfactorily explained, Antony did not keep his main fleet with him at Patras but ordered it to the Ambracian Gulf, just north of the island of Levkas. The Gulf is about ten miles long and about five miles across. It provides a safe harbor because two protruding promontories narrow the mouth to only half a mile wide. Actium is at the tip of the low, flat southern promontory. At that time, Actium was a small village used by pearl fishermen with a small five-hundred-year-old temple to Apollo nearby on the shore. Marshy, barren and dank, the area's isolation rendered it both difficult to supply and inconducive to the maintenance of morale. Octavian, on the other hand, had the advantage of wintering his troops and navy in Italy at the port cities of Brundisium and Tarentum, where facilities and health were better and morale much easier to maintain.

During the winter, when uncertain weather ruled out a major sea campaign, both sides redoubled their efforts to build new ships and to repair old ones, replacing frayed rigging, caulking leaking seams, careening the hulls and reapplying coats of pitch and wax to make the ships sail more easily and quickly through the Mediterranean waters. The Romans had by tradition been soldiers, not sailors. The long wars with the Carthaginians had taught them how to fight at sea, and their first warship designs had evolved from a close study of captured Carthaginian vessels. Roman ships were still crewed to a great extent by foreigners, some pressed, some volunteers. Octavian's navy had the great advantage of recent experience of naval warfare in the sea battles against Sextus Pompey around Sicily in which the young Agrippa had shown himself an astute admiral and naval tactician. On the other hand, Antony was able to draw on the long naval tradition of Egypt and of other of his allies and clients in the Mediterranean, such as the sailors of Rhodes.

The ships the two navies were gathering came in a variety of shapes and sizes. The large transports that, on the orders of Cleopatra, brought grain and other supplies from Egypt to Antony's armies were sail-powered vessels of around thirteen hundred tons' burden. They carried three masts, were approximately 180 feet long and 45 feet in both depth and width, had several decks divided into compartments and were well ballasted. Their pumps were based on the screw system invented by Archimedes at the Museon in Alexandria, in which a screw rotated within a pipe to pull water upward.* Supply ships would take about a week to reach Antony's forces from the Egyptian capital.

The warships on both sides were galleys and thus relied mainly on the use of oars for their propulsion. Most had more than one bank of oars, but their designation as threes, fours or sixes came not from the number of banks of oars, one above the other, but from the number of rowers who manned the oars in a particular location. For example, a five might consist of one bank of two men above another bank of two, with a further man using a single oar on the level above; or, indeed, it could designate one bank of five men pulling on a single long oar.

---

*Such devices are still in common use on the Nile today for irrigation.

Responding to the instructions of a *hortator*, who set the speed and rhythm, the rowers worked from benches, half standing to push back the oars and then falling back on their seats as they hauled the oars toward them. The bow of each ship was heavily reinforced with stout timbers and, at the waterline, a two- or three-pronged, brass-encased wooden ram protruded forward ready for use in disabling enemy vessels. According to surviving representations of them, the ships of Cleopatra's Egyptian navy, which made up at least a quarter of the fleet assembled by Antony, seem to have been distinguished by a model of a crocodile fixed to the bow above the ram and below the prow as some kind of figurehead. Cleopatra's contribution to the fleet was not limited to these ships. Many other of Antony's vessels were rowed by Egyptians.

The trireme or "three," about 150 feet long and displacing some 230 tons, was the most common type of galley on both sides. However, Antony had, in general, the larger vessels. Their sides were reinforced with ironbound beams to withstand ramming. They were so massive that they looked like fortresses and "caused the sea to groan and the wind to labor as they were carried along." Their size and weight, however, rendered them unwieldy. Agrippa, on the other hand, had introduced into Octavian's fleet a lighter, smaller version known as a Liburnian, from its place of origin on the Adriatic coast, where it had been the craft of choice for pirates. Tough enough to withstand high winds and bad weather, it had two banks of oars, was fast and maneuverable and would give Agrippa a vital advantage in the campaign to come.

On whatever part of the Mediterranean coast—Egyptian, Greek or Roman—the shipwrights working during the winter of 32–31 used very similar construction techniques. First they laid down on the stocks the keel and the stem and stern posts. Then they began assembling the outer shell of planking, which was between one and a half and four inches in thickness and joined edge to edge to its neighbor or the keel and secured by frequent mortise and tenon joints so well made and so close together that very little caulking was required. Only after the shipwrights had completed this outer shell did they begin to insert structural framing timbers to strengthen the ship and to lay the planking for the decks. All ancient ships used side rudders to steer, one on each side of the ship. They were a kind of oversized oar on a pivot operated by a tiller.

Before they launched the ships the workers coated the hulls with tar and then painted the superstructure with hot wax. A Roman work on naval warfare describes how some ships, particularly the lighter craft used for scouting and shadowing, were painted with an early version of camouflage: "Their sails and ropes are dyed blue, the color of seawater; and even the wax with which the hull is painted is similarly colored, while the soldiers and sailors aboard them likewise dye their clothes." The larger warships were painted in stronger-colored wax—purples, yellows and reds—to emphasize their size and destructive potential.

While the shipwrights labored busily that winter, neither side let up in the propaganda war. Antony had coins minted, one side of which bore his own image and titles and the other those of Cleopatra holding the ritual rattle, a symbol of Isis. Octavian challenged Antony to allow his forces to land in Greece and then to come to battle in five days or else to cross himself with his armies to Italy on the same basis. Antony responded with the very sensible question "Who is to judge between us if the agreement is broken in any way?" But he followed up with an equally empty invitation to single combat.

Octavian's propagandists began to report a series of omens favorable to their leader. (So too, presumably, did Antony's, but these are lost to us.) Octavian's spin doctors claimed sweat oozed from a statue of Antony and, however hard people tried to wipe it away, they could not make it stop for a number of days. They also claimed that a figure of Dionysus, Antony's divine counterpart, crashed to the ground, followed swiftly by one of his ancestor Heracles, and that a chasm swallowed up one of the colonies founded by Antony. According to Plutarch, Cleopatra's flagship, the *Antonias*, was also the object of a terrifying portent: "Some swallows made their nest under the stern, but others attacked them, drove them away, and killed the baby birds." Both Octavian and Antony, in his case bankrolled by Cleopatra, kept up a campaign of bribery of influential Romans and potential foreign allies.

With the arrival of the spring, the navies were readied for action. Marines, often land-loving legionaries, marched up the gangways to their stations on the decks built over the banks of rowers. Other Mediterranean navies had relied to a great extent in battle on the use of superior seamanship to vanquish their enemies. Their captains proceeded on a parallel course to an opponent before increasing speed to the maximum of which the rowers were capable—at most ten miles per hour—and swiftly changing course, either to ram the enemy or to disable them by sweeping away their oars before they could be pulled inboard. However, the Romans, being soldiers at heart, preferred to rely on the firing of arrows and other weapons from collapsible towers raised on the deck as well as the firing from deck-mounted heavy catapults of iron darts and grapnels. The latter were designed to become entangled in the opposing vessel and allow it to be winched into a position where it could be boarded. Literally to provide greater firepower, laborers carried onto the ships buckets of combustible pitch and oil. When battle was near, the crew attached these to long poles and pushed them out beyond the bow before setting them alight, so if an enemy came within range, the fire could be poured onto his decks.

Agrippa's fleet struck the first blow, crossing the Ionian Sea not by the usual northern route opposite the heel of Italy but much further south, diagonally toward the Peloponnese. Here, on its west coast, Agrippa seized Antony's naval station of Methone, killing Antony's commander there, Bogud, the deposed king of Mauretania. From here, he proceeded to harass Antony's supply route from Egypt and to make further amphibious hit-and-run raids on his bases along the coast, causing Antony to move some of his forces south. So successful were Agrippa's diversionary tactics that Octavian was able to ship his main army across the northern route to Corfu undetected by Antony's fleet, which, preoccupied with the southern threat, had failed to keep a northern shield of guard ships in place.

On reaching Corfu, Octavian found it abandoned by Antony's forces, and he crossed safely to the mainland. Octavian, perhaps on Agrippa's advice, had not brought with him all the legions he had mobilized. With a smaller, less unwieldy force, his mobility was increased and his supply problems lessened. He had about eighty thousand men compared to Antony's one hundred thousand. However, Octavian's forces were nearly all Italian, well disciplined and committed to his cause, whereas Antony's troops were drawn from all across the eastern Mediterranean and the loyalties of some, at least, were more questionable.

According to the historian Dio Cassius, Octavian brought with him to Greece "all the men who carried influence in public life, both senators and knights." His astute intention was both to ensure that they could not make trouble at home in his absence and also "to demonstrate publicly that he had on his side the largest and strongest body of support among the Roman people." He wanted to make clear that he, not Antony and the numerous renegade senators among his multinational army, represented Rome and legitimacy.

Octavian had seized the military initiative, which he would never again lose, and was quickly making his way down the mainland in a series of amphibious leaps. In response to the news of his landings, Antony mobilized his forces and, with Cleopatra at his side, moved them up toward the peninsula of Actium and the Ambracian Gulf, where his major fleet lay. Over the winter, his commanders had taken the precaution of fortifying both sides of the narrow entrance to the gulf with palisades, watchtowers and catapults.

By the time Antony reached Actium with Cleopatra, Octavian, moving with the speed and decisiveness of his adoptive father, Julius Caesar, was already on the shores of the gulf, where he had encamped some way from the mouth, on the northern side on a low hill that dominated the surrounding flats. He had also established a naval base on the open sea nearby in the Bay of Comaros. While Antony's fleet could ride safely at anchor in the gulf, if his ships attempted to put to sea, Agrippa, on Octavian's behalf, could severely maul them as they negotiated the narrow mouth and deployed. Similarly, Agrippa could harass incoming supply ships. Antony's great fleet was partially blockaded and, as a consequence, the freedom of movement of his land armies severely restricted. If his main armies marched away from the shores of the gulf, Antony's fleet would have little alternative but to surrender.

Octavian's position did have some weaknesses. His water supplies were not secure, since they came from a river about a mile to the east of his camp or from springs at least a similar distance away. Octavian had built a temporary breakwater to protect his fleet from the sea but even so, in a westerly storm—fortunately for him, rare in summer—his ships would have to quit their anchorage or face being driven ashore. It was in Octavian's interest to force a decisive battle as soon as possible while the weather was good and before Antony could marshal fully his diverse forces and summon more ships to break Agrippa's naval blockade of the gulf. Antony knew this and refused to give battle, contenting himself with harassing attacks and cavalry raids on Octavian's water supplies.

However, while Antony was assembling his troops, Agrippa struck again by sea to tilt the balance further in favor of Octavian, capturing the large craggy island of Levkas just southwest of the Actium promontory. Separated from the mainland by only a narrow channel of mudflats, the island dominates the southern approaches to the gulf. Surviving records do not recount Agrippa's feat in detail nor whether Antony had neglected to garrison the strategic island properly. However, its capture meant that not only Antony's fleet but also his army were now effectively blockaded. Agrippa's ships had secured a better anchorage and could prevent the great transports dispatched on Cleopatra's orders from Egypt with grain and other supplies from approaching the gulf or even landing supplies nearby. Only the bravest captains would attempt to run the blockade.

It was now to Octavian's advantage to defer mass combat while Antony's troops sweltered in the summer heat and caught malaria from the mosquitoes infecting the marshes and dysentery from the unsanitary conditions likely to affect any confined military camp where there was insufficient tide to wash away the feces and other waste.

These trying conditions understandably began to sap the strength and unity of Antony's multinational army and navy. Antony now had to bring in what supplies he could on the backs of local men press-ganged for the purpose. Lashed on with long whips by Antony's overseers, they struggled over the rugged mountain tracks from the nearest supply point. Among the locals was an ancestor of Plutarch—a fact that cannot have raised Antony in the historian's esteem. To try to break the deadlock, Antony ordered part of his army to march round the shores of the gulf to the northern side and, once encamped there, to launch probing attacks, partly to try to cut off Octavian's water supplies and partly to provoke Octavian to battle. Antony may even have had the idea of attempting to cut off Octavian's camp from the north and, in turn, to put him under siege if all went well. It did not.

Antony's cavalry were defeated in a major skirmish in which Octavian's troops were led by Titius, a man who had only recently deserted from Antony and been rewarded with a consulship. As a consequence of this new setback, two of Antony's client kings defected to Octavian with their men. When one attempted to curry favor with Octavian by abusing Antony, Octavian told him curtly, "I like treason but I don't like traitors."

The desertions were more damaging to the morale of Antony's army than they were in strategic terms; more seriously, Agrippa's fleet was already capturing further ports in Antony's rear, thus lengthening his overland supply routes. Agrippa's greatest success was in capturing Patras and encouraging Eurycles, ruler of Sparta, one of Antony's client states, to go over to Octavian—a decision he found easy since Antony had executed his father for piracy.

Reports of these amphibious actions in their rear, together with the worsening disease within the camp and the trickle of desertions, further eroded the morale of Antony's men. However, worse were the continuing differences within the leadership of Antony's forces between the remnants of the Roman republican faction led by Enobarbus and those who supported, or at least hoped to benefit from, the nebulous idea of an eastern Mediterranean empire being developed by Cleopatra and Antony. Even Antony's client kings were not entirely happy. They had been affronted by the diminution of their status at the Donations of Alexandria, which had subjected them to the children of Cleopatra and Antony.

Soon, a sickly Enobarbus, "angered" by some new action of Cleopatra's, decided that he stood no chance of weaning Antony from her to the republican virtues and had himself rowed in a small boat across the gulf to Octavian's camp. Even though this "upset Antony a great deal," he sent along after him all his equipment and retinue, despite Cleopatra's protests, joking that Enobarbus clearly wanted to be in the arms of his mistress in Rome. He never reached them, dying almost immediately—probably not, as Plutarch claimed, "from the shame of his disloyalty and treachery" but more prosaically from dysentery or malaria, the fever from which he was suffering before he left Antony's camp.

Even though Antony, "undermined in confidence and suspicious of everything," made an example by executing two other would-be deserters, having one, a senator, torn apart by horses and subjecting the other, an Arab ruler, to torture, presumably to find out who else was wavering, Enobarbus' was not the last defection. Antony needed quick, decisive and successful military action to prevent his forces—and with them his chances of victory—from dissipating through desertion and disease.

After an abortive attempt by the fleet to break out of the gulf, Canidius Crassus, Antony's land commander, urged him to withdraw his army northeastward over the Pindos Mountains to Macedonia and Thrace, where he could recruit further troops and face Octavian with a good chance of success. Although previously a vocal advocate of Cleopatra's presence in the camp, he now recommended to Antony that he send her home to Egypt.

The surviving accounts of the campaign (by Dio Cassius and Plutarch) record almost nothing of Cleopatra until this time. Two of the most significant glimpses of her are in the form of jokes. In the first, when Octavian's forces, in their initial advance from the Greek coast, captured a place called Toryne, whose name can mean "ladle" or "stirring spoon," she punned, "What is so terrible in Octavian sitting on a ladle?"—a joke that in translation at least says more for her courage than for her fabled wit. (In Cleopatra's defense, some scholars suggest that *toryne* was also a slang word for "penis," investing the joke with a cruder but more effective humor.) In the second incident, she was the target of a joke, or rather jibe, by Dellius, who upbraided her after they had been besieged that the wine they were now obliged to drink was sour, whereas even Sarmentus, a page at Octavian's court, whom gossip alleged was also Octavian's catamite, quaffed the best Italian vintages.

It is hard to comprehend the strength of character Cleopatra must have needed during her time at Actium, both as a woman and as the ruler of Egypt. As far as is known, none of the other leaders had their wives or mistresses with them as Antony had. There would have been no noblewomen other than those in her own retinue with whom she could discuss events. She had to be constantly alert to Antony's moods, which were probably exacerbated by drink and the paranoia and depression it induced, not to mention the inactivity he so hated and a real consciousness of his declining fortunes.

Also, Cleopatra cannot but have been aware that she was a divisive force in the testosterone-charged camp, disliked and distrusted not only by the republicans but also by her fellow eastern rulers for her privileged status. At least as important as protecting her personal position, she had to protect the interests of her Egyptian kingdom, whose treasury was funding much of the war and much of whose treasure, in the form of gold and silver, was with her in the camp. Her fate and that of her family and her kingdom were inextricably linked to Antony's. She could never succeed without him. Yet without her, Antony's position, though weakened financially, would be enhanced politically.

There was, she knew, a valid alternative to Canidius' strategy of abandoning the fleet and marching over the mountains to Macedonia. This was to load the ships with the best of the legionaries and all the treasure and head south toward Egypt, Syria and Libya, where there were at least seven legions to be added to the hardened core that got away with the fleet. Egypt was, as previous centuries had shown, easy to defend, and there they could recoup their strength. Those of Antony's legions left ashore at Actium could march back overland as best they could, since if the fleet successfully broke out, Octavian and Agrippa's best forces would be bound to follow it. Such a strategy had considerable advantages over the whole army marching to Macedonia. The latter would be risky in itself, and any victory, unless a complete rout, would be difficult to follow up because if

Antony abandoned his ships in the gulf, Octavian would have absolute dominance of the sea.

Historical accounts don't reveal whether Cleopatra made these arguments privately to Antony. However, they do record that she attended an army council where, presumably the only woman and surrounded by hostile, uniformed Romans, she put these arguments and succeeded in convincing Antony, who in turn carried most of his supporters with him. But Dellius, so adept at switching horses at the right time that one ancient writer called him "the circus rider of the civil wars," went over to Octavian and disclosed Antony's plans.

At around this time, Octavian ordered a commando squad to infiltrate Antony's camp and attempt to capture or kill him as he walked down beside the palisades to the harbor accompanied by only a single member of his staff. However, they leapt from concealment too soon and, mistaking the staff officer for Antony, carried him off while Antony made his escape with less than dignified haste.

Before Antony and his commanders could attempt a breakout, they had to review the number of ships and rowers available to them. According to Plutarch, Antony had been reduced to "press-ganging from long-suffering Greece, travellers, mule drivers, reapers and boys not yet of military age" to man his vessels. Yet even so, disease, deprivation and desertion meant that there were more ships than rowers to man them. The ships had been lying at anchor for months and some were likely to have become unseaworthy through worm infestation or slow through the accumulation of barnacles and other marine life. Antony no doubt had as many of the best ships careened and rewaxed as he could in the time available and burned the worst. Then began the process of selecting which legions were to embark. Plutarch described how those chosen were reluctant: "an infantry centurion, covered with scars from very many battles for Antony, burst into tears as Antony was passing and said, 'Imperator, why do you despise these wounds and this sword of mine and pin your hopes on wretched planks of wood. Let Egyptians and Phoenicians fight at sea but give us land, that is where we're accustomed to stand.' "

It was equally important not to alarm the soldiers, including Antony's elite legion, the Larks, into thinking that they would be left to fight their way alone over the mountains against superior forces. When galleys were prepared for battle, sails were usually left ashore to lighten the vessels and thus to make them more maneuverable as well as to free space for fighting men. However, on this occasion sails were needed, since it was a breakout that was intended and sails would allow a galley to make six knots in open waters while the rowers rested. When the legionaries spotted sails, spars and rigging being loaded aboard, Antony calmed their concerns by asserting that the added speed they would give would be necessary in a victorious pursuit so that not a single one of his enemies should escape. However, no one seems to have noticed Cleopatra's preparations. Her treasure would have been stowed on her ships discreetly and her retinue taken aboard perhaps under cover of darkness.

The battle that was at hand would decide the fate of the Mediterranean world and would be the last major naval engagement there for many hundreds of years, not surpassed until Lepanto in 1571. Antony had himself rowed around the fleet, encouraging his men to stand firm and fight exactly as if they were ashore. Octavian, all too aware of Antony's intentions and conscious of the power omens held for his superstitious troops, put it about, according to Plutarch, that as the preparations for battle were being made, "while it was still dark and he was walking towards the ships he met a man driving a donkey. He asked the man's name and the man said, 'My name is Lucky and my donkey's name is Victor.' This is why when Octavian later erected a display of captured ships' prows near by he also set up a bronze statue of a donkey and a man."

At last all was ready, and on September 2, 31, the rowers bent their backs to the oars as Antony's galleys began to move slowly through the water. The twenty thousand legionaries and two thousand auxiliaries aboard tugged nervously at their equipment, conscious that even if they could swim, if they fell into the water they would be impeded by their mail coats, which they could not discard without great risk of being wounded. After some initial maneuverings to get into formation, the ships headed slowly for the mouth of the gulf, past the encampments and fortifications of the fifty thousand or so troops who had been left to fight their way out as best they could under Canidius Crassus. As they emerged into the open sea, Antony's ships deployed into four squadrons, three of which, containing a total of perhaps 230 ships, formed a double line stretching from one shore to the other in order to protect the fourth squadron, the sixty or so Egyptian ships which were positioned to their rear.

Octavian's four hundred ships, with perhaps as many as forty thousand legionaries on board, had been early to sea and formed up in an opposing line. He stationed his vessels some way to the seaward of Antony, anxious to lure him further forward and thus to lessen his chances of retreating back into the gulf if necessary.

At first, very little happened as the seminaked rowers rested on their oars, sweating as the heat rose in the airless confines of the rowing decks. While the conditions that day were not recorded, by noon at that time of year the temperature can easily exceed 90° Fahrenheit (33° Celsius) and the difference in the temperature of the air over the sea and land produces an onshore breeze that starts to rise at about this time and strengthens as the afternoon wears on. Even though his sails were stowed, Antony was at some risk of being blown back on shore, so he could wait no longer and headed for the enemy. Plutarch described how the rowers in Antony's large ships could not get up sufficient speed, and hence momentum, to ram and that Octavian's admirals also preferred close-quarters action to ramming the reinforced sides of Antony's ships and thus risking damaging their own, more slender vessels. Hence, "the fight resembled a land battle or more precisely an assault on a walled town. Three or four of Octavian's ships would cluster round one of Antony's while the marines wielded catapults, spears, javelins and flaming missiles; the troops on Antony's ships even shot at the enemy with catapults mounted on wooden towers."

All of a sudden, Cleopatra's ships took advantage of the turn of the breeze to the northwest and a break in the lines of fighting ships to hoist their stowed sails and to make off fast southwest for the Peloponnese. Since this change of wind was a daily occurrence and would have been well known to those encamped in the area for months, this was no doubt what had been intended ever since the council of war, even if later propagandists presented her flight as outright cowardice and treachery. When he saw the Egyptian fleet was away, Antony turned his own ships to follow. Few, however, could disengage from the fierce combat. Even Antony himself pragmatically had to switch from his own massive flagship to a swifter galley before he could do so. Thus he laid himself open to the charge of deserting his men for the sake of his mistress, a charge that rang down the centuries until Shakespeare dubbed him a "doting mallard." But there was logic as well as love in his actions. If, as he planned, he could rebuild his forces, all could still be saved.

Some of Antony's ships had already been captured. Some raised their oars aloft as a token of surrender. Others took refuge back in the gulf. Yet others fought on well into the night, which Octavian spent aboard one of the swift

Liburnian vessels, supervising the closing stages of the battle. Dio Cassius probably exaggerated when he recounted how Octavian's ships turned to fire as their main weapon. But the battle continued with Octavian's sailors tossing jars of flaming pitch onto Antony's larger galleys from their more maneuverable vessels, as well as throwing torches lashed to javelins into their flammable and pitch-coated sides. When the ships were well aflame, some, presumably the rowers belowdecks, were, according to Dio, "roasted in the midst of the holocaust as if they were in ovens," while the legionaries were incinerated in their armor as it grew red-hot.

By morning, Octavian's victory was long since complete and all was quiet save for the sound of the waves lapping on the beach strewn with pieces of wreckage and the occasional sodden corpse.

CHAPTER 21

After Actium

THAT SAME MORNING, Antony was sitting in the dawn light "in silent self-absorption, holding his head in both hands" in the prow of Cleopatra's gilded flagship as its purple sails carried him southward. According to Plutarch, he had been sitting there since first coming aboard the previous evening after his vessel had come up with Cleopatra's, and had taken up his lonely position straightaway without seeing her. He had been stirred briefly into action only when a small flotilla of Octavian's fast Liburnian vessels had begun to gain on Cleopatra's fleet to harass them in their retreat. Antony rose and ordered the steersmen and rowers to turn his larger ships round to face his pursuers. All the Liburnians but one backed off, feeling themselves strong enough only to pick off stragglers, like hyenas around an animal migration, rather than to engage in a fleet action. One, however, came on, right up to Antony's ship. A man brandished his spear from its deck and yelled toward him, "I am Eurycles of Sparta and thanks to Octavian's good fortune I have the chance to avenge my father's death." For some reason, he failed to attack Antony's ship but rammed another of his largest vessels, spinning it around, and went on to attack a second, which was full of domestic equipment.

As Antony's fleet began to pull away from the frenzied mêlée around the two stricken vessels, which he had abandoned to their fate, he resumed his vigil in the prow. He would remain there without seeing or speaking to Cleopatra the whole three days it took the fleet to reach Taenarum, one of his surviving fleet bases, at the southern tip of the Peloponnese.

Both his thoughts and those of Cleopatra, keeping her distance elsewhere in the vessel, can only be imagined. The full implications of the previous day's engagement would have weighed heavily on Antony. Up until the last moment, he may well have hoped that the initial stages of the sea fight would be so successful that he could convert a planned retreat into a great victory. Now he knew he could not. He had probably at least expected that more of his fleet would have escaped with him. As it was, he was fleeing Greece just as Pompey had done seventeen years earlier, saving himself and leaving his armies behind. In doing so he was inevitably losing credibility as a Roman leader, ceding the Roman world to Octavian. Admittedly, unlike Pompey, he had left an undefeated army of fifty thousand men in Greece, but the realistic and experienced field commander within him would have known that their morale would have been further lowered by the outcome of the sea battle and the sight of him fleeing after the Egyptian queen. Perhaps he wondered whether his decision to leave Canidius Crassus in charge of the land forces had been correct or whether he might have done better going ashore himself to rally his remaining troops, leading them to Asia in person and sharing their privations as he had done in his finest hours—the retreat over the Apennines from Mutina thirteen years ago and that from Parthia four years previously. He needed time, perhaps even a drink, to compose himself.

Cleopatra's intuition would have told her not to approach her lover while he was sunk in melancholic introspection. Her own spirits would have been higher than Antony's. She was returning to her kingdom, where she still controlled immense riches and a large population in a land with good natural defenses. She was free of the carping and hostile glances of Roman senators. Previously, Antony could have hoped to succeed without her, but now their fates were inextricably linked. Any future either had would be together and in the East.

The balance of power in her relationship with Antony had tipped further. Henceforward it would lie almost exclusively with Cleopatra. Antony was now in his early fifties and his usual self-confidence in the face of adversity was crumbling. He was suffering a failure of will and did not believe, deep down, that he was making a retreat to victory.

Once they were ashore at Taenarum, Plutarch described how "Cleopatra's ladies in waiting managed to get them to talk to each other, then persuaded them to share a meal and go to bed together." Mutual love and dependence are not hard to discern amid the sulks, histrionics, recriminations and final pleasure of reconciliation. However, Antony had more to solace him than the soft words and warm embrace of Cleopatra. Quite a few transport ships and other remnants of his army gathered in the little port. Encouraging reports came in that the land army was holding together in its retreat. In return, Antony sent messages to Canidius Crassus, ordering him to bring the troops across to Asia as soon as he was able.

Even according to the critical Plutarch, Antony was "in misfortune the most nearly a virtuous man." Thus, remaining a realist about his chances, in a typical gesture of magnanimity, he publicly released many of his friends and clients from their obligations to him. Although with tears in their eyes they refused the gift of a ship filled with treasure "in coined money and valuable royal utensils of silver and gold," many took the opportunity to depart for Corinth, where Antony commended them into the safe care of his procurator while they "made their peace with Octavian." Resupplied and with political and emotional equilibrium at least somewhat restored, Cleopatra and Antony reembarked and headed for Egypt.

Back in northern Greece, Canidius Crassus had indeed started his fifty thousand troops on the northeastward crossing of the rugged hills and mountains toward Macedonia. But they had not marched far before Octavian's forces, confident and exulting in their maritime victory, overtook them. Both sides were reluctant to fight. Although Octavian would be likely to win, he could not be sure of this. As his victories in the east had shown, Canidius was an experienced and resourceful general. Therefore, Octavian sent blandishments to Canidius' troops through his heralds, appealing to them over the heads of their senior officers to come to terms. Antony's legionaries, under the leadership of their veteran centurions, drove a hard bargain in the full knowledge of the alternative price they could extract in blood. After seven days of negotiations, Octavian's wooing succeeded. Antony's legions would go over to Octavian on the condition that they would receive equal treatment with those in Octavian's ranks in terms of benefits and rewards on discharge. The most prestigious legions, such as the Larks, would be assimilated whole rather than their men being split up individually within Octavian's army. This agreement reflected not only Octavian's trust but also the esprit de corps of the legions.

While these negotiations, which he may well have tacitly condoned, were reaching their conclusion, Canidius and his senior officers, all loyal to Antony, slipped away. In promoting the negotiations and bringing them to a successful conclusion, Octavian showed his high diplomatic skills, marrying clemency and expediency to his propaganda advantage, just as he was already making the most of his victory at Actium.

The poet Horace had, it appears, been present at Actium and wrote in its immediate aftermath how "the wild queen plotting destruction to our capital and ruin to the empire with her pack of diseased half-men [eunuchs]" had had all her fleet burned. Horace went on to vilify Antony's devotion to Cleopatra, "a Roman to a woman slave by sale," and cited his passion as a central reason for Antony's defeat. However, he did not accuse Cleopatra of cowardice or treachery by flying from the battle, thus confirming that, like Octavian and others who were eyewitnesses, he was aware all along that a breakout was Antony's prime intention, whatever later historians, including Plutarch, portrayed.

Octavian did not set out in immediate pursuit of Cleopatra and Antony. He knew that his final victory was assured provided he retained control of Italy and conciliated some of those Greek and eastern states that had so recently supported them. In furtherance of this latter aim, he traveled to Eleusis, a community on a landlocked bay neighboring Athens. Here in the square stone hall of the sanctuary, once the largest public building in Greece, he sought initiation into the secret rituals of the goddesses Demeter and Kore, who were associated with both the settled rhythms of life and the seasons and the development of civilization, law and morality. He probably timed his visit to coincide with the great early autumn festival of the goddesses, to which initiates flocked from all over the Greek-speaking world. By his action, Octavian was demonstrating to a large and influential audience both his respect for Greek culture and religion and his embrace of more regular, civilized deities than the wild, anarchistic Dionysian and Bacchanalian cults of his opponents.

From Athens, Octavian traveled across to Samos, where Cleopatra and Antony had held their celebration of music and dance, and made it his winter headquarters preparatory to reordering the administration of Asia Minor, which was now swiftly falling into his hands without a fight. However, he had not been on the island long before disturbing news reached him from Rome.

Already during the Actium campaign, Marcus Lepidus, the son of the deposed triumvir and the nephew of Brutus, had been incriminated in a plot to murder Octavian on his return to Italy and been executed. Now disturbances had broken out among the veterans released from the legions and eager for their rewards, as well as among the public, resentful of the high taxation to fund the wars and fearing the expropriation of their land to assuage the veterans' demands. Octavian hastily returned to Italy to pacify his veterans with initial payments and promises of more to come in the future. He also vowed only to expropriate land from communities that had taken Antony's part and even then promised the victims land in overseas colonies. However, Octavian knew that unless he gained swift access to the great riches of Egypt, he would not be able to hold off the conflicting demands for too much longer. Returning to Samos, he began to plan his political campaign to woo away yet more of Antony and Cleopatra's remaining supporters and to consider what his military strategy should be against the rump of their forces.

On their return to Egypt from the Peloponnese, Cleopatra and Antony had separated. Cleopatra made straight for Alexandria to secure her capital. Politically astute as ever and conscious of the fickleness of the Alexandrian mob, she feared that her people might rise against her if they learned of her defeat before she landed. Therefore, according to the historian Dio Cassius, she arranged for her ships to be decked with garlands just as if she had won a great victory and had her sailors chant songs of triumph as the ships made their way past the Pharos lighthouse into the inner harbor. Once safely ashore and installed in the royal palace, she acted quickly and ruthlessly to bolster her position. Again according to Dio Cassius, she had many of "the leading Egyptians executed on the grounds that they had always been ill disposed to her and were now exulting in her setback. Their estates yielded her a great wealth, and in her efforts to equip her forces and seek fresh allies she plundered other sacred and secular sources, not even exempting the most holy shrines."

It is perhaps unlikely that Cleopatra would have risked arousing her subjects' religious sensibilities by such crude actions, but she was clearly engaged in raising funds and placing her kingdom on a war footing. In a bid to conciliate the king of Media, Cleopatra had Artavasdes, the king of Armenia, who had been a prisoner in Egypt since the time of Antony's Armenian triumph and the Donations of Alexandria, executed and she had his head sent to the Median king, his longtime adversary. Throughout she seems to have shown tenacity and determination in adversity and a single-minded desire to do everything she could to continue resistance to Octavian and to protect her kingdom and her family.

In sharp contrast, Antony's confidence had imploded as his troubles mounted. Never among the most emotionally stable of men, he had once more slumped into depression and inactivity. After leaving the Peloponnese, he had first gone to Cyrenaica in the hope of rallying his four legions stationed there. However, their commander had already declared for Octavian and refused to see Antony, killing the members of the embassy he sent ahead and executing some of his own legionaries who protested at his treatment of Antony's delegation. Plutarch describes how Antony wandered aimlessly up and down the hot, desolate and deserted beach where he had landed, with only two friends for company. One was a Greek orator and the other a Roman soldier whose devotion Antony had won by sparing his life in the aftermath of Philippi when he had impersonated Brutus to allow the republican leader to escape. Through the combined efforts of their philosophical and comradely cajoling, these two very different men dissuaded Antony from his plan to commit suicide. Eventually, he went back on board his ships for the journey of more than 160 miles east to Alexandria.

Once there, Antony relapsed into ever deeper despair. He ran a jetty out into the harbor and on it had a house built over the sea. Here, according to Plutarch, he spent his time "in exile from the world of men," calling his residence the Timoneum after that of the bad-tempered, misanthropic recluse Timon of Athens. Antony, whose paranoia was becoming more acute, claimed that, like Timon, he had reason to hate the world: "he too had been wronged and treated with ingratitude by his friends and so had come to mistrust and hate all mankind."

What Cleopatra, never mind his troops, made of Antony's overblown displays of despair is not recorded, but they can have given no one confidence in his future chances of success. Around this time, Cleopatra began to consider how she might save herself and her family if Egypt was overrun or, indeed, if Antony followed through on his threats and committed suicide in his despair. She contrived what Plutarch called "an extraordinary enterprise." She determined to move some of her fleet down through the Nile and Egypt's elaborate pattern of waterways to the Arabian Gulf, whence she could flee with her treasure "far from the dangers of slavery and war." Cleopatra may have hoped that even if she could not prevent Octavian's invasion of the Nile delta, by assembling a fleet in the Red Sea, where Octavian had no ships, she could put pressure on him to come to terms.

Either because the ships she had in mind were too big for the small canal between the Nile and the Red Sea or because it had become silted up, she had some of the ships mounted on wooden rollers and dragged overland. The Egyptians had for many centuries been skilled at moving heavy objects long distances to build their great monuments. Cleopatra probably also knew about the techniques developed to transport vessels on wheels along a paved road of some four miles between the Saronic and Corinthian gulfs to save having to circumnavigate the Peloponnesian coast.

Despite her ingenuity and the heroic efforts of her sailors, Cleopatra's plans came to nothing. Probably egged on by the Roman governor of Syria, who had just defected from Antony to Octavian, the Nabataean king Malchus and his men sallied forth on their camels from their stronghold of Petra, overcame the forces accompanying Cleopatra's ships and burned them all. Malchus' actions were an unwelcome reminder to Cleopatra of political realities. She had recently intervened with Antony to prevent Malchus' kingdom from being crushed by Herod. However, the likely outcome of Octavian's struggle with Antony weighed more heavily on the Nabataean king's mind than thoughts of gratitude, particularly since he had the prospect of recovering his income from the Dead Sea bitumen deposits that Cleopatra had persuaded Antony to make over to her.

At about this time, Canidius Crassus brought in person to Alexandria the news of the loss of his legions, which Antony must by now have long suspected. This blow was almost immediately followed by another—the news of the defection of Herod of Judaea, together with his powerful forces. Given his long-standing alliance with Antony, Herod had realized that his throne was vulnerable. He therefore determined first to remove the one credible rival to his position, the former ruler of Judaea, Hyrcanus—now in his seventies and the last survivor of the former royal line, with its evocative links to the high priesthood. Herod trumped up some charges of treachery with the help of forged letters and condemned Hyrcanus to strangulation. But he still did not think he was safe to leave his kingdom to visit Octavian. Believing his wife, Mariamme, and his mother-in-law, Alexandra, might plot against him once more, he locked the two women up in one fortress, while he placed his children by Mariamme in the fortress of Masada on the Dead Sea, some distance away, under the care of his own mother and sister Salome, as hostages for Mariamme's good behavior. Determined that Mariamme and her detested mother should not benefit from any plotting, he also left strict instructions that the two women should be summarily killed if news came of his own death.

Satisfied with his precautions, Herod set off for Rhodes to make his peace with Octavian, just as Auletes had gone to solicit Cato nearly thirty years previously. Once arrived, Herod carefully removed his royal diadem before his audience with Octavian, to demonstrate that he was counting on nothing. He then made his plea to retain his throne. He was, he claimed, a loyal man by nature, who would be as true to Octavian as he had been for so long to Antony. Playing to Octavian's propaganda that Cleopatra was the real enemy who had besotted Antony and lured him from the path of Roman virtue, he stressed, quite possibly truthfully given his strained relationship with Cleopatra, that he had frequently but fruitlessly counseled Antony to dispense with the Egyptian queen.

The politician in Octavian recognized that his interests would be best served by disturbing the eastern status quo as little as possible in the run-up to his attack on Egypt. Therefore, he graciously confirmed Herod on his throne, whereupon the latter departed well satisfied back to Judaea.

Plutarch wrote that when Antony heard of the defection of Canidius Crassus' legions and of Herod, "none of this news upset him. It was as if he was pleased to put aside his hopes since in so doing he could also let go his worries." Antony had, in the best Stoic traditions, reconciled himself to the inevitable. He abandoned the Timoneum and returned to the royal palace and Cleopatra. Together they "set the city on a course of eating, drinking and displays of generosity." Now both, not just Cleopatra alone, wore a brave face before their associates and the public alike. They dissolved their club, the Society of Inimitable Livers, but formed another, "just as devoted to sensuality, self-indulgence and extravagance as the previous one but they called it 'The Society of Partners in Death.' Their friends enrolled themselves in it as those who would die together and they all spent their time in a hedonistic round of banquets." Although Cleopatra had celebrated her own birthday quietly, she marked Antony's publicly with "extremely showy and costly festivities" to appeal to that side of his nature, which was somewhat childlike in its love of ostentation and need for attention and reassurance. In fact, many of the guests came poor to the banquets but departed rich.

Cleopatra and Antony also took a decision that would have dire consequences for Caesarion and for Antyllus, Antony's son by Fulvia. They had Caesarion, who was about sixteen, made a member of the youth organization that in the Greek world signified acceptance into manhood, while Antony gave Antyllus, only fourteen, the *toga virilis*, making him a Roman adult. The public celebrations and revelries filled the city's broad streets for many days. They were probably helpful in maintaining public morale, underlining as they did the continuance of both Cleopatra's and Antony's lines, "since [the populace] would have these boys as their leaders should any disaster overtake their parents." However, their entry into manhood made both young men formally liable to adult penalties.

At the same time as they were sponsoring this show of outward defiance, Cleopatra and Antony were privately considering whether they could come to any compromise settlement with Octavian. Although they knew they were thereby revealing their weakness, each sent peace envoys to him. The detail and sequence of their peace initiatives are obscure and vary from source to source. They clearly dispatched their children's tutor as their spokesman. He brought with him from Cleopatra one of her royal crowns and a golden scepter as well as other of the Egyptian royal insignia, asking Octavian on her behalf to allow her children to inherit the royal throne of Egypt. On behalf of Antony, the tutor asked that he might be allowed to retire into private life in Athens if not in Egypt, just as the other triumvir, Lepidus, had been allowed to do elsewhere after his defeat.

According to Dio Cassius, Octavian made no response to Antony's request but prudently kept Cleopatra's gifts: "His official response to her was a threatening one including the pronouncement that if she would disband her forces and renounce her throne he would then consider what should be done with her. But he also sent her a secret message that if she would kill Antony he would pardon her and leave her kingdom intact."

On another occasion, Antony sent his young son Antyllus to Octavian with a large sum in gold and a request for terms. Octavian again kept the money but made no reply. Later, Antony sent another emissary, once more bearing gifts of money. A measure of his despair is that this time the usually loyal Antony also sacrificed Publius Turullius, one of Julius Caesar's assassins who had been among his own entourage for some time, handing him over to Octavian, who had him executed. Antony, showing a selfless love for Cleopatra, even offered to kill himself if this meant that Cleopatra would be saved. Octavian again gave no answer.

The sources agree that Octavian was keen to wean Cleopatra away from Antony. They suggest that he thought he could flatter her and appeal to her vanity. To this end, he sent Thyrsus to her. Plutarch depicted him as a man of considerable intelligence "who could speak persuasively on his young commander's behalf to a haughty woman with an astonishingly high opinion of her own beauty." Octavian briefed Thyrsus to flatter Cleopatra by suggesting that Octavian was in love with her. "He hoped that since she believed she had the power to inspire passion in all mankind she might dispose of Antony and keep herself and her treasure unharmed."

In the event, Antony became jealous and suspicious of Thyrsus' long, private meetings with Cleopatra and had him thoroughly flogged before sending him back to Octavian with a letter at the same time ironic, sheepish and defiant, admitting that Thyrsus' insolent and supercilious behavior had infuriated him at a time when his temper was short because of all his troubles. "If you find what I've done intolerable," he added, "you've got my freedman Hipparchus. You can string him up and flog him and then we'll be quits." (Hipparchus was the son of Antony's steward and had deserted to Octavian shortly after Actium.)

Cleopatra was very unlikely to have been taken in by Octavian's protestations of love but may have been seeing what information she could charm out of Thyrsus. Other suggestions that at around this time she was actively seeking to betray Antony lack credibility since they occur only in the later sources, wherein Octavian's denigration of Cleopatra had reached its maturity. Contemporaneous writers such as Horace and Vergil, who were by no means favorable to Cleopatra, accused her of many things but not of seeking to betray Antony during these final, desperate days. Cleopatra would have known that the war had been declared on her and not Antony, that Octavian wanted Egypt's treasure and that her fate and Antony's were bound together. It also seems hard to believe that, survivor though she was, she would have considered deceiving the man to whom she had been faithful for so long—the father of three of her children and, to all intents and purposes, her husband.

By now it was the height of summer in the year 30 and Octavian had set out with his confident legions to invade Egypt. When he came ashore in Phoenicia he found King Herod awaiting him. Eager to please his new overlord, Herod provided lavish entertainments and accommodations and provisioned Octavian's armies with both water and wine as they marched onward through the hot deserts of Gaza and Sinai and on to the very borders of Egypt.

CHAPTER 22

Death on the Nile

PELUSIUM FELL QUICKLY to Octavian's forces. Cleopatra punished the town's governor for yielding too readily by ordering the execution of his wife and children. Dio Cassius claimed that Cleopatra herself had engineered the town's surrender to curry favor with Octavian and Plutarch noted a rumor that she had connived at its fall. Yet, like the earlier claims of her perfidy, this scarcely seems plausible.

Antony himself had not been at Pelusium but nearly 180 miles to the west of Alexandria at Paraetorium, the modern Mersah Matruh, trying to stem the advance of Octavian's forces from Cyrenaica. These were the four legions that had deserted from Antony only some nine months previously and were now led by Cornelius Gallus. From an unprivileged background, Gallus was nevertheless an accomplished lyric poet as well as a general. He had once composed volumes of verse to Antony's former mistress, Cytheris. In the face of Antony's advance, he showed his military skills by trapping and destroying some of Antony's galleys in a small harbor, into which he had allowed them to sail unopposed. He did so by stretching chains across the harbor mouth and lowering them beneath the water before the arrival of Antony's unsuspecting vessels, only to raise them again using a sophisticated system of winches once the galleys were inside. When, on land, Antony approached Gallus' lines to try to address the troops who had so recently been loyal to him and had served with him on so many campaigns, Gallus ordered the trumpeters to sound their bugles and to continue as long as Antony persisted in his attempt to speak. Eventually Antony gave up.

When the news of Pelusium reached him, Antony himself returned to Alexandria, leaving his subordinates to defend Egypt's western frontiers as best they could. Antony was only just in time. Octavian advanced quickly across the branches of the Nile delta toward Alexandria. Before long, in the shattering July heat, he was making camp near the hippodrome to the east of the city walls. Energized by the chance of further action, this time against Octavian in person, Antony led a sally out of Alexandria and, encountering the advance guard of Octavian's cavalry, sent them reeling back in panic to their camp.

Plutarch wrote that "Antony felt good after his victory." It was his final moment of glory. Still wearing his armor, dust-caked and sweat-soaked, and with the adrenaline of battle still pumping through his aging body, he strode into the royal palace, wrapped Cleopatra in his arms and kissed her. He then presented to her the soldier who in his view had fought the most bravely in the successful action. In a flamboyant gesture typical both of her generosity and of her ostentation, she rewarded him with a gleaming gold breastplate and helmet. However, that very night, the man quietly defected, crossing the lines to Octavian's camp, taking Cleopatra's gifts with him—a depressing sign of the faltering confidence of those close to Cleopatra and Antony and a reminder, if they needed one, to Octavian and his men of Alexandria's riches.

Nevertheless, Antony's hopes had revived, at least for a while. In a grand gesture he invited Octavian yet again to take him on in single combat. The younger man, who had no intention of agreeing to anything so foolish, replied coldly that "there were all sorts of ways for Antony to meet death." Antony next attempted a leafleting campaign, firing into the enemy camp missiles to which were attached notes offering large rewards to deserters. Octavian countered by reminding his men that the entire wealth of Antony, Cleopatra and of all Egypt would soon be theirs for the taking.

Determined to confront Octavian rather than face a siege, Antony decided to unleash a combined land and sea assault on his enemy. The night before the attack, Plutarch related that he ordered an especially sumptuous and extravagant dinner. It was, perhaps, a final gathering of the Society of Partners in Death. Once more in a fatalistic mood, Antony demanded that his servants pile his plate and fill his glass, "since there was no means of knowing whether they would be able to do so on the morrow or whether they would be serving other masters while he lay dead, a lifeless husk, a nothing." The eyes of his friends filled with tears as he told them he would be leading the attack not for the sake of victory or safety, since what he desired was "an honorable death."

At this emotional, perhaps even maudlin moment, strange sounds are said to have erupted in the otherwise subdued and apprehensive city. In the soft depths of the night, the diners heard "harmonious sounds from all manner of musical instruments, and the loud shouts of people making their way with Bacchic cries and prancing feet." It was as if "a troop of Dionysian revellers were raucously leaving the city. Their course seemed to lie more or less through the middle of the city towards the outer gate which faced the enemy camp, where the noise reached its crescendo and then died away." Plutarch continued: "Those who tried to interpret this sign concluded that the god [Dionysus], with whom Antony claimed kinship and whom he had sought above all to imitate, was now abandoning him." It was a potent image—the god of glory and conquest in the East and the patron of the Ptolemies deserting Cleopatra and Antony just as the gods had abandoned Troy the night before its fall.

As dawn broke over Alexandria on August 1, 30—ever afterward celebrated as a public holiday in Rome as the day when Octavian "rescued the state from the greatest danger"—Antony positioned his troops on high ground between the city and the hippodrome and waited as the rowers propelled his galleys out past the Pharos lighthouse into the blue waters of the Mediterranean before bearing down on Octavian's fleet. Plutarch wrote that he expected to see his fleet victorious. Instead, as the vessels came within reach of Octavian's, Antony's rowers raised their oars in salute and Octavian's men at once returned the greeting, whereupon Antony's men changed sides and all the ships combined in a single fleet to make directly for the city. Seeing the two sides fraternizing and realizing that this made defeat inevitable, Antony's cavalry also deserted, leaving only his infantry faithful to their old general. They were soon overrun by Octavian's men. Antony rushed back to the city toward the royal palace, apparently heaping reproaches on Cleopatra's head, crying out that she had betrayed him and that it was only for her sake that he had gone to war. But if they were ever spoken, they were words of abject despair uttered in the agony of the moment. Antony's love for and trust in Cleopatra were undiminished.

She was no longer in the palace but had barricaded herself with her waiting women, Iras and Charmion, in the "wonderfully imposing and beautiful" two-story stone tomb she was building, and which was now nearing completion, adjacent to the Temple of Isis, and which she had ordered to be crammed with all her royal treasure—gold, silver, emeralds, pearls, ebony, ivory and cinnamon together with containers of pitch, a great stack of firewood and oakum for kindling. If all else failed, she could order that the whole lot should go up in an expensive bonfire, taking herself with it, just as Queen Dido had died at Carthage. With the portcullises lowered and secured with bolts and bars, she was waiting anxiously on events.

Amidst all the confusion, as Antony searched for Cleopatra, a false report reached him that she had killed herself in her mausoleum. Plutarch and Dio Cassius believed she had sent it herself to deceive Antony and presumably to prompt his own suicide. Far more likely, a message sent by her to Antony that she was intending to kill herself had become confused, or perhaps reports of her death had begun circulating spontaneously. With Octavian's forces expected in Alexandria any minute and panic-stricken citizens fleeing hither and thither, the city must have teemed with all kinds of contradictory and alarming stories.

Whatever the source of the report, the distraught Antony believed it and no longer wished to live. In his despair he cried out, "It is not the loss of you that hurts. I shall be joining you very soon. What stings is that for all my great status as a commander, I have been shown inferior in courage to a woman." Unstrapping his breastplate, he asked his slave Eros, "to whom he had long ago entrusted the task of killing him in an emergency," to strike him down. Eros drew his sword, positioned it as if to kill Antony then, twisting, fell upon it himself and so died. With an agonized cry, "You have taught me what I must do," Antony thrust his sword into his own abdomen. Though grave, the wound was not immediately fatal, leaving a swooning Antony to fall backward on a couch. Eventually recovering consciousness, he cried out for someone to finish him off but no one would deliver the coup de grâce. Instead, they ran off, leaving him alone, writhing in agony and growing ever weaker from loss of blood until finally Cleopatra's scribe, Diomedes, arrived. She had sent him to bring Antony to her in the tomb. Whether she had done so because she had learned that he was dying or whether she had been hoping for a final reunion with her lover is unclear.

At the news that Cleopatra still lived, Antony struggled to his feet as if to go to her but, feeling his life ebbing away as the blood flow increased as he stood up, fell back on the couch and begged his returning slaves to take him to her. They carried him in their arms to the mausoleum, but Cleopatra refused to unlock the gates, presumably because she feared being captured. Instead she and her two waiting women let down ropes from an upper window. Antony's slaves fastened these as securely as they could around their dying master, and Cleopatra and her women began struggling and straining to haul him up. Plutarch's account has a raw vividness:

> Witnesses say that this was the most pitiful sight imaginable. Up he went, soaked in blood and in the throes of death, stretching his arms out towards her even as he dangled in the air beside the wall of the tomb. The task was no easy one for a woman: clinging to the rope as, with the strain showing on her face, Cleopatra struggled to bring the line up, while on the ground below people shared her agony and called out encouragement to her. At last she got him inside and laid him down. She tore her clothes in grief over him, beat her breasts with her hands, and scratched them with her nails. She smeared her face with his blood and called him her master, husband and commander.

The thoughts of the dying Antony were only for Cleopatra. He tried to calm her and asked for a glass of wine. After gulping it down, he warned her to save herself, "if she could do so without dishonor," and advised her that, of all Octavian's men, his officer Gaius Proculeius was the most to be trusted. With his final breaths, he begged her not to mourn his recent troubles but to think of all the good fortune he had enjoyed in his life and count him happy. "After all, supreme fame and power had been his." Moments later he was dead.

Trapped in her mausoleum, cradling her dead lover and covered in his congealing gore, Cleopatra's future had never been so bleak or so uncertain. As she sat and the first waves of numbing, paralyzing shock receded, fears over the fate of her children can only have added to her grief and agonized indecision—whether or not she should order the fire to be put to the wooden kindling in the mausoleum. Well before Octavian's arrival on the borders of the kingdom, she had dispatched Caesarion, her "King of Kings," to safety, "plentifully supplied with money" and under the protection of his tutor, Rhodon, whom she had ordered to take her son up the Nile, and over the desert to a port on the Red Sea and thence to India. Always a devoted mother and a woman with a strong sense of her lineage, she must have kept going over in her mind whether Caesarion was indeed beyond Octavian's reach and also what would happen to Alexander Helios, Cleopatra Selene and Ptolemy Philadelphus, still somewhere in the royal palace. Their fates, like hers, lay entirely in the hands of Octavian, a man not noted for his clemency.

It had not taken long for news of Antony's death to reach Octavian. One of Antony's bodyguards had grabbed the bloodstained sword with which he had stabbed himself, concealed it beneath his clothes and hastened with it to the enemy camp. Octavian apparently shed a few tears for the man who had been not only his brother-in-law but also once his partner in government. Such a magnanimous expression of sorrow over the fate of a fellow Roman was not only good manners but also good public relations—Caesar had wept when shown Pompey's crudely severed head. Equally judicious was Octavian's reading to his assembled supporters of the letters that had passed between himself and Antony to demonstrate that while he had been polite, reasonable and restrained, Antony had consistently been "rude and arrogant."

Octavian's thoughts turned very quickly to the Egyptian queen immured with the body of her dead lover in her tomb. He sent Proculeius into the city with instructions to take her alive if possible. Foremost in his mind was the need to secure Cleopatra's valuables before she had a chance to destroy them. Despite Antony's dying display of foresight in commending Proculeius to her, she refused to open the gates of the mausoleum to him, just as she had refused to unlock them to the dying Antony. However, Cleopatra agreed to talk to Proculeius as he stood outside one of the doors at ground level. She petitioned for what now mattered most to her, her children, begging that they be allowed to inherit her kingdom. Proculeius smoothly assured her she could trust Octavian absolutely and had no need to worry, but he made no specific promises.

While seeking to soothe the Egyptian queen, Proculeius took a careful look around the exterior of Cleopatra's stronghold, assessing its weak points and how best to gain entry quickly before Cleopatra had time either to kill herself or to set fire to her treasure. After rushing back outside the city to report to Octavian, Proculeius set out once more through the hushed and nervous streets of Alexandria toward the tomb. This time he was accompanied by Cornelius Gallus, the commander who had led the invasion of Egypt from the west and who had already reached the Egyptian capital. On this occasion, he was to deploy his skill with words, not weapons. Gallus' task, like a mediator in a hostage taking, was to keep Cleopatra talking and distracted from observing the activities of others. As Gallus was speaking, Proculeius quietly propped a ladder against one of the walls of the mausoleum, swiftly scaled it and climbed in through the same blood-smeared window through which Antony had been hoisted. Accompanied by the two slaves he had brought with him, Proculeius dashed past Antony's stiffening body downstairs to where Cleopatra, still unsuspecting, was deep in earnest conversation with Gallus, her face to the door and her two waiting women beside her.

As Proculeius ran toward them, one of the women turned and shrieked a warning to Cleopatra that she was about to be captured alive. Whipping around, Cleopatra pulled out the little dagger she had tucked into her belt, but before she could stab herself, the Roman had grabbed hold of her from behind, pinioned her arms and seized the knife. Then he frisked her, shaking out her clothes to check she had no poison concealed in them. Satisfied that she no longer had any means of harming herself, he left her under guard in the mausoleum.

Soon afterward, Octavian made his formal entry into the city through the Gate of the Sun. By his side were not his military staff but his adviser on Egyptian affairs, a Greek Stoic philosopher named Arius, who had studied at the Museon. His presence was a considered gesture designed to show the apprehensive population that Octavian did not hold all things Greek or Egyptian in contempt. Passing along broad Canopus Street, the conqueror's procession made its way to the Gymnasium, scene of the extravagant Donations of Alexandria. There Octavian mounted the dais that had been specially constructed for him. In somewhat shaky Greek—a language in which, according to Suetonius, he never became very fluent—he addressed the people gathered there. Fearing that their city would be given over to the soldiery for pillage and frightened out of their wits, they kept frantically prostrating themselves before Octavian until he told them to get up and announced that he was giving Alexandria "an absolute pardon." His reasons were, he said graciously, threefold—his admiration for the city's founder, Alexander, the greatness and beauty of the city and as a favor to his friend Arius.

In a decision made with regard both to public sensibilities and also to appeasing and occupying Cleopatra, Octavian allowed her to give Antony "a sumptuous, royal burial." Dio Cassius wrote that she embalmed her dead lover's body with her own hands. She was by now ill—her breast was inflamed and ulcerated where she had beaten and scratched it in her grief and she was running a high fever. She had also given up eating in hopes of hastening her death. Her doctor and confidant Olympus, whose eyewitness account of Cleopatra's last days was drawn on by Plutarch, was her accomplice. According to Plutarch, when Octavian threatened to harm her children, whom, with the exception of Caesarion, he now had under lock and key, she desisted. His well-directed threats "undermined her resolution as if they were siege-engines until she surrendered her body into the hands of those who wanted to nourish and care for it."

A week after Antony's death, to check on her mental and physical state, Octavian paid Cleopatra a visit in the palace to which she had been moved. Dio Cassius, to whom Cleopatra was "a woman of insatiable sexuality," suggested that she had prepared carefully, dressing with studied negligence in robes of mourning that "wonderfully enhanced her beauty" and that she set out to flatter and seduce Octavian, whispering tremulously of her feelings for the man who reminded her of the long-dead Julius Caesar. Plutarch's better-sourced account seems more credible. He described how Octavian found the once glamorous thirty-nine-year-old Egyptian queen sprawled on a straw mattress, clad only in a simple tunic. At the sight of him she leapt up and prostrated herself before him on the ground. "Her hair and face were unkempt and wild, her voice trembled, her eyes were sunken" and the self-inflicted bruises and lacerations on her breast were clearly visible. Octavian bade her recline once more and sat down beside her.

Despite her wretchedness, Plutarch believed something of the old Cleopatra remained. Conscious still of her charisma and doubtless hopeful of achieving something for her children, she began to justify her actions, suggesting she had acted out of necessity, even hinting that she had been afraid of Antony. Octavian, however, would have none of it, knocking down her arguments one by one. Cleopatra switched from arguing to pleading. To ingratiate herself she handed Octavian a list of her most valuable personal possessions. Her steward somewhat spoiled the gesture by pointing out that the list was incomplete—Cleopatra had secreted some valuables away. Hearing this, Cleopatra jumped up and, rushing toward him, belabored the man's face with her fists and pulled at his hair until a smiling Octavian stopped her. Thinking on her feet, she tried lamely to excuse herself by claiming that she had put aside a few of her jewels not for herself—she was far too miserable for such things—but, as she assured Octavian, "so she could give these trifles to

Octavia and your Livia and through their intercession make you more compassionate and gentle towards me."

According to Plutarch, Octavian's visit to Cleopatra convinced him that, despite her earlier displays of despair, she still valued her life. He told her that her valuables were for her to dispose of as she wished and that "he would give her more splendid treatment than she could possibly expect." Cleopatra, though, was far too experienced to be lulled by platitudes and suspected Octavian's true intentions toward her and her family. Plutarch described how she managed to worm the truth out of one of Octavian's friends, the young, aristocratic Cornelius Dolabella, who told her that Octavian planned to leave Egypt in two days' time, marching overland through Syria, and intended to pack Cleopatra and her children off to Rome, presumably by sea, in three days' time. Just like her half sister, Arsinoe, they would be paraded before the mob in a Roman Triumph.

The knowledge that her fate and that of her children would be as she feared seems to have decided Cleopatra that suicide would be preferable. Caught until then between her longing to follow her lover and her duty to her children, she may even have hoped that despite his earlier threats, with their mother dead, Octavian might spare her children. Concealing her emotions, she immediately begged Octavian's permission to go to Antony's tomb to pour libations on to his coffin. Octavian agreed and allowed Cleopatra, accompanied by her faithful ladies-in-waiting, Iras and Charmion, to make their way to the tomb. Once there, Cleopatra finally shed the carapace of regal self-reliance with which throughout her life she had sought to mask her vulnerability. Plutarch related how she fell on Antony's coffin, lamenting that she was nothing but a prisoner of fate, a captive slave, to be "closely watched and preserved for the triumph to be celebrated over your defeat . . . In life nothing could divide us but now in death it seems that we must change places: you, the Roman will lie here and I will lie in Italian soil." Though the earthly gods had abandoned them both, she begged Antony to invoke the help of the gods of the underworld and not allow "your wife," as she simply styled herself, to be the centerpiece of a Triumph.

She draped the coffin with garlands of flowers and, in a universal gesture of widow's grief, kissed it a final farewell. Then Cleopatra returned to her apartments, where she ordered a bath to be prepared. On rising from its scented depths, she once more resumed her regal dignity and prepared for the final act of her twenty-year-long reign. She ordered her attendants to fetch her royal robes, probably the brilliantly colored garb of the goddess Isis, and to dress her, taking as much care as if she were preparing once more to meet her lover at Tarsus. Next, a lavish midday meal—which some have equated to a formal funeral banquet—was served to her. Plutarch stated that in the middle of this feast a man arrived carrying a woven basket. Challenged by the guards, he raised the lid to reveal a pile of temptingly large and luscious figs beneath a layer of green leaves and invited the guards to help themselves. Suspicious no longer, the guards allowed him to enter Cleopatra's chamber.

Once she had finished eating, Cleopatra dispatched a message she had already inscribed on a tablet to Octavian. Determined that her destiny should be forever united with that of Antony, her missive was a passionate appeal to be buried with her lover. Then she ordered all her attendants except Charmion and Iras to leave her so that she could make her last preparations for death and compose herself to it. Plutarch believed that, since returning to Alexandria after Actium and establishing the Society of Partners in Death, she had been seeking a painless form of suicide. He related how, with single-minded thoroughness, she had assembled a collection of various types of lethal poisons and tested each of them to see which was painless by giving them to condemned prisoners. When she saw to her dismay that the fast-acting ones brought a swift but painful death whereas the gentler ones were slow to take effect, she continued with her experiments on one prisoner after another. This became her daily routine, and she found that "in almost every case only the bite of an asp produced a sleepy lethargy without any convulsions or groans; their faces covered with a sheen of perspiration and their senses dulled, the men painlessly lost the use of their limbs and resisted all attempts to rouse them."

But, as Plutarch acknowledged, "no one knows the truth" of what really happened in Cleopatra's apartments that day. Many in the ancient world believed that an asp was indeed responsible—smuggled in, just as Shakespeare portrays, in the basket of ripe figs. Others claimed Cleopatra had kept an asp concealed within a water jar. While she was goading it to come out by poking at it with a golden stick, "it lunged at her and fastened on her arm." Yet another theory was that Cleopatra had concealed a hollow hairpin filled with poison in her hair.

Whatever method she used, death must have come relatively quickly. Immediately on receiving her suicide note, Octavian ordered some of his men to

Cleopatra's apartments. Shouting to the guards to open the doors, the men rushed inside to find Cleopatra arrayed in her royal robes, dead upon a golden couch. Iras lay dying by her feet while Charmion, so weak she could barely stand or hold her head upright, was attempting with trembling fingers to adjust the diadem on Cleopatra's forehead. According to Plutarch, one of the men spat out, " 'A fine deed, this, Charmion!' to which she replied, 'Yes, nothing could be finer. It is no more than befits this lady, the descendant of so many kings,' " whereupon she too slumped dead by Cleopatra's couch.

And so Cleopatra staged the last great spectacle of her reign, passing from life into legend upon her golden couch as the last of the Ptolemies of Egypt and the woman who, in the words of Dio Cassius, "through her own unaided genius captivated the two greatest Romans of her time."

CHAPTER 23

"Too Many Caesars Is Not a Good Thing"

OCTAVIAN APPEARED BOTH ASTOUNDED and angered by Cleopatra's death. It was, Dio Cassius wrote, "as if all the glory of his victory had been taken away from him"—in their final tussle Cleopatra had outwitted him. This was doubtless what she had intended. Though grief at losing Antony and fears for the future had been her primary motives for choosing to die, her decision had been more than a desperate way out. Throughout her life she had struggled, sometimes fought, for control over her destiny and the right to her throne. Her death was a way of reasserting her power, of converting humbling defeat into victory, of regaining what a Roman would call her *dignitas*.

According to Suetonius, in hopes of reviving the motionless queen, Octavian summoned snake charmers "to suck the poison from her self-inflicted wound." This could, of course, have been playacting. Since his initial efforts to keep Cleopatra alive, the ever cautious Octavian might have changed his view and decided that, on balance, a dead Cleopatra was preferable to a live one. After all, the Roman crowds had not reacted well to the sight of Cleopatra's sister Arsinoe marching in chains in Caesar's Triumph. The charismatic Cleopatra similarly might have aroused their sympathy. Also, the public disgracing of her might have seemed an affront to Caesar, who had erected her glittering image in the Temple of Venus Genetrix. It is just conceivable that Octavian helped engineer Cleopatra's suicide by priming Dolabella to reveal the humiliating fate he had in store for her and her children and by relaxing the surveillance she was under. Yet more likely,

Cleopatra had indeed convinced Octavian that life was still dear to her, so he failed to anticipate her suicide.

The manner and mystery of Cleopatra's death were eagerly debated in Alexandria and in Rome. The snake idea quickly gained currency. Although those searching her apartments found no serpents lurking there, some claimed to have seen a snake's slithering track along the shore beneath the windows while others reported "two faint puncture marks" on Cleopatra's lifeless arm. Death by snakebite appears to have been the version Octavian believed—at least publicly. Plutarch noted that he ordered a gigantic image of Cleopatra with a snake clinging to her arm to be carried in his Egyptian Triumph in 29.

But if Cleopatra did indeed die by a serpent's bite, it is unlikely that an asp was responsible. Plutarch's claim that the prisoners bitten by asps on Cleopatra's instructions perished quietly and painlessly was wrong. *Asp* is a general term used to describe various small vipers of North Africa and Arabia.* A viper's venom poisons the blood, causing an immediate burning sensation and bringing on giddiness, nausea and desperate thirst. The infected part of the body turns purple and begins to swell and the victim loses all control of bodily functions, sometimes helplessly vomiting, urinating and defecating, before finally passing out. This hardly would have been the death chosen by a divine monarch so conscious of appearances.

Cleopatra more probably selected as her instrument of suicide the blackish brown or yellow Egyptian cobra or uraeus common in the marshlands of the Nile delta. Cobra venom is a nerve poison rather than a blood toxin and a cobra's bite leaves only puncture marks on the skin—like those noted by eyewitnesses on Cleopatra's body—with no discoloration or swelling. The victim begins to feel sleepy as paralysis takes hold, leading to coma and a slide into death. Such an end would have been both painless and dignified. Also, the cobra or uraeus would have appealed to Cleopatra. Not only was it sacred to Isis but it was also the symbol of the royal house of Egypt—the rearing cobras on the royal crown symbolized their protection of the wearer and a spitting defiance to any would-be enemy. Cleopatra would have considered the imagery of the cobra a suitable farewell message to Octavian.

***Cerastes vipera* (often called "Cleopatra's asp"), *Vipera berus*, *Vipera aspis* and *Cerastes cornutus* are all described as asps.

Yet even this solution begs further questions. The Egyptian cobra would have been hard for Cleopatra to conceal—the smallest cobra capable of killing a human being is around four feet long. An even bigger serpent—perhaps as long as six feet—would have been required to kill Iras and Charmion as well as their mistress. How could a reptile of such size have been smuggled into Cleopatra's chambers? Perhaps, as several writers believed, including Horace and Vergil, there was more than one snake. Whatever the case, the legendary basket of figs carried into Cleopatra's chamber of death seems an inadequate camouflage. But Cleopatra never lacked courage or ingenuity—somehow, in those burning days of high summer in Alexandria, she found a way of arranging her death to her satisfaction.

Whatever his feelings toward her in life, Octavian seems to have been impressed by Cleopatra's dignity and firmness of purpose at her end. He granted her last request to be buried beside Antony "with the kind of splendid ceremony suitable for a queen." Octavian's compassion did not, however, extend to Caesarion. Cleopatra's suicide had done nothing to protect her eldest son, around whom so many of her hopes had been built. Suetonius related how Octavian dispatched cavalry in pursuit of Caesarion with orders to kill him. Other accounts tell of how the sixteen-year-old was lured back to Alexandria, perhaps through the treachery of his tutor Rhodon. However he was captured, the results were the same. Caesarion was just too dangerous to be allowed to live and was immediately executed. Octavian's adviser Arius had counseled him that "too many Caesars is not a good thing," and Octavian had agreed.

Antony's elder son by Fulvia, Antyllus, was also murdered. He had taken refuge by a statue of Julius Caesar, probably in the Caesareum. Despite his screams for mercy, he was dragged from the statue and his head hacked off. His tutor took advantage of the scuffling and confusion surrounding his pupil's killing to steal a valuable jewel that Antyllus had always worn around his neck. Despite the tutor's attempts to conceal the stone by sewing it into his belt, his theft was discovered and Octavian ordered him to be crucified. Though he was not such a threat as Caesarion, Antyllus suffered for having donned the *toga virilis* and formally come of age during the last months of Cleopatra and Antony's rule. Octavian also would have been mindful that, several years earlier, Antony had declared Antyllus his heir and issued coins bearing both their heads.

However, Octavian spared all Antony's other children, whether by Cleopatra or by Fulvia, and of course Antony's daughters by Octavia. Cleopatra

Selene and her two full brothers, Alexander Helios and Ptolemy Philadelphus, were made to march close to the image of their dead mother in Octavian's Egyptian Triumph, which, according to Dio Cassius, "surpassed all others in luxury and magnificence." They were then placed in the care of the virtuous and maternal Octavia, together with their half brother, Antony's younger son by Fulvia, Iullus Antonius. Perhaps significantly, although she lived until 11 BC, Octavia never remarried. Perhaps she too had really loved Antony.

In his own account of his life, Octavian claimed that after the conquest of Alexandria he pardoned all Antony's Roman supporters who sought clemency, but he was, as so often, stretching the truth. He showed no mercy to the two surviving assassins of Julius Caesar who had been with Antony or to Antony's loyal general Canidius Crassus and several others, including a Roman senator who had run Cleopatra's woolen mill. All were executed.

Octavian did, however, spare Alexandria, together with its citizens, as he had promised. Although he ordered all statues of Antony to be toppled and removed, he allowed those of Cleopatra to remain—a concession secured by a rich Alexandrian for a payment of two thousand talents. Octavian also continued work on the Caesareum—Cleopatra's still incomplete memorial to his adoptive father. To make the building yet more imposing, he ordered two rose granite obelisks to be moved from Heliopolis and erected in front of it. The hieroglyphs on them reveal that they were originally erected by Tutmoses III in front of Heliopolis' temple to the sun in the first half of the fifteenth century BC.*

Octavian also put his men to work, improving Egypt's canal system and dredging the mud from some of the Nile tributaries. The purpose was not so much to benefit the Egyptians but to improve the transport of Egyptian grain

---

*The obelisks remained in their new location long after the Caesareum itself had vanished until one was acquired by a Briton, placed in a cylinder of steel on a pontoon boat suitably named *Cleopatra* and towed toward Britain. During a wild storm in the Bay of Biscay, the tow ropes broke, six men were killed or drowned and the obelisk was adrift for six days, but it was rescued and eventually reached London, where, known as Cleopatra's Needle, it still stands on the Thames embankment. The other obelisk was transported to New York at the expense of the millionaire William Vanderbilt and in 1881 erected in Central Park behind the Metropolitan Museum of Art.

to Rome, where it soon met one third of the capital's needs. Cargo fleets of up to five hundred ships at a time transported it across the Mediterranean to make Roman bread.

Territories Antony had given Cleopatra became Roman provinces once more and Herod regained the lands he had lost to the Egyptian queen. He governed Judaea with increasing ruthlessness, suppressing any dissent and killing three of his sixteen sons for plotting against him—an act that caused Octavian to remark that it was better to be Herod's pig than his child. In his final years, crazed with pain from a disease—perhaps cancer—that was putrefying his still-living body, Herod became yet more paranoid and cruel.

The fate Cleopatra had once feared for her country and striven to avoid overtook it: Egypt was annexed to Rome. However, the country remained so rich, so important and so potentially dangerous as a focal point for dissent and rebellion that Octavian appointed not a senator to govern it but a member of the knightly or *equites* class. Furthermore, he made the governor report not to the Senate but directly to himself. Egypt thus became unique in the empire as Octavian's personal fief. Senators were not even allowed to visit Egypt, never mind live there, without Octavian's explicit personal consent. The first occupant of the governor's post was Cornelius Gallus, who successfully put down rebellions and led military expeditions up the Nile and into Ethiopia. But despite his relatively humble background, Egypt appears to have seduced Gallus with delusions of grandeur, as it had so many others before him. He began openly disparaging Octavian when drunk, erecting great numbers of statues of himself throughout the country and having a list of his achievements chiseled into one of the pyramids. Octavian summoned him to Rome, where in 26 he was forced to commit suicide for his hubris.

Octavian's personal attitude toward Egypt was equivocal but pragmatic. Before leaving the country he had visited Alexander's mausoleum, where he inspected the iconic leader's embalmed body and, according to Suetonius, showed his veneration by crowning the head with a golden diadem and strewing the body with flowers. Dio Cassius claimed he went further, inadvertently breaking off a piece of Alexander's nose, which he had touched, no doubt, out of curiosity. Octavian refused an invitation to view the bodies of the Ptolemies in their mausolea, insisting that he "came to see a King, not a row of corpses." Nor would he visit the Apis bull, remarking that he was "accustomed to worship gods not cattle."

Yet Octavian was sufficiently concerned with administrative continuity to allow—no doubt with an appropriate show of reluctance—for the last regnal year of Cleopatra's rule to be followed in the official Egyptian calendar by the first year of his own, as well as allowing himself to be referred to formally as the "father of the country." He added his name to those inscribed on the Temple of Dendera, the exterior walls of which depicted the graceful forms of Cleopatra and Caesarion, and placed his granite portrait next to that of Cleopatra's father, Auletes, in a temple he had built to Isis. Later he permitted his wife, Livia, to appear on the Egyptian coinage—something that never occurred elsewhere and which may have been a concession to the Egyptian concept of joint rule. Such Egyptian coins even bore the double cornucopia—the badge of the Ptolemies—on the reverse.

In Rome, the conquest of Egypt and, in particular, the acquisition of the contents of Cleopatra's vast treasuries triggered a financial boom. Allegedly keeping only one of Cleopatra's jeweled drinking cups for himself, Octavian ordered all the rest of her opulent gold and silverware to be melted down. Keen to retain the loyalty of his legions, he paid a special premium of about a year's pay to the soldiers who had participated in the Alexandrian campaign as well as a general premium of the same amount to all his soldiers. He also spent a great deal of money buying land on which to settle his veterans, since he was eager to reduce the size of the armies swiftly to peacetime levels and thus lessen the potential for revolt. Rates of interest in Rome and Italy tumbled from 12 to 4 percent and the price of land doubled, producing a feel-good effect throughout the country. Octavian took the opportunity to underline his own part in this prosperity by minting coins as a beneficent victor and the founder of a new, yet stronger, prouder Rome. He also gave four hundred sesterces to each male citizen of Rome. The Roman population, which had yearned for so long for an end to civil wars and anarchic upheavals, was content even at the price of losing some liberties as Octavian strengthened his grip. As Dio Cassius wrote, "They forgot all the hardships they had suffered and accepted Octavian's triumph with pleasure as though the enemies he had conquered had all been foreigners."

Octavian had, like his adoptive father Julius Caesar, shown a single-minded focus in the fourteen years since Caesar's murder. He had been determined throughout to achieve his ambition of sole power. To do so, he had chosen well in his supporters, in particular Agrippa, and had delegated to them sufficient authority—but no more—to achieve his purposes. He had been prepared to trim to the prevailing winds in his early alliances with Caesar's murderers but had never lost sight of his ultimate objective. Perhaps, unlike Antony, he had never seen the triumvirate as anything other than an expedient and temporary arrangement. He had been prepared cynically to break commitments he made to Antony during this period despite his sister Octavia's intervention on her husband's behalf. He had an innate hypocrisy that allowed him to square in his mind his own ambition with the public good and his version of events with the truth. As a consequence, he had shown himself a master of public relations and propaganda. Unlike Antony, who emerges from all the accounts as the more impulsive and warmhearted personality and, to most tastes, the more likeable, the buttoned-up, self-contained Octavian never took a decision without, like a chess player, weighing not just its immediate impact but also its long-term strategic benefit. He never made a speech without calculating its effect. Suetonius alleged that Octavian "did not even make statements to individuals, or even to his wife Livia, except by writing them down and reading them aloud, lest he say too much or too little by speaking casually."

As a consequence of his defeat of Cleopatra and Antony, Octavian was now well on his way to becoming the princeps, or chief citizen, of the Roman state, a title he assumed in 27, together with the appellation "Augustus," with its implication of dignity, stateliness, even sanctity. As de facto first emperor of Rome, he remained, just as Cleopatra and Antony had been, conscious of his image—sufficiently so, in fact, to order an official portrait of himself depicting a calm, elevated leader to be widely copied and circulated throughout the Roman world. It served as the basis for a variety of surviving sculptures and other portrayals. Significantly, when the Senate offered to name one of the months after him, he asked that it should not be the month of his birth, as in the case of Julius Caesar and July, but Sextillis, the old sixth month but now, under the Julian calendar, the eighth—the month of his victory over Cleopatra and Antony. This became August.

After forty-four years of successful autocratic rule, during which he centralized the administration of the empire and banished conflict to its borders, where skirmishes with barbarians continued but did not threaten, Augustus died in AD 14. Ironically, many of his centralizing measures and, in particular, his concentration of all power in the hands of a single unelected leader resembled the way the Ptolemies had ruled Egypt. After Augustus' cremation, his ashes were placed in his great round mausoleum set in a public park, which, it was said, he had designed taking the tomb of Alexander in Alexandria as his inspiration.

By now Rome also contained many artifacts transported from Egypt. Immediately following the return to Italy of Augustus and his veterans and over the subsequent decades a sort of "Egyptmania" had taken hold. Citizens eagerly imported pharaonic works of art. Sometimes obelisks were reerected in Roman squares to celebrate victories, sometimes in temples to Roman gods and at other times simply to beautify public spaces or to act as giant sundials.* Rarely did those installing them in their picturesque new settings have any consciousness of the original purpose of the works, a sphinx being considered a must-have for any large Roman garden. Egyptian landscapes incorporating such elements as Nile scenes, lotuses, pyramids and crocodiles became commonplace in frescoes and decorative relief sculptures. There was also a fashion for Egyptian jewelry in the form of scarab rings and amulets.

Many Romans even chose to have their ashes buried in pyramid-shaped tombs. They did so irrespective of their religion, but the other major Egyptian exports to Rome were the cults of Isis, Osiris and other gods. These gods had initially been imported at the beginning of the first century BC but after Cleopatra's defeat freed them from association with a foreign enemy they began to flourish. The cult of Isis offered life after death to its converts, together with exotic and elaborate rituals accompanied by music, chanting and the burning of incense. Each day before sunrise, the priests presented the statue of Isis to her seated followers who had gathered, shaking their metal rattles in her honor and to drown out any extraneous sounds intruding into the complex rites of the cult. They remained deep in prayer until the sun had risen to be blessed by the assembled worshippers who also celebrated the resurrection of Osiris, god of the underworld, at the daily rebirth of the sun. At two o'clock in the afternoon, a second ceremony was held for the adoration of the sacred water of the Nile. So popular were the cults that the worship of these Egyptian deities continued in some quarters of Rome until the city's fall.

The eventual fates of the surviving children of Cleopatra, Antony and Octavian were various and in some cases curious. Cleopatra Selene was married to

---

*One such sundial, which Octavian ordered to be brought to Rome and placed in the Campus Martius, is now in the city's Piazza di Monte Citorio.

a young man who as a small boy had, like her, been displayed in a Roman Triumph. This was Juba, the erudite Numidian prince who in 25 was made the ruler of the client kingdom of Mauretania (in present-day Morocco). Their son, whom they named Ptolemy, succeeded his father in AD 23. Cleopatra Selene's two brothers are assumed to have accompanied her to her new kingdom and, from here, the boys for whom such grand futures were announced by Antony on his silver dais at the Donations of Alexandria passed into obscurity.

Antony's two daughters by Octavia left a greater mark on history. Both remained in Rome and one became the mother and both became grandmothers of emperors, albeit notorious ones. The elder Antonia became the grandmother of Nero, while the younger Antonia became the mother of Claudius and grandmother of Caligula.* Octavian allowed Antony's surviving son by Fulvia, Iullus Antonius, to claim his family inheritance. Under Octavian's patronage he enjoyed a successful career in Rome, becoming a consul and governor in Asia Minor as well as a poet. However, in 2 BC, age forty-one, he became caught up in a sex scandal involving Octavian's thirty-six-year-old daughter, Julia. She had first been married to Octavian's faithful school friend and admiral Agrippa, who died in 12 BC, and at the time of the scandal was wife to Tiberius, the son of her stepmother, Livia, by her first husband.

Like several other well-born men, Antonius was accused of indulging in sexual debauches with Julia, "who refrained from no sex act possible to a woman." Allegedly, she had been seen in the dead of night carousing and fornicating in the Forum with Antonius and the others, as well as drunkenly clambering and cavorting over the rostra where Cicero's head had once been nailed and from which her father had addressed the populace urging the moral regeneration of Rome. The men were charged with treason and some, including Antonius, were forced to commit suicide or executed. Tiberius divorced Julia. As unforgiving of his only daughter's weaknesses as he was of those of others, Octavian exiled her to an offshore island. Presumably because drink had played a part in her downfall, rather than just for spite, he ordered her guards to allow her no wine. She shared her abstemious life with her mother, Scribonia, abruptly divorced herself

---

*In AD 40 Caligula murdered Ptolemy of Mauretania—Cleopatra and Antony's grandson and so, of course, his cousin. The reason was that Ptolemy had dared to wear a more gorgeous purple mantle to the amphitheater than Caligula.

by Octavian so many years previously and who voluntarily followed her daughter into exile. Although eventually allowed to return to the mainland, Julia remained in close confinement until she died fourteen years later. She lived to see her former husband, Tiberius, succeed Octavian as emperor since her sons by Agrippa had died before their grandfather.

Sexual excess continued to play a part in Roman politics. Other women of the imperial family were banished for their appetites. As emperor, Octavian introduced legislation governing the behavior of women, promoting marriage, punishing adultery and generally emphasizing that a woman's place was in the home bearing children. Nevertheless, Suetonius alleged that well into old age Octavian himself retained "a passion for deflowering girls—who were collected for him from every quarter, even by his wife."

Predictably, it was Cleopatra who was the ultimate icon of sexual depravity in Roman eyes. Oil lamps depicted her squatting on a giant phallus. Stripped of humanity, intellect and feeling, she was beginning her long, distorted journey through history as the epitome of the scheming, predatory whore, her true story ignored and then forgotten.

Postscript: "This Pair So Famous"

In the closing scene of Shakespeare's *Antony and Cleopatra*, Octavian orders a fitting burial for the man and woman he refers to as "this pair so famous." Amidst all the confusions and contradictions, propaganda and prejudice that have clouded the story of Cleopatra and Antony for over two millennia, this, at least, is unarguable. They are one of the most enduringly famous couples of history. It is also undoubtedly true that their lives were turbulent and eventful, played out against a backdrop of bitter power struggles, complex conspiracies and bloody battles at a defining time in Rome's history.

In analyzing the relationship between Cleopatra and Antony, certain elements always come through, whatever the source and however favorable or unfavorable the author. Their names are always linked—even in the earliest sources—as lovers. There was an undoubted chemistry between them that endured over a decade and produced three children. In many ways they were very similar: charismatic, with an ability to charm; risk takers, sometimes thrill seekers; ambitious and disposed to scheme on a grand scale; passionate lovers of life and relishers of excess. They were also loyal to one another.

Cleopatra was not the "bitch in heat" nymphomaniac so often portrayed. She had two men in her life, Caesar and then Antony. Neither—moving to the other end of the spectrum—was she the cold-blooded schemer and manipulator of men as she is equally frequently depicted to be. Certainly, she took her first lover, Caesar, because she feared for her throne, indeed her life, and there was an element of calculation. But she developed feelings for the man who fathered her beloved Caesarion and who was, in many ways, her own father figure. When she joined Caesar in Rome, so great was their empathy that he discussed with her his plans for remodeling Rome and for introducing a new calendar. Her influence with Caesar was one of the reasons she was so feared and disliked in Rome. Later, during the civil war that followed her lover's murder, Cleopatra did not accede to the requests of his assassins for aid, despite the proximity of their armies to Egypt and the consequent risks to herself and her throne. Instead, she attempted to lead her navy to support Antony and Octavian.

Cleopatra's relationship with Antony was very different. Though again it began with an element of calculation and self-interest, it developed and transmuted into deep and passionate love. With Caesar, Cleopatra had been the junior and very much younger partner. With Antony, she came to enjoy a relationship of equals unique for the time—a true partnership sexually, emotionally, intellectually, politically, in which each came to depend on the other. She was his daily companion. Unlike his Roman wives, Cleopatra usually accompanied Antony on his campaigns.

Something of Antony's attachment to Cleopatra also penetrates the fog of Octavian's misogynistic propaganda and the centuries of myth building. His feelings for her developed over time. Antony was clearly susceptible to attractive women and would not have been hard to seduce. He also admired and was accustomed to being guided by strong-minded, patrician women. Cleopatra fitted a mold he was used to, with the additional allure that she was a queen and the living incarnation of a goddess. It is not surprising that he fell heavily for her in Tarsus and followed her back to Alexandria for a period of sexual abandon. But his feelings at this early stage, though strong, did not, of course, prevent him from returning to Rome and settling down with Octavia.

Yet Antony could not forget Cleopatra, to whom, of all the many women in his life, he would make the greatest commitment. That was why he took the politically dangerous step of sending Octavia away and binding himself totally to the Egyptian queen, to whom thereafter he remained uniquely faithful. Sexual passion turned into a bond so strong that together they formulated a novel concept under which Egypt would become almost an equal partner with Rome in the East. Unlike Octavian, Antony had always been comfortable working in a team and sharing ideas—he had been a loyal second in command to Caesar—and had no difficulty regarding Cleopatra, though a woman, as his partner. She guided and reassured him, kept him focused and mitigated the mood swings of his mercurial, seemingly somewhat manic-depressive temperament. That was one reason—though of course there were others—why, when told Cleopatra was dead, he fell on his sword. The thought of life without the lover and friend with whom he had shared everything seemed unendurable.

There is, of course, much that we can never know and only guess at. That is part of our fascination with this couple whose lives still radiate such sensual, sexual glamour that we sometimes forget the bigger picture. Cleopatra and Antony were not romantic victims being swept to an inevitable doom in some epic tragedy. Almost uniquely in the ancient world, Cleopatra was a female ruler in her own right of a major economic power. Many centuries would pass—perhaps until the time of Elizabeth I—before another woman would show such political shrewdness and staying power. Antony was for a time the most powerful man in the Western world. The motivations and ambitions, decisions and actions of these lovers shaped one of the great power struggles of history—a struggle that, had Cleopatra and Antony succeeded, might have produced a world somewhat different from the one we know today.

Typical of the mass of myth and propaganda that surrounds Cleopatra, one of the most remembered historical conundrums centers on her and is itself based on a historical inaccuracy. In his *Pensées*, Pascal asked, what if Cleopatra had had a smaller nose? Would the course of history have been different? Would Antony still have fallen in love with her, or would he have stayed in Rome and overcome Octavian? The question spawned the "Cleopatra's nose theory of history," highlighting both how great events depend on small details and the personal relationships behind history, and launching a deluge of modern discussion of historical what-ifs. However, the conundrum ignores evidence from coins showing that Cleopatra had a prominent, long, hooked nose, a reduction in the size of which might have been beneficial, as well as Plutarch's comment that it was Cleopatra's personality and voice—not her middling looks—that gave her such charisma.

Pascal's question misunderstands the nature of romantic love and physical attraction if not of the symmetry that underlies so much of our appreciation of beauty. It also prompts delightful if idle speculation about the role of personal chemistry, itself as impossible to dissect as love between political leaders. For example, what made Churchill and Roosevelt kindred spirits and, even more, what gave Margaret Thatcher such influence with Reagan and Gorbachev? However, it is perhaps more profitable to speculate what would have happened had Antony been victorious with Cleopatra's assistance over Octavian.

Octavian's triumph marked the ascendance of occidental Rome over the Greeks and the eastern states that had absorbed Greek culture. It allowed Vergil, following Octavian's imperialistic and chauvinistic party line, first to admit condescendingly that the East might supply better artists, sculptors, rhetoricians and even astronomers but that:

. . . yours my Roman is the gift of government,
That is your bent—to impose upon the nations
The code of peace; to be clement to the conquered,
But utterly to crush the intransigent.

More than three hundred years would pass before the East would, with the rise of Constantinople and the subsequent establishment of the Byzantine empire, once more take a share of political power in the Mediterranean.

Scholars, as well as defining the battle of Actium as one of the major tipping points of history, have argued about what would have happened had Antony been victorious, either at Actium or earlier. Part of the answer depends on at what stage and how he would have won, with its consequences for the balance of power between the two lovers and leaders. If Antony had routed the Parthians and opened up Rome's path to India and beyond, he could have returned to Rome. His triumph would have easily eclipsed Octavian's victory over Sextus Pompey and the inhabitants of Illyricum. He would have had much less political need for Cleopatra than if together they had defeated Octavian in a close-fought series of naval and land engagements around Actium.

In the event of a complete victory over Parthia and the establishment of a Roman hegemony reaching as far as India, both contemporary and ancient history show that one of the most difficult feats would have been to retain order and control over such a vast dominion after the initial military victory. If Antony had done so, it is possible that he would have come to an agreement with Octavian establishing a duumvirate whereby Octavian ruled his existing western possessions from Rome and Antony an eastern empire consisting of a combination of Roman provinces and client kingdoms from Alexandria.

While Antony still would have needed Cleopatra emotionally, he would have been unlikely to have needed politically to move so quickly to please her with such an ostentatious and elaborate ceremony as the Donations of Alexandria—such anathema to Roman society. Their ideas for a partnership between Rome and Egypt could have been developed more slowly and privately. In these circumstances, Antony and Octavian might have coexisted uneasily until Antony's death—the latter would have been around fifty at the time of his Triumph and had lived a dissipated life. Depending on how long Antony in fact lived, the two halves of the empire might have become so distinct in culture and administration that Octavian would not have felt able to confront Antony's successor, leading to a much earlier development of separate empires in the east and west.

A victory for Antony's forces around Actium in 31, with the assumed death of Octavian by his own or another's hand, poses a completely different set of questions. Crucially, Antony's supporters were, in addition to Cleopatra, a mixed bag of eastern client kings and the remnants of the Roman republicans. If the Actium campaign had gone well, there would have been no republican defections from Antony, and it is hard to envisage that after his victory such elements would not have agitated for a resurrection of at least some of the senatorial powers.

Antony's views on how Rome should have been governed are not clear. He offered Caesar the crown. However, nearly all the staunch republicans flocked to him as a better hope for the preservation of the republic than Octavian, perhaps indicating that his approach was more evolutionary than the revolution of his rival. Perhaps like Pompey, Antony would have been uncertain what to do with supreme power when he acquired it, relishing the respect and status his position afforded more than anything else. Unlike Octavian, Antony's views were influenced by a succession of close associates: first his mother, Julia, then Curio, Julius Caesar, Fulvia and finally Cleopatra. Since she would have been his dominant influence after Actium, she would have pushed him toward autocracy and probably monarchy, a pressure that could have been reinforced by the practicalities of the new empire, which would have demanded a strong and stable administration and a clear, swift and decisive command structure. Rome would have found, just as it did with Octavian, that the republic's lingering death had become inevitable—at least after the Senate's supine approval of the Second Triumvirate. The republicans had been fractious, small-minded and far too inclined to focus on detail and petty jealousies to see the big picture and the consequences of their incessant squabblings on it. By refusing to pool some of their prerogatives and to sacrifice some of their privileges and even some minor liberties, they had rendered autocracy inevitable.

Given that Octavian's propaganda against Cleopatra had built on deeply held xenophobic and misogynistic prejudices that would not easily have been dispelled, and given Antony's preferences for the East, it is quite likely that after some time in Rome, he with Cleopatra's strong backing would have chosen to make their capital in Alexandria, with that city becoming at least Rome's equal, as Constantinople later became in reality. Bearing in mind the monarchical dynastic tradition of Cleopatra, it is highly likely that the two would have become hereditary rulers, indeed just as Octavian did, with Antyllus perhaps succeeding in Rome while Caesarion ruled in Alexandria.

Antony with Cleopatra at his side would have governed through a combination of direct rule and a hierarchy of client kingdoms as foreshadowed by Pompey and basically continued in practice by Octavian. However, their rule would have been founded more on a partnership between Greeks, Hellenes and Romans. It would have drawn on the Hellenic concept of *harmonia*—a community of outlook and interest—and would have shown a greater tolerance of difference and of local customs. Greeks and the other peoples of the region would have had more political power, avoiding much of the resentment that built up against the imperialist, cold and alien rule of Rome. Alexandria would have flourished as a center of learning and culture. Distinctions and prejudices between East and West, as apparent in those times as now, might have become blurred, to the benefit of all. As a consequence of Cleopatra's longer rule, even women's position in society might have changed.

One interesting sidelight is that Cleopatra might well have in the end succeeded in deposing Herod in Judaea. She had the wealth, power and determination. If she had, the area certainly would have developed in a less militaristic and antagonistic way. Jesus of Nazareth would then have been born into a more tolerant environment and, just perhaps, his reception might have been different.

ACKNOWLEDGMENTS

I wrote this book with my husband, Michael.

In the United Kingdom I would like to thank the staff of the London Library, the British Library, the Bodleian Library and the British Museum for their kind, patient help. I would also like to thank Dr. Martin Weaver for applying his expertise in archaeological facial reconstruction to the creation of an image of Cleopatra that suggests she may not have looked quite as we had imagined.

In Egypt I am indebted to Ibrahim Ahmed Metwalli of the National Maritime Museum for so generously giving his time to explain about recent marine excavations in the harbor of Alexandria and how this has been clarifying knowledge of the royal quarter of Alexandria in Cleopatra's day. I am also most grateful to the staff of the Library of Alexandria, in particular Badrya Serry, director of the library's Antiquities Museum, and Darin Hassan for information on the original Library of Alexandria and its location. The staff of the Alexandria National Museum showed us artifacts recovered from the harbor of Alexandria. Our research in Egypt would not have been half so enjoyable without the expert advice of our guide, Mohamed Younis, and the assistance of Voyages Jules Verne in allowing us, like Cleopatra and Caesar, to sail down the Nile and visit Alexandria and the temples of Upper Egypt.

Friends have, as always, been extremely kind and supportive, not least in reading the text at a formative stage, and I would like to express my appreciation to Kim Lewison, Neil Munro, Edmund Griffiths, St. John and Krystyna Brown and Robin Binks in particular.

Lastly, my warm thanks to George Gibson and his colleagues at Walker & Company and Bloomsbury USA, to Marianne Velmans, Michèle David and all the team at Transworld Publishers and to my agents, Bill Hamilton of A. M. Heath and Co. in London and Michael Carlisle of Inkwell Management in New York.

APPENDIX: PUTTING A FACE TO A FAMOUS NAME

Though she died more than two thousand years ago, Cleopatra's appearance still fascinates us. The ancient sources—even those hostile to her—acknowledge her charisma, intelligence and powers of attraction. During my research, I began to build up a mental picture of Cleopatra and to feel that I understood at least a little of her psyche. This made me all the more curious about her physical appearance. How did this woman whose gilded statue was erected by Julius Caesar in Rome's main temple to Venus and who captivated Mark Antony actually look?

I was fortunate to meet an archaeologist—Dr. Martin Weaver—as intrigued as I was by Cleopatra and ready to apply his scientific expertise to creating the first three-dimensional model of her. Dr. Weaver, an archaeologist for thirty years, is a specialist in archaeosteology—reconstructions based on evidence from human bones.

Of course, the usual starting point for an archaeological facial reconstruction would be the individual's skull but Cleopatra's vanished long ago. Dr. Weaver therefore decided to "reverse-engineer" her. The most reliable sources of information about how Cleopatra looked are the numerous coin depictions throughout her twenty-year reign. These vary in appearance depending on her age at the time and whether she is depicted in Hellenistic or Egyptian pose. But they all suggest she had high cheekbones, a pronounced nose and chin and a slight underhang beneath the jaw.

As well as analyzing these coin images, Dr, Weaver also examined the many sculptures of other members of Cleopatra's dynasty—the ultra-inbred Ptolemies—that have survived. The evidence from these suggests—just like the coins—that Cleopatra was a woman of strong facial features and very probably—at least in later years—quite plump. In addition, Dr. Weaver looked at the surviving sculptures generally considered to be of Cleopatra—some in Egyptian and some in Greco-Roman style—but these are few in number and less helpful than the other evidence.

Dr. Weaver concluded that Cleopatra was broadly of the "dolichocephalic" type—that is, with a long, high-cheekboned face with protrusive features. Since this type is highly characteristic of people of Macedonian stock and Cleopatra was, of course, of mainly Macedonian descent, he selected a cast of a female Macedonian skull with these traits as the basic structure on which to "hang" Cleopatra's face.

To adapt the skull to his observations from the surviving evidence, Dr. Weaver made the chin and jaw more pronounced and the cheekbones even more prominent. Next, he applied known facial skin depth measurements to the model, selecting those most appropriate to a woman of Cleopatra's known appearance and genealogy. Fixing "skin pegs" to the model, he smoothed plastic clay over them to create the basic external structure of Cleopatra's face.

His next step was to model the soft tissue of Cleopatra's nose, basing the shape on her profile on coins and on the very strong Ptolemaic family traits he had observed.

To calculate the space between her eyes, Dr. Weaver drew notional lines upward from where her canine incisors would have been since in humans these lines pass through the center of the pupil. To determine the shape of Cleopatra's eyes, Dr. Weaver applied to his deductions from his observations some additional information from studies of generic ratios in human skulls from which the distance from cheek to brow in humans is known to be an indicator of the degree of protuberance of the eyes.

To re-create Cleopatra's ears, Dr. Weaver calculated the angle by following the jaw line—a standard technique in archaeological facial reconstruction. He then took standard "ear frames" (developed by the FBI to help in the identification process of criminals), attached these to the model at the correct angle and built up the ears by smoothing layers of clay over the frames.

The dimensions of a human being's lips can be calculated according to the length of their teeth. As this was not possible in Cleopatra's case, Dr. Weaver based his reconstruction of Cleopatra's mouth on coin evidence, making it quite wide.

Dr. Weaver chose as Cleopatra's hairstyle the so-called melon style she often wore in coin depictions and which has tight braids segmenting her hair into sections like the markings on a melon, hence the name, and with the ends of her hair gathered into a bun on the nape of the neck. This style requires so much hair that—unless Cleopatra habitually wore wigs, which the ancient sources suggest she probably did not—her hair must have been abundant, reaching almost to her waist. To create the melon hairstyle, Cleopatra's maids probably oiled her hair to make it easier to work with. These oils would have further darkened her already dark hair to black.

In accordance with Cleopatra's probable genealogy, Dr. Weaver gave Cleopatra olive skin and brown eyes. Her makeup was applied by an expert in cosmetics of the time. The model was completed with a gold filet around the head, long blue and gold earrings and a heavy gold necklace.

Is she beautiful? From certain angles, yes. She certainly has a compelling, even commanding presence, and shrewdness and intelligence look out from those dark brown eyes. At present she sits on a windowsill in Dr. Weaver's office. As he works he finds it hard to forget she is there—probably exactly what the real Cleopatra would have expected.

NOTES AND SOURCES

I have used the Loeb Classics Series for the text of the classical sources. In these notes the references relate to the classical author, the relevant work, then the book and chapter/section references, as appropriate. I have used the following abbreviations: Plu.Ant for Plutarch's *Life of Antony*, Plu.Ca for Plutarch's *Life of Cato the Younger*, Plu.Pomp for Plutarch's *Life of Pompey* and Plu.JC for his *Life of Julius Caesar*; in the case of Suetonius, Suet.JC for his *Life of Julius Caesar* and Suet.A for his *Life of Augustus/Octavian*. App is Appian's *Civil Wars* from his *Roman History*. DioCass.RH is Dio Cassius' *Roman History*. Cic.LA is Cicero's *Letters to Atticus*; Cic.LF his *Letters to Friends*; Cic.Phil his *Philippics*. Luc.Phar is Lucan's *Pharsalia*.

As well as the Loeb translations, I have drawn on those of myself, my husband, Michael, and kind friends and advisers. I have also found the following works invaluable: the translation of Plutarch's *Lives* by Robin Waterfield in Oxford World Classics; Robert Graves' translation of Suetonius' *The Twelve Caesars* in Penguin Classics; Ian Scott-Kilvert's translation of Dio Cassius' *Roman History—The Reign of Augustus*, also in Penguin Classics; and P. Jones, *Cleopatra: A Source Book*, University of Oklahoma Press. I have also found the older Bohn series of translations very helpful in several cases.

Prologue

1 "They opened . . . kings": Plu.Ant, 85.

4 "royal progress": Suet.JC, 32.

5 In early Christian times: Lucy Hughes-Hallett's excellent book *Cleopatra—Histories, Dreams and Distortions* reviews the way Cleopatra's image has developed over the centuries.

5 "licentious": Dante, *Inferno,* Canto V, line 63.

6 The four main classical sources: Each of the classical authors has his own emphasis. For example, Plutarch is keen to draw moral comparisons and to tell a good story; Dio Cassius to create set pieces, whether speeches or battles; and Appian to focus on military matters. Provided one allows for his personal views, Cicero, who was writing as events unfolded, is incomparable in giving insights into characters and into the political ebb and flow leading up to the creation

of the Second Triumvirate. His witticisms are as fresh today as they were then. Michael Grant's *Greek and Roman Historians* is valuable to any author in its analysis of the motivations and foibles of ancient historians. Anthony Everitt's *Cicero* is an excellent biography.

1: Keeping It in the Family

11 Egypt's final pharaoh: The word *pharaoh* had come to mean "king." Its original meaning was "palace" or "great house."

12 "the river . . . silt": Vergil, *Georgics*, IV.290–4.

13 His new subjects' . . . openly": Herodotus, History, II.35–6.

13 "the most religious men": ibid, II.58.

14 mummified animals: Mummification of humans had become customary in Egypt as early as 3500 BC. The ancient Egyptians believed that, as long as the body remained intact, the soul too would live. Various methods of preservation were used. The process for mummifying humans took seventy days. Priests wearing the masks of the jackal-headed Anubis removed the internal organs, which were placed in four jars to be "entrusted" to the four sons of the god Horus. The body was then dried and purified using natron, a carbonate of sodium. Next, the body was treated with oils and resins and stuffed to preserve its shape. Then came the process of wrapping it in hundreds of yards of fine linen. The word *mummy* comes from *mummiya*, the black adhesive resin used to coat the linen. (In medieval times the color brown for use in paints and dyes was extracted from old mummies.) Finally, the body's face was painted with cosmetics and, if the family was rich enough, further embellished with artificial eyes and a funerary mask and wig. The body was then encased in a double coffin and placed inside a sarcophagus, on the lid of which were painted two eyes to enable the deceased to gaze out on the world.

14 Another serapeum: The Serapeum of Alexandria is thought to have stood near the site still occupied by Pompey's Pillar, erected in the time of the emperor Diocletian. The rectangular serapeum housed a daughter library of the great Library of Alexandria and survived until AD 391, when Theophilus, bishop of Alexandria, ordered its destruction as a pagan temple.

15 "the growing . . . in return": DioCass.RH, Book X, fragment 41.

16 "in difficult . . . faith": Livy, *History of Rome*, XXXI.2.

17 "to deprive . . . life . . . If . . . sincerity": A copy of this will was found at Cyrene.

18 "a size . . . around him": Athenaeus, *Banquet of the Learned*, XII.549.

18 "as though . . . to hide": Marcus Justinianus Justinus, *Epitome of the Philippic History of Pompeius Trogus*, XXXVIII.8.10.

18 "the sight . . . a walk": Quoted M. Grant, *Cleopatra*, p. 10. The amused commentator was Scipio Africanus the Younger.

18 "the number . . . leaders": Diodorus Sicculus, XXXIII.28b.

2: Siblings and Sibylline Prophecies

20 "the most . . . race": Cato the Elder, quoted Pliny the Elder, *Natural History*, 29.14

21 six thousand talents: A talent was a Greek coin worth 24,000 Roman sesterces. One sesterce equates to perhaps three to four dollars today.

21 to the island of Rhodes: Sailing into the harbor of Rhodes, Auletes would have passed the fragments of the Colossus of Rhodes. Originally over a hundred feet high, it had broken off at the knees during an earthquake in 224, only half a century after its completion, and still lay

where it had fallen. Pliny the Elder described how "its fingers are larger than most statues . . . as for its broken limbs, their insides look like caves."
22 "Libyan princess": M. Grant, *Cleopatra*, p. 15.
23 "succor . . . multitude": Cic.LF, I.7.
23 "a thieving . . . curlers": Cicero quoted in M. Foss, *The Search for Cleopatra*, p. 55.
24 "devoid . . . moment": Sallust, *Conspiracy of Catiline*, xvii.
24 outpost at Pelusium: Pelusium was near the modern town of Tell el-Farana, east of Port Said.
24 "It is said . . . Alexandria": App, V.8.
24–25 "which are . . . nature": App, IV.16.
25 "a princess . . . philosophy": al-Masudi, *Les Prairies d'Or*, pp. 287–88.
27 "the queen . . . father . . . on to . . . see her": Inscription on a stele from the Bucheum, which is today in Copenhagen.
27–28 "the crowd . . . life": Diodorus Sicculus, I.83.
29 "acting . . . friends": Caesar, *Civil War*, III.103.

3: The Race for Glory

30 "the slight . . . eyes . . . which contributed . . . popularity": Plu.Pomp, 2.
40 "Jupiter . . . greatest . . . because . . . prosperous": Cicero, *On the Nature of the Gods*, III.87.
41 "Keep him . . . in him": Suet.JC, 1.
41 "this youth . . . girdled . . . Caesar . . . tweezers": ibid., 45.
42 "the female . . . queen . . . the bottom . . . bed": ibid., 49.
43 "In his . . . influence": Plu.JC, 4.

4: "Odi et Amo"

44 "the greatest . . . art": Suet.JC, 4.
45 The dinner menu survives: The menu is described by Macrobius in his *Saturnalia*, 3.13.10–12.
46 "he gave . . . event]": Pliny the Elder, *Natural History*, 14.66.
48 "foolish vanity": Cic.LA, II.18.
48 "Have . . . idiot": Sallust, *Conspiracy of Catiline*, 53.4.
49 "a mystery . . . to know": Quoted E. Bradford, *Julius Caesar*, p. 43.
49 The most famous of these sisters was Clodia: Cicero called Clodia "cow-eyed" and his wife, perhaps unfairly, suggested that he too was having an affair with her.
49 "after . . . husbands . . . Caesar's . . . suspicion": Plu.JC, 10.
49–50 "settled . . . reputations": Cic.LA, I.16.
50 "Pompey . . . girl": Plu.Ca, 30.
50 "He is apt . . . from showing": Cic.LF, VIII.1.
50–51 "As for . . . cesspit": Cic.LA, II.1.
51 "It . . . resources": Plu.JC, 14.
51 "talking . . . intemperate": Cicero, "Speech Before the Senate on his Return from Exile," VI.14.
52 "the queen . . . to be one": Suet.JC, 49.
52 "a high . . . brightness": Sallust, op. cit., 54.

52 The word *fascist*: R. Syme's *The Roman Revolution*, first published in 1939 and still in print, is preeminent among those works highlighting the resemblances between the fall of the Roman republic and the rise of fascism in Europe.
54 "Avoid . . . rocks": Caesar quoted by Aulus Gelius, *Attic Nights*, 1.10.
54 "Regions . . . people": Cicero, *On the Consular Provinces*, 33.

5: Crossing the Rubicon

55 "The Tiber . . . sponges": Cicero, *Pro Sestio*, 77.
57 battle in Gaul at Alesia: Prior to Alesia, believing that the rebellious Gauls had received help from Britain, Caesar had decided on an invasion of the island. Perhaps more importantly, he had heard that Britain was rich in minerals such as iron and tin as well as in gold, silver and freshwater pearls of a particularly fine quality and large size. Caesar was known for his admiration of pearls. In 55, attempting a landing at Dover, Caesar's troops received a severe shock, as he admitted in his *Gallic Wars*: "The natives sent in their cavalry and chariots which frightened the Romans who were quite unaccustomed to this type of fighting." The Britons' appearance, wild-haired and painted all over with blue woad, also discouraged the invaders, who only gradually made progress, winning small victories and burning farms but soon retreating back across the Channel. Caesar came in greater force the following year, landing from an armada of eight hundred ships with five legions and two thousand cavalry. This time he, in turn, shocked the Britons by bringing over a war elephant, the first of any kind to reach the island. His troops advanced much further, crossing the Thames, but the Britons usually refused pitched battles, using their chariots to deploy small numbers of men in harassing raids on the less mobile Romans. Storms in the Channel, probably not for the first and certainly not for the last time, saved Britain. Many of Caesar's ships were wrecked and, as autumn approached, Caesar prudently withdrew.
59 "I only . . . ground": Plu.Pomp, 57.
59 "a struggle . . . expense": Cic.LA, VII.3.
60 "Let the dice . . . high": Plu.JC, 32.
61 "total . . . winner": Suet.JC, 36.
61 "he was . . . mind": Plu.Pomp, 67.
61 "next to . . . army": Plu.Ant, 9.
61 "young dandies . . . unused . . . hair . . . the glint . . . eyes": ibid., 69.
61 "turning . . . faces": ibid., 71.
62 "It . . . for help": Plu.JC, 46.

6: Like a Virgin

65–67 Pompey's arrival . . . murderer": All quotes in these seven paragraphs are from Plu.Pomp, 77–79.
68 "it seemed . . . city": Arrian, *History of Alexander*, III.1–2.
68 "birds . . . numbers . . . Even . . . nation": Plutarch's *Life of Alexander*, 26.
68 "the city . . . across": Strabo, *Geography*, 17.1.8.
68 "entering . . . angles": Quoted in J-Y. Empereur, *Alexandria Rediscovered*, p. 57.
69 "the greatest . . . world": Strabo, op. cit., 17.1.13.
70 recent underwater archaeology: In the 1960s, while exploring the underwater site around Fort Qait Bey, Egyptian archaeologist and diver Kamel Abouel-Saadat found chunks of statu-

ary, including pieces of a sphinx that clearly had been cut for use in the construction of the Pharos. More recently, an Egyptian and French team exploring the Pharos area has also made interesting discoveries. Finds from this part of the harbor are on display at the Roman theater in Alexandria. They include statues that were clearly decorative rather than used as building materials, such as a red granite sphinx and two huge heads of male figures that once would have stood over twenty feet high and, honed by the waves, resemble Henry Moore sculptures. A tall carved figure of Ptolemy II with a beautifully modeled, muscular torso also found near the site of the Pharos today stands outside the new Library of Alexandria. Another Egyptian and French team has been diving on the eastern side of the Great Harbor and has done much to clarify the geography of this area in Ptolemaic times. They believe that much of it now lies beneath the corniche along Alexandria's waterfront. They have identified Cape Silsileh as the likely site of the royal harbor and have found traces of what they believe was the Timoneum built by Antony in his final days, which would have been very close to Cleopatra's palace. Some of their findings suggest that Strabo made errors when describing the location of the Timoneum.

70 "a quarter . . . third": ibid., 17.1.8.
70 "on sailing . . . colours": ibid., 17.1.9.
71 "in . . . cone": Strabo, op. cit., 17.1.10.
73 "A large . . . community": Strabo, quoted by Josephus, Antiquities, XIV.7.2.
73 "his words . . . offensive . . . told . . . eating": Plu.JC, 48.
74 As tensions . . . assassins: All quotes in these two paragraphs are from Suet.JC, 50–1.
75 Their first encounter . . . corrupted": The quotes in this paragraph are from Luc.Phar, X, lines 70–108. Apart from certain temple carvings, which are anyway in a highly stylized pharaonic style and give little clue to Cleopatra's real appearance, the only certain representations of Cleopatra are those on coins. The marble head in the Vatican is one of three sculptures generally, though not universally, accepted by scholars to be depictions of Cleopatra. Here, the face looks youthful, rounded and alluring, with full, sensuous lips and large eyes. The other representations are a marble bust in the Staatliche Museen zu Berlin, which has a delicately modeled, slightly thinner face and a more studiedly composed expression, and a marble head depicting a rather older woman with the same large eyes but a more pronounced chin in the Cherchel Museum in Algeria (though some believe the latter in fact depicts Cleopatra's daughter, Cleopatra Selene). In addition, a small marble head in the Department of Greek, Roman and Etruscan Antiquities in the Louvre shares some notable similarities with the Vatican, Berlin and Cherchel sculptures and, it has recently been claimed, may also be a representation of Cleopatra. (See Peter Higgs and Susan Walker's article "Cleopatra VII at the Louvre," in *British Museum Occasional Paper* no. 103.)

Other claimants to come into the frame as likenesses of Cleopatra but then to be dismissed by the majority of academics (though the arguments go on) include a marble head with melon hairstyle that Heinrich Schliemann, the excavator of Troy, claimed to have discovered in Alexandria but which was later found to be a Roman copy of a Greek sculpture of the fourth century BC; a small, high-cheekboned, hawk-nosed marble head of a woman found on Delos; and the travertine Castellani head with its distinctive aquiline nose (named for the Roman dealer Alessandro Castellani, who acquired it), currently in the British Museum. Less well known is a wooden statue now in the Seattle Art Museum carved and painted in the Egyptian style and bearing Cleopatra's name in a cartouche on the biceps but which is widely believed to be a forgery.

For a further commentary on images of Cleopatra, both Hellenic and Egyptian, see J. Tyldesley, *Cleopatra*, pp. 60–69.

76 "according . . . charming . . . which . . . Egyptian": Plu.Ant, 27–8.
76 "intellectual . . . charm": Sallust, *Conspiracy of Catiline*, 25.
77 Though some . . . mixed stock: For a discussion of Cleopatra's possible ethnicity see J. Tyldesley, op. cit., pp 27–32.
77 "This ruse . . . fall for her": Plu.JC, 49.
78 "His baldness . . . of it": Suet.JC, 45.
78 a bizarre lotion: The baldness cure is given in M. Grant, *Cleopatra*, p. 67.
78–79 "Believe . . . comes": Ovid, *Art of Love,* II, lines 717–32.

7: The Alexandrian War

Unless otherwise stated below, the source for the quotes in this chapter is *The Alexandrian War*, believed to have been written by one of Caesar's officers.

80–81 The rapprochement . . . world': The quotes in these three paragraphs are from Luc.Phar, X, lines 109–72.
82 "he damaged . . . Cleopatra": Plu.JC, 48.
82 "weapons . . . palace": Luc.Phar, X, lines 478–84.
82 "a most . . . enemy": Suet.JC, 35.
83 "from roof . . . heavens": Luc.Phar, X, lines 500–2.
83 "because . . . Pharos": Caesar, Civil War, III.112.
84 "habitually . . . affairs": Plu.JC, 49.
85 "was towing . . . Egyptians": Suet.JC, 64.
87 "Cleopatra's wicked beauty": Luc.Phar, X, line 137.
87 "it might . . . governor-general": Suet.JC, 35.
88 "Why . . . instruments?": Ovid, *Amores*, II.14, lines 27–28.
89 "nearly to Ethiopia": Suet.JC, 52.
89 "Caesar seems . . . situation there": Cic.LA, XI.15.
90 An inscription in Memphis: For an alternative view of the significance of the inscription for the date of Caesarion's birth see J. Tyldesley, *Cleopatra*, pp. 101–3.
90 the Temple of Hathor: This temple, at Dendera, some forty miles north of Luxor and lying amidst fields of sesame, is one of the most complete remaining temples of the Ptolemaic period. Built on the granite foundations of an earlier temple dating from the time of Cheops, it is still ringed by three mud-brick enclosure walls. Its huge columns are decorated with carvings of the smooth-featured, half-smiling, cow-eared face of Hathor, traces of the original blue paint of pounded lapis lazuli still visible. Long, shallow flights of stone stairs lead up past life-size bas-reliefs of priests, the treads smoothed and worn by thousands of feet. On the ceiling of a chamber on the upper story, the figure of the goddess Nut stretches out, her arms extended, as she swallows the disc of the sun that will travel through her body during the hours of darkness and that she will give birth to as the dawn rises. A wall carving depicts Isis lovingly embalming the body of her husband, Osiris. To the back of the main temple, opposite the reliefs of Cleopatra and Caesarion, is Octavian's temple to Isis, where he is depicted offering a mirror to Hathor and Horus.

8: "Veni, Vidi, Vici"

92 "there . . . Rome . . . dangerous rifts": *The Alexandrian War*, 65.

92 "Veni . . . vici": Plu.JC, 50.

93 "his swaggering . . . him": Plu.Ant, 4.

94 "as if . . . was": Plu.JC, 51.

94 "one . . . fits": ibid., 53.

95 Epicureanism: It is ironic that *epicurean* has come to mean a sensualist who is, as often as not, greedy.

96 "opened . . . entrails": App, II.99.

96 "In present . . . disgraceful": Plu.Ca, 66.

96 "I am . . . over them": ibid.

98 "it was . . . Greece": Plu.JC, 55.

99 "a feeling . . . human about them": Cicero, LF, VII.1.

99 "Such huge . . . senators": Suet.JC, 39.

9: "Slave of the Times"

101 "I hate . . . bitterness . . . Her . . . speech": Cic.LA, XV.15.

102 "No boy . . . Curio's": Cic.Phil, II.18.

102 "a private . . . generals . . . owed . . . women": Plu.Ant, 10.

103 "those filthy . . . tombs": Martial, quoted A. Dalby, *Empire of Pleasures*, p. 31.

104–4 "two . . . tenants . . . a building . . . profit": Cic.LA, XIV.9.

105 To the east . . . price list": All quotes in this paragraph come from Martial, quoted in A. Dalby, op. cit., pp. 216–18.

109 "the last year of confusions": Quoted D. Ewing-Duncan, *The Calendar*, p. 45.

109 "Yes . . . edict": Plu.JC, 59.

109 "the slave of the times": Quoted T. Holland, *Rubicon*, p. 338.

10: The Ides of March

112 "provided . . . himself": Suet.JC, 83.

112 "more succulent provender": ibid., 38.

113 "admitted . . . children": ibid., 52.

114 "only . . . Parthians": ibid., 79.

116 "a groan . . . Forum": Cic.Phil, II.34.

116 "The amazing . . . freedom": Plu.Ant, 12.

116 "Where . . . from . . . it . . . advance": Cic.Phil, II.34.

116 "was . . . substance": Suet.JC, 77.

117 "I'm not . . . lean ones": Plu.JC, 62.

117 "if only . . . now . . . Brutus . . . today": Suet.JC, 80.

118 Just before . . . gone": The quotes in this paragraph are from Plu.JC, 63 and 65.

118 "Caesar . . . my son!' ": ibid., 84.

11: "Flight of the Queen"

123 "Antony asked . . . tyrant": DioCass. RH, XLIV.34.

123 "the spirit . . . boys . . . absurd": Cic.AT, XIV.21.

125 "Freedom . . . not": ibid., XIV.4. (What, one wonders, would Cicero have made of the follow-up to the toppling of Saddam Hussein in Iraq?)
126 "She'll . . . tomorrow": Cicero, *Quintilianus*, VI.3.75.
126 "I see . . . queen": Cic.AT, XIV.8.
126 "I am hoping . . . Caesar": ibid., XIV.20.
127 "I am hoping . . . queen": ibid., XV.4.
127 "If she . . . lacked everything": Josephus, *Antiquities*, XV.4.1.
127 "With regard . . . their security": Plutarch, *Life of Demetrius*, 3.
129 "the seams . . . feet": Suet.A, 94.
129 "I shall . . . feet": DioCass.RH, XLV.2.
129 Busts . . . together: The quotes in this paragraph are from Suet.A, 73, 79, 80 and 83.
130 "I cannot . . . place": Cic.AT, XIV.12.
130 "The young . . . to me": ibid., XIV.11.
130 "spurned . . . obscurity": Velleius Paterculus, *History of Rome*, II.60.
132 "had been . . . moneychanger": Suet.A, 2.
132 "Julius . . . adoption": ibid., 68.
132 "used . . . shells": ibid..
132 "that Caesar . . . paternity": Suet.JC, 52.
132 "I found . . . no method": Cic.AT, XV.11.
133 "You, boy . . . name": Cic.Phil, XIII.11.
134 "We are amazed . . . Caesar": Cic.LF, XI.3.
135 "Life . . . breathing . . . The slave . . . not": Cic.Phil, X.10.
135 "not to speak . . . words": Cic.LF, XII.2.
135 "gladiator . . . massacre": ibid.
136 "to subjugate us": Cic.LF, XII.23.
137 "have the city . . . sincerity": Cic.AT, XVI.8.
137 "asked . . . their homes": App, III.42.
137 "He got . . . send-off": App, III.46.
138 feathery papyrus: Papyrus has recently been reintroduced to Egypt from Kenya.
138 "No one . . . best": quoted H. Volkmann, *Cleopatra*, p. 23.

12: Ruler of the East

141 "set . . . them": App, III.70.
141 "Antony's . . . circumstances . . . Antony . . . eaten . . . ate . . . man": Plu.Ant, 17.
142 "this heaven-sent boy": Cic.Phil, V.16.
142 "Octavian must . . . extolled": Cic.LF, XI.20.
143 "If you . . . this will": Suet.A, 26.
143–44 "as if . . . estate": Plu.Ant, 19.
144–45 The troops . . . murder him: The quotes in these five paragraphs come from App, IV.5–30.
145 "terrible . . . plans": Quoted A. Everitt, *Cicero*, p. 308.
146 "What gladiator . . . stroke?": Cicero, *Tusculum Disputations*, II.41.
146 "You . . . crimes?: App, IV.32.
151 "he placed . . . sword in": Plutarch, *Life of Brutus*, 52.

151 "they courteously . . . epithets": Suet.A, 13.
152 "a puny . . . body . . . has . . . defeated": DioCass.RH, L.18.
152 "The city . . . wind-pipes": Plu.Ant, 24.
153 "Kings . . . by him": ibid.
154 "His weakness . . . families": Plu.Ant, 4 and 36.

13: Mighty Aphrodite

Unless stated otherwise below, the quotes in this chapter come from Plu.Ant, 24–27.
157 The quotes in the first paragraph are from App, IV.64.
160 Plutarch lusciously . . . Tarsus: For Enobarbus' report of Cleopatra's arrival in Tarsus in *Antony and Cleopatra* Shakespeare drew heavily on Sir Thomas North's lyrical translation of Plutarch's account.
162 Appian believed . . . sex: The quotes in this paragraph are from App, V.1 and 8–9.
163 "the topmost . . . pearls": Pliny the Elder, *Natural History*, IX.54.
163 An American academic: The article on how pearls dissolve is by B. L. Ullman in *The Classical Journal*, February 1957, Vol. 52, pp. 193–201.
163 "prepared . . . region": Socrates of Rhodes quoted in Athenaeus, *Banquet of the Learned*, IV.147.

14: "Give It to Fulvia"

167 Antony . . . sandals: The quotes in this paragraph are from App, V.11.
167–68 During . . . to be": The quotes in these two paragraphs are from Plu.Ant, 28.
170 "in the robe . . . Isis": Plu.Ant, 54.
170 Isis' "many-colored . . . moon": The description of Isis comes from Apuleius, *The Golden Ass*, XI. 3–4.
170 "concerned . . . death": Plutarch, *Of Isis and Osiris*, 78.
171–72 She and Antony . . . pleasure: The quotes in these three paragraphs are from Plu.Ant, 29–30.
171 Lake Mareotis: Today Lake Mareotis is in the middle of an industrial area dotted with the flares of oil refineries, but fishermen still pole their puntlike boats through the reeds.
173 "like . . . night . . . a miserable letter": Plu.Ant, 30.
173 "a partaker . . . showed": Velleius Paterculus, *History of Rome, II*.74.
174 "A godless . . . hand": Vergil, *Eclogue*, I, lines 71–7.
174–75 "in crowds . . . war": App, V.12.
175 At the same . . . withdrew: The quotes in this paragraph are from App, V.16.
176 "Glaphyra's . . . sound": Martial, *Epigrams*, XI.20.
176 slingshots . . . dick": The Latin text of the messages on the slingshots are given in the *Corpus Inscriptorium Latinarium* of 1901, XI or II.2.1.
177 "as long . . . speedily . . . moved . . . jealousy": App, V.19.
177 "that Fulvia . . . Italy": Plu.Ant, 30.
177 "laid . . . general . . . on falling . . . dwindle": App, V.9 and 11.
178 "She girded . . . them": DioCass.RH, XXXXVIII.10.
178 "had . . . sex . . . was . . . violence": Velleius Paterculus, *History of Rome,* II.74.

15: Single Mother

180 "delivered . . . fight": App, V.51.
182 "had become . . . anger": ibid., 59.
183 "generally . . . wife": Plu.Ant, 31.
184 "dignity . . . beauty . . . she . . . affairs": ibid.
184 "a lover . . . outrageous": Plutarch, *Life of Demetrius*, I.
185 "His rational . . . Egyptian": Plu.Ant, 31.
185 "we must . . . performed": Vitruvius, *On Architecture*, VI.5. (Vitruvius drew on the ideas of earlier Greek writers but this is the earliest surviving architectural work.)

16: "The Awful Calamity"

189 "Now . . . world": Vergil, Eclogue, IV, line 4 ff. Medieval Christians took these lines as a prophecy of Christ.
190–91 "Nor . . . whatsoever": The decree is reproduced in several places in translation, for example, P. Jones, *Cleopatra: A Source Book*, pp. 205–6.
192 "very . . . disorder": Josephus, *Antiquities*, XIV.14.2.
193 To celebrate . . . promise": The quotes in this paragraph are from Plu.Ant, 32.
193–94 "I could . . . at me . . . the one . . . death": Suet.A, 62.
194 "Either . . . man": Plu.Ant, 33.
195 "He . . . women": App, V.76.
195 "beneficent gods": Quoted M. Grant, *Cleopatra*, p. 130.
196 "full . . . dead": App, V.89.
196 "into fighting condition": Suet.A, 16.
197 "not to . . . wretched": Plu.Ant, 35.
198 "a hundred . . . warships": ibid.
199 "The awful . . . Syria": Plu.Ant, 36.

17: Sun and Moon

Unless otherwise stated below, the source for the quotes in this chapter is Plu.Ant, 36–51. Plutarch's account of the Parthian campaign is based on a work by one of Antony's generals, Dellius, now lost.
206 "cut . . . ears . . . complete . . . blemish": Josephus, *Antiquities*, XIV.13.10.
207 Silver coins . . . Antony: One of the silver coins—a drachm—minted in Antioch and depicting Cleopatra on one side and Antony on the other can be seen in the British Museum.

18: "Theatrical, Overdone, and Anti-Roman"

216–17 "When she . . . had a great . . . to Egypt": Josephus, *Antiquities*, XV.4.2.
219 "realized . . . shock": Plu.Ant, 53.
220 As Antony . . . attain': The quotes in these two paragraphs are from Plu.Ant, 54.
221 "it was not . . . use it": Josephus, *Antiquities*, XV.3.8.
222 "he . . . war": Plu.Ant, 52.
224 Cleopatra . . . state: The quotes in this paragraph are from DioCass.RH, XLIX.40.
224 "in very . . . wife . . . the son . . . for Caesar's sake": ibid., 41.
224–25 Plutarch . . . costume: The quotes in this paragraph are from Plu.Ant, 54.

225 the triple uraeus . . . of Kings": For a discussion of the linkage by S.-A. Ashton of the triple uraeus with Cleopatra and of Cleopatra's possible motives for adopting this insignia, see her article in the *British Museum Occasional Paper*, no. 103, p. 26, and D. E. E. Kleiner's *Cleopatra and Rome*, pp. 140–42. The chief evidence for associating the triple uraeus with Cleopatra is provided by a piece of a limestone crown found in a shrine in a temple to Isis at Coptos by Sir Flinders Petrie, the front of which bears three uraei. Sally-Ann Ashton dismisses the view that the crown might have belonged to the earlier Ptolemaic queen Arsinoe II, arguing that evidence from relief carvings in the temple and from the crown itself suggest that the shrine was dedicated early in Cleopatra's reign when she was sharing the throne with one of her two half brothers. She has also identified a blue glass intaglio in the British Museum depicting an Egyptian queen wearing a magnificent headdress with triple uraeus as a representation of Cleopatra and has linked this to a series of statues of a queen of the late Ptolemaic period, again prominently displaying the triple uraeus.

227 "was only . . . son": DioCass.RH., XLIX.41.

228 And now . . . tolerate: The quotes in this paragraph are from Plu.Ant, 50 and 54.

19: "A Woman of Egypt"

229 "to avoid . . . speech": Suet.A, 84.

229 Parts . . . done so: The quotes in this paragraph are from Suet.A, 69.

230 "at a feast . . . twelve . . . The gods . . . grain": ibid., 70.

230 "like the slave . . . sale": ibid., 69.

232 "that it . . . matters": Plu.Ant, 56.

233 Whether bribed . . . decree: A papyrus granting land to Canidius Crassus is reproduced and translated in P. Jones, *Cleopatra: A Source Book*, pp. 205–6.

233 "carefully . . . Antony": Josephus, *Antiquities*, XV.5.1.

233 "to her . . . possible": ibid.

234 "Every practitioner . . . victories?": Plu.Ant, 56.

235 "She left . . . war": ibid., 57.

235 "diseased with desertion": Velleius Paterculus, *Roman History*, II.83.

236 "one . . . world": ibid., 85.

237 "the Egyptian . . . things": DioCass. RH, XLVIII.24.

237 "a slave . . . Cleopatra": ibid., XLIX.34.

237 "degenerated . . . monster . . . a crown . . . queen": Florus, *Epitome of Roman History*, II.21.

237 "an enormity . . . ashamed": Pliny the Elder, *Natural History*, XXXIII.50.

237 "to be . . . understood . . . our . . . Asiatic orators": Suet.A, 86.

237 "Who would not . . . Egyptian": DioCass.RH, L.25–7.

238 "We . . . eunuchs?": ibid., 24–5.

238 "so as . . . wiles . . . no . . . treacherous": *The Alexandrian War*, 24.

238 "he plays . . . lust": DioCass.RH, L.27.

238 "unchastity . . . dear": Luc.Phar, X, line 58.

238–39 "Antony . . . Nile": Plutarch, *Comparison of Demetrius and Antony*, 3.

239 "as surely . . . Capitol": DioCass.RH, L.5.

239–240 "And . . . curse": *Oracula Sibyllina*, III.75 ff.

240 "the whole . . . way": *Res Gestae Divi Augustus*, 25.

241 Geminius . . . from you": Plu.Ant, 59.

242 "that Antony's . . . deserted him": DioCass.RH, L.4.

20: The Battle of Actium

245 "caused . . . along": Florus, *Epitome of Roman History*, II.21.

246 "Their . . . clothes": Quoted E. Bradford, *Cleopatra*, p. 205.

246 "Who . . . way?": DioCass.RH, L.9.

246 "Some . . . birds": Plu.Ant, 60.

247 "all . . . knights . . . to demonstrate . . . people": DioCass. RH, L.11.

249 "I like . . . traitors": Quoted M. Foss, *The Search for Cleopatra*, p. 157.

250 "angered": DioCass.RH, L.13.

250 "upset . . . deal . . . from . . . treachery": Plu.Ant, 63.

250 "undermined . . . everything": DioCass.RH, L.13.

250 "What . . . ladle?": Plu.Ant, 62.

252 "the circus . . . civil wars": Seneca (the Elder), *Suasoriae*, I.7.

252 "press-ganging . . . age": Plu.Ant, 62.

252 "an infantry . . . stand": ibid., 64.

253 "while it . . . a man": ibid., 65.

254 "the fight . . . towers": ibid., 66.

254 "doting mallard": W. Shakespeare, *Antony and Cleopatra*, Act III, scene 10, line 20.

255 "roasted . . . ovens": DioCass.RH, L.34.

21: After Actium

Unless otherwise stated below the source for the quotes in this chapter is Plu.Ant, 67–73.

259 "the wild . . . eunuchs": Horace, "Ode," I.37.

259 "a Roman . . . by sale": Horace, "Epode," IX.

260 "the leading . . . shrines": DioCass.RH, LI.5.

264 "since . . . parents": ibid., 6.

264 "His official . . . intact": ibid.

265 "He . . . unharmed": ibid., 8.

22: Death on the Nile

Unless otherwise stated below the source for the quotes in this chapter is Plu.Ant, 71–84.

269 "rescued . . . danger": Quoted M. Grant, *Cleopatra*, p. 223.

274 "a woman of insatiable sexuality": DioCass.RH, LI.15

274 "wonderfully enhanced . . . beauty": DioCass.RH, LI.12.

23: "Too Many Caesars Is Not a Good Thing"

278 "as if . . . him": DioCass.RH, LI.14.

278 "to suck . . . wound": Suet.A, 17.

279 "two . . . marks": Plu.Ant, 86.

279 Asp is a . . . Octavian: The information on the various effects of snakebite draws on Lucy Hughes-Hallett, *Cleopatra—Histories*, pp. 106–7, and her source, F. W. Fitzsimmons, *Snakes and the Treatment of Snakebite*, Cape Town, 1929.

280 "with the . . . queen": Plu.Ant, 86.
280 "too . . . good thing": ibid., 81.
281 "surpassed . . . magnificence": DioCass.RH, LI.21.
282 "came . . . corpses . . . accustomed . . . cattle": ibid., 16.
283 "They forgot . . . foreigners": ibid., 21.
284 "did not . . . casually": Suet.A, 84.
285 By now Rome . . . amulets: In the centuries following Cleopatra's death, Egyptian and Roman art fused intriguingly in Alexandria. Catacombs built in the second century AD are decorated with carvings of cobras and of the Apis bull but also with Medusa heads. A tunic-clad figure of the god Anubis is depicted mummifying a body, while another figure of Anubis is dressed as a Roman soldier.
286 "who refrained . . . woman": Suet.A, 65.
287 "a passion . . . wife": ibid., 71.

Postscript: "This Pair So Famous"

288 "this pair so famous": W. Shakespeare, *Antony and Cleopatra*, Act V, Scene 2, line 357.
290 In his *Pensées*: Pascal's reflections on the size of Cleopatra's nose are in *Pensées* ref. S. 32 (p. 6 of the edition listed in the bibliography). See also *Pensées* ref. S. 228 (p. 57).
291 "yours my Roman . . . intransigent": Vergil, *Aeneid*, Book VI, lines 853ff.

BIBLIOGRAPHY

Classical Sources

The Alexandrian War
Appian, *Roman History*
Apuleius, *The Golden Ass*
Arrian, *History of Alexander*
Athenaeus, *Banquet of the Learned (The Deipnosophists)*
Augustus (Octavian), *Res Gestae Divi Augustus*
Aulus Gelius, *Attic Nights*
Catullus, *Poems*
Cicero, *Tusculum Disputations*, *Letters to Atticus*, *Letters to Friends*, *Quintilianus*, *On the Consular Provinces*, *On the Nature of the Gods*, *Philippics*, *Pro Sestio*, "Speech Before the Senate on His Return from Exile," et al.
Dio Cassius, *Roman History*
Diodorus Sicculus, *History*
Florus, *Epitome of Roman History*
Herodotus, *History*
Horace, *Odes and Epodes*
Josephus, *Antiquities*, *Wars of the Jews*
Julius Caesar, *The Gallic Wars*, *The Civil Wars*
Livy, *History of Rome*
Lucan, *Pharsalia*
Macrobius, *Saturnalia*
Martial, *Poems*
Ovid, *Art of Love*, *Amores*
Pliny the Elder, *Natural History*
Plutarch's *Lives*, in particular those of Antony, Julius Caesar, Pompey, Brutus, Cato the Younger, Demetrius and Alexander

Sallust, *Conspiracy of Catiline*
Seneca the Elder, *Suasoriae*
Strabo, *Geography*
Suetonius, *The Lives of the Twelve Caesars*
Velleius Paterculus, *History of Rome*
Vergil, *The Aeneid*, *Eclogues*, *Georgics*

Secondary Sources

Balsdon, J. P. V. D. *Life and Leisure in Ancient Rome*. London: Phoenix, 2002.
Bauman, R. A. *Women and Politics in Ancient Rome*. London: Routledge, 1992.
Bevan, E. R. *A History of Egypt Under the Ptolemaic Dynasty*. London: Methuen, 1927.
Blond, A. A. *Scandalous History of the Roman Emperors*. London: Constable, 2000.
Boardman, J., J. Griffin, and O. Murray, eds. *The Oxford History of the Roman World*. Oxford: Oxford University Press, 1991.
Bowman, A. K. *Egypt After the Pharaohs*. London: British Museum Publications, 1986.
Bowman, A. K., E. Champlin, and A. Lintott, eds. *The Cambridge Ancient History*, vol. X: *The Augustan Empire*. Cambridge: Cambridge University Press, 1996.
Bradford, E. *Cleopatra*. New York: Harcourt Brace Jovanovich, 1972.
———. *Julius Caesar*. London: Hamish Hamilton, 1984.
Braund, D., and C. Gill, eds. *Myth, History and Culture in Republican Rome*. Exeter: University of Exeter Press, 2003.
Carcopino, J. *Daily Life in Ancient Rome*. London: Routledge, 1941.
Carter, J. M. *The Battle of Actium*. New York: Weybright and Talley, 1970.
Casson, L. *Ships and Seamanship in the Ancient World*. Princeton, NJ: Princeton University Press, 1971.
Chaveau, M. *Cleopatra Beyond the Myth*. Ithaca, NY: Cornell University Press, 2004.
———. *Egypt in the Age of Cleopatra*. Ithaca, NY: Cornell University Press, 2000.
Clarke, J. R. *Roman Sex*. New York: Harry N. Abrams, 2003.
Connolly, P. *Coliseum—Rome's Arena of Death*. London: BBC Books, 2003.
Cook, S. A., F. E. Adcock, and M. P. Charlesworth, eds. *The Cambridge Ancient History*, vol. X: *The Augustan Empire*. Cambridge: Cambridge University Press, 1934.
Cowley, E., ed. *More What If?* London: Pan, 2002.
Dalby, A. *Empire of Pleasures: Luxury and Indulgence in the Roman World*. London: Routledge, 2000.
———. *Food in the Ancient World from A to Z*. London: Routledge, 2003.
Dando-Collins, S. *Cleopatra's Kidnappers*. Hoboken, N.J.: John Wiley and Sons, 2006.
Dupont, F. *Daily Life in Ancient Rome*. Oxford: Blackwell, 1992.
Empereur, J.-Y. *Alexandria Rediscovered*. London: British Museum Press, 1998.
Everitt, A. *Cicero—A Turbulent Life*. London: John Murray, 2001.
———. *The First Emperor*. London: John Murray, 2006.
Flamarion, E. *Cleopatra: The Life and Death of a Pharaoh*. New York: Harry N. Abrams, 1997.
Foreman, L. *Cleopatra's Palace*. New York: Discovery Books, 1999.
Foss, M. *The Search for Cleopatra*. London: Michael O'Mara Books, 1997.
Fraser, P. M. *Ptolemaic Alexandria*, vol I. London: Oxford University Press, 1972.

Gill, A. *Ancient Egyptians*. London: HarperCollins, 2003.

Goddio, F., and A. Bernand, *Sunken Egypt: Alexandria*. London: Periplus, 2004.

Grant, M. *Cleopatra*. London: Phoenix Press, 2000.

———. *Greek and Roman Historians*. London: Routledge, 1995.

———. *Herod the Great*. London: Weidenfeld and Nicolson, 1971.

———. *History of Rome*. London: Weidenfeld and Nicolson, 1978.

Gurval, R. A. *Actium and Augustus*. Ann Arbor: University of Michigan Press, 1995.

Hamer, M. *Signs of Cleopatra*. London: Routledge, 1993.

Holland, R. *Augustus*. Gloucestershire, England: Sutton, 2005.

Holland, T. *Rubicon*. London: Abacus, 2004.

Hughes-Hallett, L. *Cleopatra—Histories, Dreams and Distortions*. London: Bloomsbury, 1990.

Huzar, E. G. *Mark Antony—A Biography*. Beckenham, Kent: Croom Helm, 1978.

Jones, P. *Cleopatra: A Source Book*. Norman: University of Oklahoma Press, 2006.

Jones, P., and K. Sidwell, eds. *The World of Rome*. Cambridge: Cambridge University Press, 1997.

Kleiner, D. E. *Cleopatra and Rome*. Cambridge, Mass.: Harvard University Press, 2005.

Lane Fox, R. *The Classical World*. London: Allen Lane, 2005.

Lewis, J. E., ed. *The Mammoth Book of It Happened in Ancient Rome*. London: Robinson, 2003.

Licht, H. *Sexual Life in Ancient Greece*. London: Constable, 1994.

Lindsay, J. *Cleopatra*. London: Constable, 1971.

Meier, C. *Caesar*. London: Fontana, 1996.

Mossman, J., ed. *Plutarch and His Intellectual World*. London: Duckworth, 1997.

Pascal, B. *Pensées*. Edited and translated by R. Arieu. Indianapolis, In.: Hackett, 2005.

Pomeroy, S. *Goddesses, Whores, Wives and Slaves*. London, Robert Hale, 1976.

———. *Women in Hellenic Egypt*. New York: Schocken Books, 1984.

———. ed. *Women's History and Ancient History*. Chapel Hill: University of North Carolina Press, 1991.

Powell, A., ed. *Roman Poetry and Propaganda in the Age of Augustus*. London: Bristol Classical Press, Duckworth and Co., 1992. ("Augustan Cleopatras: Female Power and Poetic Authority," Maria Wyke, pp. 98–134.)

Richlin, A. *The Garden of Priapus*. London: Yale University Press, 1983.

Royster, F. *Becoming Cleopatra: The Shifting Image of an Icon*. New York: Palgrave, 2003.

Syme, R. *The Roman Revolution*. Oxford: Oxford University Press, 1939.

Southern, P. *Cleopatra*. Gloucestershire, England: Tempus, 2000.

———. *Mark Antony*. Gloucestershire, England: Tempus, 1998.

Stadter, P. A., ed. *Plutarch and the Historical Tradition*. London: Routledge, 1992. ("Antony-Osiris, Cleopatra-Isis: The End of Plutarch's Antony," F. E. Brenk, pp. 159–82.)

Stanwick, P. A. *Portraits of the Ptolemies*. Austin: University of Texas Press, 2002.

Tannahill, R. *Food in History*. London: Review, 2002.

———. *Sex in History*. London: Abacus, 1992.

Tyldesley, J. *Cleopatra, Last Queen of Egypt*. London: Profile Books, 2008.

Volkmann, H. *Cleopatra*. New York: Sagamore, 1958.

Walker, S., and S.-A. Ashton, eds. *Cleopatra Reassessed*. London: British Museum Occasional Paper, British Museum, 2003.

Walker, S., and P. Higgs, eds. *Cleopatra of Egypt from History to Myth*. London: British Museum Press, 2001.

Winkes, R. *Livia, Octavia, Iulia—Porträts und Darstellungen*. Louvain: Archaeologica Transatlantica XIII, Publications d'Histoire de L'Art et d'Archéologie de l'Université Catholique de Louvain, 1995.

Journals

Art in America
The Classical Journal
Historia
Latomus
Smithsonian

PICTURE CREDITS

1 Sandstone relief: photo Michael Preston.

2/3 Green basanite bust of Julius Caesar, beginning of first century AD, Antikensammlung, Staatliche Museen, Berlin: photo Scala/Bildarchiv Preussischer Kulturbesitz Berlin; head from a full-length bronze statue of the Emperor Augustus (eyes inlaid with alabaster, colored stone and glass), c. 30–25 BC, found at Meroe, Sudan: British Museum, London/Bridgeman Art Library; marble bust of Octavia, wife of Mark Antony, from Velletre, c. 39 BC, Museo Nazionale Romano delle Terme, Rome: akg-images; bust of Antony: The Art Archive/Museo Capitolino, Rome/Gianni Dagli Orti.

4/5 Pompey's pillar with sphinx in the foreground, Alexandria: photo Michael Preston; upper arm bracelet of Queen Amanishakete of Nubia as the goddess Nut, gold set with paste, end of the first century BC, Meroe, Sudan, Staatliche Sammlung Ägyptischer Kunst, Munich: INTERPHOTO Pressebildagentur/Alamy; Horus and Caesarion: photo Michael Preston; reconstruction of Alexandria seen from the south: watercolor by J-C Colvin.

6/7 Reconstruction bust of Cleopatra by Dr. Martin Weaver: photo Michael Preston; Roman terra-cotta lamp with a caricatured scene, c. AD 40–80, British Museum: British Museum Images; Giambattista Tiepolo, Cleopatra's Banquet, detail, 1746–47, Palazzo Labia, Venice: Cameraphoto Arte Venezia/Bridgeman Art Library; Jean-André Rixens, *The Death of Cleopatra*, 1874, Musée des Augustins, Toulouse: © Visual Arts Library (London)/Alamy.

8 Fritz Leiber and Theda Bara in *Cleopatra*, 1917: Fox Films/The Kobal Collection; Elizabeth Taylor and Richard Burton in *Cleopatra*, 1963: 20th Century Fox/The Kobal Collection.

WHO WAS WHO IN THE FIRST CENTURY BC

The Romans

Agrippa, Marcus Vipsanius. Loyal friend of Octavian and his chief commander.

Antonia the Elder and Antonia the Younger. Antony's daughters by Octavia.

Antonius, Lucius. Mark Antony's brother.

Antonius, Marcus (Mark Antony). Caesar's loyal general; member of the Second Triumvirate with Octavian and Lepidus; husband of, among others, Fulvia and Octavia and lover of Cleopatra.

Antyllus. Antony's son by Fulvia.

Atia. Niece of Julius Caesar and mother of Octavian and Octavia.

Aurelia. Mother of Julius Caesar.

Brutus, Decimus. One of Caesar's murderers and later governor of Cisalpine Gaul and opponent of Antony.

Brutus, Marcus Junius. Son of Servilia, rumored to be fathered by Julius Caesar and a ringleader of his assassins. Also a nephew of Cato the Younger.

Caesar, Gaius Julius. Politician, general and author; member of the First Triumvirate and later dictator for life; father of Julia and of Cleopatra's son Caesarion.

Calpurnia. Daughter of Piso and wife of Julius Caesar.

Canidius Crassus, Publius. One of Antony's chief generals, faithful to him to the end.

Cassius Longinus, Caius. With Marcus Brutus a ringleader of the plot to kill Caesar.

Catiline, Lucius. Demagogue and instigator of a conspiracy.

Cato, Marcus Porcius (Cato the Younger). Republican, constitutionalist and guardian of old moral values.

Cicero, Marcus Tullius. Politician, author, orator and defender of republican orthodoxies.

Cinna, Lucius Cornelius. Politician, later ally of Marius.

Clodia. One of the sisters of Clodius, with whom she is said to have committed incest.

Clodia. Daughter of Clodius and Fulvia, stepdaughter of Antony and first wife of Octavian.

Clodius Pulcher, Publius. Demagogue, street fighter and husband of Fulvia.

Cornelia. Daughter of Cinna and first wife of Julius Caesar.

Cornelia. Wife of Publius Crassus and later of Pompey the Great.

Crassus, Marcus Licinius. Richest man in Rome; member of the First Triumvirate; killed at Carrhae fighting the Parthians.

Crassus, Publius. Son of Marcus Licinius Crassus; also killed at Carrhae.

Curio, Gaius Scribonius. Politician, youthful friend of Antony and Clodius and second husband of Fulvia.

Dellius, Quintus. One of Antony's leading generals and advisers who later defected to Octavian.

Enobarbus (Ahenobarbus), Lucius Domitius. Republican and later ally of Antony before defecting to Octavian.

Fulvia. Politically ambitious wife of, successively, Clodius, Curio and Antony.

Gabinius, Aulus. Politician, general and Roman governor of Syria.

Julia. Daughter of Julius Caesar by Cornelia and wife of Pompey the Great.

Julia. Mother of Antony.

Julia. Daughter of Octavian and Scribonia.

Labienus, Quintus. Former republican; later in the pay of the Parthians.

Lepidus, Marcus Aemilius. Politician and Caesar's master of horse; later member with Antony and Octavian of the Second Triumvirate.

Livia. Third wife of Octavian.

Marius, Gaius. General and politician; Julius Caesar's uncle by marriage.

Milo, Titus Annius. Politician, street fighter and enemy of Clodius.

Octavia. Sister of Octavian; later wife of Antony and mother of two daughters by him.

Octavian. Caesar's great-nephew and heir; member of the Second Triumvirate with Antony and Lepidus and later the Emperor Augustus.

Piso, Calpurnius Lucius. Politician and Caesar's father-in-law.

Pompeia. Granddaughter of Sulla and second wife of Julius Caesar.

Pompeius, Gnaeus. Elder son of Pompey the Great.

Pompeius Magnus, Gnaeus (Pompey the Great). Politician, general, "conqueror of the east," member of the First Triumvirate with Caesar and Crassus, later leader of the republican army against Caesar.

Pompeius, Sextus. Younger son of Pompey the Great; opponent of the Second Triumvirate.

Rabirius Postumus. Roman banker who lent money to Cleopatra's father, Auletes.

Scribonia. Relative of Sextus Pompeius, Octavian's second wife and mother of their daughter, Julia.

Servilia. Caesar's mistress and mother of Marcus Brutus.

Sosius, Gaius. Politician, general and ally of Antony.

Sulla, Lucius Cornelius. General and politician; the first man to bring the legions onto Rome's streets; later dictator.

The Ptolemies

Alexander Helios. Cleopatra VII's elder son by Antony and twin brother of Cleopatra Selene.

Arsinoe. Younger half sister of Cleopatra VII.

Auletes (Ptolemy XII). Father of Cleopatra VII.

Berenike IV. Elder sister of Cleopatra VII.

Caesarion (Ptolemy XV of Egypt). Cleopatra VII's son by Julius Caesar.

Cleopatra V. Wife of Ptolemy XII and probable mother of Cleopatra VII.

Cleopatra VI. Elder sister of Cleopatra VII.

Cleopatra VII. Final queen of the Ptolemaic dynasty.

Cleopatra Selene. Cleopatra VII's daughter by Antony and twin sister of Alexander Helios.

Ptolemy XIII. Younger half brother of Cleopatra VII and her co-ruler; killed during the Alexandrian War.

Ptolemy XIV. Younger half brother of Cleopatra VII, her co-ruler, probably killed on her orders.

Ptolemy Philadelphus. Cleopatra VII's younger son by Antony.

The Ptolemaic Court

Achillas. Military commander, member of Ptolemy XIII's regency council and chief instigator of the assassination of Pompey the Great.

Ganymedes. Eunuch, military commander and adviser to Arsinoe.

Charmion. Cleopatra's waiting woman.

Iras. Cleopatra's waiting woman. Some modern scholars have suggested that Iras' name derives from the Greek word for wool and means "wool-head," suggesting that Iras may have been black and perhaps from Nubia.

Pothinus. Eunuch and member of Ptolemy XIII's regency council.

Sosigenes. Celebrated astronomer from the Museon of Alexandria.

Theodotus. Professor of rhetoric and member of Ptolemy XIII's regency council.

Judaeans

Alexandra. Friend of Cleopatra and mother-in-law of Herod.

Antigonus. Nephew of Hyrcanus of Judaea and usurper of his throne.

Antipater. Minister to Hyrcanus of Judaea and father of Herod and Phasael.

Aristobolus. Grandson of Hyrcanus and son of Alexandra; probably murdered by Herod.

Herod. Son of Antipater and appointed king of Judaea by the Roman Senate.

Hyrcanus. Ruler of Judaea and member of the priestly Hasmonaean dynasty.

Mariamme. Granddaughter of Hyrcanus, daughter of Alexandra and wife of Herod.

Phasael. Son of Antipater, brother of Herod.

Others

Amyntas. Appointed ruler of Galatia by Antony.

Artavasdes. King of Armenia.

Artavasdes. King of Media.

Bogud. King of Mauretania.

Eunoe. Queen of Mauretania and Caesar's mistress.

Eurycles. Ruler of Sparta and later ally of Octavian.

Glaphyra. A princess of Cappadocia and reputed mistress of Antony.

Juba II, Numidian prince, later made king of Mauretania. Husband of Cleopatra Selene.

Malchus. King of the Nabataean Arabs.

Mithridates. King of Pontus.
Mithridates. King of Pergamum.
Nicomedes. King of Bithynia.
Orodes. King of Parthia.
Pacorus. Son of Orodes of Parthia.
Pharnaces. King of Pontus and son of Mithridates of Pontus.
Phraates. Son of Orodes of Parthia, whom he later murdered to take the throne.
Polemo. Appointed ruler of Pontus by Antony.
Vercingetorix. Chieftain of the Gauls.

INDEX

A NOTE ON THE AUTHOR

Diana Preston is an Oxford University–educated historian and author of *Before the Fallout: From Marie Curie to Hiroshima*, which won the 2006 *Los Angeles Times* Book Prize for Science and Technology; *Lusitania: An Epic Tragedy*; *The Boxer Rebellion*; *A First Rate Tragedy*; and *The Road to Culloden Moor*. With her husband, Michael Preston, she has coauthored *A Pirate of Exquisite Mind* and *Taj Mahal*.